公式 *TOEIC*®
Listening & Reading
問題集

7

一般財団法人 国際ビジネスコミュニケーション協会

はじめに

本書は『公式 *TOEIC*® Listening & Reading 問題集』シリーズの第7弾です。2016年5月実施の公開テストから加わった新しい出題形式に対応し、実際と同じテスト形式で2回分の問題を掲載しています。*TOEIC*® Listening & Reading Test の受験準備にお使いください。

本シリーズの特長

- 問題は全て、ETSが実際のテストと同じプロセスで制作しています。
- サンプル問題とテスト2回分の問題(200問×2回、計400問)を掲載し、リスニングセクションは*TOEIC*®公式スピーカーによる音声が収録されています。
  - *実際のテストでは、担当スピーカーや発音の種類(どの国の発音か)の割合が変更される場合があります。
- 素点から参考スコア範囲が算出可能です。
- 正解を導くための詳しい解説の他、学習の助けとなる語注「Words & Phrases」(Part 3、4、6、7)や表現紹介のコーナー「Expressions」(Part 6、7)を掲載しています。

付属CD・特典の音声について

- CDは一般的なプレーヤーで再生できます。また、CDの音声をパソコンなどの機器に取り込んで再生することもできます。
- 『公式*TOEIC*® Listening & Reading問題集7』の特典として、TEST 1、2のリーディングセクションの以下の音声をダウンロードすることができます。問題に解答した後の学習用教材としてご活用ください。
  - 正解が入った問題音声(Part 5、6)
  - 文書の音声(Part 7)

*株式会社 Globee が提供するサービス abceed への会員登録(無料)が必要です。

音声ダウンロードの手順:

1. パソコンまたはスマートフォンで音声ダウンロード用のサイトにアクセスします。
   (右のQRコードまたはブラウザから https://app.abceed.com/audio/iibc-officialprep へ)
2. 表示されたページから、abceed の新規会員登録を行います。既に会員の場合は、ログイン情報を入力して上記1.のサイトへアクセスします。
3. 上記1.のサイトにアクセス後、「公式*TOEIC*® Listening & Reading 問題集7」の画像をクリックします。クリックすると、教材詳細画面へ遷移します。
4. スマートフォンの場合は、アプリ「abceed」の案内が出ますので、アプリからご利用ください。パソコンの場合は、教材詳細画面の「音声」のアイコンからご利用ください。

   *音声は何度でもダウンロード・再生ができます。ダウンロードについてのお問い合わせは下記へ
    Eメール:support@globeejphelp.zendesk.com(お問い合わせ窓口の営業日:祝日を除く月～金曜日)
   *特典音声は、必ず一度TEST 1、2 のリーディングセクションの問題に解答した後に、ご利用ください。詳しい使い方は、
    別冊『解答・解説』p.200 をご参照ください。

本書が、*TOEIC*® Listening & Reading Testの出題形式の理解と受験準備、そして皆さまの英語学習のお役に立つことを願っております。

2020年12月
一般財団法人 国際ビジネスコミュニケーション協会

目　次

本誌

＊解答用紙は112ページの後ろに綴じ込まれています。

別冊 『解答・解説』

- 解答・解説で使われている表記の説明
- 参考スコア範囲の算出方法
- 正解一覧
- 解答・解説
- CDトラック・特典音声ファイル 一覧表
- 音声を使った学習例の紹介

TOEIC® Listening & Reading Test について

TOEIC® Listening & Reading Test とは？

TOEIC® Listening & Reading Test（以下、TOEIC® L&R）は、TOEIC® Programのテストの一つで、英語における Listening（聞く）と Reading（読む）の力を測定します。結果は合格・不合格ではなく、リスニングセクション5～495点、リーディングセクション5～495点、トータル10～990点のスコアで評価されます。スコアの基準は常に一定であり、 英語能力に変化がない限りスコアも一定に保たれます。知識・教養としての英語ではなく、オフィスや日常生活における英語によるコミュニケーション能力を幅広く測定するテストです。特定の文化を知らないと理解できない表現を排除しているので、誰もが公平に受けることができる「グローバルスタンダード」として活用されています。

問題形式

● リスニングセクション（約45分間・100問）とリーディングセクション（75分間・100問）から成り、約2時間で200問に解答します。

● テストは英文のみで構成されており、英文和訳や和文英訳といった設問はありません。

● マークシート方式の一斉客観テストです。

● リスニングセクションにおける発音は、米国・英国・カナダ・オーストラリアが使われています。

＊テスト中、問題用紙への書き込みは一切禁じられています。

リスニングセクション（約45分間）

パート	Part Name	パート名	問題数
1	Photographs	写真描写問題	6
2	Question-Response	応答問題	25
3	Conversations	会話問題	39
4	Talks	説明文問題	30

リーディングセクション（75分間）

パート	Part Name	パート名	問題数
5	Incomplete Sentences	短文穴埋め問題	30
6	Text Completion	長文穴埋め問題	16
7	• Single passages • Multiple passages	1つの文書 複数の文書	29 25

開発・運営団体について

TOEIC® L&Rは、ETSによって開発・制作されています。ETSは、米国ニュージャージー州プリンストンに拠点を置き、TOEIC® ProgramやTOEFL、GRE（大学院入学共通試験）を含む約200のテストプログラムを開発している世界最大の非営利テスト開発機関です。

日本におけるTOEIC® L&Rを含むTOEIC® Programの実施・運営は、一般財団法人 国際ビジネスコミュニケーション協会（IIBC）が行っています。IIBCは、公式教材の出版やグローバル人材育成など、「人と企業の国際化」の推進に貢献するための活動を展開しています。

本書の構成と使い方

本書は、本誌と別冊に分かれています。それぞれの主な内容は以下の通りです。

- 本誌 …… 「サンプル問題」「TEST 1」「TEST 2」「解答用紙」
- 別冊『解答・解説』…… 「参考スコア範囲の算出方法」「正解一覧」「解答・解説」「CDトラック・特典音声ファイル 一覧表」「音声を使った学習例の紹介」

本誌

サンプル問題（29問）［本誌p.8-27] 全パートから合計29問を掲載しています。　CD 1 02-10

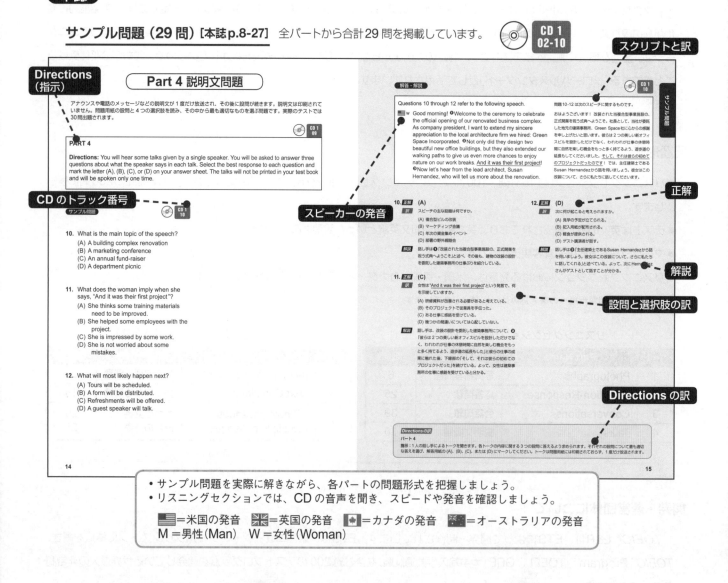

・サンプル問題を実際に解きながら、各パートの問題形式を把握しましょう。
・リスニングセクションでは、CDの音声を聞き、スピードや発音を確認しましょう。

🇺🇸＝米国の発音　🇬🇧＝英国の発音　🇨🇦＝カナダの発音　🇦🇺＝オーストラリアの発音
M＝男性（Man）　W＝女性（Woman）

TEST 1 ［本誌p.29-70] CD 1 11-92　　### TEST 2 ［本誌p.71-111] CD 2 01-82

TEST 1、2ともに、実際のテストと同じ、合計200問で構成されています。

リスニングセクション　　100問　　約45分間
リーディングセクション　100問　　75分間

予行演習として時間を計って解答し、時間配分の参考にしたり、伸ばしたい分野や弱点を把握したり、使い方を工夫してみましょう。

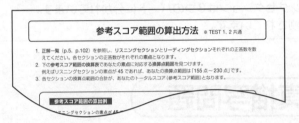
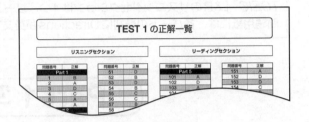

別冊『解答・解説』

参考スコア範囲の算出方法 [別冊 p.4]

正解数を基に、参考スコア範囲を算出できます。

> **参考スコア範囲の算出方法** ※ TEST 1, 2 共通
>
> 1. 正解一覧（p.5, p.102）を参照し、リスニングセクションとリーディングセクションそれぞれの正答数を数えてください。各セクションの正答数がそれぞれの素点となります。
> 2. 下の参考スコア範囲の換算表であなたの素点に対応する換算点範囲を見つけます。
>   例えばリスニングセクションの素点が45であれば、あなたの換算点範囲は [155点～230点] です。
> 3. 各セクションの換算点範囲の合計が、あなたのトータルスコア（参考スコア範囲）となります。
>
> **参考スコア範囲の算出例**
> リスニングセクションの素点が45

正解一覧 [TEST 1 ➡ 別冊 p.5　TEST 2 ➡ 別冊 p.102]

> **TEST 1 の正解一覧**
>
> | リスニングセクション | | リーディングセクション | |
> | --- | --- | --- | --- |

解答・解説 [TEST 1 ➡ 別冊 p.6-101　　TEST 2 ➡ 別冊 p.103-197]

表記の説明は、別冊 p.2-3 をご覧ください。

問題の再掲載

問題の訳

設問と選択肢の訳

正解と解説

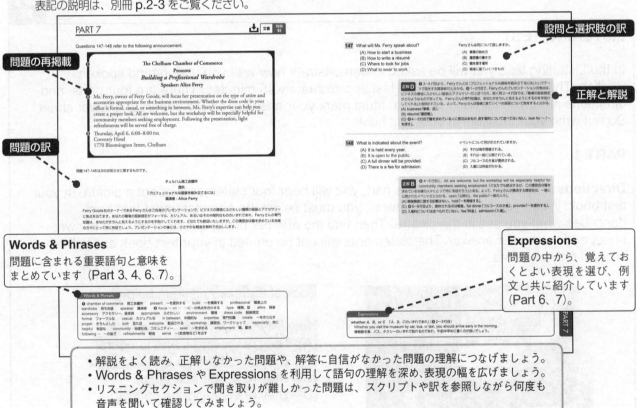

Words & Phrases
問題に含まれる重要語句と意味をまとめています（Part 3、4、6、7）。

Expressions
問題の中から、覚えておくとよい表現を選び、例文と共に紹介しています（Part 6、7）。

- 解説をよく読み、正解しなかった問題や、解答に自信がなかった問題の理解につなげましょう。
- Words & Phrases や Expressions を利用して語句の理解を深め、表現の幅を広げましょう。
- リスニングセクションで聞き取りが難しかった問題は、スクリプトや訳を参照しながら何度も音声を聞いて確認してみましょう。

CD トラック・特典音声ファイル 一覧表
[別冊 p.198-199]

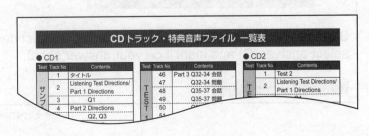

> **CD トラック・特典音声ファイル 一覧表**

サンプル問題

TOEIC® Listening & Reading Test（以下、*TOEIC®* L&R）の問題形式を、サンプル問題を使ってご紹介します。サンプル問題は、全部で29問（リスニングセクション12問、リーディングセクション17問）です。問題の番号は連番になっており、実際のテストの問題番号とは異なります。

TOEIC® L&Rのリスニングセクションは4つ、リーディングセクションは3つのパートに分かれています。問題用紙には、各パートの最初にDirectionsが英文で印刷されています。

Part 1 写真描写問題

1枚の写真について4つの短い説明文が1度だけ放送されます。説明文は印刷されていません。4つのうち写真を最も適切に描写しているものを選ぶ問題です。実際のテストでは6問出題されます。

CD 1
02

LISTENING TEST

In the Listening test, you will be asked to demonstrate how well you understand spoken English. The entire Listening test will last approximately 45 minutes. There are four parts, and directions are given for each part. You must mark your answers on the separate answer sheet. Do not write your answers in your test book.

PART 1

Directions: For each question in this part, you will hear four statements about a picture in your test book. When you hear the statements, you must select the one statement that best describes what you see in the picture. Then find the number of the question on your answer sheet and mark your answer. The statements will not be printed in your test book and will be spoken only one time.

Look at the example item below.

Now listen to the four statements.
(A) They're moving some furniture.
(B) They're entering a meeting room.
(C) They're sitting at a table.
(D) They're cleaning the carpet.

Statement (C), "They're sitting at a table," is the best description of the picture, so you should select answer (C) and mark it on your answer sheet.

Now Part 1 will begin.

＊上記枠内の網掛けの部分は音声のみで、問題用紙には印刷されていません。

Part 2 応答問題

1.

解答・解説

1. Look at the picture marked number 1 in your test book.

M (A) A truck is stopped at a stoplight.
(B) A man is using a gardening tool.
(C) Some people are sitting on the grass.
(D) Some workers are cutting down a tree.

正解 (B)

解説 gardeningは「造園、園芸」、toolは「用具、道具」という意味。

訳 問題用紙にある問題1の写真を見てください。

(A) トラックが停止信号で止まっている。
(B) 男性が造園用具を使っている。
(C) 何人かの人々が芝生の上に座っている。
(D) 何人かの作業員が木を切り倒している。

Directionsの訳

リスニングテスト

リスニングテストでは、話されている英語をどのくらいよく理解しているかが問われます。リスニングテストは全体で約45分間です。4つのパートがあり、各パートにおいて指示が与えられます。答えは、別紙の解答用紙にマークしてください。問題用紙に答えを書き込んではいけません。

パート1

指示：このパートの各設問では、問題用紙にある写真について、4つの説明文を聞きます。説明文を聞いて、写真の内容を最も適切に描写しているものを選んでください。そして解答用紙の該当する問題番号にあなたの答えをマークしてください。説明文は問題用紙には印刷されておらず、1度だけ放送されます。

下の例題を見てください。

では4つの説明文を聞きましょう。
　(A) 彼らは家具を動かしている。
　(B) 彼らは会議室に入ろうとしている。
　(C) 彼らはテーブルのところに座っている。
　(D) 彼らはカーペットを掃除している。

(C)の文、"They're sitting at a table"(彼らはテーブルのところに座っている)がこの写真を最も適切に描写しているので、(C)を選び、解答用紙にマークします。

ではパート1が始まります。

Part 2 応答問題

1つの質問または発言と、3つの応答がそれぞれ1度だけ放送されます。質問も応答も印刷されていません。質問に対して最も適切な応答を選ぶ問題です。実際のテストでは25問出題されます。

> **PART 2**
>
> **Directions:** You will hear a question or statement and three responses spoken in English. They will not be printed in your test book and will be spoken only one time. Select the best response to the question or statement and mark the letter (A), (B), or (C) on your answer sheet.
>
> Now let us begin with question number 2.

＊上記枠内の網掛けの部分は音声のみで、問題用紙には印刷されていません。

サンプル問題

2. Mark your answer on your answer sheet.
3. Mark your answer on your answer sheet.

解答・解説

2. W Are you taking an international or a domestic flight?

 M (A) I'd prefer a window seat.
(B) He moved there last year.
(C) I'm flying internationally.

訳 あなたは国際線の便に乗りますか、それとも国内線の便ですか。

(A) 私は窓側の席を希望します。
(B) 彼は昨年、そこへ引っ越しました。
(C) 私は国際線の飛行機で行きます。

正解 (C)

解説 A or B? の形で、国際線と国内線のどちらの便に乗るのかを尋ねているのに対し、「国際線の飛行機で行く」と答えている (C) が正解。

3. M Shouldn't we hire more salespeople?

W (A) I'm glad they went.
(B) A higher profit.
(C) Let's look at the budget.

訳 私たちはもっと販売員を雇った方がいいのではありませんか。

(A) 私は、彼らが行ってうれしいです。
(B) より高い利益です。
(C) 予算を見てみましょう。

正解 (C)

解説 「もっと販売員を雇った方がいいのではないか」という男性の発言に対し、「予算を見てみよう」と雇用の検討を示唆している (C) が正解。

Directionsの訳

パート2

指示：英語による1つの質問または発言と、3つの応答を聞きます。それらは問題用紙には印刷されておらず、1度だけ放送されます。質問または発言に対して最も適切な応答を選び、解答用紙の (A)、(B)、または (C) にマークしてください。

では、問題2から始めましょう。

問題の訳

答えを解答用紙にマークしてください。

Part 3 会話問題

会話が1度だけ放送され、その後に設問が続きます。会話は印刷されていません。問題用紙の設問と4つの選択肢を読み、その中から最も適切なものを選ぶ問題です。実際のテストでは39問出題されます。

 CD 1 06

PART 3

Directions: You will hear some conversations between two or more people. You will be asked to answer three questions about what the speakers say in each conversation. Select the best response to each question and mark the letter (A), (B), (C), or (D) on your answer sheet. The conversations will not be printed in your test book and will be spoken only one time.

 CD 1 07   CD 1 08

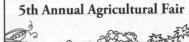

4. Which department is the man most likely calling?

   (A) Receiving
   (B) Catering
   (C) Security
   (D) Finance

5. Why does the man apologize?

   (A) He has forgotten his badge.
   (B) His report will be late.
   (C) A meeting location has to be changed.
   (D) A shipment must be delivered after business hours.

6. What does the woman say she will do?

   (A) Arrange additional workspace
   (B) Publish some materials
   (C) Issue a temporary pass
   (D) Ask staff to work late

5th Annual Agricultural Fair

Day 1—Vegetables
Day 2—Dairy
Day 3—Flowers
Day 4—Baked goods

7. Why do the speakers want to attend the fair?

   (A) To advertise a new business
   (B) To find local food suppliers
   (C) To sell some products
   (D) To participate in a workshop

8. What does the man say he has downloaded?

   (A) An electronic book
   (B) A mobile phone application
   (C) Some photographs
   (D) Some tickets

9. Look at the graphic. Which day do the speakers decide to attend the fair?

   (A) Day 1
   (B) Day 2
   (C) Day 3
   (D) Day 4

Questions 4 through 6 refer to the following conversation.   問題4-6は次の会話に関するものです。

M Hello. ❶I'm expecting an extra-large load of clothing racks delivered to the store today, and they'll arrive after business hours. Are you the person I should inform about this?

もしもし。今日お店に、洋服ラックの特大の積み荷が配達される予定ですが、それらは営業時間の後に着きます。あなたがこの件についてお知らせすべき方でしょうか。

W Yes, ❷I'm head of Receiving. But ❸you're supposed to have suppliers make deliveries during business hours.

はい、私が荷受け部門の責任者です。でも、供給業者には、営業時間中に配達してもらうことになっているはずですが。

M ❹I'm sorry, but this is the only time the supplier can deliver them, and we need the racks for a fashion show we're having tomorrow.

申し訳ありません。しかし、これが、供給業者がそれらを配達できる唯一の時間帯で、私たちが明日開催するファッションショーには、そのラックが必要なんです。

W I understand. ❺I'm not sure which of my staff members is working tonight, but I'll ask one of them to stay late to accept the delivery.

分かりました。今夜うちのスタッフの誰が勤務するのか定かではありませんが、配達物を受け取るために遅くまで残るよう、彼らのうちの1人に頼みます。

---

4. 正解 **(A)**

訳 男性はどの部署に電話をかけていると考えられますか。

(A) 荷受け
(B) ケータリング
(C) 警備
(D) 財務

解説 男性からの電話に応答した女性は❷「私が荷受け部門の責任者だ」と答え、その後も2人は配達物の受け取りについて話をしている。

5. 正解 **(D)**

訳 男性はなぜ謝罪していますか。

(A) 自分のバッジを忘れたから。
(B) 報告書が遅れるから。
(C) 会議の場所が変更されなければならないから。
(D) 荷物が営業時間の後に配達されざるを得ないから。

解説 ❶「積み荷が配達される予定だが、それらは営業時間の後に着く」という男性の報告に対し、女性が❸「供給業者には、営業時間中に配達してもらうことになっているはず」と指摘している。それに対して男性は❹で、「申し訳ない」と謝罪後「これが、供給業者がそれらを配達できる唯一の時間帯で、私たちが明日開催するファッションショーには、そのラックが必要だ」と事情を説明している。よって、正解は(D)。

6. 正解 **(D)**

訳 女性は何をすると言っていますか。

(A) 追加の作業スペースを手配する。
(B) 資料を公表する。
(C) 臨時の通行証を発行する。
(D) スタッフに遅くまで勤務するよう頼む。

解説 女性は❺「今夜うちのスタッフの誰が勤務するのか定かではないが、配達物を受け取るために遅くまで残るよう、彼らのうちの1人に頼む」と述べている。stay lateをwork late「遅くまで勤務する」と表した(D)が正解。

Directionsの訳

パート3

指示：2人あるいはそれ以上の人々の会話を聞きます。各会話の内容に関する3つの設問に答えるよう求められます。それぞれの設問について最も適切な答えを選び、解答用紙の (A)、(B)、(C)、または (D) にマークしてください。会話は問題用紙には印刷されておらず、1度だけ放送されます。

Questions 7 through 9 refer to the following conversation and schedule.

🇺🇸 w Pedro, ❶I know we're still looking for local fresh food suppliers for our new restaurant. We should check out the Agricultural Fair next month.

🇨🇦 M That's a good idea. It's a major event, so many local farmers will be there. ❷I downloaded the fair's mobile phone application. The app has a lot of helpful information, including a schedule. Which day do you think we should go?

🇺🇸 w Well, it looks like they'll have dairy vendors on the second day.

🇨🇦 M Hmm, I just contacted a dairy company that might work for us. ❸We really need a vegetable supplier though…

🇺🇸 w Oh, OK. ❹They have a day for showcasing vegetable farmers. Let's go then.

問題7-9は次の会話と予定表に関するものです。

Pedro、私たちはまだ、うちの新しいレストランのために、地元の生鮮食品の供給業者を探しているわよね。来月の農業フェアを見てみるべきだわ。

それは良い考えだね。大きなイベントだから、多数の地元の農業経営者たちがそこにいるだろう。僕はフェアの携帯電話用アプリをダウンロードしたよ。このアプリには、予定表を含め、役立つ情報がたくさんあるんだ。僕たちはどの日に行くべきだと思う？

そうね、乳製品の販売業者は2日目にいるみたいね。

うーん、僕はうちに合いそうな乳製品会社に連絡を取ったばかりなんだ。僕たちには野菜の供給業者はぜひとも必要だけど…。

ああ、分かったわ。野菜農家の出展日があるわ。そのときに行きましょう。

---

7. 正解 **(B)**

訳 なぜ話し手たちはフェアに行きたいと思っていますか。

(A) 新しい店を宣伝するため。
(B) 地元の食品供給業者を見つけるため。
(C) 製品を販売するため。
(D) 講習会に参加するため。

解説 女性は❶「私たちはまだ、うちの新しいレストランのために、地元の生鮮食品の供給業者を探している。来月の農業フェアを見てみるべきだ」と提案し、男性もそれに同意している。よって、(B)が適切。

8. 正解 **(B)**

訳 男性は何をダウンロードしたと言っていますか。

(A) 電子書籍
(B) 携帯電話用アプリ
(C) 数枚の写真
(D) 数枚のチケット

解説 男性は❷「僕はフェアの携帯電話用アプリをダウンロードした」と述べている。

9. 正解 **(A)**

訳 図を見てください。話し手たちはどの日にフェアへ行くことに決めますか。

(A) 1日目
(B) 2日目
(C) 3日目
(D) 4日目

解説 ❸「僕たちには野菜の供給業者がぜひとも必要だ」という男性の発言に対し、女性は❹「野菜農家の出展日がある。そのときに行こう」と提案している。予定表から、野菜農家が集まる日は1日目だと分かる。予定表のbaked goodsはクッキーやパンなどのオーブンで焼いた食品を指す。

図の訳

第5回　年次農業フェア
1日目 ― 野菜
2日目 ― 乳製品
3日目 ― 花
4日目 ― パン・焼き菓子

Part 4 説明文問題

アナウンスや電話のメッセージなどの説明文が1度だけ放送され、その後に設問が続きます。説明文は印刷されていません。問題用紙の設問と4つの選択肢を読み、その中から最も適切なものを選ぶ問題です。実際のテストでは30問出題されます。

PART 4

Directions: You will hear some talks given by a single speaker. You will be asked to answer three questions about what the speaker says in each talk. Select the best response to each question and mark the letter (A), (B), (C), or (D) on your answer sheet. The talks will not be printed in your test book and will be spoken only one time.

サンプル問題

10. What is the main topic of the speech?
    (A) A building complex renovation
    (B) A marketing conference
    (C) An annual fund-raiser
    (D) A department picnic

11. What does the woman imply when she says, "And it was their first project"?
    (A) She thinks some training materials need to be improved.
    (B) She helped some employees with the project.
    (C) She is impressed by some work.
    (D) She is not worried about some mistakes.

12. What will most likely happen next?
    (A) Tours will be scheduled.
    (B) A form will be distributed.
    (C) Refreshments will be offered.
    (D) A guest speaker will talk.

Questions 10 through 12 refer to the following speech.

🇺🇸 w　Good morning! ❶Welcome to the ceremony to celebrate the official opening of our renovated business complex. As company president, I want to extend my sincere appreciation to the local architecture firm we hired: Green Space Incorporated. ❷Not only did they design two beautiful new office buildings, but they also extended our walking paths to give us even more chances to enjoy nature on our work breaks. And it was their first project! ❸Now let's hear from the lead architect, Susan Hernandez, who will tell us more about the renovation.

問題 10-12 は次のスピーチに関するものです。

おはようございます！ 改装された当複合型事業施設の、正式開業を祝う式典へようこそ。社長として、当社が委託した地元の建築事務所、Green Space 社に心からの感謝を申し上げたいと思います。彼らは 2 つの美しい新オフィスビルを設計しただけでなく、われわれが仕事の休憩時間に自然を楽しむ機会をもっと多く持てるよう、遊歩道の延長もしてくださいました。そして、それは彼らの初めてのプロジェクトだったのです！ では、主任建築士である Susan Hernandez から話を伺いましょう。彼女はこの改装について、さらに私たちに話してくださいます。

10. 正解 **(A)**

訳　スピーチの主な話題は何ですか。

(A) 複合型ビルの改装
(B) マーケティング会議
(C) 年次の資金集めイベント
(D) 部署の野外親睦会

解説　話し手は❶「改装された当複合型事業施設の、正式開業を祝う式典へようこそ」と述べ、その後も、建物の改装の設計を委託した建築事務所の仕事ぶりを紹介している。

11. 正解 **(C)**

訳　女性は "And it was their first project" という発言で、何を示唆していますか。

(A) 研修資料が改善される必要があると考えている。
(B) そのプロジェクトで従業員を手伝った。
(C) ある仕事に感銘を受けている。
(D) 幾つかの間違いについては心配していない。

解説　話し手は、改装の設計を委託した建築事務所について、❷「彼らは 2 つの美しい新オフィスビルを設計しただけでなく、われわれが仕事の休憩時間に自然を楽しむ機会をもっと多く持てるよう、遊歩道の延長もした」と彼らの仕事の成果に触れた後、下線部の「そして、それは彼らの初めてのプロジェクトだった」を続けている。よって、女性は建築事務所の仕事に感銘を受けていると分かる。

12. 正解 **(D)**

訳　次に何が起こると考えられますか。

(A) 見学の予定が立てられる。
(B) 記入用紙が配布される。
(C) 軽食が提供される。
(D) ゲスト講演者が話す。

解説　話し手は❸「主任建築士である Susan Hernandez から話を伺いましょう。彼女はこの改装について、さらに私たちに話してくれる」と述べている。よって、次に Hernandez さんがゲストとして話すことが分かる。

Directionsの訳

パート 4

指示：1 人の話し手によるトークを聞きます。各トークの内容に関する 3 つの設問に答えるよう求められます。それぞれの設問について最も適切な答えを選び、解答用紙の (A)、(B)、(C)、または (D) にマークしてください。トークは問題用紙には印刷されておらず、1 度だけ放送されます。

ここからはリーディングセクションです。
実際のテストでは、リスニングセクションの終わりに"This is the end of the Listening test. Turn to Part 5 in your test book."(これでリスニングテストは終了です。問題用紙のパート5に進んでください。)というアナウンスがありますので、それが聞こえたらリーディングセクションの解答を始めます。

Part 5 短文穴埋め問題

4つの選択肢の中から最も適切なものを選び、不完全な文を完成させる問題です。実際のテストでは30問出題されます。

READING TEST

In the Reading test, you will read a variety of texts and answer several different types of reading comprehension questions. The entire Reading test will last 75 minutes. There are three parts, and directions are given for each part. You are encouraged to answer as many questions as possible within the time allowed.

You must mark your answers on the separate answer sheet. Do not write your answers in your test book.

PART 5

Directions: A word or phrase is missing in each of the sentences below. Four answer choices are given below each sentence. Select the best answer to complete the sentence. Then mark the letter (A), (B), (C), or (D) on your answer sheet.

サンプル問題

13. Before ------- with the recruiter, applicants should sign in at the personnel department's reception desk.

    (A) meets
    (B) meeting
    (C) to meet
    (D) was met

14. Stefano Linen Company suggests requesting a small fabric ------- before placing your final order.

    (A) bonus
    (B) sample
    (C) feature
    (D) model

13. **正解** **(B)**

訳 採用担当者と会う前に、応募者の方々は人事部の受付で署名して到着を記録してください。

(A) 動詞の三人称単数現在形
(B) 動名詞
(C) to不定詞
(D) 受動態の過去形

解説 選択肢は全て動詞 meet「会う」の変化した形。文頭からカンマまでの部分に主語と動詞がないため、Before は前置詞と考えられる。前置詞に続く空所には名詞の働きをする語句が入るので、動名詞の (B) meeting が適切である。sign in「署名して到着を記録する」。

14. **正解** **(B)**

訳 Stefano リネン社は、お客さまが最終的な注文をなさる前に、小さな布地見本をご要望になることをお勧めしています。

(A) 特別手当
(B) 見本
(C) 特徴
(D) 模型

解説 選択肢は全て名詞。空所の後ろは「お客さまが最終的な注文をする前に」という意味。(B) sample「見本」を空所に入れると small fabric sample「小さな布地見本」となり、注文前に要望するものとして適切で、意味が通る。

Directionsの訳

リーディングテスト

リーディングテストでは、さまざまな文章を読んで、読解力を測る何種類かの問題に答えます。リーディングテストは全体で75分間です。3つのパートがあり、各パートにおいて指示が与えられます。制限時間内に、できるだけ多くの設問に答えてください。

答えは、別紙の解答用紙にマークしてください。問題用紙に答えを書き込んではいけません。

パート5

指示：以下の各文において語や句が抜けています。各文の下には選択肢が4つ与えられています。文を完成させるのに最も適切な答えを選びます。そして解答用紙の (A)、(B)、(C)、または (D) にマークしてください。

Part 6 長文穴埋め問題

4つの選択肢の中から最も適切なものを選び、不完全な文書を完成させる問題です。実際のテストでは16問出題されます。

PART 6

Directions: Read the texts that follow. A word, phrase, or sentence is missing in parts of each text. Four answer choices for each question are given below the text. Select the best answer to complete the text. Then mark the letter (A), (B), (C), or (D) on your answer sheet.

サンプル問題

Questions 15-18 refer to the following article.

---

❶ SAN DIEGO (May 5)—Matino Industries has just bolstered its image with environmentally conscious customers thanks to its ------- to reduce its use of nonrenewable energy to less than 20 percent within five years. -------. Best practices guidelines are already being revised ------- powering down and disconnecting equipment when not in use. In addition, solar-panel arrays are slated for installation on-site as early as next year. When weather ------- are clear, these panels will offset Matino's reliance on the power grid, as they already do for a growing list of companies.

15. / 16. / 17. / 18.

*❶は解説の中で説明している文書中の段落番号等を示しています。問題用紙には印刷されていません。

---

15. (A) product
    (B) commitment
    (C) contest
    (D) workforce

16. (A) Discounts on all its products have increased Matino's customer base.
    (B) Management predicts that the takeover will result in a net financial gain.
    (C) To achieve this goal, the company will begin by improving its energy efficiency.
    (D) The initial step will involve redesigning the company's logo and slogans.

17. (A) been encouraging
    (B) have encouraged
    (C) encourages
    (D) to encourage

18. (A) conditions
    (B) instructions
    (C) views
    (D) reports

問題15-18は次の記事に関するものです。

サンディエゴ（5月5日）——Matino産業社は、同社の再生不能エネルギーの使用を5年以内に20パーセント未満に削減するという公約のおかげで、環境意識の高い顧客にとっての同社のイメージを強化したところである。*この目標を達成するために同社は、自社のエネルギー効率を改善することから始める予定だ。機器を使用していないときには電源を落として接続を切ることを推奨するために、最良実践ガイドラインがすでに改定されているところである。さらに、早くも来年には、ソーラーパネルの列が構内に設置される予定である。天候条件が晴れのときには、これらのパネルが、増え続ける多くの企業に対してすでにそうしているように、Matino社の送電網依存を弱めることになる。

*問題16の挿入文の訳

15. 正解 **(B)**

訳
(A) 製品
(B) 公約
(C) 競争
(D) 全従業員

解説 ❶の1～3行目は「Matino産業社は、同社の-------のおかげで、同社のイメージを強化したところだ」というのが、文の中心の意味。空所の後ろの「同社の再生不能エネルギーの使用を5年以内に20パーセント未満に削減すること」は、空所に入る名詞の内容を示していると考えられるので、文意から(B) commitment「公約」が適切。

16. 正解 **(C)**

訳
(A) 全ての自社製品に対する割引が、Matino社の顧客基盤を拡大してきた。
(B) 経営陣は、その企業買収は財務上の純利益をもたらすと予測している。
(C) この目標を達成するために同社は、自社のエネルギー効率を改善することから始める予定だ。
(D) 第1段階には、会社のロゴとスローガンを作り直すことが含まれる予定だ。

解説 空所の前の文では、Matino産業社が同社の再生不能エネルギーの使用を5年以内に20パーセント未満に削減することが述べられている。この内容をthis goalで受けて、目標達成のために同社がこれから取り組むことを挙げている(C)が流れとして適切。

17. 正解 **(D)**

訳
(A) 〈be動詞の過去分詞＋現在分詞〉
(B) 現在完了形
(C) 動詞の三人称単数現在形
(D) to不定詞

解説 選択肢は全て動詞encourage「～を推奨する」が変化した形。空所の前に〈主語＋動詞〉の形があり、andやorなどの接続詞もないことから、空所に動詞は入らない。空所には、to不定詞の(D) to encourageが適切。

18. 正解 **(A)**

訳
(A) 条件
(B) 指示
(C) 見解
(D) 報道

解説 空所を含む文の、文頭からカンマまでは「天候-------が晴れのときには」という意味。these panels以降では、その際にソーラーパネルがもたらす効果について述べられている。「天候条件が晴れのときには」とすると意味が通るため、(A) conditions「条件」が適切。

Directionsの訳

パート6
指示：以下の文書を読んでください。各文書の中で語や句、または文が部分的に抜けています。文書の下には各設問の選択肢が4つ与えられています。文書を完成させるのに最も適切な答えを選びます。そして解答用紙の (A)、(B)、(C)、または (D) にマークしてください。

Part 7 読解問題

いろいろな形式の、1つもしくは複数の文書に関する問題が出題されます。設問と4つの選択肢を読み、その中から最も適切なものを選ぶ問題です。実際のテストでは1つの文書に関する問題が29問、複数の文書に関する問題が25問出題されます。

PART 7

Directions: In this part you will read a selection of texts, such as magazine and newspaper articles, e-mails, and instant messages. Each text or set of texts is followed by several questions. Select the best answer for each question and mark the letter (A), (B), (C), or (D) on your answer sheet.

サンプル問題

Questions 19-20 refer to the following text-message chain.

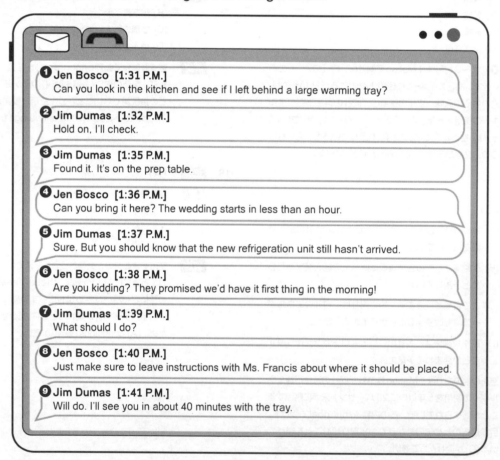

Jen Bosco [1:31 P.M.]
Can you look in the kitchen and see if I left behind a large warming tray?

Jim Dumas [1:32 P.M.]
Hold on, I'll check.

Jim Dumas [1:35 P.M.]
Found it. It's on the prep table.

Jen Bosco [1:36 P.M.]
Can you bring it here? The wedding starts in less than an hour.

Jim Dumas [1:37 P.M.]
Sure. But you should know that the new refrigeration unit still hasn't arrived.

Jen Bosco [1:38 P.M.]
Are you kidding? They promised we'd have it first thing in the morning!

Jim Dumas [1:39 P.M.]
What should I do?

Jen Bosco [1:40 P.M.]
Just make sure to leave instructions with Ms. Francis about where it should be placed.

Jim Dumas [1:41 P.M.]
Will do. I'll see you in about 40 minutes with the tray.

19. For whom do the writers most likely work?

(A) A catering company
(B) A home-improvement store
(C) A kitchen-design company
(D) An appliance manufacturer

20. At 1:38 P.M., what does Ms. Bosco most likely mean when she writes, "Are you kidding"?

(A) She thinks Mr. Dumas is exaggerating.
(B) She knew she would have to wait a long time.
(C) She expects the refrigeration unit to arrive soon.
(D) She is upset that a delivery has not been made.

解答・解説

問題 19-20 は次のテキストメッセージのやり取りに関するものです。

Jen Bosco [午後 1 時 31 分]
調理場の中をのぞいて、私が大きな保温トレーを置き忘れたかどうかを確かめてくれるかしら。

Jim Dumas [午後 1 時 32 分]
待ってて。確認するよ。

Jim Dumas [午後 1 時 35 分]
見つけた。調理台の上にあるよ。

Jen Bosco [午後 1 時 36 分]
それをここに持ってきてくれる？ 結婚式が 1 時間足らずで始まるの。

Jim Dumas [午後 1 時 37 分]
もちろん。でも、新しい冷蔵装置がまだ届いていないことを知っておいた方がいいよ。

Jen Bosco [午後 1 時 38 分]
冗談でしょう？ 朝一番には私たちにそれを届けてくれると、彼らは約束したのよ。

Jim Dumas [午後 1 時 39 分]
僕はどうしたらいい？

Jen Bosco [午後 1 時 40 分]
とにかく、どこにそれを置けばいいか、Francis さんに必ず指示を残しておいて。

Jim Dumas [午後 1 時 41 分]
そうするよ。約 40 分後にトレーを持って君に会うね。

---

19. 正解 **(A)**

訳 書き手たちはどこに勤めていると考えられますか。

(A) ケータリング会社
(B) ホームセンター
(C) キッチン設計会社
(D) 電化製品メーカー

解説 ❶と❷のやり取りから、書き手たちの職場には調理場があることが分かる。また❹で、Bosco さんが Dumas さんに保温トレーを結婚式の場に持ってくるよう伝えていることから、書き手たちは料理を作り配達を行っていると考えられる。よって、(A) が適切。

20. 正解 **(D)**

訳 午後 1 時 38 分に Bosco さんは、"Are you kidding" という発言で、何を意味していると考えられますか。

(A) Dumas さんが誇張していると思っている。
(B) 長い間待たなくてはならないことを知っていた。
(C) 冷蔵装置がもうすぐ届くだろうと見込んでいる。
(D) 配達が行われていないことに動揺している。

解説 Dumas さんが❺「新しい冷蔵装置がまだ届いていないことを知っておいた方がいい」と伝えたのに対して、Bosco さんは「冗談でしょう？」と驚きを示し、「朝一番には私たちにそれを届けてくれると、彼らは約束した」と続けている。つまり、Bosco さんは配達が約束通りに行われていないことに動揺していると考えられる。

Directions の訳

パート 7

指示：このパートでは、雑誌や新聞の記事、E メールやインスタントメッセージなどのさまざまな文書を読みます。1 つの文書または複数の文書のセットにはそれぞれ、幾つかの設問が続いています。各設問について最も適切な答えを選び、解答用紙の (A)、(B)、(C)、または (D) にマークしてください。

Questions 21-24 refer to the following Web page.

---

http://straubuniversityschoolofmedicine.edu/vendors/rfp0023

❶ Straub University School of Medicine is currently seeking a vendor to provide surgical gloves, laboratory coats, and protective goggles. The university requires high-quality, hospital-grade equipment for its students and faculty and is especially interested in providers who currently work with local hospitals and clinics.

❷ You can download the complete Request for Proposal (RFP) instructions from our Web site. Below is a summary of the proposal requirements. — [1] —.

• A standard proposal form, which can be downloaded from our Web site
• A general description of the provider and its experience in the industry
• Product descriptions with a complete list of specifications and prices
• Contact information of three current or recent clients who are able to speak to the quality of the provider's products or services

❸ If you have any questions about the RFP, please submit them in writing to queries@straub.edu by July 20. — [2] —. Responses to questions will be posted publicly on the Straub University School of Medicine's Web page on August 4.

❹ Proposals must be received no later than August 15. — [3] —. All submissions will be thoroughly reviewed, and the winning proposal will be announced on September 10. A contract will be finalized with the strongest candidate that same month, and the agreement will take effect starting October 1. — [4] —.

---

21. Who are the instructions intended for?

(A) Sellers of medical supplies
(B) Applicants for hospital jobs
(C) Hospital administrators
(D) Medical students

22. What are candidates required to submit?

(A) Questions about the proposal
(B) Professional references
(C) An application fee
(D) Product samples

23. When will candidates learn if they have been selected?

(A) In July
(B) In August
(C) In September
(D) In October

24. In which of the positions marked [1], [2], [3], and [4] does the following sentence best belong?

"All documentation must arrive by this date in a sealed envelope addressed to the School of Medicine's Purchasing Department."

(A) [1]
(B) [2]
(C) [3]
(D) [4]

解答・解説

問題21-24は次のウェブページに関するものです。

http://straubuniversityschoolofmedicine.edu/vendors/rfp0023

Straub 大学医学部は現在、手術用手袋、白衣、保護用ゴーグルを供給してくれる業者を求めています。本学は、学生と教授陣向けの、高品質で病院仕様の備品を必要としており、特に、地元の病院や診療所と現在取引をしている販売会社に関心があります。

本学のウェブサイトから、提案依頼書（RFP）の指示一式をダウンロードすることができます。以下は提案要件の概略です。

・定型の提案書式。本学のウェブサイトからダウンロード可能
・販売会社の概要および業界における同社の経験
・仕様および価格の全一覧を付した、製品の説明
・販売会社の製品あるいはサービスの質について述べることのできる、現在もしくは最近の顧客3社の連絡先

RFP について何かご質問がございましたら、それらを文書で7月20日までに queries@straub.edu 宛てにご提出ください。ご質問に対する回答は、8月4日に Straub 大学医学部のウェブページ上で公開されます。

提案書は8月15日必着です。*全ての書類は、封書でこの日付までに医学部の購買部宛てに到着しなければなりません。全ての提出物は入念に検討され、採用された提案書は9月10日に発表されます。契約書は最有力候補業者とその同月に最終的な形にされ、契約は10月1日より発効します。

*問題24の挿入文の訳

---

21. 正解 **(A)**

訳　この指示は誰に向けられていますか。

(A) 医療用品の販売会社
(B) 病院の職への応募者
(C) 病院の管理者
(D) 医学生

解説　❶1～2行目に「Straub 大学医学部は現在、手術用手袋、白衣、保護用ゴーグルを供給する業者を求めている」とあり、❷では提案要件の概略について、❹では提出期日や選考過程などについて説明されている。よって、この指示は医療用品の販売会社に向けたものだと分かる。

22. 正解 **(B)**

訳　候補者は何を提出することを求められていますか。

(A) 提案書に関する質問
(B) 取引上の照会先
(C) 申込金
(D) 製品の見本

解説　❷で提案要件の概略として挙げられている箇条書きの4点目に、「販売会社の製品あるいはサービスの質について述べることのできる、現在もしくは最近の顧客3社の連絡先」とある。

23. 正解 **(C)**

訳　候補者はいつ、自分が選出されたかどうかを知りますか。

(A) 7月
(B) 8月
(C) 9月
(D) 10月

解説　❹2行目に、the winning proposal will be announced on September 10「採用された提案書は9月10日に発表される」とある。

24. 正解 **(C)**

訳　[1]、[2]、[3]、[4]と記載された箇所のうち、次の文が入るのに最もふさわしいのはどれですか。

「全ての書類は、封書でこの日付までに医学部の購買部宛てに到着しなければなりません」

(A) [1]
(B) [2]
(C) [3]
(D) [4]

解説　挿入文は書類の提出方法と宛先を伝えている。(C) [3]に入れると、挿入文中の this date「この日付」が❹1行目のAugust 15 を指し、提案書の提出期日に続けて提出方法と宛先を伝える自然な流れとなる。

Questions 25-29 refer to the following article, e-mail, and Web page.

❶ (November 6)—The Rudi's store at 47 Kask Highway in Glencoe Park will shut its doors next Saturday, adding another empty building to the local landscape. The shutdown is one of a rash of store closings in the greater Billington area and is a result of two major forces. First, Rudi's has changed its business plan, relying increasingly on online sales. Second, much of the traffic on Kask Highway has been rerouted to the recently completed bypass, resulting in fewer potential customers passing through Billington.

❷ Other Rudi's closings over the past two years include the store at 38 Quail Hill Road, the store at 21 Lowell Boulevard, and the downtown megastore at 59 Claremont Street on the banks of the Corks River. A Rudi's spokesperson stated that no further closures are expected.

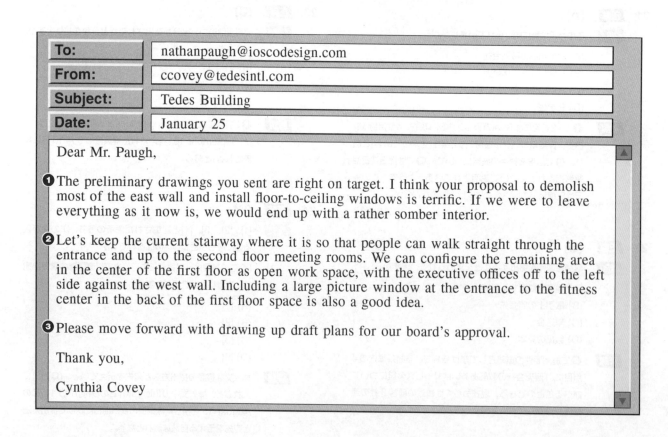

To:	nathanpaugh@ioscodesign.com
From:	ccovey@tedesintl.com
Subject:	Tedes Building
Date:	January 25

Dear Mr. Paugh,

❶ The preliminary drawings you sent are right on target. I think your proposal to demolish most of the east wall and install floor-to-ceiling windows is terrific. If we were to leave everything as it now is, we would end up with a rather somber interior.

❷ Let's keep the current stairway where it is so that people can walk straight through the entrance and up to the second floor meeting rooms. We can configure the remaining area in the center of the first floor as open work space, with the executive offices off to the left side against the west wall. Including a large picture window at the entrance to the fitness center in the back of the first floor space is also a good idea.

❸ Please move forward with drawing up draft plans for our board's approval.

Thank you,

Cynthia Covey

http://www.buildingmonthly.com/readersreviews

| HOME | LATEST ISSUE | **READERS' REVIEWS** | ADVERTISERS |

The new Tedes corporate building
Posted by Monty K.

❶ Tedes International has opened its corporate headquarters in a former Rudi's megastore building. In an area with many vacated retail buildings, one is now a workplace for over 400 Tedes employees. Corporations looking for prime real estate should take notice.

❷ The interior design of the Tedes Building is notable for its mixed use of open and closed space. The entrance is open and inviting and leads to a wide staircase up to the second floor, which houses offices for upper management. Large windows installed as one of the exterior walls create a bright atmosphere in the open work space and nearby meeting rooms, while boats glide by on the river right in front of them. On my visit, several employees were exercising on fitness bikes in full view at the rear of the first-floor space.

25. What is the purpose of the article?

(A) To notify readers of recent job openings
(B) To publicize an online sale
(C) To report on a store closing
(D) To alert motorists to changing traffic patterns

26. Who most likely is Mr. Paugh?

(A) An artist
(B) An architect
(C) A real estate agent
(D) A reporter

27. Which former Rudi's location did Tedes International choose for its headquarters?

(A) 47 Kask Highway
(B) 38 Quail Hill Road
(C) 21 Lowell Boulevard
(D) 59 Claremont Street

28. What aspect of the design suggested by Ms. Covey was ultimately rejected?

(A) The replacement of a wall with windows
(B) The layout of the entrance
(C) The inclusion of a fitness center
(D) The location of the offices

29. What is implied by the reviewer?

(A) Tedes International is planning to expand.
(B) Tedes International wants to sell its property.
(C) Vacant buildings have great potential.
(D) Local businesses may experience reduced profits.

問題25-29は次の記事、Eメール、ウェブページに関するものです。

1. 記事

（11月6日）——グレンコーパークのカスク街道47番地にあるRudi's社の店舗は、次の土曜日に扉を閉ざし、その地域の風景にもう1棟空きビルを加えることになる。この閉店は、ビリントン広域圏で頻発する店舗の閉鎖の1つであり、2つの大きな影響力によるものである。第1に、Rudi's社が事業計画を変更し、オンライン販売に一層依存するようになったこと。第2に、カスク街道の交通の大部分が、最近完成した迂回路の方へ流れ、ビリントンを通る潜在顧客が減少する結果となったことだ。

過去2年間のRudi's社の他の閉店には、クウェイルヒル通り38番地の店舗、ローウェル大通り21番地の店舗、そしてコークス川岸のクレアモント通り59番地にあった中心街の超大型店舗が含まれる。Rudi's社の広報担当者は、これ以上の閉店は一切予定されていないと明言した。

2. Eメール

受信者：nathanpaugh@ioscodesign.com
送信者：ccovey@tedesintl.com
件名：Tedes ビル
日付：1月25日

Paugh様

お送りくださった仮の図面は、まさに期待通りのものです。東側の壁の大半を取り壊し、床から天井までの窓を設置するという貴殿のご提案は素晴らしいと思います。もし何もかも現状のままにしておいたとしたら、最終的にかなり陰気な内装になってしまうでしょう。

今の階段は、そのままの場所で残しましょう。そうすれば人々が入り口をまっすぐ通り抜け、2階の会議室に歩いて上がっていけます。1階の中央にある残りの区域は開放的な作業スペースとし、重役の執務室を左側へ、西の壁際に配置することができます。1階スペースの奥にあるフィットネスセンターへの入り口に大きな一枚ガラスの窓を入れることも良いアイデアです。

当社役員会の承認に向けて、設計図の草案の作成を進めてください。

よろしくお願いいたします。

Cynthia Covey

3. ウェブページ

http://www.buildingmonthly.com/readersreviews

| ホーム | 最新号 | 読者レビュー | 広告主 |

Tedes 社の新しいビル
Monty K. 投稿

Tedesインターナショナル社は、かつてRudi's社の超大型店舗だった建物に本社を開設した。空き家となった小売店のビルが多数ある地域において、1棟は今や400名超のTedes社の従業員の職場である。優良な不動産を求めている企業は注目すべきである。

Tedes ビルの内部設計は、開放的スペースと閉鎖的スペースを取り混ぜて使用していることで注目に値する。入り口は広々として、いざなうようであり、2階に至る広い階段に通じている。2階には、経営上層部のための執務室が入っている。外壁の一部として設置された大型の窓は、開放的な作業スペースと近くの会議室に明るい雰囲気を作り出し、他方で、すぐ目の前にある川をボートが滑るように進む。私の訪問時には、数名の従業員が1階スペースの奥で、よく見える所でフィットネスバイクで運動をしていた。

25. **正解** **(C)**

訳 記事の目的は何ですか。

(A) 読者に最近の求人を知らせること。
(B) オンラインのセールを宣伝すること。
(C) 店舗の閉鎖を報道すること。
(D) 車を運転する人に、交通パターンの変化について注意を喚起すること。

解説 **1**の記事の**❶** 1～3行目に、「グレンコーパークのカスク街道47番地にあるRudi's社の店舗は、次の土曜日に扉を閉ざす」とあり、その後も閉店の要因などが述べられている。よって、記事の目的はRudi's社の店舗の閉鎖を報道することだと分かる。

26. **正解** **(B)**

訳 Paughさんとは誰だと考えられますか。

(A) 芸術家
(B) 建築家
(C) 不動産仲介人
(D) 記者

解説 Paughさんは**2**のEメールの受信者。Eメールの本文では、**❶** 1行目で「お送りくださった仮の図面は、まさに期待通りのものだ」と伝えられ、建物の設計についての話が続いている。さらに、**❸**で「設計図の草案の作成を進めてほしい」と依頼を受けていることから、Paughさんは建築家と考えられる。

27. **正解** **(D)**

訳 Tedesインターナショナル社は、かつてのRudi's社のどの場所を本社に選びましたか。

(A) カスク街道47番地
(B) クウェイルヒル通り38番地
(C) ローウェル大通り21番地
(D) クレアモント通り59番地

解説 **3**のウェブページの**❶** 1～2行目に、「Tedesインターナショナル社は、かつてRudi's社の超大型店舗だった建物に本社を開設した」とある。**1**の記事の**❷** 3～5行目に、閉店したRudi's社の店舗の1つとして、「コークス川岸のクレアモント通り59番地にあった中心街の超大型店舗」が挙げられているので、(D)が正解。

28. **正解** **(D)**

訳 Coveyさんによって示された設計のどの点が、最終的に不採用とされましたか。

(A) 壁を窓で置き換えること
(B) 入り口の配置
(C) フィットネスセンターを含めること
(D) 執務室の位置

解説 Coveyさんは**2**のEメールの送信者。仮の図面を作ったPaughさんに対して、**❷** 2～4行目で「1階の中央にある残りの区域は開放的な作業スペースとし、重役の執務室を左側へ、西の壁際に配置することができる」と述べている。一方、完成したビルの読者レビューを載せた**3**のウェブページには、**❷** 2～3行目に「入り口は広々として、いざなうようであり、2階に至る広い階段に通じている。2階には、経営上層部のための執務室が入っている」とあることから、重役の執務室はCoveyさんが提案した1階ではなく、2階に配置されたと分かる。

29. **正解** **(C)**

訳 レビュー投稿者によって何が示唆されていますか。

(A) Tedesインターナショナル社は拡大する予定である。
(B) Tedesインターナショナル社は同社の不動産を売却したいと思っている。
(C) 空きビルは大きな可能性を持っている。
(D) 地元の企業は減益を経験するかもしれない。

解説 **3**のウェブページの読者レビューの**❶** 1～3行目で、Tedesインターナショナル社がかつてRudi's社の超大型店舗だった建物に本社を開設したことで、空きビル1棟が今や多数の従業員の職場へと変化したことが述べられている。続けて「優良な不動産を求めている企業は注目すべきだ」とあることから、レビュー投稿者は空きビルに大きな可能性があることを示唆していると考えられる。

採点・結果について

TOEIC® Listening & Reading Test のテスト結果は合格・不合格ではなく、リスニングセクション5〜495点、リーディングセクション5〜495点、トータル10〜990点のスコアで、5点刻みで表示されます。このスコアは、常に評価基準を一定に保つために統計処理が行われ、英語能力に変化がない限りスコアも一定に保たれる点が大きな特長です。

テスト結果はOfficial Score Certificate（公式認定証）として、試験日から30日以内に発送されます。また、インターネットからお申し込みいただく際、「テスト結果のインターネット表示」で「利用する」を選択すると、試験日から17日後にインターネットでスコアを確認することが可能です。（日米の祝日の影響により、遅れる場合がございます。）

Official Score Certificate（公式認定証）のサンプル

Your Score（スコア）：
今回取得したリスニング、リーディングの各セクションスコアです。右側にトータルスコアが記載されます。

Percentile Rank（パーセンタイルランク）：
あなたが取得したスコアに満たない受験者が全体でどのくらいを占めているかをパーセンテージで示しています。例えば、リスニングでスコア300点、パーセンタイルランクが41%という場合には、リスニングスコア300点未満の受験者が全体の41%いることを示します。つまり、リスニングスコア300点を取得した受験者は上位59%に位置することになります。

Score Descriptors（スコアディスクリプターズ）：
レベル別評価です。今回取得したスコアをもとに、あなたの英語運用能力上の長所が書かれています。

Abilities Measured（アビリティーズメジャード）：
項目別正答率です。リスニング、リーディングの5つの項目における正答率を示しています。

TOEIC® Listening & Reading 公開テストのお申し込み

IIBC公式サイト **https://www.iibc-global.org** にてテスト日程、申込方法、注意事項をご確認の上、申込受付期間内にお申し込みください。試験の実施方法などに変更があった場合には IIBC 公式サイト等でご案内いたします。

お問い合わせ

一般財団法人 国際ビジネスコミュニケーション協会　IIBC 試験運営センター
〒100-0014　東京都千代田区永田町 2-14-2　山王グランドビル
TEL：03-5521-6033（土・日・祝日・年末年始を除く 10:00 〜 17:00）

TEST 1

 **CD 1 11-92**

LISTENING TEST ·························· p.30

READING TEST ·························· p.42

＊解答用紙は本誌 p.112 の後ろに綴じ込まれています。

実際のテストでは問題用紙の裏側に、以下のようなテスト全体についての指示が印刷されています。
この指示を念頭においてテストに取り組みましょう。

General Directions

This test is designed to measure your English language ability. The test is divided into two sections: Listening and Reading.

You must mark all of your answers on the separate answer sheet. For each question, you should select the best answer from the answer choices given. Then, on your answer sheet, you should find the number of the question and fill in the space that corresponds to the letter of the answer that you have selected. If you decide to change an answer, completely erase your old answer and then mark your new answer.

訳 ### 全体についての指示

このテストはあなたの英語言語能力を測定するよう設計されています。テストはリスニングとリーディングという2つのセクションに分けられています。

答えは全て別紙の解答用紙にマークしてください。それぞれの設問について、与えられた選択肢から最も適切な答えを選びます。そして解答用紙の該当する問題番号に、選択した答えを塗りつぶしてください。答えを修正する場合は、元の答えを完全に消してから新しい答えをマークしてください。

LISTENING TEST

In the Listening test, you will be asked to demonstrate how well you understand spoken English. The entire Listening test will last approximately 45 minutes. There are four parts, and directions are given for each part. You must mark your answers on the separate answer sheet. Do not write your answers in your test book.

PART 1

Directions: For each question in this part, you will hear four statements about a picture in your test book. When you hear the statements, you must select the one statement that best describes what you see in the picture. Then find the number of the question on your answer sheet and mark your answer. The statements will not be printed in your test book and will be spoken only one time.

Statement (C), "They're sitting at a table," is the best description of the picture, so you should select answer (C) and mark it on your answer sheet.

1.

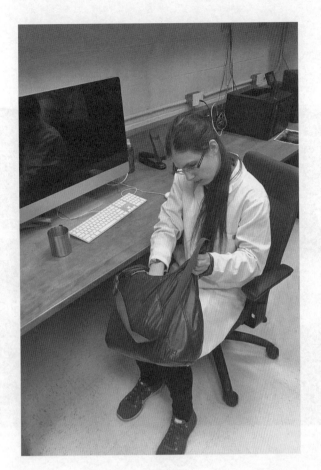

2.

GO ON TO THE NEXT PAGE ➔

3.

4.

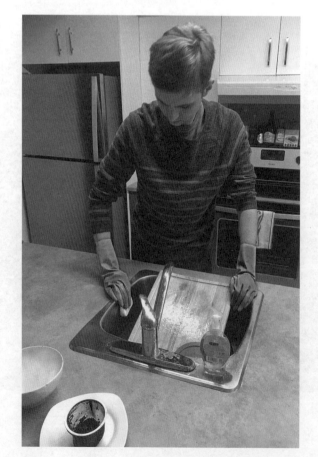

5.

6.

GO ON TO THE NEXT PAGE ➡

PART 2

Directions: You will hear a question or statement and three responses spoken in English. They will not be printed in your test book and will be spoken only one time. Select the best response to the question or statement and mark the letter (A), (B), or (C) on your answer sheet.

7. Mark your answer on your answer sheet.

8. Mark your answer on your answer sheet.

9. Mark your answer on your answer sheet.

10. Mark your answer on your answer sheet.

11. Mark your answer on your answer sheet.

12. Mark your answer on your answer sheet.

13. Mark your answer on your answer sheet.

14. Mark your answer on your answer sheet.

15. Mark your answer on your answer sheet.

16. Mark your answer on your answer sheet.

17. Mark your answer on your answer sheet.

18. Mark your answer on your answer sheet.

19. Mark your answer on your answer sheet.

20. Mark your answer on your answer sheet.

21. Mark your answer on your answer sheet.

22. Mark your answer on your answer sheet.

23. Mark your answer on your answer sheet.

24. Mark your answer on your answer sheet.

25. Mark your answer on your answer sheet.

26. Mark your answer on your answer sheet.

27. Mark your answer on your answer sheet.

28. Mark your answer on your answer sheet.

29. Mark your answer on your answer sheet.

30. Mark your answer on your answer sheet.

31. Mark your answer on your answer sheet.

PART 3

Directions: You will hear some conversations between two or more people. You will be asked to answer three questions about what the speakers say in each conversation. Select the best response to each question and mark the letter (A), (B), (C), or (D) on your answer sheet. The conversations will not be printed in your test book and will be spoken only one time.

32. Where is the conversation taking place?
(A) At a supermarket
(B) At a shoe store
(C) At a repair shop
(D) At a shipping company

33. What does the man explain to the woman?
(A) A new location recently opened.
(B) Express delivery will cost extra.
(C) Some items are out of stock.
(D) Some merchandise was moved.

34. What does the man offer to do?
(A) Call another location
(B) Reduce a price
(C) Check a Web site
(D) Cancel an order

35. Where does the man most likely work?
(A) At an auto repair shop
(B) At a construction site
(C) At a factory
(D) At an airport

36. What does the woman say she needs to do tomorrow?
(A) Conduct an inspection
(B) Meet a client
(C) Reserve a parking space
(D) Make a payment

37. What does the man offer the woman?
(A) Some safety glasses
(B) Express delivery
(C) Another vehicle
(D) An alternate date

38. What are the women surprised about?
(A) A line is long.
(B) An exhibit is closed.
(C) A sign is missing.
(D) A speaker is delayed.

39. According to the man, what will take place at noon?
(A) A lecture
(B) A tour
(C) A concert
(D) An art sale

40. Where will the women probably go next?
(A) To a park
(B) To a theater
(C) To a restaurant
(D) To a school

41. Why is the man calling?
(A) To check the status of an order
(B) To report a computer problem
(C) To propose a policy change
(D) To discuss a software installation

42. What information does the woman request?
(A) A username
(B) A call-back number
(C) An office location
(D) An identification number

43. Why does the man say, "I'm presenting at a meeting in 30 minutes"?
(A) To express urgency
(B) To decline an invitation
(C) To correct a misunderstanding
(D) To request a deadline extension

GO ON TO THE NEXT PAGE

44. Where do the speakers work?

(A) At an art gallery
(B) At a library
(C) At a cafeteria
(D) At a bus station

45. What do the speakers plan to purchase?

(A) Some furniture
(B) Laptop computers
(C) Additional lighting
(D) Some artwork

46. Where will the woman go next?

(A) To a budget meeting
(B) To a training session
(C) To a department store
(D) To a supply room

---

47. Where do the women most likely work?

(A) At a hotel
(B) At an airport
(C) At a car rental service
(D) At a travel agency

48. What problem does the man mention?

(A) He cannot connect to the Internet.
(B) He cannot make a reservation.
(C) A key is not working properly.
(D) A restaurant is closed.

49. What does Isabel give the man?

(A) A discount coupon
(B) A free upgrade
(C) A brochure
(D) A souvenir

---

50. According to the woman, what will the company do next week?

(A) Repave a parking area
(B) Hold an annual staff meeting
(C) Update a vacation policy
(D) Have an anniversary celebration

51. What are employees encouraged to do?

(A) Sign up for additional tasks
(B) Complete a questionnaire
(C) Apply for a business course
(D) Work from home

52. Who will the man most likely talk to?

(A) A building contractor
(B) An office manager
(C) A training coordinator
(D) A computer salesperson

---

53. Which city department does the woman work for?

(A) Health
(B) Housing
(C) Finance
(D) Transportation

54. What does the man say he has been trying to do?

(A) Renew a lease
(B) Respond to a survey
(C) Buy a monthly pass
(D) Find a map

55. Why does the woman apologize?

(A) A payment method has been declined.
(B) A remodeling project must be postponed.
(C) A Web page is not working.
(D) A street has been closed.

---

56. Why does the woman say, "That place has been for sale for quite a while"?

(A) She is disappointed by a decision.
(B) She will visit a location soon.
(C) She is surprised at some news.
(D) She plans to make an offer.

57. What is special about the Fontana Theater?

(A) It is close to the city center.
(B) It is a historic landmark.
(C) It is near public transportation.
(D) It is owned by a celebrity.

58. What does the woman say she would look forward to seeing?

(A) A historic tour of the city
(B) The draft of a contract
(C) A theater production
(D) The view from a rooftop

59. Who most likely is the man?

(A) A musician
(B) A radio announcer
(C) A film critic
(D) A photographer

60. According to the woman, what will the man have to do to get a permit?

(A) Pay a processing fee
(B) Submit a work sample
(C) Attend an orientation session
(D) Provide a letter from an employer

61. Why should the man contact the Help Desk?

(A) To buy recordings of previous events
(B) To pick up free tickets to shows
(C) To get advice on planning local trips
(D) To schedule interviews with performers

Art Center Pottery Classes	
Class	Dates
Level 1	April 1- April 30
Level 2	May 1 – May 31
Level 3	June 1 – June 30
Level 4	July 1 – July 31

62. What does the man say about all of the classes?

(A) They include free materials.
(B) They take place in the morning.
(C) They can be repeated.
(D) They are still available.

63. Look at the graphic. Which class level will the woman most likely choose?

(A) Level 1
(B) Level 2
(C) Level 3
(D) Level 4

64. What does the man say about a payment?

(A) It can be paid in installments.
(B) It must be paid by credit card.
(C) It is refundable.
(D) It will be collected on the first day of class.

TEST 1

GO ON TO THE NEXT PAGE

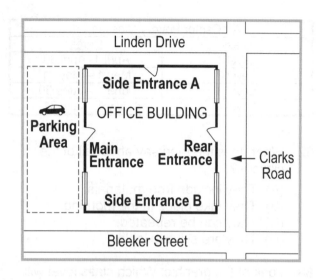

65. Who is the man?

(A) A construction worker
(B) A repair technician
(C) A security guard
(D) An office manager

66. Look at the graphic. Where will a delivery be made?

(A) At side entrance A
(B) At the rear entrance
(C) At side entrance B
(D) At the main entrance

67. What does the woman say the driver will do?

(A) Provide an invoice
(B) Install some equipment
(C) Make a phone call
(D) Show identification

68. What field does the woman most likely work in?

(A) Hospitality
(B) Finance
(C) Education
(D) Transportation

69. What does the woman say she is hoping to do?

(A) Publish an article
(B) Reduce expenses
(C) Change a date
(D) Increase membership

70. Look at the graphic. What is the woman's travel destination?

(A) Boston
(B) Los Angeles
(C) Chicago
(D) Philadelphia

PART 4

Directions: You will hear some talks given by a single speaker. You will be asked to answer three questions about what the speaker says in each talk. Select the best response to each question and mark the letter (A), (B), (C), or (D) on your answer sheet. The talks will not be printed in your test book and will be spoken only one time.

71. What is being advertised?

(A) A convention center
(B) A shopping mall
(C) An apartment building
(D) An amusement park

72. What will the listeners appreciate the most about Bora Park Tower?

(A) The convenient location
(B) The low prices
(C) The free parking
(D) The fast Internet access

73. What does the speaker suggest the listeners do online?

(A) Download discount coupons
(B) Watch some videos
(C) Apply for a job
(D) Schedule a visit

74. What does the company make?

(A) Furniture
(B) Electronics
(C) Cars
(D) Toys

75. According to the speaker, what will happen next quarter?

(A) Factory machinery will be upgraded.
(B) Assembly of a new product will begin.
(C) New-hire training will take place.
(D) A vacation policy will be updated.

76. What are the listeners asked to do?

(A) Reassign some work
(B) Draft a cost estimate
(C) Prepare a safety manual
(D) Conduct an inventory

77. Who most likely is Fernando Ortiz?

(A) An actor
(B) A chef
(C) A gardener
(D) An architect

78. According to the speaker, what can the listeners purchase during the break?

(A) Maps
(B) Souvenirs
(C) Refreshments
(D) Transportation passes

79. Why does the speaker say, "the sun is shining"?

(A) To make a recommendation
(B) To disagree with a weather report
(C) To ask for assistance
(D) To explain why an itinerary has changed

80. Where does the talk most likely take place?

(A) At a bank
(B) At a storage facility
(C) At a hardware store
(D) At a real estate office

81. What added benefit of a system does the speaker mention?

(A) It records all visitors.
(B) It turns off automatically.
(C) It is easy to upgrade.
(D) It is portable.

82. Why are employees asked to see Hao Nan?

(A) To get a parking pass
(B) To sign up for training
(C) To update payroll information
(D) To have a photograph taken

GO ON TO THE NEXT PAGE

83. What type of product does the speaker sell?

(A) Food
(B) Clothing
(C) Kitchen appliances
(D) Cookbooks

84. What achievement is the speaker proud of?

(A) His products broke a sales record.
(B) His products have become widely available.
(C) His products were featured in a news article.
(D) His products won an industry award.

85. What does the speaker say he will do in the future?

(A) Work with local farms
(B) Raise funds for charities
(C) Continue using traditional techniques
(D) Try different business models

---

86. What is the main topic of the workshop?

(A) Photo editing
(B) Cooking
(C) Computer repair
(D) Nutrition

87. What does the speaker mean when he says, "we'd like to have the computers for future classes"?

(A) The speaker is requesting donations.
(B) The speaker wants to renew a contract.
(C) The listeners should be careful.
(D) The listeners should complete a questionnaire.

88. What does the speaker say is discounted?

(A) A software program
(B) A library membership
(C) A magazine subscription
(D) A workshop registration

---

89. According to the speaker, why is a change in strategy needed?

(A) Sales results have been disappointing.
(B) Competition in the technology field has increased.
(C) An overseas office has recently opened.
(D) A manufacturing process has changed.

90. According to the speaker, what has research indicated?

(A) Television sets are decreasing in price.
(B) Online advertising is successful.
(C) Customers prefer to pay with credit cards.
(D) Most consumers own several mobile devices.

91. What is the company planning to do?

(A) Upgrade its computer system
(B) Merge with another company
(C) Conduct a customer survey
(D) Hire specialized employees

---

92. What project is being discussed?

(A) The opening of a town library
(B) The construction of a new bus station
(C) The conversion of a railroad line
(D) The demolition of a historic building

93. According to the speaker, what can the listeners view on the town's Web site?

(A) A map
(B) Some images
(C) The annual budget
(D) A list of upcoming events

94. What does the speaker imply when she says, "construction will begin in two months"?

(A) Some work is on schedule.
(B) Noise in an area will likely increase.
(C) The listeners might experience traffic delays.
(D) The listeners should make a choice soon.

Conference Room Arrangements

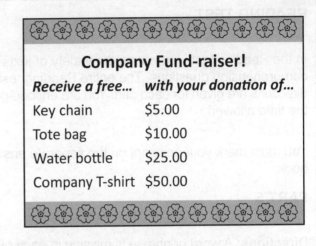

Chairs only	Chairs and tables
①	②
③	④

Company Fund-raiser!

Receive a free...	with your donation of...
Key chain	$5.00
Tote bag	$10.00
Water bottle	$25.00
Company T-shirt	$50.00

95. What is the caller pleased about?

(A) A high attendance rate
(B) An award nomination
(C) A convention location
(D) A presentation topic

96. Look at the graphic. Which room arrangement does the caller recommend?

(A) Arrangement 1
(B) Arrangement 2
(C) Arrangement 3
(D) Arrangement 4

97. What needs to be updated in the program booklet?

(A) Some agenda items
(B) A registration deadline
(C) A biography
(D) A city map

98. What is the company raising money for?

(A) A mobile health clinic
(B) A music school
(C) A summer camp program
(D) A library computer room

99. Look at the graphic. Which thank-you gift has the company run out of?

(A) Key chains
(B) Tote bags
(C) Water bottles
(D) Company T-shirts

100. What does the speaker ask the listeners to do?

(A) Order more supplies
(B) Choose a design
(C) Complete a survey
(D) Run a report

This is the end of the Listening test. Turn to Part 5 in your test book.

GO ON TO THE NEXT PAGE

READING TEST

In the Reading test, you will read a variety of texts and answer several different types of reading comprehension questions. The entire Reading test will last 75 minutes. There are three parts, and directions are given for each part. You are encouraged to answer as many questions as possible within the time allowed.

You must mark your answers on the separate answer sheet. Do not write your answers in your test book.

PART 5

Directions: A word or phrase is missing in each of the sentences below. Four answer choices are given below each sentence. Select the best answer to complete the sentence. Then mark the letter (A), (B), (C), or (D) on your answer sheet.

101. All FFP employees are encouraged to participate ------- in community programs.

(A) regularly
(B) regular
(C) regulation
(D) regularity

102. Please inspect the contents of the package and contact us with any -------.

(A) questionable
(B) questioning
(C) questioned
(D) questions

103. The training instructors will stay at the ------- renovated guest house.

(A) newly
(B) enough
(C) directly
(D) exactly

104. Sunnyville Public Library is ------- today because of a problem with the electrical system.

(A) certain
(B) closed
(C) returned
(D) simple

105. Ms. Suzuki ------- as a leader in the Asian financial services industry.

(A) recognizes
(B) recognizing
(C) is recognized
(D) has recognized

106. Before meeting with the board, Mr. Ortiz practiced his ------- several times.

(A) presentation
(B) leader
(C) setting
(D) education

107. The firm's ------- strategy is quite different from that of its competitors.

(A) hired
(B) to hire
(C) hires
(D) hiring

108. Before the cafeteria's expansion, a limited number of employees could ------- the seating area at one time.

(A) access
(B) accessibly
(C) accessing
(D) to access

109. The proposal from ------- development team was met with great enthusiasm.

(A) us
(B) we
(C) ours
(D) our

110. At Triton Bank, new employees have 30 days to ------- in the company's benefits program.

    (A) credit
    (B) renew
    (C) commit
    (D) enroll

111. Epiquick Production Services hired a ------- speaker to boost employee morale.

    (A) motivational
    (B) motivate
    (C) to motivate
    (D) motivates

112. The branch office in Riyadh will be closed on Thursday and Friday ------- a national holiday.

    (A) at
    (B) of
    (C) for
    (D) with

113. Ms. Patel ------- offered to share the results of her research with the planning board.

    (A) generosity
    (B) most generous
    (C) generously
    (D) generous

114. The training session will begin fifteen minutes late ------- Ms. Stumpff is still in a meeting.

    (A) as
    (B) then
    (C) or
    (D) but

115. Skyspan Airlines compensated passengers whose flights ------- due to crew shortage.

    (A) cancel
    (B) to be canceled
    (C) were canceled
    (D) canceling

116. Over the past six months, there has been a tremendous ------- for Hudson's motorized bicycles.

    (A) amount
    (B) demand
    (C) speed
    (D) service

117. The marketing director is ------- in the latest Web site design than in the previous ones.

    (A) more interested
    (B) most interested
    (C) too interested
    (D) interested

118. November's sales figures were ------- high given the poor weather conditions during that month.

    (A) primarily
    (B) surprisingly
    (C) separately
    (D) accurately

119. Camico Broadband Services earned excellent ratings for ------- on the latest consumer survey.

    (A) reliable
    (B) reliability
    (C) reliably
    (D) rely

120. ------- volunteered to complete the report, so Ms. Hughes assigned it to Mr. Nakamura.

    (A) Have not
    (B) Having nobody
    (C) No one
    (D) No

121. ------- the guidance of a talented coach, Belfast's chess team has made great progress.

    (A) Under
    (B) Along
    (C) Toward
    (D) Among

122. Mr. Lukas e-mailed his staff to ask whether ------- would be available to cover the front desk from noon to 1 P.M.

    (A) other
    (B) himself
    (C) few
    (D) anyone

123. Bluing, Inc., combined its two warehouses in order to ------- the efficiency of its operations.

(A) collapse
(B) maximize
(C) astonish
(D) resemble

124. ------- he is scheduled for a promotion, Anton Shaqua plans to leave the law firm soon.

(A) Although
(B) Prior to
(C) From
(D) Perhaps

125. Margolex' survey results were ------- analyzed using state-of-the-art software.

(A) brightly
(B) thickly
(C) boastfully
(D) effortlessly

126. ------- Zamlo toys are sold primarily in Australia, they are manufactured in Malaysia.

(A) Despite
(B) Even
(C) While
(D) That

127. Ms. Cho asked her secretary to compile a list of caterers ------- menus include vegetarian options.

(A) who
(B) whom
(C) whose
(D) whoever

128. The customer who called to complain had received an ------- tracking number.

(A) unheard
(B) absent
(C) inaccurate
(D) opposite

129. After 25 years of use, Burl Business Solutions has decided to ------- its well-known logo.

(A) approach
(B) retire
(C) reduce
(D) appoint

130. Any ------- to the company's work-from-home policy must be approved by the Human Resources Department.

(A) inspection
(B) exception
(C) acquisition
(D) correlation

PART 6

Directions: Read the texts that follow. A word, phrase, or sentence is missing in parts of each text. Four answer choices for each question are given below the text. Select the best answer to complete the text. Then mark the letter (A), (B), (C), or (D) on your answer sheet.

Questions 131-134 refer to the following instructions.

Residential Garbage and Recycling Disposal

Garbage and recycling are picked up on ------- days, depending on your address. Check our
                                   131.

Web site to find your designated pickup day. All residents receive a large blue container for

regular household garbage and a large green container for material to be recycled. -------. For
                                                                                   132.

recyclables, do not include plastic bags. ------- may get caught in the sorting machinery at the
                                          133.

processing plant. Please also try to reduce the number of items you throw away. -------, old
                                                                                134.

furniture or clothing that is still usable can be donated to one of our many local charity

organizations or secondhand shops.

131. (A) strict
     (B) different
     (C) recent
     (D) direct

132. (A) If there are any problems with the
         payment, you will be notified.
     (B) The calendar is updated regularly.
     (C) They are free initially, but there is a
         fee for replacements.
     (D) By all accounts, the program was a
         success.

133. (A) What
     (B) These
     (C) Theirs
     (D) Either

134. (A) Otherwise
     (B) Nevertheless
     (C) Instead
     (D) For example

GO ON TO THE NEXT PAGE

To: <hiddenlist>
From: events@estoncity.gov
Date: July 1
Subject: Scavenger hunt

Dear Residents,

This year's Eston City Scavenger Hunt (ECSH) is coming soon! Now in its seventh year, the ECSH has become a ------- for local residents. Gather clues, solve challenges, and uncover
135.
hidden details about historical sites throughout the city.

The ECSH starts in Founders Park at 10:00 A.M. on July 20. ------- takes two to four hours to
136.
complete, and a smartphone is required. -------. All of the sites are within walking distance of
137.
the park. -------, join your neighbors to celebrate with refreshments and music in the park.
138.
Register online at www.estoncity.gov/ecsh by July 18 or in person on the day of the event.

We hope to see you there!

Eston City Events Office

135. (A) tradition
(B) traditional
(C) traditions
(D) traditionally

136. (A) Another
(B) Each
(C) Mine
(D) It

137. (A) The park map is very detailed.
(B) City hall was built 75 years ago.
(C) You will need only one device per team.
(D) Feedback from participants would be helpful.

138. (A) Afterward
(B) However
(C) Similarly
(D) Rather

Questions 139-142 refer to the following letter.

Matisson Tire Supply
37 Fieldcrest Pike
Milwaukee, WI 53205

January 15

Dear Valued Customer,

You may have heard recent news reports about a ------- of the raw materials needed to make
                                             139.
our products. -------, we purchase our materials three months in advance and will not need to
              140.
increase our prices at this time. However, given the increase in our costs, we anticipate a

slight price increase of 5 percent beginning on May 1. -------.
                                                       141.

We ------- your business and look forward to your continued patronage. If you have any
   142.
questions or concerns, please feel free to contact me.

Sincerely,

Hugh Toussaint
Wholesale Manager, Matisson Tire Supply

---

139. (A) short
(B) shortage
(C) shortly
(D) shortening

140. (A) Unexpectedly
(B) Besides
(C) Fortunately
(D) Likewise

141. (A) These materials are sourced
underground.
(B) We will let you know if the situation
changes.
(C) We guarantee all of our tires for one
year.
(D) Our products are the best on the
market.

142. (A) values
(B) valuation
(C) valuing
(D) value

GO ON TO THE NEXT PAGE

Questions 143-146 refer to the following article.

Heswall Natural Foods (HNF), a Liverpool-based food retailer, announced yesterday that it has

appointed Sven Larsen as vice president. -------. Larsen has twenty years of experience in the
143.

food industry and will be ------- for the company's York facility. He will report directly to CEO
144.

Wilma Collins. "We are delighted to welcome Mr. Larsen to head our York operations," said

Collins. "His ------- in the natural and organic food business is legendary."
145.

Prior to accepting the position at HNF, Larsen worked for Simcox Foods, where he rose through

the ranks to become senior director of marketing. ------- working at Simcox, Larsen designed
146.

magazine advertisements for the food industry.

---

143. (A) He is replacing Judith Middleton, who is retiring.
    (B) HNF entered the Canadian market last year.
    (C) Simcox Foods is engaged in merger talks with a former competitor.
    (D) Collins has been CEO for more than a decade.

144. (A) responsibility
    (B) responsibly
    (C) responsibleness
    (D) responsible

145. (A) purpose
    (B) observation
    (C) leadership
    (D) calculation

146. (A) Until
    (B) Without
    (C) Near
    (D) Before

PART 7

Directions: In this part you will read a selection of texts, such as magazine and newspaper articles, e-mails, and instant messages. Each text or set of texts is followed by several questions. Select the best answer for each question and mark the letter (A), (B), (C), or (D) on your answer sheet.

Questions 147-148 refer to the following sign.

> **Attention All Zandpro Technology**
> **Employees and Visitors**
>
> Welcome to our Product Innovation Factory.
>
> • To safeguard our designs, no cameras or audio- and video-recording devices are permitted on the factory floor.
>
> • Please leave all such devices, including mobile phones, in the safe in room 332.

147. According to the sign, why most likely are recording devices prohibited on the factory floor?

(A) To ensure privacy for factory floor workers

(B) To minimize distractions for factory floor workers

(C) To avoid interference with assembly line equipment

(D) To protect unreleased product information

148. What is suggested about room 332?

(A) It has no Internet access.

(B) It contains a secure storage location.

(C) It is available to employees only.

(D) It is used for large meetings.

GO ON TO THE NEXT PAGE

Arstonia, Inc.
ID Request Form

Please complete the top portion of this form and bring it with you on your first day of work. You will be escorted to Corporate Security, where you will submit the form and obtain your employee identification badge.

Name: **Martin McGuigan**

Department: **Research & Development**

Supervisor: **Lakeisha Washington**

License plate: **G98 MDL**

Badge number: **59756**

Date of hire: **June 1**

- -

Approved by: Nancy Arusyak   Date: June 1

---

149. What does the form indicate about Mr. McGuigan?

(A) He reports to Ms. Washington.
(B) He comes to work by bus.
(C) He started a special project in June.
(D) He has worked at Arstonia for many years.

150. What department will most likely process the form?

(A) Personnel
(B) Corporate Security
(C) Legal
(D) Facilities Management

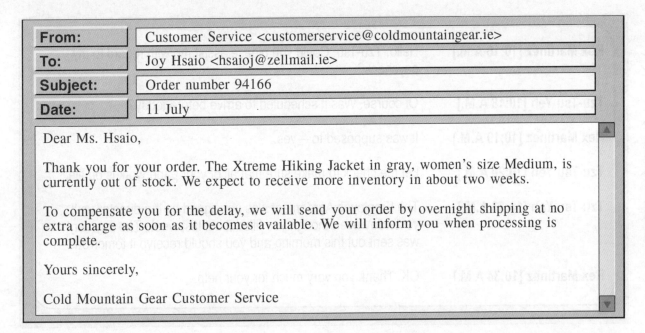

From:	Customer Service <customerservice@coldmountaingear.ie>
To:	Joy Hsaio <hsaioj@zellmail.ie>
Subject:	Order number 94166
Date:	11 July

Dear Ms. Hsaio,

Thank you for your order. The Xtreme Hiking Jacket in gray, women's size Medium, is currently out of stock. We expect to receive more inventory in about two weeks.

To compensate you for the delay, we will send your order by overnight shipping at no extra charge as soon as it becomes available. We will inform you when processing is complete.

Yours sincerely,

Cold Mountain Gear Customer Service

151. What is indicated about Ms. Hsaio's order?

(A) It will arrive later than expected.
(B) It was sent to the wrong address.
(C) It was damaged during shipping.
(D) It is an unusual color.

152. What does Cold Mountain Gear offer Ms. Hsaio?

(A) A replacement item
(B) A frequent-customer membership
(C) A discount on her next order
(D) A shipping service upgrade

GO ON TO THE NEXT PAGE

TEST 1

Rex Martinez [10:16 A.M.]	Hello, Tzu-Tsu. Could you please assist me with regard to my paycheck?
Tzu-Tsu Yeh [10:18 A.M.]	Of course. Was it scheduled to arrive before today?
Rex Martinez [10:19 A.M.]	It was supposed to—yes.
Tzu-Tsu Yeh [10:20 A.M.]	Let me check to make sure that all of your paperwork is on file.
Tzu-Tsu Yeh [10:33 A.M.]	The Employee Agreement was not signed by the director until yesterday even though you filled it out last week. The payment was sent out this morning and you should receive it tomorrow.
Rex Martinez [10:34 A.M.]	OK. Thank you very much for your help.

153. At 10:19 A.M., what does Mr. Martinez most likely mean when he writes, "It was supposed to"?

(A) His paperwork should have been completed sooner.
(B) He received a different amount of money than he agreed to.
(C) His bank account should have been set up last week.
(D) He expected to have already received a payment.

154. In what department does Ms. Yeh most likely work?

(A) Sales
(B) Advertising
(C) Payroll
(D) Customer Relations

Questions 155-157 refer to the following letter.

Lavenham Management Services
5 Bennett Park
Ipswich IP1 2AL
01632 960862 (phone)
01632 960863 (fax)
info@lavenhamservices.co.uk

10 August

Ruby S. Brown
67 Cloch Road
Peterborough
PE1 1XQ

Dear Ms. Brown,

We are pleased to announce the move of our headquarters. Since launching our consulting practice five years ago, we have rapidly expanded our customer base, and our staff has grown accordingly. As a result, our current facility is no longer adequate for our needs, and we have spent the last six months in search of a new home.

Our staff will officially move to Colchester on 10 September. From that date on, please address all correspondence to our new address listed on the enclosed card. Our phone and fax numbers will also change at that time. All other contact information will stay the same. Mail sent to our Ipswich address will be forwarded for two months following the move.

We look forward to serving you from our new and improved headquarters.

Sincerely,

Lavenham Management Services

Enclosure

155. What does the letter suggest about Lavenham's new headquarters facility?

(A) It will be in the same city as the current one.
(B) It will offer additional parking spaces for visitors.
(C) It will feature state-of-the-art technology.
(D) It will be larger than the current one.

156. The word "spent" in paragraph 1, line 4, is closest in meaning to

(A) paid
(B) gone
(C) used
(D) wasted

157. When will the move take place?

(A) In one week
(B) In one month
(C) In two months
(D) In six months

GO ON TO THE NEXT PAGE

Questions 158-160 refer to the following article.

KINGSTON (1 July)—On a street corner in downtown Kingston, the noise of hammers, drills, and saws can be heard from behind a large blue tarp. Above the tarp hangs a banner announcing the future home of the first Taco Park franchise in Kingston, Jamaica.

According to its marketing plan, Taco Park will launch the restaurant next month, just in time for the Independence Day holiday. The construction is expected to be finished by the end of this month.

"Few people here are familiar with Taco Park, since this is the first one in the city," explained Darryl Grange, general manager of Taco Park Jamaica. "We hope that by placing friendly greeters outside for the grand opening and offering samples from our regular menu we can create a new generation of Taco Park fans right here in Kingston."

The new restaurant will hire more than 50 employees, including cooks, servers, and cashiers. Interested candidates can apply at www.tacopark.com.jm. They must indicate their job skills, work experience, and provide a brief explanation of why they want to work at Taco Park. Applicants who are invited to interview for a position must provide two references from former places of employment.

158. What is the article mainly about?

(A) A new trend in the construction industry
(B) The reorganization of a company's marketing department
(C) A proposed solution to a neighborhood's noise issue
(D) The opening of a new business

159. According to the article, what most likely will happen by the end of July?

(A) A city ordinance will be revised.
(B) A menu will be updated for the holiday.
(C) A construction project will be completed.
(D) An employee training program will begin.

160. What does the article indicate must be included with the online application?

(A) Areas of expertise
(B) Proof of residency
(C) A copy of a current driver's license
(D) A preference for full-time or part-time employment

To: All employees
From: Patricia Ogdencort, CEO
Date: 22 June
Subject: Company-wide discussion

Here at Ogdencort, we believe in partnering with our employees to make positive changes. — [1] —. As such, we would like one representative from each department to participate in company-wide discussions on reducing costs.

Employees interested in serving as a representative must have worked at Ogdencort for a minimum of one year. — [2] —. Also, they must have received positive performance reviews and must be able to attend four meetings during one calendar year. Department heads are asked to withhold from serving as representatives. Please submit your name for consideration to your department head no later than 20 August. — [3] —. Successful applicants will be notified within one week of the deadline.

We will also be creating a suggestion box. — [4] —. Further information will be provided soon.

161. What is the purpose of the memo?

(A) To request ideas for reducing costs
(B) To announce a company initiative
(C) To offer training for future leaders
(D) To collect data on employee performance reviews

162. What is NOT a requirement for participation?

(A) A leadership position
(B) One year of employment at the company
(C) A positive performance review
(D) Availability to attend four meetings

163. In which of the positions marked [1], [2], [3], and [4] does the following sentence best belong?

"Each department head will make the final decision."

(A) [1]
(B) [2]
(C) [3]
(D) [4]

GO ON TO THE NEXT PAGE

https://www.lkjsportswear.com.br/about/founders ▼

Company Founders

Matheus Mori was a standout business student at Lowell University in Toronto, Canada. After graduating, he received funding from a regional business organisation to launch a travel software business. — [1] —. Four years later, he realised that he wanted to do more than just make money. He wanted to pursue his interests and dreams. So he sold his business and entered into a period of travel and cycling.

— [2] —. While at a sports conference in Brazil, Mr. Mori attended a presentation by Gustavo Santana, who had recently developed three-dimensional body-scanning software to create custom athletic wear. After the presentation, Mr. Mori introduced himself to Mr. Santana, and the two got into an in-depth conversation. — [3] —. In subsequent months, more exchanges between the two men followed, ultimately leading them to create LKJ Sportswear. Mr. Mori's travels had helped him formulate crucial ideas for revamping cycling apparel, which he was able to realise in collaboration with Mr. Santana, using Mr. Santana's software. — [4] —. Today, after 25 years in business, LKJ Sportswear continues to be a leader in sports apparel in Brazil and throughout South America, while sales of its products, most notably the cycling and tennis lines, continue to grow in Europe.

164. According to the Web page, why did Mr. Mori sell his first business?

(A) To pay some debts
(B) To return to his studies
(C) To spend time traveling
(D) To establish a new business

165. Where did LKJ Sportswear's founders meet?

(A) At a university
(B) At a conference
(C) At a cycling race
(D) At a sportswear store

166. What is indicated about LKJ Sportswear?

(A) It sells its products in multiple countries.
(B) It now makes only cycling apparel.
(C) Its products are often sold at a discount.
(D) Its founders are both from Canada.

167. In which of the positions marked [1], [2], [3], and [4] does the following sentence best belong?

"They discovered that they shared an interest in high-performance sportswear."

(A) [1]
(B) [2]
(C) [3]
(D) [4]

Questions 168-171 refer to the following online chat discussion.

Gail Oneta (1:20 P.M.) Hi, Mary. Can you send me a copy of the client questionnaire you mentioned during our meeting yesterday?

Mary Huang (1:21 P.M.) Sure. I will e-mail you the link to it right now.

Gail Oneta (1:22 P.M.) OK. Got it. But I can't edit the document for some reason.

Mary Huang (1:23 P.M.) Let me check with Brian Becker. Brian, I just sent Gail a link to the client questionnaire, but she cannot edit it.

Brian Becker (1:24 P.M.) It's probably because Gail has not been approved as an editor. Gail, I'll enter your name in the system now.

Gail Oneta (1:25 P.M.) OK. Thanks. I'm able to edit now. Would it be OK for me to add a few more questions to the document?

Brian Becker (1:26 P.M.) That's fine. But I would limit it to two or three at most. We promised the client that the questionnaire will take only ten minutes to complete.

Gail Oneta (1:27 P.M.) OK, understood. I'll keep that in mind.

Mary Huang (1:28 P.M.) So Brian, we will see you next on Tuesday at the Querol Health Services Center for the meeting with their team. It will be our first meeting with them, so it's important for us all to be there.

Brian Becker (1:29 P.M.)
Right. Thanks for reminding me. I'll put it on my calendar.

168. What problem does Ms. Oneta have?

(A) Meeting notes have been misplaced.
(B) An important meeting was canceled.
(C) She is unable to update a document.
(D) She has accidentally deleted an electronic file.

169. At 1:27 P.M., what does Ms. Oneta mean when she writes, "I'll keep that in mind"?

(A) She must ask permission to access a report.
(B) She will limit the number of changes she makes to a questionnaire.
(C) She will remember the password to open a document.
(D) She has been given a strict deadline to complete a task.

170. How long should it take to complete the questionnaire?

(A) Two minutes
(B) Three minutes
(C) Five minutes
(D) Ten minutes

171. What is Mr. Becker going to note on his calendar?

(A) A team review of a document
(B) An appointment with a new client
(C) A celebration of a new contract
(D) A consultation with a medical professional

GO ON TO THE NEXT PAGE

FOR IMMEDIATE RELEASE   **Contact:** Carla Guerra 512-555-0172,
c_guerra@dupontcamera.com

<u>Dupont Camera Store Hosts Its Tenth Annual Photography Equipment Swap and Sell</u>

(Monday, June 12)—Dupont Camera Store is once again hosting its photography equipment Swap and Sell event. On Friday, June 16, the store's showroom will be packed with tables of new and used photography gear from various vendors and hobbyists. Entry is $6 cash. Doors open at 10:00 A.M., and the event lasts until 5:00 P.M.

"This is an event people look forward to all year," said Dupont Camera Store's marketing manager Don Bergner. "Every time we've hosted it, a line has started forming about an hour before we even open the doors."

Professional dealers and camera companies can rent tables for $250 as an official vendor. Tables are 6 meters by 2 meters and include clear plastic clips for attaching a company banner or poster. Hobby photographers wanting to sell or trade a few handheld items can pay an entry fee of $50 and bring crates or camera bags of gear to set up in a designated area on the floor.

"I went to the event last year and definitely plan to go again," said Jonathan McDougall. "I didn't have anything to sell, but I got to meet some interesting people. I also ended up finding some accessories for my outdated camera model that I hadn't been able to find online."

---

172. What does Mr. Bergner imply about the event?

(A) Tickets sell out within a few days.
(B) Attendees start arriving before 10:00 A.M.
(C) It is hosted by a different camera company each year.
(D) Store staff will unload the vendors' items.

173. According to the press release, what is the purpose of the table clips?

(A) To display marketing materials
(B) To promote the Dupont logo
(C) To hold gift bags together
(D) To keep the tablecloths in place

174. What is suggested about hobby photographers?

(A) They will not be provided with a table.
(B) They can sell only certain items.
(C) They pay the same entry fee as the public.
(D) They have to sign up online.

175. What does Mr. McDougall mention about his experience at the event last year?

(A) He was representing his employer.
(B) He learned about new online camera stores.
(C) He found some rare items he wanted.
(D) He sold an old camera and bag.

GO ON TO THE NEXT PAGE

To:	alee@terratasker.com
From:	jaznar@dynaston.com
Date:	5 March
Subject:	Order number 329XSU

Dear Ms. Lee,

I have been in communication with the shipping company, Marsantis, over the past week about your order of trucks. Apparently, the earliest we can get the TC73 trucks to you is 8 May, which puts us three days behind our estimated delivery date. Unfortunately, the only other ship departing from Valencia in April with enough clearance for the TC73 trucks was cancelled. Only certain ships can transport these trucks because of their height of 4.5 metres. In any case, I apologise for the inconvenience. I will work with our team on waiving some of your transport fees on this order.

Best regards,

Javier Aznar
Assistant Sales Director, Dynaston

Marsantis Shipping
Valencia to Toyohashi Service
Spring Schedule

Voyage Number	Ship Name	Maximum Cargo Height	Valencia (Spain)	Halifax (Canada)	Veracruz (Mexico)	San Diego (USA)	Toyohashi (Japan)
22	Olympia	5 metres	16 March	25 March	30 March	—	17 April
48	Pegasus	4 metres	2 April	9 April	—	cancelled	5 May
33	Karenga IV	5 metres	13 April	20 April	27 April	cancelled	16 May
57	Yoshimo	5 metres	14 April	cancelled	30 April	8 May	19 May

176. Why did Mr. Aznar most likely write the e-mail?

(A) To explain a delay
(B) To request a shipment
(C) To offer a discount
(D) To clarify a policy

177. In the e-mail, the word "clearance" in paragraph 1, line 4, is closest in meaning to

(A) removal
(B) permission
(C) experience
(D) space

178. What is the shipping destination for the TC73 trucks?

(A) Canada
(B) Mexico
(C) United States
(D) Japan

179. When is the Olympia scheduled to arrive at its final destination?

(A) On March 16
(B) On April 17
(C) On May 16
(D) On May 19

180. According to the schedule, what ship will travel directly from Canada to Japan?

(A) The Olympia
(B) The Pegasus
(C) The Karenga IV
(D) The Yoshimo

GO ON TO THE NEXT PAGE

KELLER ATTIRE

Renting a suit from Keller Attire has never been easier! We now have an expanded range of men's formal wear in sizes XS to XXL, all available to rent online.

Whether you are attending a wedding, a black-tie event, or some other special occasion, we have the right suit for you. Visit our Web site at www.kellerattire.com to see our full range of styles, colors, and fabrics. One of our style experts is ready to chat with you about your choices and walk you through our super accurate online Measuring Wizard. We will help you find a great suit that fits you perfectly!

Our standard delivery service will get your order to you in three to five days. For faster service, we offer overnight delivery for an additional charge of $50.

Antonio Varela
808 Avenue K, Apt. 5B
Dallas, TX 75246

October 14

Joanne Ford, President
Keller Attire, Inc.
2200 East Fourth Street
Chicago, IL 60611

Dear Ms. Ford,

I recently ordered a suit from Keller Attire to wear to an important client dinner in New York. I chose your overnight delivery service and provided a New York address for delivery. However, the suit was delivered to my home address in Dallas instead—I was already on my way to New York at the time.

Your customer service team handled the problem with spotless professionalism. As there was not enough time to send a replacement, they arranged for a local rental company to deliver a similar suit to my hotel at no additional cost to me.

I am extremely grateful for your team's superior customer service. I will certainly use Keller Attire again in the future.

Yours sincerely,

Antonio Varela

Antonio Varela

181. What would NOT be available to customers who visit Keller Attire's Web site?

(A) Shoes to match a suit
(B) Professional advice
(C) Images of clothes
(D) A way to find correct sizes

182. In the advertisement, the word "standard" in paragraph 3, line 1, is closest in meaning to

(A) basic
(B) valuable
(C) average
(D) affordable

183. Why did Mr. Varela write to Ms. Ford?

(A) To report a mistake in an advertisement
(B) To express his concern about a policy
(C) To invite her to meet his clients
(D) To praise her company's customer service

184. What is suggested about Mr. Varela?

(A) He lives in New York.
(B) He is dissatisfied with a service.
(C) He was unable to attend a dinner.
(D) He paid $50 for delivery.

185. What problem did Mr. Varela have with the suit he ordered?

(A) It did not fit.
(B) It was the wrong color.
(C) It was delivered to the wrong address.
(D) It arrived late.

GO ON TO THE NEXT PAGE

TEST 1

Hendriks Chemicals Corporate Sales Meeting
Amsterdam Centre Hotel
12–14 May
Day 1 Agenda—Conference Room C

Time	Subject/Activity	Facilitator
8:30 A.M.	*Using the Sales Process to Win*	Anika De Vries
10:00 A.M.	Break	
10:30 A.M.	*Preparing to Call on the Customer*	Hasen Alghamdi
12:30 P.M.	Lunch	
1:30 P.M.	*Planning to Win the Contract*	Lucas Bakker
3:00 P.M.	Break	
3:30 P.M.	*Best Practices Discussion*	Sofie Meijer
5:30 P.M.	End of Day 1	
7:00 P.M.	Dinner—Old Canal Restaurant	

To:	Thomas Visser
From:	Emma Jansen
Date:	23 April
Subject:	Sales meeting agenda—Day 1

Thomas:

Gerritt Smit has put together a proposed agenda for Day 1 of the corporate sales meeting next month. After looking it over, I would like to switch the 10:30 A.M. and 1:30 P.M. sessions, so the order makes more sense.

Gerritt has made a reservation for a group dinner that night at a well-known restaurant in Amsterdam. The plan is to have another group dinner on the second night, and everyone is free to make his or her own dinner plans on the third night.

I still do not have the agendas for Days 2 and 3. Gerritt indicated that he is waiting on confirmation from at least one facilitator before sending them out.

Regards,

Emma Jansen
Regional Sales Manager

To:	Emma Jansen
From:	Thomas Visser
Date:	23 April
Subject:	RE: Sales meeting agenda—Day 1

Emma:

I agree with your proposed change to the agenda for Day 1. Please note that Anika De Vries is no longer able to facilitate her session, but she still plans to participate in the meeting via videoconferencing. Sofie Meijer will now lead Anika's session. She has done it before, so I do not anticipate any issues with this. However, I would like to take a few minutes at the beginning of the day to give a short introduction to the sales process before turning the session over to Ms. Meijer.

Please forward the agendas for Day 2 and Day 3 to me when you receive them.

Best,

Thomas Visser
Vice President of Sales

---

186. What session does Ms. Jansen want to move to the 1:30 P.M. time slot?

(A) *Using the Sales Process to Win*
(B) *Preparing to Call on the Customer*
(C) *Planning to Win the Contract*
(D) *Best Practices Discussion*

187. According to the first e-mail, what is the plan for dinner on Day 3?

(A) It will be held at the Old Canal Restaurant.
(B) It will be served at 7:00 P.M.
(C) Participants will make their own arrangements.
(D) Mr. Smit will reserve a table at the hotel dining room.

188. What does the first e-mail mention about the agendas for Day 2 and Day 3?

(A) Mr. Visser wants to add an activity to both of them.
(B) Ms. Jansen has already seen them.
(C) Lunch will not be included.
(D) The facilitators have not been finalized.

189. What does the second e-mail indicate about Ms. De Vries?

(A) She recently started working at Hendriks Chemicals.
(B) She has never led a sales session before.
(C) She will give a brief overview before the first session begins.
(D) She will not attend the meeting in person.

190. Who will lead the *Using the Sales Process to Win* session?

(A) Ms. De Vries
(B) Mr. Alghamdi
(C) Ms. Meijer
(D) Mr. Bakker

GO ON TO THE NEXT PAGE

Fairview Bicycle Share (FBS): *Become a Rider!*

Get an FBS pass to ride to work, school, or around the city. Then select a bicycle from one of our 40 FBS stations in the city and return it to any station by the end of the day.

■ **Yearly pass**—$800/year—Commuters' top choice.

■ **Three-month pass**—$200—Available only to students over the summer.

■ **Weekly pass**—$18/week—Tourists love this option.

■ **Pay-per-ride**—$2/ride—Affordable option for occasional users.

Fairview Daily News
Happy Birthday to FBS

December 17 (FAIRVIEW)—The Fairview Bicycle Share program (FBS) turns one today, and yesterday Mayor Mahdasian provided her thoughts on the program's success.

"Before we got started, we proposed the idea for the FBS program to Fairview residents at a planning meeting. Critics said a program like FBS would work only in big cities, such as New York and San Francisco. They thought that a small city like ours would not have enough riders to cover the costs," said the mayor, who has made the launch of FBS a priority since starting her second term in office. She noted that she herself uses a Pay-per-ride card.

The city's Office of Transport conducted random polling this month to measure the success of FBS. Our journalists are compiling the information, and the full findings will be released tomorrow.

December 18

Report on Year One of Fairview Bicycle Share

The following statistics were gathered to help capture and analyze the role of FBS one year after its launch.

- Individuals who have used FBS since it began: 2,638
- Estimated number of users who report now using FBS more than their cars: 310
- Percent of users who report that FBS has reduced their commute time: 12 percent
- Percent of Fairview University students who report using FBS at least once a week: 19 percent
- Summary of types of passes sold over the first year:
    —Weekly pass: 7 percent
    —Three-month pass: 24 percent
    —Annual pass: 30 percent
    —Pay-per-ride card: 39 percent

191. What does the advertisement indicate about FBS bicycles?

(A) They cannot be kept overnight.
(B) They are mostly used by tourists.
(C) They are stored in one location.
(D) They are not available in different sizes.

192. According to the article, why did some local residents think FBS would not succeed?

(A) The planning team was not experienced.
(B) The market was too competitive.
(C) The city was not large enough.
(D) The advertising budget was too low.

193. What is suggested about Mayor Mahdasian?

(A) She recently celebrated her birthday.
(B) She occasionally uses an FBS bicycle.
(C) She is in her first term as mayor.
(D) She has visited San Francisco.

194. What is implied in the report?

(A) Some people are using their car less frequently.
(B) Students are attending more classes.
(C) Commuters are saving money on public transportation.
(D) Some workers are getting to work early.

195. What is suggested about 24 percent of FBS passes?

(A) The passes were sold to tourists.
(B) The passes were sold to students.
(C) The passes were sold during the first half of the year.
(D) The passes were sold to people who live outside of Fairview.

GO ON TO THE NEXT PAGE

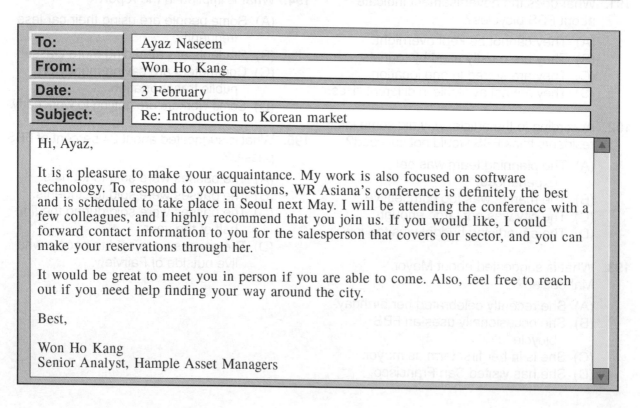

To:	Won Ho Kang
From:	Ayaz Naseem
Date:	2 February
Subject:	Introduction to Korean market

Dear Won Ho,

I recently joined Hample Asset Managers in Sydney as an emerging business analyst with a particular focus on software technology companies. I would like to research some of the new related small businesses in Korea and have a couple of questions for you. In your opinion, what brokerage firm runs the best technology conference there? And are there any software startups that you know of that I should focus on?

I look forward to hearing from you.

Many thanks,

Ayaz Naseem
Analyst, Hample Asset Managers

To:	Ayaz Naseem
From:	Won Ho Kang
Date:	3 February
Subject:	Re: Introduction to Korean market

Hi, Ayaz,

It is a pleasure to make your acquaintance. My work is also focused on software technology. To respond to your questions, WR Asiana's conference is definitely the best and is scheduled to take place in Seoul next May. I will be attending the conference with a few colleagues, and I highly recommend that you join us. If you would like, I could forward contact information to you for the salesperson that covers our sector, and you can make your reservations through her.

It would be great to meet you in person if you are able to come. Also, feel free to reach out if you need help finding your way around the city.

Best,

Won Ho Kang
Senior Analyst, Hample Asset Managers

WR Asiana Technology Conference, Thursday, 8 May
Afternoon schedule, continued
Concurrent Business Sessions—2:00 to 3:00 P.M.

	1	**2**	**3**	**4**
Sector	Internet	Software	Hardware	Mobile Phones
Company	Wingbae Tech	Kedia	Namhaejin Max	Vindoh
Room	Petunia Room	Rose Hall	Lily Suite	Tulip Salon

196. What is indicated about Mr. Naseem?

(A) He is a new employee at Hample Asset Managers.
(B) He used to work closely with Mr. Kang.
(C) He has worked as an analyst for many years.
(D) He recently moved to Sydney.

197. Why did Mr. Naseem write the first e-mail?

(A) To ask for directions to a meeting
(B) To request information on companies
(C) To offer investment advice
(D) To learn more about Mr. Kang's job

198. According to Mr. Kang, how should Mr. Naseem arrange his attendance at a conference?

(A) By calling a customer service department
(B) By speaking with a travel agent
(C) By contacting a salesperson
(D) By visiting WR Asiana's Web site

199. What is suggested about Mr. Kang?

(A) He travels regularly to Sydney.
(B) He does not like attending professional conferences.
(C) He lives outside of Seoul.
(D) He forgot to answer all of Mr. Naseem's questions.

200. What session will Mr. Kang most likely attend at 2 P.M. on May 8?

(A) Wingbae Tech's session
(B) Kedia's session
(C) Namhaejin Max's session
(D) Vindoh's session

Stop! This is the end of the test. If you finish before time is called, you may go back to Parts 5, 6, and 7 and check your work.

NO TEST MATERIAL ON THIS PAGE

TEST 2

CD 2 01-82

LISTENING TEST ·· p.72

READING TEST ·· p.84

＊解答用紙は本誌 p.112 の後ろに綴じ込まれています。

実際のテストでは問題用紙の裏側に、以下のようなテスト全体についての指示が印刷されています。
この指示を念頭においてテストに取り組みましょう。

General Directions

This test is designed to measure your English language ability. The test is divided into two sections: Listening and Reading.

You must mark all of your answers on the separate answer sheet. For each question, you should select the best answer from the answer choices given. Then, on your answer sheet, you should find the number of the question and fill in the space that corresponds to the letter of the answer that you have selected. If you decide to change an answer, completely erase your old answer and then mark your new answer.

訳 ### 全体についての指示

このテストはあなたの英語言語能力を測定するよう設計されています。テストはリスニングとリーディングという 2 つのセクションに分けられています。

答えは全て別紙の解答用紙にマークしてください。それぞれの設問について、与えられた選択肢から最も適切な答えを選びます。そして解答用紙の該当する問題番号に、選択した答えを塗りつぶしてください。答えを修正する場合は、元の答えを完全に消してから新しい答えをマークしてください。

LISTENING TEST

In the Listening test, you will be asked to demonstrate how well you understand spoken English. The entire Listening test will last approximately 45 minutes. There are four parts, and directions are given for each part. You must mark your answers on the separate answer sheet. Do not write your answers in your test book.

PART 1

Directions: For each question in this part, you will hear four statements about a picture in your test book. When you hear the statements, you must select the one statement that best describes what you see in the picture. Then find the number of the question on your answer sheet and mark your answer. The statements will not be printed in your test book and will be spoken only one time.

Statement (C), "They're sitting at a table," is the best description of the picture, so you should select answer (C) and mark it on your answer sheet.

1.

2.

TEST 2

GO ON TO THE NEXT PAGE

3.

4.

5.

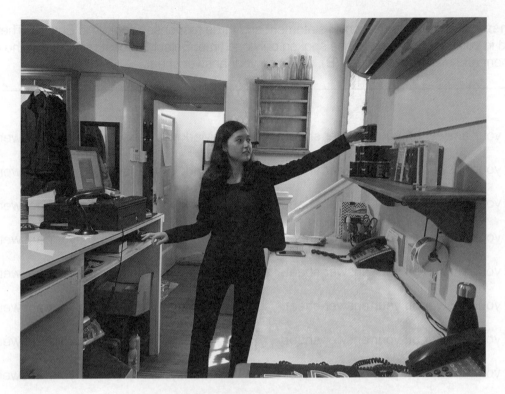

6.

GO ON TO THE NEXT PAGE ➡

PART 2

Directions: You will hear a question or statement and three responses spoken in English. They will not be printed in your test book and will be spoken only one time. Select the best response to the question or statement and mark the letter (A), (B), or (C) on your answer sheet.

7. Mark your answer on your answer sheet.

8. Mark your answer on your answer sheet.

9. Mark your answer on your answer sheet.

10. Mark your answer on your answer sheet.

11. Mark your answer on your answer sheet.

12. Mark your answer on your answer sheet.

13. Mark your answer on your answer sheet.

14. Mark your answer on your answer sheet.

15. Mark your answer on your answer sheet.

16. Mark your answer on your answer sheet.

17. Mark your answer on your answer sheet.

18. Mark your answer on your answer sheet.

19. Mark your answer on your answer sheet.

20. Mark your answer on your answer sheet.

21. Mark your answer on your answer sheet.

22. Mark your answer on your answer sheet.

23. Mark your answer on your answer sheet.

24. Mark your answer on your answer sheet.

25. Mark your answer on your answer sheet.

26. Mark your answer on your answer sheet.

27. Mark your answer on your answer sheet.

28. Mark your answer on your answer sheet.

29. Mark your answer on your answer sheet.

30. Mark your answer on your answer sheet.

31. Mark your answer on your answer sheet.

PART 3

Directions: You will hear some conversations between two or more people. You will be asked to answer three questions about what the speakers say in each conversation. Select the best response to each question and mark the letter (A), (B), (C), or (D) on your answer sheet. The conversations will not be printed in your test book and will be spoken only one time.

32. What is the man's job?

(A) Computer programmer
(B) Travel agent
(C) Photographer
(D) Product tester

33. What product feature is most important to the man?

(A) Weight
(B) Color
(C) Battery life
(D) Reliability

34. What does the woman suggest that the man do?

(A) Talk to her colleague
(B) Use a coupon code
(C) Consider a different product
(D) Purchase an extended warranty

35. What are the speakers preparing for?

(A) A staff meeting
(B) A company picnic
(C) A business trip
(D) A product demonstration

36. What will happen next week?

(A) A photocopier will be replaced.
(B) An office will be renovated.
(C) A company policy will change.
(D) A client will visit.

37. What does the man ask the woman to do?

(A) Visit an event location
(B) Leave documents for a coworker
(C) Set up a display
(D) Check a reservation

38. What news does the man share?

(A) A delivery will be delayed.
(B) A store has extended its hours.
(C) A parking garage is being built.
(D) A new business will open.

39. Why does the woman dislike shopping at Paxton's Drug Store?

(A) Its prices are high.
(B) It is difficult to find parking.
(C) It has poor customer service.
(D) It has a small selection of products.

40. What does the man want to learn more about?

(A) Some journalists
(B) A bus schedule
(C) Some classes
(D) A medication

41. Where most likely are the speakers?

(A) At an art museum
(B) At an employment agency
(C) At an airport
(D) At a hotel

42. Why is a change requested?

(A) A space is unavailable.
(B) Some employees are on vacation.
(C) An appointment was rescheduled.
(D) An announcement was postponed.

43. What does Mr. Aziz tell the woman about?

(A) A pamphlet
(B) Transportation
(C) Computer access
(D) A voucher

GO ON TO THE NEXT PAGE

44. What products does the company sell?

(A) Furniture
(B) Electronics
(C) Automobiles
(D) Appliances

45. What does the man want to change?

(A) A script
(B) A contract
(C) A product name
(D) A company logo

46. What concern does the woman have?

(A) A budget is too small.
(B) A deadline is approaching.
(C) Some actors are not available.
(D) Some equipment is not working.

47. Where does the woman work?

(A) At a cleaning service
(B) At an advertising agency
(C) At a plumbing company
(D) At a property management company

48. What does the man imply when he says, "I run a car wash"?

(A) His problem is urgent.
(B) He is correcting some misinformation.
(C) He needs to hire more workers.
(D) He is too busy to help.

49. What will the woman do next?

(A) Conduct a training
(B) Transfer a call
(C) Prepare an invoice
(D) Update a Web site

50. What type of meeting is taking place?

(A) A midyear performance review
(B) A policy planning meeting
(C) A training session
(D) A job interview

51. What does the man ask about?

(A) A salary increase
(B) A vacation policy
(C) A security guideline
(D) A telecommuting arrangement

52. What is the man reminded to submit?

(A) A time sheet
(B) A work sample
(C) An authorization request
(D) A project timeline

53. What most likely is the woman's occupation?

(A) Weather forecaster
(B) Computer programmer
(C) Scientist
(D) Photographer

54. What does the woman say is beneficial about a location?

(A) It is near the ocean.
(B) It has a dry climate.
(C) It is accessible using public transportation.
(D) It has a renewable energy source.

55. What will the woman do tomorrow?

(A) Edit some images
(B) Start a new project
(C) Present at a conference
(D) Install some software

56. What type of business do the speakers probably work for?

(A) A music school
(B) A manufacturing company
(C) A construction firm
(D) A travel agency

57. Why does the man say, "I'm working on a financial report"?

(A) To offer help
(B) To share an accomplishment
(C) To decline an invitation
(D) To make a request

58. What is the woman worried about?

(A) Whether an investment is worth the cost
(B) Whether a job applicant is qualified
(C) Whether a flight will arrive on time
(D) Whether a customer will complain

59. What department does the man most likely work in?

(A) Groundskeeping
(B) Human Resources
(C) Transportation
(D) Information Technology

60. What does the man ask about?

(A) How much some equipment will cost
(B) What time a colleague will arrive
(C) What will happen if it rains
(D) Why a repair is being delayed

61. What is the woman going to give to Karima?

(A) Some keys
(B) A receipt
(C) A book order
(D) Some money

Store Directory

Aisle 1 –Beauty supplies	**Aisle 2** –Paper products
Aisle 3 –Cleaning supplies	**Aisle 4** –Pet food

62. Why is the woman surprised?

(A) Customers have complained about a brand.
(B) An inspection will take place soon.
(C) Some merchandise is not selling well.
(D) A supplier has gone out of business.

63. Look at the graphic. Which aisle will some products be moved to?

(A) Aisle 1
(B) Aisle 2
(C) Aisle 3
(D) Aisle 4

64. What is scheduled to happen on Thursday?

(A) A training will be held.
(B) A shipment will arrive.
(C) A promotional event will begin.
(D) A budget report will be updated.

TEST 2

GO ON TO THE NEXT PAGE

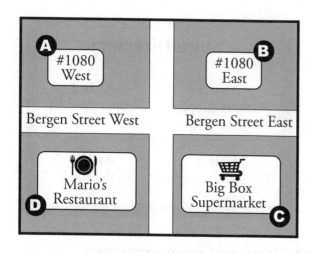

Bixter Web Site Builder				
	Design Tools	Unlimited Storage Capacity	Video Capable	Tech Support
Package 1 $10/month	✓			
Package 2 $15/month	✓	✓		
Package 3 $20/month	✓	✓	✓	
Package 4 $35/month	✓	✓	✓	✓

65. Look at the graphic. Where will the man pick the woman up?

(A) At location A
(B) At location B
(C) At location C
(D) At location D

66. Why is the man relieved?

(A) A colleague will take over an assignment.
(B) A parking spot is available.
(C) A business is already open.
(D) A drive will be short.

67. What does the man say he will provide?

(A) Some water
(B) Some coupons
(C) An umbrella
(D) A phone charger

68. What type of business do the speakers most likely own?

(A) A computer repair store
(B) An online newspaper
(C) A bakery
(D) A medical supply company

69. Look at the graphic. Which package will the speakers most likely choose?

(A) Package 1
(B) Package 2
(C) Package 3
(D) Package 4

70. What does the man say he will do after lunch?

(A) Pick up a permit
(B) Make a call
(C) Watch a video
(D) Repair a device

PART 4

Directions: You will hear some talks given by a single speaker. You will be asked to answer three questions about what the speaker says in each talk. Select the best response to each question and mark the letter (A), (B), (C), or (D) on your answer sheet. The talks will not be printed in your test book and will be spoken only one time.

71. Who most likely are the listeners?

(A) Ticket agents
(B) Art critics
(C) Janitorial staff
(D) Museum guides

72. What does the speaker hand out?

(A) New uniforms
(B) Instructor evaluations
(C) Fact sheets
(D) Security badges

73. What are the listeners reminded to do?

(A) Submit application forms
(B) Print out brochures
(C) Prepare for an inspection
(D) Collect visitor passes

74. What kind of store does the speaker most likely manage?

(A) A stationery store
(B) An electronics store
(C) A grocery store
(D) A clothing store

75. What are customers having difficulty with?

(A) Submitting orders
(B) Finding items
(C) Returning products
(D) Contacting staff

76. According to the speaker, what should the listeners do?

(A) Be helpful
(B) Arrive early
(C) Dress neatly
(D) Eat quickly

77. Where does the speaker work?

(A) At a newspaper
(B) At a travel agency
(C) At a hotel
(D) At a technology company

78. What does the speaker mean when he says, "you have a lot of experience"?

(A) The listener should take over a project.
(B) The listener will not need any assistance.
(C) The listener deserves a pay raise.
(D) The listener should teach an upcoming class.

79. What does the speaker say he is doing tomorrow?

(A) Attending a meeting
(B) Organizing a party
(C) Going on vacation
(D) Visiting a school

80. What is the topic of today's broadcast?

(A) Unusual desserts
(B) Breakfast foods
(C) Homemade energy drinks
(D) Cold vegetable soups

81. What does the speaker say she likes about a recipe?

(A) It won an award.
(B) Its ingredients are inexpensive.
(C) It is low in sugar.
(D) It is easy to prepare.

82. What will the speaker do next?

(A) Interview a guest
(B) Recommend an appliance
(C) Explain contest rules
(D) Provide a discount code

TEST 2

GO ON TO THE NEXT PAGE

83. Where does the speaker most likely work?

(A) At a printing business
(B) At a video game company
(C) At a plastics manufacturer
(D) At an employment agency

84. What is the speaker concerned about?

(A) A timeline may need to be revised.
(B) Some prototypes are very heavy.
(C) Some specifications are incorrect.
(D) A material is currently unavailable.

85. Why does the speaker say, "our junior designer has just left"?

(A) To explain why she is busy
(B) To complain about a delay
(C) To request that the listener return the next day
(D) To suggest that the listener apply for a job

86. What benefit is being discussed?

(A) A shuttle service
(B) A fitness center membership
(C) Additional vacation days
(D) Free financial advice

87. What will employees have to show to receive the benefit?

(A) A letter from their supervisor
(B) A recent bank statement
(C) A driver's license
(D) A company identification card

88. What should some of the listeners do by Friday?

(A) Complete a survey
(B) Read an informational brochure
(C) Sign a contract
(D) Speak to a manager

89. What is the topic of the workshop?

(A) Testing water
(B) Preserving food
(C) Conserving energy
(D) Cleaning up a work site

90. What advantage does the speaker mention about the equipment?

(A) It comes with accessories.
(B) It is inexpensive.
(C) It is lightweight.
(D) It is easy to use.

91. What will happen at the end of the workshop?

(A) Photographs will be taken.
(B) Certificates will be awarded.
(C) Lunch will be served.
(D) Projects will be assigned.

92. Who most likely is the speaker?

(A) A musician
(B) A painter
(C) An athlete
(D) A photographer

93. What does the speaker imply when he says, "I can go to a restaurant now"?

(A) He is not available for an interview.
(B) He is not recognized by fans.
(C) He is ready to start a project.
(D) He is receiving payments.

94. Who does the speaker thank?

(A) His family
(B) His manager
(C) A reporter
(D) A competitor

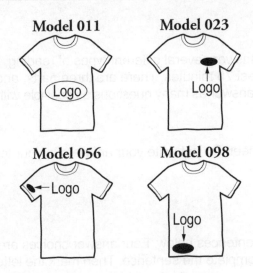

Model 011   Model 023

Model 056   Model 098

Upcoming Client Meetings	
August 3	Chung Associates
August 14	Bedham Corporation
August 18	Marsten Company
August 24	Satero Construction

98. What type of business does the speaker work for?

(A) A marketing firm
(B) A Web-design company
(C) A shipping service
(D) A law firm

95. What will the speaker's employees do next month?

(A) Receive annual bonuses
(B) Act in a commercial
(C) Attend a trade show
(D) Celebrate an anniversary

99. Look at the graphic. What day are the listeners asked to be available?

(A) August 3
(B) August 14
(C) August 18
(D) August 24

96. Look at the graphic. Which shirt design does the speaker prefer?

(A) Model 011
(B) Model 023
(C) Model 098
(D) Model 056

100. What will the listeners find at the back of the room?

(A) Name tags
(B) Some product samples
(C) Some refreshments
(D) Information packets

97. What does the speaker ask about?

(A) A delivery date
(B) A payment method
(C) Color options
(D) Shirt sizes

This is the end of the Listening test. Turn to Part 5 in your test book.

GO ON TO THE NEXT PAGE

READING TEST

In the Reading test, you will read a variety of texts and answer several different types of reading comprehension questions. The entire Reading test will last 75 minutes. There are three parts, and directions are given for each part. You are encouraged to answer as many questions as possible within the time allowed.

You must mark your answers on the separate answer sheet. Do not write your answers in your test book.

PART 5

Directions: A word or phrase is missing in each of the sentences below. Four answer choices are given below each sentence. Select the best answer to complete the sentence. Then mark the letter (A), (B), (C), or (D) on your answer sheet.

101. Summer interns at Fairview City Hall must ------- all city council meetings.

(A) attend
(B) attending
(C) to attend
(D) attends

102. A ------- analysis of market trends can lead retailers to profitable results.

(A) careful
(B) care
(C) carefully
(D) cared

103. Please ------- a copy of each sales report on a separate piece of paper.

(A) pick
(B) tell
(C) reply
(D) print

104. Ms. Wendt's -------, Daniel Novianto, will be answering her e-mails while she is on leave.

(A) assistant
(B) assistance
(C) assisting
(D) assists

105. Do not keep perishable foods in the cooler beyond ------- expiration date.

(A) they
(B) their
(C) them
(D) themselves

106. Erico Costa's new work of fiction is an ------- tale of mistaken identity.

(A) amuse
(B) amusement
(C) amusingly
(D) amusing

107. Zantos Network is moving forward with the ------- to purchase a local radio station.

(A) property
(B) advancement
(C) proposal
(D) signature

108. Over 95 percent of Kapp Hardware's clients have responded ------- in online reviews.

(A) favorable
(B) favorably
(C) favored
(D) to favor

109. Ms. Kean mentioned the improved tool kit ------- at the meeting but did not discuss how we will promote it.

(A) closely
(B) repeatedly
(C) upwardly
(D) neatly

110. Once Mr. Braun had toured the conference -------, he paid the deposit fee.

(A) location
(B) locate
(C) locating
(D) locator

111. Management has asked Ms. Leung to meet ------- the new office supply vendor tomorrow.

(A) at
(B) with
(C) for
(D) of

112. Mr. Farmingham will rearrange his schedule to have lunch at 2:00 P.M. ------- you are available then.

(A) if
(B) by
(C) without
(D) during

113. Please include your employee number ------- filling out the room reservation form.

(A) although
(B) so
(C) when
(D) however

114. Be sure to pack a water bottle for tomorrow's mountain hike, as it is ------- to stay hydrated.

(A) nutritious
(B) sensitive
(C) direct
(D) crucial

115. Westmont Hospital announced that leading heart ------- Dr. Emily Chow will be joining the staff next month.

(A) special
(B) specialize
(C) specialist
(D) specialized

116. The Midosuji branch of Tsurutani Bank is closed ------- because of a problem with the electrical system.

(A) slightly
(B) temporarily
(C) universally
(D) terminally

117. Funds raised by the community auction will be used to maintain the ------- Quill Street playground.

(A) aging
(B) glad
(C) utter
(D) brief

118. United Carpet West received ------- higher customer satisfaction ratings than its competitors did.

(A) signify
(B) significance
(C) signifying
(D) significantly

119. This month's tool catalog was edited to reflect that two items are not in -------.

(A) situation
(B) stock
(C) action
(D) asset

120. On-site training programs are associated with ------- employee motivation.

(A) to increase
(B) increases
(C) increased
(D) increase

121. The catering contract calls for flowers to be arranged ------- in a vase on each banquet table.

(A) honestly
(B) enormously
(C) hungrily
(D) attractively

122. Fifty percent of the total landscaping cost is required now, and the ------- is due upon completion of the project.

(A) remains
(B) remain
(C) remained
(D) remainder

GO ON TO THE NEXT PAGE

123. The date of the building's grand opening was moved ------- President Daniels could be there to officiate.

    (A) so that
    (B) such as
    (C) due to
    (D) except for

124. New patients ------- miss their initial visit at Pratha Medical Clinic without advance notice will not be rescheduled.

    (A) what
    (B) where
    (C) who
    (D) why

125. Mr. Lewis deserves ------- for the thoughtful service he always provides to customers.

    (A) content
    (B) experience
    (C) community
    (D) recognition

126. ------- the growing demand for steel, there is still a large supply available.

    (A) Likewise
    (B) Despite
    (C) Though
    (D) While

127. Maria Pennfield's Star Signs Company ------- two decades ago.

    (A) has established
    (B) establishes
    (C) was established
    (D) establishing

128. The paintings ------- the outside wall of the Klampton Hotel feature the art of Ah Lam Zhang.

    (A) unto
    (B) instead of
    (C) in case of
    (D) along

129. Please ------- the handrail when going down the Palmer Theater's marble staircase.

    (A) catch up
    (B) run out of
    (C) find out
    (D) hold on to

130. Until the office heating system ------- , employees are permitted to work from home.

    (A) will be fixed
    (B) is being fixed
    (C) has been fixed
    (D) had been fixed

Questions 139-142 refer to the following e-mail.

To: Leni Bischof <lbischof@curiousgardengoods.de>
From: Brian Adler <badler@curiousgardengoods.co.uk>
Subject: Information
Date: 31 March
Attachment: Adler_1

Dear Ms. Bischof:

After our meeting in London last week, I did some research into the feasibility of using robots in the Hamburg warehouse. -------. Despite the initial expenditure we would have to make, I think we would end up saving money in the long run. -------, robots can be programmed to accomplish simple, automated tasks. Robots can also perform the same task over and over again. This allows employees to concentrate on jobs that require more ------- skills. I have attached a brief report on the costs and benefits of ------- robotic technology. Please let me know what you think.

Sincerely,

Brian Adler

139. (A) I think it is an idea worth considering.
(B) It is the oldest building on the campus.
(C) I saw a photo of robots in a magazine.
(D) Technology changes rapidly these days.

140. (A) Otherwise
(B) Even so
(C) Nevertheless
(D) For one thing

141. (A) analyze
(B) have analyzed
(C) analytical
(D) to analyze

142. (A) used
(B) using
(C) to use
(D) being used

Anabel Faren
183 Maple Road
Irvine, CA 92621

September 12

Arun Khatri
Product Development
Better Barley Company
2800 Clearview Drive
Los Angeles, CA 90040

Dear Mr. Khatri,

Thank you for your interest in my food blog, *Cooking with Anabel 365*. I am a trained chef who has been creating original recipes for the home cook for the past eleven years. I currently have more than 50,000 followers who respond ------- to my posts. From their many comments, one
143.
fact stands out—they are eager to purchase the products I -------.
144.

-------. I can create recipes using your products and feature your products on my site. I use the
145.
services of a professional photographer ------- the products I use to their best advantage.
146.
Please let me know if you would like to talk further about the brands I work with or about using your products on my blog.

Very truly yours,

Anabel Faren

143. (A) quietly
(B) frequently
(C) negatively
(D) aggressively

144. (A) design
(B) restore
(C) recommend
(D) manufacture

145. (A) Original recipes are often preferred.
(B) I would be happy to work with you.
(C) Many have eaten in the best restaurants.
(D) I will soon rearrange my kitchen.

146. (A) to display
(B) it displays
(C) a display of
(D) has displayed

Directions: In this part you will read a selection of texts, such as magazine and newspaper articles, e-mails, and instant messages. Each text or set of texts is followed by several questions. Select the best answer for each question and mark the letter (A), (B), (C), or (D) on your answer sheet.

Questions 147-148 refer to the following announcement.

The Chelham Chamber of Commerce
Presents
Building a Professional Wardrobe
Speaker: Alice Ferry

Ms. Ferry, owner of Ferry Goods, will focus her presentation on the type of attire and accessories appropriate for the business environment. Whether the dress code in your office is formal, casual, or something in between, Ms. Ferry's expertise can help you create a proper look. All are welcome, but the workshop will be especially helpful for community members seeking employment. Following the presentation, light refreshments will be served free of charge.

Thursday, April 6, 6:00–8:00 P.M.
Coventry Hotel
1770 Bloomington Street, Chelham

147. What will Ms. Ferry speak about?

(A) How to start a business
(B) How to write a résumé
(C) Where to look for jobs
(D) What to wear to work

148. What is indicated about the event?

(A) It is held every year.
(B) It is open to the public.
(C) A full dinner will be provided.
(D) There is a fee for admission.

GO ON TO THE NEXT PAGE

Questions 149-150 refer to the following online customer-service exchange.

Mariam Abebe (9:05 A.M.): Hello. I'm Mariam Abebe with Heisler & Wilcox. Since last week my staff members and I have been having trouble accessing one of our bank accounts electronically.

Josue Martin (9:07 A.M.): Sorry to hear that, Ms. Abebe. Let me look into this for you.

Josue Martin (9:09 A.M.): Your publishing company has a few accounts with us. Which one are you referring to?

Mariam Abebe (9:09 A.M.): The one ending in 8409.

Josue Martin (9:11 A.M.): It looks like that account has been locked due to multiple failed log-in attempts. To unlock the account, the password must be reset.

Mariam Abebe (9:12 A.M.): Actually, my assistants and I have taken great care to enter the password correctly. Besides, we've tried changing it already, but we weren't able to.

Josue Martin (9:13 A.M.): I see. I will report your problem to our Enhanced Technical Support team. A technician will be contacting you within two hours.

Mariam Abebe (9:14 A.M.): Thank you.

149. What most likely is true about Ms. Abebe?
   (A) She has been locked out of her office before.
   (B) She oversees staff at a publishing company.
   (C) She will be submitting a report in two hours.
   (D) She had contacted Mr. Martin last week.

150. At 9:13 A.M., what does Mr. Martin most likely mean when he writes, "I see"?
   (A) He knows that Ms. Abebe tried to access the account repeatedly.
   (B) He noticed that Ms. Abebe had changed her password.
   (C) He understands why Ms. Abebe rejects his suggestion.
   (D) He realizes why Ms. Abebe needs on-site assistance.

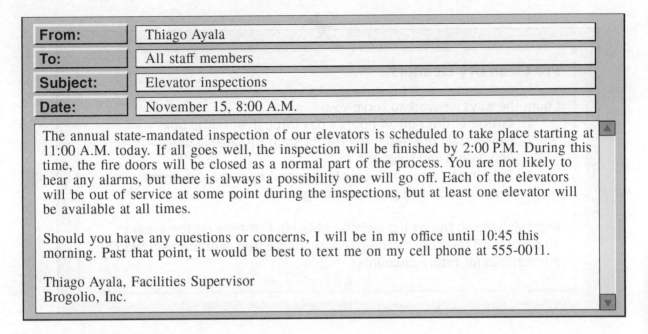

From:	Thiago Ayala
To:	All staff members
Subject:	Elevator inspections
Date:	November 15, 8:00 A.M.

The annual state-mandated inspection of our elevators is scheduled to take place starting at 11:00 A.M. today. If all goes well, the inspection will be finished by 2:00 P.M. During this time, the fire doors will be closed as a normal part of the process. You are not likely to hear any alarms, but there is always a possibility one will go off. Each of the elevators will be out of service at some point during the inspections, but at least one elevator will be available at all times.

Should you have any questions or concerns, I will be in my office until 10:45 this morning. Past that point, it would be best to text me on my cell phone at 555-0011.

Thiago Ayala, Facilities Supervisor
Brogolio, Inc.

TEST 2

151. What is indicated about the inspection?

(A) It takes place every two years.
(B) It involves checks over a two-day period.
(C) It includes testing the alarm system.
(D) It is required by a government agency.

152. When are both elevators anticipated to be operational again?

(A) At 8:00 A.M.
(B) At 10:45 A.M.
(C) At 11:00 A.M.
(D) At 2:00 P.M.

GO ON TO THE NEXT PAGE

Pro Clean Dry Cleaners

Count the ways we work to serve you!
1. Customer drop-off 24 hours a day through our drop box
2. Expert stain removal using the most up-to-date cleaning equipment and solutions
3. Tailoring services, including button and zipper replacement
4. Long-term on-site garment storage

Monthly special: During the month of March, first-time customers get 30 percent off their dry-cleaning service, plus a free garment bag! Watch our mailings for future discounts.

---

153. What service does Pro Clean Dry Cleaners offer?

(A) Delivery of orders to customers' homes
(B) Removal of stains using current processes
(C) Free replacement of buttons and zippers
(D) Advice on proper long-term garment storage

154. How can some customers receive a discount?

(A) By placing their first order in March
(B) By spending more than $30
(C) By responding to a customer survey
(D) By purchasing a garment bag

Burger City Bistro to Become BC Bistro

By Lola Jimenez

Burger City Bistro has announced that it will soon be known as BC Bistro. All advertisements, packaging, signage, and social media accounts are being updated in line with the new name. — [1] —.

"Over the years, our organization has expanded its menu to feature healthful items such as salads, sandwich wraps, and grilled chicken, in addition to burgers," company president Howard Shuman said. "We want our guests to think of us as a place where everyone can find tasty options." — [2] —.

Burger City Bistro has traditionally appealed to young adults and teenagers. But women aged 25–49 currently make up only 23 percent of the company's annual sales. — [3] —. The company recently announced that it had hired celebrity Isobel Wu as a spokesperson to help appeal to that market segment. Ms. Wu, who performs on the television program *Star Dancers*, will appear in television and print advertisements featuring BC Bistro as part of a healthy lifestyle.

"Ms. Wu will bring a new voice to our company that will reach potential customers who don't yet know that our menu has shifted away from what it was years ago," Mr. Shuman noted. — [4] —.

155. According to the article, why is the company changing its name?

(A) To make the name easier to remember
(B) To better reflect the company's current image
(C) Because it has been sold to another company
(D) Because it is no longer selling burgers

156. According to the article, what does the company hope to accomplish by hiring Ms. Wu?

(A) More women will visit BC Bistro locations.
(B) More teenagers will become interested in BC Bistro.
(C) There will be a larger audience for *Star Dancers*.
(D) Free dance classes will be held at all locations.

157. In which of the positions marked [1], [2], [3], and [4] does the following sentence best belong?

"Advertisements featuring Ms. Wu are set to begin when the name changes."

(A) [1]
(B) [2]
(C) [3]
(D) [4]

TEST 2

GO ON TO THE NEXT PAGE

Questions 158-160 refer to the following invoice.

All Sounds Music
Equipment, repairs, and rentals
Established 1954

All Sounds Music
4 Oak Street
Foustown, Pennsylvania 17404

Store Hours
10:00 A.M. – 6:00 P.M., seven days a week

Date: *March 14*

Phone: *717-555-0102*

Salesperson: *Winston Sajek*

Customer: *Karen Ahn*

QUANTITY	DESCRIPTION	PRICE
2	GR-48 Speakers	$160.00
	Subtotal	$160.00
	Sales tax	$9.60
	Total refund	-$169.60
	In-store credit	$169.60

Return policy:
No returns on discounted sale items.
All other items may be returned as long as they are in the same condition as purchased and an original receipt is submitted.
Customers returning items up to 14 days after purchase will receive a full refund.
Customers returning items between 15 and 30 days after purchase are eligible for in-store credit only. Store credit is good for 90 days from the date it was issued.
Repaired items not picked up within 60 days become the property of All Sounds Music.

158. What is indicated about All Sounds Music?
(A) Its store in Foustown is new.
(B) Its owner is Mr. Sajek.
(C) It has multiple locations.
(D) It is open every day.

159. What is suggested about the GR-48 speakers?
(A) They were purchased at a discount.
(B) They were returned in damaged condition.
(C) They were returned with a purchase receipt.
(D) They were rented from All Sounds Music.

160. For how long is Ms. Ahn's store credit valid?
(A) 14 days
(B) 30 days
(C) 60 days
(D) 90 days

Questions 161-163 refer to the following memo.

MEMO

To: All Lawson's Repair Technicians
From: Joel Gaos
Subject: New Process
Date: 3 April

Beginning on 5 April, our cost estimates for repairs will be processed electronically and sent to customers via e-mail. Whenever you visit customers to assess damage to their items, be sure to have your mobile phone or a tablet with you so that you can take pictures of the damage. You will fill out the estimate form on our Web site, attach the photos, and e-mail the estimate to the customer. Estimates should be filled out within 24 hours of your visit to a customer's home or business. We will likely have a few customers who will want handwritten estimates. If this is the case, you will still need to fill out the electronic form for our records and upload a copy of the handwritten estimate.

As always, carefully check warranties to find out which repairs are covered and which repairs the customer is responsible for. The computer desks now have only a three-month warranty, and the sofas, chairs, and dining sets have a much more limited warranty than before.

---

161. What is indicated about Lawson's customers?

(A) They must provide photographs of damaged items.
(B) They must send an e-mail request for repair service.
(C) They may request that technicians write out an estimate.
(D) They may record complaints about the warranties electronically.

162. The word "covered" in paragraph 2, line 1, is closest in meaning to

(A) replaced
(B) included
(C) retrieved
(D) concealed

163. What do Lawson's technicians repair?

(A) Cameras
(B) Mobile phones
(C) Homes
(D) Furniture

GO ON TO THE NEXT PAGE

Questions 164-167 refer to the following text-message chain.

Linda Farr (8:48 A.M.) Megumi and Ricardo, I suggest going to Sofia's Place for our weekly meeting instead of gathering here in our usual conference room. The three of us could easily report on progress made on the Humbert project over lunch. Thoughts?

Megumi Sugiyama (8:50 A.M.) I could use a break from the office.

Ricardo Thompson (8:51 A.M.) Alright by me. But what about staying close by and going to Crab Bay Café?

Linda Farr (8:52 A.M.) It's closer, but there's usually a wait because seating is limited. I don't want to go over an hour. Plus, I love the salads at Sofia's.

Ricardo Thompson (8:53 A.M.) True. They're great.

Megumi Sugiyama (8:55 A.M.) Sofia's it is then! But could we change the time? I find our usual meeting time a bit early for lunch.

Linda Farr (8:56 A.M.) Yes, 11:00 is a bit early for lunch, isn't it? OK, what time works best? 11:30? 12:00?

Ricardo Thompson (8:57 A.M.) Hmmm. How about 12:30?

Megumi Sugiyama (8:58 A.M.) Perfect!

Linda Farr (8:59 A.M.) Sounds good. See you then!

164. What is indicated about the upcoming meeting?

(A) Staff will give updates on a project.
(B) Staff will be joined by several clients.
(C) Staff will celebrate a recent success.
(D) Staff will make some important decisions.

165. At 8:50 A.M., what does Ms. Sugiyama mean when she writes, "I could use a break from the office"?

(A) She approves of meeting elsewhere.
(B) She wants to ask for time off from work.
(C) She is looking forward to her vacation.
(D) She is happy to run an errand for Ms. Farr.

166. What concern does Ms. Farr express about Crab Bay Café?

(A) It is too expensive.
(B) It is somewhat noisy.
(C) It does not offer Internet service.
(D) It cannot accommodate many people.

167. What time does the group normally meet?

(A) At 11:00 A.M.
(B) At 11:30 A.M.
(C) At 12:00 noon
(D) At 12:30 P.M.

Crofton Power

Crofton Power is consistently given high ratings for its commitment to customers. Service representatives are available at all times to promptly address power concerns. Customer satisfaction is backed with several key guarantees. — [1] —. Our assurances to customers are outlined below.

Billing: Customer inquiries should be directed to the billing department at 604-555-0101 or made online through the Crofton Power customer portal. — [2] —. If your question requires further investigation, please allow up to three business days for a response. Should the response be delayed by more than three days, the customer's account will be credited $25.

Appointments: Crofton Power aims to keep all appointments with customers. Crofton service technicians are scheduled to arrive within a two-hour time frame. On any occasion that this time frame is not honored, the customer's account will be credited $40.

Planned Outages: If Crofton Power needs to turn off power temporarily for construction or maintenance work, customers who may be affected will be notified at least 48 hours in advance. — [3] —. In the rare case that a service interruption notice has not been provided and a power outage occurs, the customer's account will be credited $80.

The aim of Crofton Power is to provide service that is fair and transparent. — [4] —. Thank you for trusting Crofton Power with your energy needs.

TEST 2

168. What is suggested in the information?

(A) Equipment has been recently upgraded.
(B) Delayed bill payments may result in a late fee.
(C) Quality service is a priority.
(D) A service area has expanded.

169. In what case will a customer receive a $40 credit from Crofton Power?

(A) When a power outage lasts more than three days
(B) When an inquiry is not addressed quickly
(C) When equipment requires emergency maintenance
(D) When a service technician's arrival is delayed

170. What will Crofton Power do when a power outage is planned?

(A) Renew a service contract
(B) Update a billing cycle
(C) Give advance notice
(D) Hire additional technicians

171. In which of the positions marked [1], [2], [3], and [4] does the following sentence best belong?

"Customers typically receive a response within two hours after an online request is made."

(A) [1]
(B) [2]
(C) [3]
(D) [4]

GO ON TO THE NEXT PAGE

Home	Products	**Reviews**	Contact Us

Adrianna Rossi ★ ★ ★ ★ ★

Mr. Prescott runs a top-notch online business. I have never worked with a designer this talented before. I was able to give a very specific description of what I wanted and my expectations were exceeded. I could have never imagined my wedding invitations turning out so beautiful! A friend needs new brochures for her business, and I will definitely refer her to this shop. Thanks!

Prisha Deol ★ ★ ☆ ☆ ☆

I am not pleased with my recent order. I had bought birthday party invitations previously from this store and was satisfied. This time, I ordered customized programs for my piano recital. I loved the proof that I was sent, but these do not look like the proof at all. The printing looks grainy and cheap. Also, the programs have a white mark at the top on the front and the back. It just does not look very professional.

Isak Larsson ★ ★ ★ ★ ★

The owner was fast to respond to my questions before I had even purchased anything. My business cards were designed in days and arrived quickly, even with international shipping to Sweden. They were exactly how I wanted them, even though I gave the designer only a few details and asked whether they could be completed in a hurry. This was a great experience.

172. What type of service does the business most likely provide?

(A) Home decorating
(B) Event planning
(C) Custom printing
(D) Fashion accessorizing

173. What does Ms. Rossi indicate about her items?

(A) They were made according to her instructions.
(B) They were shipped to another country.
(C) They were constructed with inexpensive materials.
(D) They were not the correct color.

174. What made a customer unhappy?

(A) A product option
(B) Business hours
(C) A party venue
(D) Recital programs

175. What does Mr. Larsson discuss in his review?

(A) The instructions for placing an order
(B) The variety of product choices
(C) The efficiency of the business
(D) The weight of the merchandise

GO ON TO THE NEXT PAGE

National Package Service (NPS) Package Tracking
Shipment number: DM5671

Location	Date	Local time	Action
Baltimore, MD	May 2	7:15 A.M.	Origin scan
Baltimore, MD	May 2	8:22 A.M.	Departure scan
Hartford, CT	May 3	4:48 P.M.	Arrival scan
Hartford, CT	May 4	6:30 A.M.	Departure scan
Lowell, MA	May 4	3:43 P.M.	Arrival scan
Lowell, MA	May 5	9:47 A.M.	Departure scan
Windham, NH	May 5	1:26 P.M.	Arrival scan
Windham, NH	May 5	5:17 P.M.	Loaded for delivery
Windham, NH	May 6	7:34 A.M.	Delivered

Shipped by: Deymantis, Inc.
Shipment category: Package
Billed on: May 1

Weight: 23.5 kilograms
Service: Ground shipment
Message on package:
Shipment of part number 264

To:	Mervin Hartley
From:	Caroline Launey
Date:	May 11
Subject:	Re: Deymantis package

Dear Mr. Hartley,

We received the package ahead of schedule and were able to install the Deymantis blade (part 264) on the day it arrived and test it the next day. We closed the mill to test the blade on various lengths and types of damaged lumber. The tests with the new cutting blade were successful, and so Monday was our first day at full operational status. I will send you an initial report on our revised processing times by the end of this week.

Sincerely,

Caroline Launey
Milford Lumber Mill

176. According to the tracking information, where was the package on the evening of May 4?

(A) In Baltimore
(B) In Hartford
(C) In Lowell
(D) In Windham

177. According to the tracking information, how was the package most likely transported?

(A) By NPS airplane
(B) By NPS truck
(C) By Deymantis airplane
(D) By Deymantis truck

178. Why did Ms. Launey write the e-mail?

(A) To provide an update
(B) To explain a delay
(C) To order a new part
(D) To request a report

179. When was part number 264 tested?

(A) On May 2
(B) On May 6
(C) On May 7
(D) On May 11

180. According to the e-mail, what will part number 264 most likely be used for?

(A) Breaking concrete
(B) Polishing metal
(C) Shaping glass
(D) Cutting wood

GO ON TO THE NEXT PAGE

From:	Month of Giving Committee
To:	All Vernment Employees
Date:	April 26
Subject:	Only a few days left

As our company's Month of Giving comes to a close, I would like to draw your attention to one more charity to consider. We have been profiling some of the lesser-known, but well-respected, organizations that are important to our colleagues. If you have not already made your voluntary contribution, take a moment to learn about this worthy cause. Remember that as your employer, Vernment, Inc., will match up to $100 of your contributions to eligible charities during this month.

Arborlee International works with communities in North America, South America, and Asia to establish young trees in areas that need to be reforested. Experts assist their partners in choosing the most appropriate native trees to plant. Local citizens are hired and taught the skills required to plant the trees and to care for them. Arborlee wants the trees to grow strong and provide shade, oxygen, and soil stabilization for previously barren areas. Every dollar donated goes toward the planting of trees; a gift of $1,000, for example, funds the planting of 1,000 trees. Go to www.arborlee.org to learn more.

ARBORLEE INTERNATIONAL

CERTIFICATE OF APPRECIATION

FOR

Vernment, Inc.

Many thanks for the generous gift of $7,260 generated by your company and for spreading the word about Arborlee International and its mission. In recognition of your contribution, your company's name will be displayed on a plaque at the entrance gate of the Rio Alto Forest Reserve in Bolivia, a project completed with the help of your funds.

Jennifer Price

Jennifer Price, President, Arborlee International

181. What is the purpose of the e-mail?

(A) To announce a business acquisition
(B) To inform employees of a charitable giving option
(C) To recognize an employee's community service
(D) To encourage organizations to conserve resources

182. In the e-mail, the word "draw" in paragraph 1, line 1, is closest in meaning to

(A) provide
(B) picture
(C) create
(D) attract

183. According to the e-mail, who will plant trees?

(A) People living in deforested areas
(B) Representatives from government agencies
(C) The Month of Giving committee
(D) Volunteers from Vernment, Inc.

184. What is the purpose of planting the trees?

(A) To provide inexpensive building materials
(B) To increase incomes in an area
(C) To improve the environment
(D) To beautify a city

185. For what was the contribution from Vernment, Inc., most likely used?

(A) Planting thousands of new trees
(B) Making improvements to the landscaping on a corporate campus
(C) Saving native trees from being harvested
(D) Printing materials that outline the mission of Arborlee International

GO ON TO THE NEXT PAGE

GREEN LYRE OFFICE FURNITURE DECEMBER SALE

We are making room for new models and products. Save 40 percent off all in-stock Green Lyre brand furniture, and save 30 percent off all other furniture brands in stock. All sales are final.

Delivery service is available and free to locations within Somerfield city limits. Pick-up and disposal of old furniture is also offered.

Start shopping now! Go to www.greenlyreofficefurniture.com or visit our showroom at 174 E. Landover Street.

Green Lyre Office Furniture Invoice

Purchased by:
Jasmine Kai, Office Manager
Hainey Medical Clinic

Phone: (210) 555-0108

Order number: G90123

Description	Item Number	Color	Quantity	Total Price
Reception Chair	MT-5047	Gray	2	$376.00
Lounge Chair	MT-2956	Gray	2	$1,100.00
Accent Chair	MT-0632	Black	1	$330.00
Leather Sofa	MT-4278	Gray	1	$1,325.00

Subtotal: $3,131.00
Discount (40%): - $1,252.40
Delivery: + $100.00
Total Charges: $1,978.60

To:	Jasmine Kai <jkai@haineymed.com>
From:	Colin Byrne <cbyrne@greenlyreofficefurniture.com>
Date:	December 10
Subject:	Your recent voicemail

Dear Ms. Kai:

I received your voicemail regarding your order number G90123, but your office was closed when I tried to return your call. You mentioned that you realized the sofa you ordered is unlikely to fit in the intended space in your clinic's waiting area. Then you asked whether you could receive a refund. Unfortunately, your purchase is not refundable, but I would like to accommodate you by offering an exchange. I can provide you with a Green Lyre Leather Love Seat in place of the sofa. And if you accept the love seat, I would also let you have an additional Green Lyre Reception Chair, all for the same total price as on the original invoice. Let me know if this will work.

Thank you for shopping at Green Lyre Office Furniture.

Sincerely yours,

Colin Byrne, Sales Manager

186. What is indicated about Green Lyre Office Furniture?

(A) It will soon close one of its stores.
(B) It accepts online orders only.
(C) It is offering a 40 percent discount on all merchandise.
(D) It offers to remove used furniture.

187. What is suggested about Hainey Medical Clinic?

(A) It is not located in Somerfield.
(B) Its waiting room includes a children's play area.
(C) It has just enlarged its waiting room.
(D) It has recently moved to a new location.

188. Why did Mr. Byrne send the e-mail?

(A) To make a purchase
(B) To answer a question
(C) To schedule an appointment
(D) To describe some product features

189. What did Ms. Kai indicate about the leather sofa?

(A) It was not the correct item.
(B) It was the wrong color.
(C) It was somewhat damaged.
(D) It was not suitable for the space.

190. What extra item does the store offer to add to the order?

(A) MT-5047
(B) MT-2956
(C) MT-0632
(D) MT-4278

GO ON TO THE NEXT PAGE

From:	mdavies@wafrennewsletter.com
To:	eskens@netsailos.com
Subject:	Old library
Date:	23 May
Attachment:	🔗 Permission form

Dear Mr. Eskens,

Thank you for agreeing to grant the *Wafren City Newsletter* permission to use your archival photographs of the old library. They will be included in an article about the history of local buildings. The article will appear in the July issue. So that we may complete our records, please print and sign the attached permission form and return it to us by post or as an attachment.

Best regards,

Mona Davies, Art Coordinator

From the Editorial Board

Welcome to the July issue of the *Wafren City Newsletter*. Featured on the front page is a photo of the renovated City Park. Read about how it has been transformed to better serve our community. This year, for the first time, it will host the popular Vegetable and Fruit Market, featuring produce from local farmers. Also covered in this issue are music performances and a drama festival.

Learn more about how City Hall works closely with local businesses. For example, you can read about a recent job-training initiative, fully financed by City Hall, which resulted in a number of Wafren residents being hired as drivers by transport companies in the area.

We welcome contributions from our readers, which can be found on pages 2–3. Letters to the editor, notices, and other submissions must be received by the tenth of the month to be considered for the next issue.

Also in this issue:
Street Improvements Pending–Page 4
Then and Now: Wafren Historical Landmarks–Page 6
Food Trucks: Locations and Schedules–Page 9
City Calendar and Phone Directory–Page 14

▲

Rolph Transport

In the News: Posted 1 July, 7:00 A.M.

This past spring, several graduates of the local career training program were hired by Rolph Transport. Read the July issue of the *Wafren City Newsletter* to learn about the training conducted by our own Aiden Lothar.

▼

191. In the e-mail, what is Mr. Eskens asked to do?

(A) Subscribe to a newsletter
(B) Update his photograph
(C) Sign a document
(D) Visit the library

192. According to the article, what will take place at a new location?

(A) A food market
(B) A training program
(C) A drama festival
(D) A music concert

193. What page in the newsletter most likely features materials provided by Mr. Eskens?

(A) Page 4
(B) Page 6
(C) Page 9
(D) Page 14

194. Who must follow the deadline mentioned in the article?

(A) Workers applying for jobs
(B) Artists requesting funds
(C) Readers canceling subscriptions
(D) Writers submitting articles

195. What is indicated about the training given by Mr. Lothar?

(A) Residents requested it.
(B) Local authorities paid for it.
(C) It can be attended online.
(D) It will be postponed.

TEST 2

GO ON TO THE NEXT PAGE

ADELETTO AND SONS

Our family business has been processing and dyeing fine leather since 1849. Whatever your factory product line, our experts will help you to wrap and finish your items beautifully by providing you with the highest-quality leather tailored to your specifications. Speedy worldwide shipping is guaranteed. Choose from the following collections, all of which are available in a variety of finishes and in over 100 designer colors.

- ROMA COLLECTION, for automotive, aviation, and seagoing use

- GENOA COLLECTION, for fine furniture

- VICENZA COLLECTION, for both dress shoes and casual footwear

- MILANO COLLECTION, for handbags and personal accessories

To:	Domenico Grande <d.grande@adeletto.it>
From:	Youngjoon Cho <yjcho@jaehakmarine.co.kr>
Date:	15 February
Subject:	Touring Line seating

Dear Mr. Grande:

We received the sample shipment of leather for the seats in our line of touring boats. While the color and texture are very pleasing, this leather is much too fine and thin for our purposes. It seems to be more like a glove leather, appropriate for small personal items. We are concerned that it will easily tear and become worn out, even with normal use.

Jaehak Marine builds boats for touring companies to use for weddings, corporate parties, and gala events. Naturally, the seating must be comfortable, but the surface should be sturdy and durable enough to withstand weight and friction as well as continual exposure to moisture. Most importantly, we must choose a leather that will stand up to the frequent spills that occur when food and beverages are served. Damage from spills is an issue we have had with our seats in the past, so we want to be certain to make the right choice this time. Please help us identify the best Adeletto and Sons material to meet these needs.

We look forward to your recommendation.

Sincerely,

Youngjoon Cho
Product Development, Jaehak Marine

```
┌─────────────────────────────────────────────────────────────────┐
│ ════════════════        *E-mail*        ════════════════         │
├─────────────────────────────────────────────────────────────────┤
│   To:       │ Youngjoon Cho <yjcho@jaehakmarine.co.kr>           │
│   From:     │ Domenico Grande <d.grande@adeletto.it>             │
│   Date:     │ 16 February                                        │
│   Subject:  │ RE: Touring Line seating                           │
├─────────────────────────────────────────────────────────────────┤
│                                                                   │
│  Dear Mr. Cho:                                                    │
│                                                                   │
│  We are so sorry for the error. Your sample should never have     │
│  been prepared with our softest and most delicate leather         │
│  product. We will send you new samples.                           │
│                                                                   │
│  Given what you have said about the usage your seating must       │
│  withstand, we think you may also be interested in our special    │
│  stain-resistant leather treatment. This type of finishing        │
│  treatment is very popular with clients whose products are        │
│  subject to heavy, repeated use. Please let us know if you would  │
│  like to add this option to your sample order. Also, let us know  │
│  if you would like your new samples in the same neutral color     │
│  that you originally requested.                                   │
│                                                                   │
│  Adeletto and Sons can have your samples delivered to you in      │
│  Jeju City within three days, and we will offer a 10 percent      │
│  discount when you are ready to place a full order.               │
│                                                                   │
│  Thank you,                                                       │
│                                                                   │
│  Domenico Grande                                                  │
│  Director of Client Relations, Adeletto and Sons                  │
│                                                                   │
└─────────────────────────────────────────────────────────────────┘
```

TEST 2

196. What is suggested about Adeletto and Sons?

(A) It creates products made of artificial leather.
(B) It produces shoes and handbags.
(C) It plans to open a new international office soon.
(D) It sells leather to manufacturing companies.

197. What is one purpose of the first e-mail?

(A) To promote boat rentals for events
(B) To complain about a late shipment
(C) To ask for advice about seat coverings
(D) To request instructions for preserving a delicate material

198. What collection best suits Mr. Cho's needs?

(A) Roma
(B) Genoa
(C) Vicenza
(D) Milano

199. What is the reason for Mr. Grande's apology in the second e-mail?

(A) A sample arrived with significant water damage.
(B) The wrong material was used in preparing a sample.
(C) An order confirmation was not sent.
(D) A discount was not applied to an order.

200. What will probably be most important to Mr. Cho when he places a full order?

(A) The shipping time
(B) The amount of the discount
(C) The color selection
(D) The finishing treatment

Stop! This is the end of the test. If you finish before time is called, you may go back to Parts 5, 6, and 7 and check your work.

公式 TOEIC® Listening & Reading 問題集 7 （音声 CD 2 枚付）

2020 年 12 月 10 日　第 1 版 第 1 刷発行
2023 年　5 月 15 日　第 1 版 第 6 刷発行

著者　　ETS

発行元　一般財団法人 国際ビジネスコミュニケーション協会

　　　　〒 100-0014

　　　　東京都千代田区永田町 2-14-2

　　　　山王グランドビル

　　　　電話　(03) 5521-5935

　　　　FAX　(03) 3581-9801

印刷　　凸版印刷株式会社

ISBN 978-4-906033-61-4

TEST 1

解答用紙

REGISTRATION No.
受験番号

フリガナ

NAME 氏名

LISTENING SECTION

Part 1

No.	ANSWER A B C D
1	Ⓐ Ⓑ Ⓒ Ⓓ
2	Ⓐ Ⓑ Ⓒ Ⓓ
3	Ⓐ Ⓑ Ⓒ Ⓓ
4	Ⓐ Ⓑ Ⓒ Ⓓ
5	Ⓐ Ⓑ Ⓒ Ⓓ
6	Ⓐ Ⓑ Ⓒ Ⓓ
7	Ⓐ Ⓑ Ⓒ
8	Ⓐ Ⓑ Ⓒ
9	Ⓐ Ⓑ Ⓒ
10	Ⓐ Ⓑ Ⓒ

Part 2

No.	ANSWER A B C
11	Ⓐ Ⓑ Ⓒ
12	Ⓐ Ⓑ Ⓒ
13	Ⓐ Ⓑ Ⓒ
14	Ⓐ Ⓑ Ⓒ
15	Ⓐ Ⓑ Ⓒ
16	Ⓐ Ⓑ Ⓒ
17	Ⓐ Ⓑ Ⓒ
18	Ⓐ Ⓑ Ⓒ
19	Ⓐ Ⓑ Ⓒ
20	Ⓐ Ⓑ Ⓒ

No.	ANSWER A B C
21	Ⓐ Ⓑ Ⓒ
22	Ⓐ Ⓑ Ⓒ
23	Ⓐ Ⓑ Ⓒ
24	Ⓐ Ⓑ Ⓒ
25	Ⓐ Ⓑ Ⓒ
26	Ⓐ Ⓑ Ⓒ
27	Ⓐ Ⓑ Ⓒ
28	Ⓐ Ⓑ Ⓒ
29	Ⓐ Ⓑ Ⓒ
30	Ⓐ Ⓑ Ⓒ

Part 3

No.	ANSWER A B C D
31	Ⓐ Ⓑ Ⓒ
32	Ⓐ Ⓑ Ⓒ Ⓓ
33	Ⓐ Ⓑ Ⓒ Ⓓ
34	Ⓐ Ⓑ Ⓒ Ⓓ
35	Ⓐ Ⓑ Ⓒ Ⓓ
36	Ⓐ Ⓑ Ⓒ Ⓓ
37	Ⓐ Ⓑ Ⓒ Ⓓ
38	Ⓐ Ⓑ Ⓒ Ⓓ
39	Ⓐ Ⓑ Ⓒ Ⓓ
40	Ⓐ Ⓑ Ⓒ Ⓓ

No.	ANSWER A B C D
41	Ⓐ Ⓑ Ⓒ Ⓓ
42	Ⓐ Ⓑ Ⓒ Ⓓ
43	Ⓐ Ⓑ Ⓒ Ⓓ
44	Ⓐ Ⓑ Ⓒ Ⓓ
45	Ⓐ Ⓑ Ⓒ Ⓓ
46	Ⓐ Ⓑ Ⓒ Ⓓ
47	Ⓐ Ⓑ Ⓒ Ⓓ
48	Ⓐ Ⓑ Ⓒ Ⓓ
49	Ⓐ Ⓑ Ⓒ Ⓓ
50	Ⓐ Ⓑ Ⓒ Ⓓ

No.	ANSWER A B C D
51	Ⓐ Ⓑ Ⓒ Ⓓ
52	Ⓐ Ⓑ Ⓒ Ⓓ
53	Ⓐ Ⓑ Ⓒ Ⓓ
54	Ⓐ Ⓑ Ⓒ Ⓓ
55	Ⓐ Ⓑ Ⓒ Ⓓ
56	Ⓐ Ⓑ Ⓒ Ⓓ
57	Ⓐ Ⓑ Ⓒ Ⓓ
58	Ⓐ Ⓑ Ⓒ Ⓓ
59	Ⓐ Ⓑ Ⓒ Ⓓ
60	Ⓐ Ⓑ Ⓒ Ⓓ

No.	ANSWER A B C D
61	Ⓐ Ⓑ Ⓒ Ⓓ
62	Ⓐ Ⓑ Ⓒ Ⓓ
63	Ⓐ Ⓑ Ⓒ Ⓓ
64	Ⓐ Ⓑ Ⓒ Ⓓ
65	Ⓐ Ⓑ Ⓒ Ⓓ
66	Ⓐ Ⓑ Ⓒ Ⓓ
67	Ⓐ Ⓑ Ⓒ Ⓓ
68	Ⓐ Ⓑ Ⓒ Ⓓ
69	Ⓐ Ⓑ Ⓒ Ⓓ
70	Ⓐ Ⓑ Ⓒ Ⓓ

Part 4

No.	ANSWER A B C D
71	Ⓐ Ⓑ Ⓒ Ⓓ
72	Ⓐ Ⓑ Ⓒ Ⓓ
73	Ⓐ Ⓑ Ⓒ Ⓓ
74	Ⓐ Ⓑ Ⓒ Ⓓ
75	Ⓐ Ⓑ Ⓒ Ⓓ
76	Ⓐ Ⓑ Ⓒ Ⓓ
77	Ⓐ Ⓑ Ⓒ Ⓓ
78	Ⓐ Ⓑ Ⓒ Ⓓ
79	Ⓐ Ⓑ Ⓒ Ⓓ
80	Ⓐ Ⓑ Ⓒ Ⓓ

No.	ANSWER A B C D
81	Ⓐ Ⓑ Ⓒ Ⓓ
82	Ⓐ Ⓑ Ⓒ Ⓓ
83	Ⓐ Ⓑ Ⓒ Ⓓ
84	Ⓐ Ⓑ Ⓒ Ⓓ
85	Ⓐ Ⓑ Ⓒ Ⓓ
86	Ⓐ Ⓑ Ⓒ Ⓓ
87	Ⓐ Ⓑ Ⓒ Ⓓ
88	Ⓐ Ⓑ Ⓒ Ⓓ
89	Ⓐ Ⓑ Ⓒ Ⓓ
90	Ⓐ Ⓑ Ⓒ Ⓓ

No.	ANSWER A B C D
91	Ⓐ Ⓑ Ⓒ Ⓓ
92	Ⓐ Ⓑ Ⓒ Ⓓ
93	Ⓐ Ⓑ Ⓒ Ⓓ
94	Ⓐ Ⓑ Ⓒ Ⓓ
95	Ⓐ Ⓑ Ⓒ Ⓓ
96	Ⓐ Ⓑ Ⓒ Ⓓ
97	Ⓐ Ⓑ Ⓒ Ⓓ
98	Ⓐ Ⓑ Ⓒ Ⓓ
99	Ⓐ Ⓑ Ⓒ Ⓓ
100	Ⓐ Ⓑ Ⓒ Ⓓ

READING SECTION

Part 5

No.	ANSWER A B C D
101	Ⓐ Ⓑ Ⓒ Ⓓ
102	Ⓐ Ⓑ Ⓒ Ⓓ
103	Ⓐ Ⓑ Ⓒ Ⓓ
104	Ⓐ Ⓑ Ⓒ Ⓓ
105	Ⓐ Ⓑ Ⓒ Ⓓ
106	Ⓐ Ⓑ Ⓒ Ⓓ
107	Ⓐ Ⓑ Ⓒ Ⓓ
108	Ⓐ Ⓑ Ⓒ Ⓓ
109	Ⓐ Ⓑ Ⓒ Ⓓ
110	Ⓐ Ⓑ Ⓒ Ⓓ

No.	ANSWER A B C D
111	Ⓐ Ⓑ Ⓒ Ⓓ
112	Ⓐ Ⓑ Ⓒ Ⓓ
113	Ⓐ Ⓑ Ⓒ Ⓓ
114	Ⓐ Ⓑ Ⓒ Ⓓ
115	Ⓐ Ⓑ Ⓒ Ⓓ
116	Ⓐ Ⓑ Ⓒ Ⓓ
117	Ⓐ Ⓑ Ⓒ Ⓓ
118	Ⓐ Ⓑ Ⓒ Ⓓ
119	Ⓐ Ⓑ Ⓒ Ⓓ
120	Ⓐ Ⓑ Ⓒ Ⓓ

No.	ANSWER A B C D
121	Ⓐ Ⓑ Ⓒ Ⓓ
122	Ⓐ Ⓑ Ⓒ Ⓓ
123	Ⓐ Ⓑ Ⓒ Ⓓ
124	Ⓐ Ⓑ Ⓒ Ⓓ
125	Ⓐ Ⓑ Ⓒ Ⓓ
126	Ⓐ Ⓑ Ⓒ Ⓓ
127	Ⓐ Ⓑ Ⓒ Ⓓ
128	Ⓐ Ⓑ Ⓒ Ⓓ
129	Ⓐ Ⓑ Ⓒ Ⓓ
130	Ⓐ Ⓑ Ⓒ Ⓓ

Part 6

No.	ANSWER A B C D
131	Ⓐ Ⓑ Ⓒ Ⓓ
132	Ⓐ Ⓑ Ⓒ Ⓓ
133	Ⓐ Ⓑ Ⓒ Ⓓ
134	Ⓐ Ⓑ Ⓒ Ⓓ
135	Ⓐ Ⓑ Ⓒ Ⓓ
136	Ⓐ Ⓑ Ⓒ Ⓓ
137	Ⓐ Ⓑ Ⓒ Ⓓ
138	Ⓐ Ⓑ Ⓒ Ⓓ
139	Ⓐ Ⓑ Ⓒ Ⓓ
140	Ⓐ Ⓑ Ⓒ Ⓓ

Part 7

No.	ANSWER A B C D
141	Ⓐ Ⓑ Ⓒ Ⓓ
142	Ⓐ Ⓑ Ⓒ Ⓓ
143	Ⓐ Ⓑ Ⓒ Ⓓ
144	Ⓐ Ⓑ Ⓒ Ⓓ
145	Ⓐ Ⓑ Ⓒ Ⓓ
146	Ⓐ Ⓑ Ⓒ Ⓓ
147	Ⓐ Ⓑ Ⓒ Ⓓ
148	Ⓐ Ⓑ Ⓒ Ⓓ
149	Ⓐ Ⓑ Ⓒ Ⓓ
150	Ⓐ Ⓑ Ⓒ Ⓓ

No.	ANSWER A B C D
151	Ⓐ Ⓑ Ⓒ Ⓓ
152	Ⓐ Ⓑ Ⓒ Ⓓ
153	Ⓐ Ⓑ Ⓒ Ⓓ
154	Ⓐ Ⓑ Ⓒ Ⓓ
155	Ⓐ Ⓑ Ⓒ Ⓓ
156	Ⓐ Ⓑ Ⓒ Ⓓ
157	Ⓐ Ⓑ Ⓒ Ⓓ
158	Ⓐ Ⓑ Ⓒ Ⓓ
159	Ⓐ Ⓑ Ⓒ Ⓓ
160	Ⓐ Ⓑ Ⓒ Ⓓ

No.	ANSWER A B C D
161	Ⓐ Ⓑ Ⓒ Ⓓ
162	Ⓐ Ⓑ Ⓒ Ⓓ
163	Ⓐ Ⓑ Ⓒ Ⓓ
164	Ⓐ Ⓑ Ⓒ Ⓓ
165	Ⓐ Ⓑ Ⓒ Ⓓ
166	Ⓐ Ⓑ Ⓒ Ⓓ
167	Ⓐ Ⓑ Ⓒ Ⓓ
168	Ⓐ Ⓑ Ⓒ Ⓓ
169	Ⓐ Ⓑ Ⓒ Ⓓ
170	Ⓐ Ⓑ Ⓒ Ⓓ

No.	ANSWER A B C D
171	Ⓐ Ⓑ Ⓒ Ⓓ
172	Ⓐ Ⓑ Ⓒ Ⓓ
173	Ⓐ Ⓑ Ⓒ Ⓓ
174	Ⓐ Ⓑ Ⓒ Ⓓ
175	Ⓐ Ⓑ Ⓒ Ⓓ
176	Ⓐ Ⓑ Ⓒ Ⓓ
177	Ⓐ Ⓑ Ⓒ Ⓓ
178	Ⓐ Ⓑ Ⓒ Ⓓ
179	Ⓐ Ⓑ Ⓒ Ⓓ
180	Ⓐ Ⓑ Ⓒ Ⓓ

No.	ANSWER A B C D
181	Ⓐ Ⓑ Ⓒ Ⓓ
182	Ⓐ Ⓑ Ⓒ Ⓓ
183	Ⓐ Ⓑ Ⓒ Ⓓ
184	Ⓐ Ⓑ Ⓒ Ⓓ
185	Ⓐ Ⓑ Ⓒ Ⓓ
186	Ⓐ Ⓑ Ⓒ Ⓓ
187	Ⓐ Ⓑ Ⓒ Ⓓ
188	Ⓐ Ⓑ Ⓒ Ⓓ
189	Ⓐ Ⓑ Ⓒ Ⓓ
190	Ⓐ Ⓑ Ⓒ Ⓓ

No.	ANSWER A B C D
191	Ⓐ Ⓑ Ⓒ Ⓓ
192	Ⓐ Ⓑ Ⓒ Ⓓ
193	Ⓐ Ⓑ Ⓒ Ⓓ
194	Ⓐ Ⓑ Ⓒ Ⓓ
195	Ⓐ Ⓑ Ⓒ Ⓓ
196	Ⓐ Ⓑ Ⓒ Ⓓ
197	Ⓐ Ⓑ Ⓒ Ⓓ
198	Ⓐ Ⓑ Ⓒ Ⓓ
199	Ⓐ Ⓑ Ⓒ Ⓓ
200	Ⓐ Ⓑ Ⓒ Ⓓ

TEST 2

解答用紙

REGISTRATION No. 受験番号

フリガナ

NAME 氏名

LISTENING SECTION

Part 1

No.	ANSWER
1	A B C D
2	A B C D
3	A B C D
4	A B C D
5	A B C D
6	A B C D
7	A B C D
8	A B C D
9	A B C D
10	A B C D

Part 2

No.	ANSWER
11	A B C
12	A B C
13	A B C
14	A B C
15	A B C
16	A B C
17	A B C
18	A B C
19	A B C
20	A B C

No.	ANSWER
21	A B C
22	A B C
23	A B C
24	A B C
25	A B C
26	A B C
27	A B C
28	A B C
29	A B C
30	A B C

Part 3

No.	ANSWER
31	A B C D
32	A B C D
33	A B C D
34	A B C D
35	A B C D
36	A B C D
37	A B C D
38	A B C D
39	A B C D
40	A B C D

No.	ANSWER
41	A B C D
42	A B C D
43	A B C D
44	A B C D
45	A B C D
46	A B C D
47	A B C D
48	A B C D
49	A B C D
50	A B C D

No.	ANSWER
51	A B C D
52	A B C D
53	A B C D
54	A B C D
55	A B C D
56	A B C D
57	A B C D
58	A B C D
59	A B C D
60	A B C D

Part 4

No.	ANSWER
61	A B C D
62	A B C D
63	A B C D
64	A B C D
65	A B C D
66	A B C D
67	A B C D
68	A B C D
69	A B C D
70	A B C D

No.	ANSWER
71	A B C D
72	A B C D
73	A B C D
74	A B C D
75	A B C D
76	A B C D
77	A B C D
78	A B C D
79	A B C D
80	A B C D

No.	ANSWER
81	A B C D
82	A B C D
83	A B C D
84	A B C D
85	A B C D
86	A B C D
87	A B C D
88	A B C D
89	A B C D
90	A B C D

No.	ANSWER
91	A B C D
92	A B C D
93	A B C D
94	A B C D
95	A B C D
96	A B C D
97	A B C D
98	A B C D
99	A B C D
100	A B C D

READING SECTION

Part 5

No.	ANSWER
101	A B C D
102	A B C D
103	A B C D
104	A B C D
105	A B C D
106	A B C D
107	A B C D
108	A B C D
109	A B C D
110	A B C D

No.	ANSWER
111	A B C D
112	A B C D
113	A B C D
114	A B C D
115	A B C D
116	A B C D
117	A B C D
118	A B C D
119	A B C D
120	A B C D

Part 6

No.	ANSWER
121	A B C D
122	A B C D
123	A B C D
124	A B C D
125	A B C D
126	A B C D
127	A B C D
128	A B C D
129	A B C D
130	A B C D

No.	ANSWER
131	A B C D
132	A B C D
133	A B C D
134	A B C D
135	A B C D
136	A B C D
137	A B C D
138	A B C D
139	A B C D
140	A B C D

Part 7

No.	ANSWER
141	A B C D
142	A B C D
143	A B C D
144	A B C D
145	A B C D
146	A B C D
147	A B C D
148	A B C D
149	A B C D
150	A B C D

No.	ANSWER
151	A B C D
152	A B C D
153	A B C D
154	A B C D
155	A B C D
156	A B C D
157	A B C D
158	A B C D
159	A B C D
160	A B C D

No.	ANSWER
161	A B C D
162	A B C D
163	A B C D
164	A B C D
165	A B C D
166	A B C D
167	A B C D
168	A B C D
169	A B C D
170	A B C D

No.	ANSWER
171	A B C D
172	A B C D
173	A B C D
174	A B C D
175	A B C D
176	A B C D
177	A B C D
178	A B C D
179	A B C D
180	A B C D

No.	ANSWER
181	A B C D
182	A B C D
183	A B C D
184	A B C D
185	A B C D
186	A B C D
187	A B C D
188	A B C D
189	A B C D
190	A B C D

No.	ANSWER
191	A B C D
192	A B C D
193	A B C D
194	A B C D
195	A B C D
196	A B C D
197	A B C D
198	A B C D
199	A B C D
200	A B C D

公式 *TOEIC*®
Listening & Reading
問題集

7

別冊 『解答・解説』

目　次

解答・解説で使われている表記の説明

● **CDのトラック番号（Part 1～4）**

会話の音声が CD 2 のトラック番号 40 に、
問題の音声が CD 2 のトラック番号 41 に入っていることを示しています。

● **スクリプトの前の記号（Part 1～4）**

🇺🇸 = 米国の発音
🇬🇧 = 英国の発音
🇨🇦 = カナダの発音
🇦🇺 = オーストラリアの発音

M = 男性（Man）
W = 女性（Woman）

● **スクリプト中の ❶❷ 等の番号（Part 3、4）**

解説の中で説明している箇所を示しています。

| | 会話 | CD 2 40 | 問題 | CD 2 41 |

Questions 38 through 40 refer to the following conversation.

🇨🇦 M Emily, ❶did you hear that a new pharmacy's opening on West Avenue?

🇬🇧 W No, but that's great news. ❷I usually go to Paxton's Drug Store on Main Street. It has a very friendly staff, ❸but the parking downtown is so inconvenient. There's never anywhere to park there!

🇨🇦 M I agree! Plus ❹the article I read about the pharmacy on West Avenue said it's supposed to have wellness classes every week. ❺It'll be great to learn more about them.

問題38-40は次の会話に関するものです。

Emily、ウェスト大通りに新しい薬局が開業することを聞きましたか？

いいえ、でも素晴らしいニュースですね。私は普段、メイン通りにあるPaxton'sドラッグストアに行きます。そこはとても親切なスタッフがいますが、中心街の駐車場はとても不便です。あそこには駐車できる場所がどこにもあったためしがありませんから。

同感です。それに、ウェスト大通りの薬局について僕が読んだ記事には、そこが毎週、健康推進講座を開催することになっていると書いてありましたよ。それらについて、もっと知ることができたらいいですよね。

38 What news does the man share?

(A) A delivery will be delayed.
(B) A store has extended its hours.
(C) A parking garage is being built.
(D) A new business will open.

男性はどんな知らせを共有していますか。

(A) 配達が遅延する。
(B) 店が営業時間を延長した。
(C) 駐車場が建設中である。
(D) 新しい店が開業する。

正解 D 男性は❶「ウェスト大通りに新しい薬局が開業することを聞いたか」と女性に尋ねている。a new pharmacyをa new businessと表している(D)が正解。❶のpharmacy's openingは pharmacy is opening の短縮形で近い未来の予定を表している。share「～を共有する」。business「店、事業」。

(A) delivery「配達」、delay「～を遅らせる」。
(B) extend「～を延長する」、hours「営業時間」。
(C) parking garage「駐車場」。

39 Why does the woman dislike shopping at Paxton's Drug

女性は❷で、普段利用するPaxton'sド

● **色の区別**

青字：正答に関する解説
黒字：誤答に関する解説や語句の意味

● **特典音声ファイルの番号（Part 5 〜 7）**

「52-54」は特典音声のファイル番号を示しています。ダウンロード音声ファイルのタイトル名に、「特典52」、「特典53」、「特典54」と表示されています。

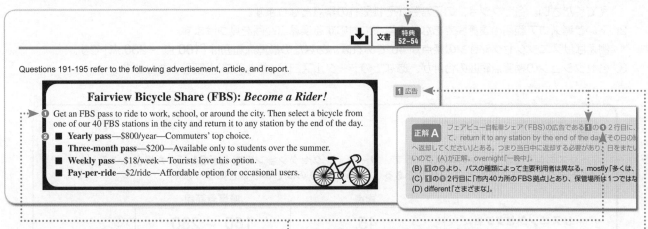

Questions 191-195 refer to the following advertisement, article, and report.

Fairview Bicycle Share (FBS): *Become a Rider!*

❶ Get an FBS pass to ride to work, school, or around the city. Then select a bicycle from one of our 40 FBS stations in the city and return it to any station by the end of the day.

❷ ■ **Yearly pass**—$800/year—Commuters' top choice.
■ **Three-month pass**—$200—Available only to students over the summer.
■ **Weekly pass**—$18/week—Tourists love this option.
■ **Pay-per-ride**—$2/ride—Affordable option for occasional users.

正解 A フェアビュー自転車シェア（FBS）の広告である**1**の❶2行目に、て、return it to any station by the end of the day、その日の〜へ返却してください」とある。つまり当日中に返却する必要があり、日をまたしいので、(A)が正解。overnight「一晩中」。
(B) **1**の❷より、パスの種類によって主要利用者は異なる。mostly「多くは、
(C) **1**の❶1行目に「市内40カ所のFBS拠点」とあり、保管場所は1つではな
(D) different「さまざまな」。

● **文書中の ❶❷ 等の番号（Part 6、7）**

解説の中で説明している文書中の段落番号等を示しています。解説文中の段落番号に続く行数は、英文中の各段落の何行目かを表しています。

● **文書を示す 1 2 等の番号（Part 7）**

解説の中で説明している文書を示しています。

● **Words & Phrases（Part 3、4、6、7）**

会話やトーク、文書などに含まれる重要な語句と意味を紹介しています。Part 6、7 では、上記に示した **1 2** や ❶❷ の番号により、本文で使われている場所が参照できます。

Words & Phrases

1 広告 share 共有 rider 乗り手 ❶ pass 乗車券、定期券 select 〜を選ぶ station 拠点
❷ yearly 年間の commuter 通勤通学者 choice 選択肢 available 利用できる、求めに応じられる
weekly 週単位の option 選択肢 pay-per-ride 乗る都度支払う affordable 手頃な価格の
occasional 不定期の、時折の

2 記事 ❶ turn 〜になる mayor 市長 thoughts on 〜 〜についての考え ❷ get started 始める
propose 〜を提案する resident 住民 planning meeting 企画会議 critic 批判する人

● **Expressions（Part 6、7）**

文書の中から、知っておくと便利な表現を例文とともに紹介しています。覚えて使えるようになると、大変便利です。

Expressions

such as 〜 「例えば〜など、〜のような」（**2**の❷④〜5行目）
XYZ company exports a lot of fruits, such as lemons, oranges, and apples.
XYZ社はレモン、オレンジ、りんごなどの果物をたくさん輸出しています。

＊『公式 *TOEIC*® Listening & Reading 問題集7』の特典として、ダウンロード音声の中には、TEST 1、2 のリーディングセクションの以下の音声が入っています。音声ダウンロードの手順は本誌 p. 3 をご参照ください。
　・正解が入った問題音声（Part 5、6）
　・文書の音声（Part 7）

参考スコア範囲の算出方法 ※ TEST 1、2 共通

1. 正解一覧（p.5、p.102）を参照し、リスニングセクションとリーディングセクションそれぞれの正答数を数えてください。各セクションの正答数がそれぞれの素点となります。
2. 下の参考スコア範囲の換算表であなたの素点に対応する換算点範囲を見つけます。
   例えばリスニングセクションの素点が45であれば、あなたの換算点範囲は「160点～230点」です。
3. 各セクションの換算点範囲の合計が、あなたのトータルスコア（参考スコア範囲）となります。

参考スコア範囲の算出例

リスニングセクションの素点が **45** で、リーディングセクションの素点が **64** だった場合、
トータルスコアは①と②の合計である③ **415—570** の間ということになります。

	素点	換算点範囲	
リスニングセクション	45	160 — 230	①
リーディングセクション	64	255 — 340	②
トータルスコア（参考スコア範囲）		415 — 570	③（①＋②）

参考スコア範囲の換算表

リスニングセクション		リーディングセクション	
素点	換算点範囲	素点	換算点範囲
96 － 100	475 － 495	96 － 100	460 － 495
91 － 95	435 － 495	91 － 95	425 － 490
86 － 90	405 － 470	86 － 90	400 － 465
81 － 85	370 － 450	81 － 85	375 － 440
76 － 80	345 － 420	76 － 80	340 － 415
71 － 75	320 － 390	71 － 75	310 － 390
66 － 70	290 － 360	66 － 70	285 － 370
61 － 65	265 － 335	61 － 65	255 － 340 （算出例②）
56 － 60	240 － 310	56 － 60	230 － 310
51 － 55	215 － 280	51 － 55	200 － 275
46 － 50	190 － 255	46 － 50	170 － 245
41 － 45	160 － 230 （算出例①）	41 － 45	140 － 215
36 － 40	130 － 205	36 － 40	115 － 180
31 － 35	105 － 175	31 － 35	95 － 150
26 － 30	85 － 145	26 － 30	75 － 120
21 － 25	60 － 115	21 － 25	60 － 95
16 － 20	30 － 90	16 － 20	45 － 75
11 － 15	5 － 70	11 － 15	30 － 55
6 － 10	5 － 60	6 － 10	10 － 40
1 － 5	5 － 50	1 － 5	5 － 30
0	5 － 35	0	5 － 15

TEST 1 の正解一覧

リスニングセクション

問題番号	正解
Part 1	
1	B
2	A
3	D
4	C
5	A
6	A
Part 2	
7	B
8	C
9	B
10	A
11	B
12	B
13	A
14	B
15	B
16	B
17	C
18	B
19	B
20	A
21	A
22	C
23	C
24	A
25	C
26	A
27	A
28	A
29	C
30	C
31	A
Part 3	
32	B
33	C
34	A
35	A
36	B
37	C
38	A
39	B
40	C
41	B
42	D
43	A
44	B
45	A
46	D
47	A
48	C
49	A
50	A

問題番号	正解
51	D
52	B
53	D
54	B
55	C
56	C
57	B
58	D
59	D
60	D
61	D
62	D
63	B
64	C
65	D
66	A
67	C
68	C
69	B
70	A
Part 4	
71	C
72	A
73	B
74	C
75	B
76	A
77	D
78	C
79	A
80	B
81	A
82	D
83	A
84	B
85	C
86	A
87	C
88	A
89	A
90	B
91	D
92	C
93	B
94	D
95	D
96	D
97	C
98	C
99	B
100	C

リーディングセクション

問題番号	正解
Part 5	
101	A
102	D
103	A
104	B
105	C
106	A
107	D
108	A
109	D
110	D
111	A
112	C
113	C
114	A
115	C
116	B
117	A
118	B
119	B
120	C
121	A
122	D
123	B
124	A
125	D
126	C
127	C
128	C
129	B
130	B
Part 6	
131	B
132	C
133	B
134	D
135	A
136	D
137	C
138	A
139	B
140	C
141	B
142	D
143	A
144	D
145	C
146	D
Part 7	
147	D
148	B
149	A
150	B

問題番号	正解
151	A
152	D
153	D
154	C
155	D
156	C
157	B
158	D
159	C
160	A
161	B
162	A
163	C
164	C
165	B
166	A
167	C
168	C
169	B
170	D
171	B
172	B
173	A
174	A
175	C
176	A
177	D
178	C
179	B
180	B
181	A
182	A
183	D
184	D
185	C
186	B
187	C
188	D
189	D
190	C
191	A
192	C
193	B
194	A
195	B
196	A
197	B
198	C
199	D
200	B

1

2

3

---

1 🇺🇸 W

(A) She's changing her shoes.
(B) She's reaching into her bag.
(C) She's adjusting her chair.
(D) She's typing on a keyboard.

(A) 彼女は自分の靴を履き替えている。
(B) 彼女は自分のバッグの中に手を入れている。
(C) 彼女は自分の椅子を調節している。
(D) 彼女はキーボードで入力している。

> **正解 B** 女性は膝上にあるバッグの中に右手を入れている。reach into ～「～の中に手を入れる」。
> (A) 女性は靴をすでに履いており、履き替えているところではない。
> (C) 女性は椅子に座っているが、それを調節してはいない。adjust「～を調節する」。
> (D) type on a keyboard「キーボードで入力する」。

---

2 🇨🇦 M

(A) He's carrying a shopping basket.
(B) He's wiping some shelves.
(C) He's paying for a purchase.
(D) He's sampling a product.

(A) 彼は買い物かごを持ち歩いている。
(B) 彼は幾つかの棚を拭いている。
(C) 彼は買い物の支払いをしている。
(D) 彼は製品を試食している。

> **正解 A** 男性は店内で右手に買い物かごを持ち歩いている。carry「～を持ち歩く」、shopping basket「買い物かご」。
> (B) wipe「～を拭く」、shelvesはshelf「棚」の複数形。
> (C) 男性は買い物の最中だが、支払いをしているところではない。pay for ～「～の支払いをする」、purchase「買い物、購入品」。
> (D) sample「～を試食する」、product「製品」。

---

3 🇬🇧 W

(A) One of the men is buying a ticket.
(B) One of the men is sweeping the floor.
(C) Some people are having a meal.
(D) Some people are seated in a waiting area.

(A) 男性の1人はチケットを買っている。
(B) 男性の1人は床を掃いている。
(C) 何人かの人々が食事をしている。
(D) 何人かの人々が待合エリアで座っている。

> **正解 D** 複数の人々が待合スペースのような場所にある椅子に腰掛けている。be seated「座っている」、waiting area「待合エリア、待合所」。
> (A) チケットを買っている男性は写っていない。
> (B) floor「床」は写っているが、男性が床を掃除してはいない。sweep「～を掃く」。
> (C) have a meal「食事をする」。

4 　　　**5** 　　　**6**

4 🏴 M

(A) He's turning on a water faucet.
(B) He's cleaning a stove top.
(C) He's wearing a pair of gloves.
(D) He's filling a bottle with dish soap.

(A) 彼は水道の蛇口を開けている。
(B) 彼はコンロの上面を掃除している。
(C) 彼は1組の手袋を着用している。
(D) 彼はボトルを食器用洗剤で満たしている。

> 正解 **C**　男性は両手に手袋を着用している。a pair of ~「1組の~」、glove「手袋」。
> (A) 男性はwater faucet「水道の蛇口」に触れておらず、水も出ていない。turn on ~「~(蛇口など)を開ける」。
> (B) 男性が前に立って作業をしているのはシンクであり、コンロではない。stove「(料理用の)コンロ、レンジ」、top「上面」。
> (D) fill ~ with …「~を…で満たす」、dish soap「食器用洗剤」。

5 🇺🇸 W

(A) A wooden ladder is leaning against a wall.
(B) A piano is positioned in the center of the room.
(C) An audio speaker is mounted on the ceiling.
(D) Some drums are being put away in cases.

(A) 木製のはしごが壁に立て掛けられている。
(B) ピアノが部屋の中央に置かれている。
(C) オーディオスピーカーが天井に取り付けられている。
(D) 幾つかのドラムがケースにしまわれているところである。

> 正解 **A**　右壁に木製のはしごが立て掛けてある。wooden「木製の」、ladder「はしご」、lean against ~「~にもたれる」。
> (B) ピアノは部屋の窓側の隅にあり、中央に置かれてはいない。position「~を置く」。
> (C) audio speaker「オーディオスピーカー」、be mounted on ~「~に取り付けられている」、ceiling「天井」。
> (D) drum「ドラム」、put away ~「~をしまう、~を片付ける」、case「ケース」。

6 🏴 M

(A) They're looking down at the front page of a newspaper.
(B) They're setting a package on top of a mailbox.
(C) They're standing in front of a stoplight.
(D) They're climbing the stairs to an apartment building.

(A) 彼女らは新聞の第1面に視線を落としている。
(B) 彼女らは小包を郵便受けの上に載せている。
(C) 彼女らは交通信号の前に立っている。
(D) 彼女らはアパートへの階段を上っている。

> 正解 **A**　2人の女性が新聞の表面に視線を落としている。look down at ~「~に視線を落とす」、front page「(新聞の)第1面」。
> (B) package「小包」、mailbox「郵便受け」。
> (C) 奥にstoplight「交通信号」のようなものは写っているが、2人はその前に立ってはいない。
> (D) 建物の前に階段はあるが、2人はそれを上ってはいない。climb「~を上る」、stairs「階段」、apartment building「アパート、集合住宅」。

PART 2

7 W Who is Paul's supervisor?

M (A) The product launch is next month.
(B) It's Ms. Ito.
(C) No, they're down the hall.

誰がPaulの上司ですか。

(A) 製品の発売は来月です。
(B) それはItoさんです。
(C) いいえ、それらは廊下の先にあります。

正解 **B** Who ～?で誰がPaulの上司か尋ねているのに対し、「それはItoさんだ」と人物名を伝えている(B)が正解。Itは質問にあるPaul's supervisorを指す。supervisor「上司、管理者」。
(A) 製品の発売時期は尋ねられていない。launch「発売」。
(C) 人物を尋ねられているので、Yes、Noでは応答にならない。down the hall「廊下の先に」。

8 W Where can I find copy paper?

M (A) Some new chairs.
(B) Just sign at the bottom.
(C) In aisle twelve.

コピー用紙はどこで見つけることができますか。

(A) 数脚の新しい椅子です。
(B) 下部に署名するだけです。
(C) 12番通路です。

正解 **C** Where ～?でコピー用紙がどこにあるか尋ねているのに対し、「12番通路」と具体的な場所を答えている(C)が正解。copy paper「コピー用紙」。aisle「通路」。
(B) 場所に関する応答だが、質問に対する答えになっていない。sign「署名する」、bottom「下部」。

9 W What was David's major in college?

W (A) A good starting salary.
(B) Business administration, I think.
(C) At university job fairs.

Davidの大学での専攻は何でしたか。

(A) 初任給は良いです。
(B) 経営学だと思います。
(C) 大学での就職フェアです。

正解 **B** Davidが大学で何を専攻したかを尋ねているのに対し、「経営学だと思う」と、専攻していたと思われる分野を伝えている(B)が正解。major「専攻」、college「大学」。business administration「経営学、企業経営」。
(A) starting salary「初任給」。
(C) 質問にあるcollegeと関連するuniversityが含まれるが、応答になっていない。job fair「就職フェア」。

10 M Are you going to eat that sandwich?

M (A) You can have it.
(B) No, it doesn't.
(C) Mexican food.

そのサンドイッチをあなたは食べるつもりですか。

(A) あなたがそれを食べてもいいですよ。
(B) いいえ、それはそうではありません。
(C) メキシコ料理です。

正解 **A** そのサンドイッチを食べるつもりか相手の意志を尋ねているのに対し、「あなたがそれを食べてもいい」と答え、質問した人物にそのサンドイッチを食べるよう勧めている(A)が正解。itは質問にあるthat sandwichを指す。
(B) itがサンドイッチを指すとしても、doesn'tで何を否定しているのか不明。
(C) Mexican food「メキシコ料理」。

11 M When did you last update your software?

W (A) A new uniform.
(B) Two months ago.
(C) Above the printers.

あなたは自分のソフトウエアをいつ最後に更新しましたか。

(A) 新しい制服です。
(B) 2カ月前です。
(C) プリンターの上方です。

正解 **B** When ～?でソフトウエアをいつ最後に更新したのか尋ねているのに対し、「2カ月前だ」と時期を伝えている(B)が正解。last「最後に」、update「～を更新する」。
(A) uniform「制服」。
(C) 位置は尋ねられていない。printer「プリンター、印刷機」。

12 🇦🇺 M Isn't the firm planning to hire more staff?

🇬🇧 W (A) No, it's quite soft.

(B) Absolutely, that's our top priority.

(C) I can't reach it.

会社はもっとスタッフを雇用する計画ではないのですか。

(A) いいえ、それはかなり柔らかいです。

(B) 全くその通り、それが私たちの最優先事項です。

(C) 私はそれに届きません。

正解 **B** 否定疑問文で、「会社はもっとスタッフを雇用する計画ではないのか」と確認しているのに対し、Absolutely「全くその通り」と強く肯定して、「それが私たちの最優先事項だ」と補足している(B)が正解。thatは質問にある、追加のスタッフを雇用することを指す。firm「会社」、plan to do「～する計画である」、hire「～を雇用する」。

(A) 質問にあるfirmを「堅い」と捉えて、それと関連するsoftから判断して選ばないこと。

(C) reach「～に届く」。

13 🇺🇸 W Who sent you this lovely gift basket?

🇨🇦 M (A) It's actually for Anna.

(B) Thanks for taking my shift.

(C) Some fruit and nuts.

誰があなたに、この素敵な贈り物の詰め合わせを送ったのですか。

(A) 実は、それはAnna宛てのものです。

(B) 私のシフトの代わりを務めてくれてありがとう。

(C) 幾つかの果物とナッツ類です。

正解 **A** Who ～?で贈り物をくれた人物を尋ねているのに対し、「実は、それはAnna宛てのものだ」と、贈り物の宛先が自分ではなくAnnaであると訂正をしている(A)が正解。lovely「素敵な」、gift basket「贈り物の詰め合わせ」。

(B) 質問にあるgiftと似た音のshiftに注意。take one's shift「～のシフトの代わりを務める」。

(C) 贈り物の詰め合わせに関する質問だが、中身は尋ねられていない。nut「ナッツ」。

14 🇨🇦 M Would you like to take a tour of the office space?

🇦🇺 M (A) A follow-up interview.

(B) Yes, I'd like to see it.

(C) The memo is three pages.

オフィススペースを見学なさりたいですか。

(A) 再度の面接です。

(B) はい、それを見たいと思っています。

(C) メモは3ページあります。

正解 **B** Would you like to do ～?「～したいですか」は、丁寧に相手の意向を尋ねる表現。オフィススペースを見学したいかと相手の意向を尋ねているのに対し、Yesと肯定し、「それを見たいと思っている」と自分の希望を伝えている(B)が正解。itは質問にあるthe office spaceを指す。take a tour of ～「～の中を見て回る」。

(A) follow-up「再度の、重ねて行う」、interview「面接」。

(C) memo「メモ」については言及がない。

15 🇦🇺 M What time is the concert?

🇬🇧 W (A) No, I need a new one.

(B) The tickets were sold out.

(C) The workshop next month.

コンサートは何時ですか。

(A) いいえ、私は新しいものが必要です。

(B) チケットは売り切れました。

(C) 来月の講習会です。

正解 **B** What time ～?でコンサートの開演時刻を尋ねているのに対し、「チケットは売り切れた」と伝え、もはやチケットが購入できないため、コンサートへの入場ができないことを示唆している(B)が正解。be sold out「売り切れている」。

(A) 時刻を尋ねられているので、Yes、Noでは応答にならない。また、oneが何を指すのか不明。

(C) workshop「講習会、ワークショップ」。

TEST1 PART 2

16 🇬🇧 W Why is the history museum closed today?

🇨🇦 M (A) Usually around six o'clock.

(B) Because they're hosting a private event.

(C) Oh, yes, we really enjoyed it!

なぜ歴史博物館は今日閉まっているのですか。

(A) いつも6時ごろです。

(B) 私的なイベントを開催しているところだからです。

(C) ああ、はい、私たちはそれをとても楽しみました。

正解 **B** Why ～?で、今日歴史博物館が閉まっている理由を尋ねている。これに対し、同博物館をtheyで表し、Because ～を用いて、「私的なイベントを開催しているところだからだ」と答えている(B)が正解。host「～を主催する」、private「私的な」。

(A) 時刻は尋ねられていない。

(C) 理由を尋ねられているので、Yes、Noでは応答にならない。

---

17 🇺🇸 W Should I buy this black jacket or the blue one?

🇬🇧 W (A) Less than ten miles away.

(B) Because it's sunny outside.

(C) Which one is warmer?

私はこの黒いジャケットを買うべきですか、それとも青いものを買うべきですか。

(A) 10マイルも離れていません。

(B) 外が晴れているからです。

(C) どちらの方が暖かいですか。

正解 **C** A or B?の形で、黒いジャケットと青いジャケットのどちらを購入すべきか尋ねている。これに対し、「どちらの方が暖かいか」と判断材料を求めて聞き返している(C)が正解。oneは質問にあるjacket「ジャケット、上着」を指す。

(A) 距離は尋ねられていない。less than ～「～未満」、mile「マイル（約1.6キロメートル）」。

(B) sunny「晴れた」。

---

18 🇨🇦 M I can recycle this milk container, right?

🇺🇸 W (A) I rode my bicycle yesterday.

(B) Correct, so please put it in this bin.

(C) I prefer to drink tea.

この牛乳容器はリサイクルできるのですよね？

(A) 私は昨日、自分の自転車に乗りました。

(B) その通りなので、それをこの箱に入れてください。

(C) 私は紅茶を飲む方が好きです。

正解 **B** 肯定文の文末に ～, right?を付けて「～ですよね」と、牛乳の製品容器がリサイクル可能か確認している。これに対し、Correctと肯定してから、「だから、それをこの箱に入れてください」と容器を捨てるべき箱を示している(B)が正解。itは質問にあるthis milk containerを指す。recycle「～をリサイクルする」、container「容器」。bin「（ふた付きの）大箱、集積貯蔵容器」。

(A) 質問にあるrecycleと似た音の名詞bicycleに注意。

(C) prefer to do「～する方を好む」。

---

19 🇺🇸 W Are you available at three P.M. on Thursday for a final briefing?

🇦🇺 M (A) The fifth floor security desk.

(B) Yes, I can be there.

(C) I'm sorry, it's out of stock.

木曜日の午後3時の最終打ち合わせに出ることができますか。

(A) 5階の警備デスクです。

(B) はい、そちらに出席できます。

(C) 申し訳ありません、それは在庫切れです。

正解 **B** 木曜日の午後3時からの最終打ち合わせに出席できるか尋ねているのに対し、Yesと肯定した上で、打ち合わせに出席可能だと述べている(B)が正解。thereは木曜日午後3時の最終打ち合わせの場を表している。available「都合がつく、求めに応じられる」、briefing「打ち合わせ、ブリーフィング」。

(A) 場所は尋ねられていない。security「警備」。

(C) itが何を指すか不明。out of stock「在庫切れで」。

20 M How long will we have to wait for a table?

W (A) Do you want to sit inside or outside?

(B) The food was delicious.

(C) About fourteen meters.

私たちはどれくらいの間、席が空くのを待つ必要がありますか。

(A) 中にお座りになりますか、それとも外にですか。

(B) 食べ物はおいしかったです。

(C) 約14メートルです。

正解 **A** How long ～?で席が空くまでの待ち時間を尋ねているのに対し、*A or B?* の形で、店の中と外のどちらの席を希望しているか聞き返している(A)が正解。wait for a table「(レストランなどの)席が空くのを待つ」。

(B) 食べ物の感想は尋ねられていない。

(C) 距離や長さは尋ねられていない。

21 W I'm trying a vegetarian diet for the next month.

M (A) I have some recipes you could try.

(B) The next appointment.

(C) Sure, I'll buy it.

私は、来月ベジタリアンの食生活を試してみます。

(A) 試すと良さそうなレシピを幾つか知っていますよ。

(B) 次の予約です。

(C) いいですよ、私はそれを購入します。

正解 **A** 「来月ベジタリアンの食生活を試してみます」という発言に対し、「あなたが試すと良さそうなレシピを幾つか知っている」と、ベジタリアンの食生活を送る上で役立ちそうなレシピの情報提供を申し出ている(A)が正解。vegetarian「ベジタリアン(の)、菜食主義(の)」、diet「(日頃の)食事」。

(B) appointment「予約」。

(C) itが何を指すのか不明で、相手の発言とかみ合わない。

22 W This store has been here for many years, hasn't it?

M (A) Those are discounted today only.

(B) Are you sure she's free right now?

(C) I haven't lived in this neighborhood long.

この店は長年ここにありますよね?

(A) それらは本日限り、割引になっています。

(B) 彼女がちょうど今空いているというのは確かですか。

(C) 私はこの辺りに長く住んではいないのです。

正解 **C** 肯定文の文末に ～, hasn't it?を付けて、「～ですよね?」と店が長年この場所にあることを確認している。これに対し、「私はこの辺りに長く住んではいない」と答え、その店が長い間この場所にあるかどうか知らないことを示唆している(C)が正解。neighborhood「近辺」。

(A) Thoseが何を指すのか不明。discount「～を割引して売る」。

(B) sure (that)～「～と確信している」、right now「ちょうど今」。

23 M Where can I catch a bus to the airport?

W (A) The nine o'clock flight.

(B) Two tickets, please.

(C) You'll have to take a taxi.

空港行きのバスにはどこで乗ることができますか。

(A) 9時の便です。

(B) 切符を2枚、お願いします。

(C) あなたはタクシーに乗る必要があるでしょう。

正解 **C** Where ～?で空港行きのバスの乗車場所を尋ねているのに対し、「あなたはタクシーに乗る必要があるだろう」と、別の交通手段を使う必要性を伝えている(C)が正解。catch a bus「バスに乗る」。

(A) 質問にあるairportに関連したflight「(航空機の)便、フライト」を含むが、応答になっていない。

TEST 1 PART 2

24 🇬🇧 W Can you ask the legal team when they'll have the contract ready?

🇺🇸 W (A) Yes, I'll give them a call this afternoon.
(B) Try the storage closet down the hall.
(C) My favorite sports team won this weekend.

法務チームにいつ契約書の準備が整うか聞いてもらえますか。

(A) はい、今日の午後、彼らに電話をします。
(B) 廊下の先にある収納保管庫を見てみてください。
(C) 私の好きなスポーツチームはこの週末、勝ちました。

正解 A Can you 〜?で書類の準備がいつ整うか法務チームに尋ねるよう頼んでいるのに対し、Yesと答えて、「今日の午後、彼らに電話をする」と確認を引き受けている（A）が正解。themは質問にあるthe legal teamを指す。legal「法律の」、contract「契約書」、ready「準備のできた」。give 〜 a call「〜に電話する」。
(B) 保管場所は尋ねられていない。storage「保管」、closet「収納室、押し入れ」。
(C) 質問にあるteamが含まれるが、スポーツは話題に上っていない。

25 🇺🇸 W How many mobile phones can your factory produce and ship each month?

🇨🇦 M (A) Usually on the first Friday.
(B) From here they're shipped directly to Milford.
(C) Between 300 and 500.

御社の工場では毎月、何台の携帯電話の生産と出荷が可能ですか。

(A) 通例は第1金曜日にします。
(B) ここからミルフォードへそれらは直接出荷されます。
(C) 300台から500台の間です。

正解 C How many 〜?で相手の工場で、月ごとに何台の携帯電話の生産と出荷が可能か尋ねているのに対し、「300台から500台の間だ」と、その台数を範囲で答えている（C）が正解。ship「〜を出荷する、〜を発送する」。between 〜 and …「〜と…の間で」。
(A) 時期は尋ねられていない。
(B) 質問にあるshipの過去分詞shippedが含まれるが、出荷先は尋ねられていない。directly「直接」。

26 🇦🇺 M Wasn't the sales report due yesterday?

🇺🇸 W (A) Bernard doesn't have all the numbers yet.
(B) Let's take the A train.
(C) Only twenty percent off.

営業報告書は、昨日が期限ではありませんでしたか。

(A) Bernardはまだ、全ての数値がそろっていないのです。
(B) A列車に乗りましょう。
(C) わずか20パーセント引きです。

正解 A 否定疑問文で、「営業報告書は、昨日が期限ではなかったか」と確認しているのに対し、「Bernardはまだ、全ての数値がそろっていない」と説明し、報告書がまだ仕上がっていないことを示唆している（A）が正解。due「期限で」。
(B) 質問にあるdueを「(乗り物が)到着予定で」と捉え、それと関連するtrainから判断して選ばないこと。
(C) 割引率は尋ねられていない。

27 🇨🇦 M Does your plane leave in the morning or in the evening?

🇺🇸 W (A) At eight o'clock tomorrow morning.
(B) Sure, that'd be great.
(C) A window seat.

あなたが乗る飛行機が出発するのは午前中ですか、それとも夜間ですか。

(A) 明朝の8時です。
(B) もちろんです、そうしていただけるとうれしいです。
(C) 窓側の座席です。

正解 A A or B?の形で、搭乗予定の飛行機の出発時刻が午前中か夜間のどちらか尋ねている。これに対し、「明朝の8時だ」と具体的な時刻を伝えている（A）が正解。
(B) Sureで何を肯定しているのか、thatが何を指すのか不明。
(C) 質問にあるplaneと関連するwindow seat「(飛行機やバスなどの)窓側の席」が含まれるが、応答になっていない。

28 🇦🇺 M What topics should we cover in the next staff meeting?

🇬🇧 W (A) We should talk about the new payroll procedures.
(B) Yes, I think it went well today.
(C) Either in the auditorium or the lobby.

私たちは次回のスタッフ会議で、どんな題目を取り上げるべきですか。
(A) 私たちは新しい給与計算方法について話すべきです。
(B) はい、今日、それはうまくいったと思います。
(C) 講堂内もしくはロビー内です。

正解 A 次回のスタッフ会議で取り上げるべき題目について尋ねているのに対し、「私たちは新しい給与計算方法について話すべきだ」と具体的な議題を提案している(A)が正解。topic「題目」、cover「～を取り上げる」。payroll「給与」、procedure「方法、手順」。
(B) itが会議を指すとしても、次回の会議について尋ねられているので、過去の感想は応答にならない。go well「うまくいく」。
(C) 場所は尋ねられていない。either ～ or …「～か…」、auditorium「講堂」。

29 🇺🇸 W The bookstore is hosting a writing workshop on Wednesday night.

🇨🇦 M (A) They're children's books.
(B) No, I haven't been there before.
(C) Do you have to register to attend?

その書店は、水曜日の夜に執筆のワークショップを主催します。
(A) それらは児童書です。
(B) いいえ、私はこれまでにそこへ行ったことがありません。
(C) 出席するには登録が必要ですか。

正解 C 水曜日の夜に書店がワークショップを主催する予定だと知らせる発言に対し、「出席するには登録が必要か」と、ワークショップへの出席方法を尋ねている(C)が正解。host「～を主催する」。register「登録する」、attend「出席する」。
(A) 発言にあるbookstoreと関連するbooksが含まれるが、Theyが何を指すのか不明。
(B) 書店を訪れた経験は尋ねられていない。

30 🇨🇦 M Did Dolores process the orders that came in yesterday?

🇦🇺 M (A) The employee of the month award.
(B) We agreed on the red logo.
(C) She's been out sick all week.

Doloresは昨日入った注文を処理しましたか。
(A) 月間最優秀従業員賞です。
(B) 私たちは、その赤いロゴに関して意見が一致しました。
(C) 彼女は1週間ずっと、病欠しています。

正解 C Doloresが昨日受けた注文を処理したかを尋ねているのに対し、「彼女は1週間ずっと、病欠している」と答え、Doloresが注文を処理していないことを示唆している(C)が正解。process「～を処理する」、order「注文」、come in「入る」。be out sick「病欠している」、all week「1週間ずっと」。
(A) the employee of the month「月間最優秀従業員」、award「賞」。
(B) agree on ～「～に関して意見が一致する」。

31 🇨🇦 M Why are we replacing the packaging machine?

🇬🇧 W (A) Actually, we were able to fix it.
(B) I'll check the inventory.
(C) Yes, the package just arrived.

私たちはなぜ包装機を交換するのですか。
(A) 実は、私たちはそれを修理することができました。
(B) 私が在庫を確認してみます。
(C) はい、小包はちょうど届いたところです。

正解 A Why ～?で包装機を交換する理由を尋ねているのに対し、実はそれを修理することができたと伝えて、もはや交換の必要がなくなったことを示唆している(A)が正解。itは質問にあるthe packaging machineを指す。replace「～を交換する」、packaging machine「包装機」。be able to do「～することができる」、fix「～を修理する」。
(B) inventory「在庫」。
(C) 質問にあるpackaging machineと関連するpackage「小包」を含むが、応答になっていない。

13

Questions 32 through 34 refer to the following conversation.

問題32-34は次の会話に関するものです。

🇨🇦 M ❶Welcome to Comfortable Footwear. **Can I help you find something?**

Comfortable履物店へようこそ。何かお探しでしょうか。

🇺🇸 W Yes, ❷I know you carry a wide selection of shoes, but I'm wondering if you also sell socks. ❸I'm looking for athletic socks to wear while running.

はい、こちらが幅広い品ぞろえの靴を扱っていることは知っていますが、靴下も販売していますか。私はランニング中に着用する運動用靴下を探しているのです。

🇨🇦 M ❹We usually do, but unfortunately we don't have any athletic socks in stock right now.

当店では通常は販売しておりますが、あいにく、ただいま運動用靴下が在庫に全くございません。

🇺🇸 W Oh no! I'm running in a race this weekend.

ああ、なんてこと! 私は今週末、レースで走ることになっているのです。

🇨🇦 M Well, ❺I'll check if our second store location has any. They can send them here this afternoon if they do.

なるほど、うちの2号店に幾つかないか調べてみます。そちらにあれば、今日の午後ここに送ってもらえます。

---

32 Where is the conversation taking place?

(A) At a supermarket
(B) At a shoe store
(C) At a repair shop
(D) At a shipping company

会話はどこで行われていますか。

(A) スーパーマーケット
(B) 靴屋
(C) 修理店
(D) 運送会社

正解 B 男性は❶「Comfortable履物店へようこそ」と女性に声を掛けている。それに対し、女性は❷「こちらが幅広い品ぞろえの靴を扱っていることは知っているが、靴下も販売しているか」と尋ねているので、会話は靴屋で行われていると考えられる。take place「行われる」。
(C) repair「修理」。
(D) shipping company「運送会社」。

---

33 What does the man explain to the woman?

(A) A new location recently opened.
(B) Express delivery will cost extra.
(C) Some items are out of stock.
(D) Some merchandise was moved.

男性は女性に何を説明していますか。

(A) 最近、新しい店舗が開業した。
(B) 速達便には割増料金がかかる。
(C) 一部の品が在庫切れである。
(D) 一部の商品が移された。

正解 C ❸で、ランニング中に着用する運動用靴下を探していると伝えた女性に対し、男性は❹で、ちょうど今運動用靴下が在庫にないと説明している。このことをsome itemsとout of stock「在庫切れで」を用いて言い換えている(C)が正解。explain「~を説明する」。item「品物、品目」。
(A) 別の店舗に言及があるが、それが最近開業したとは述べていない。recently「最近」。
(B) express delivery「速達便」、extra「割増料金」。
(D) merchandise「商品、製品」。

---

34 What does the man offer to do?

(A) Call another location
(B) Reduce a price
(C) Check a Web site
(D) Cancel an order

男性は何をすることを申し出ていますか。

(A) 別の店舗に電話する
(B) 価格を下げる
(C) ウェブサイトを確認する
(D) 注文をキャンセルする

正解 A 女性が今週末のレースで走る予定だと聞いた男性は、現在在庫を切らしている運動用靴下について、❺「うちの2号店に幾つかないか調べてみる」と申し出ているので、系列店に連絡すると分かる。our second store locationをanother locationと表している(A)が正解。
(B) reduce「~(価格など)を下げる」、price「価格」。
(D) cancel「~をキャンセルする」、order「注文」。

Words & Phrases

footwear 履物 ★靴・ブーツなどの履物全般を指す   carry ~(商品など)を扱っている
wide 幅広い   selection 品ぞろえ   socks 靴下   look for ~ ~を探す   athletic 運動(競技)用の
wear ~を着用する   unfortunately あいにく、残念ながら   have ~ in stock ~が在庫にある   right now ちょうど今
race レース、競争   check ~を調べる   location 店舗、所在地

Questions 35 through 37 refer to the following conversation.

🇬🇧 W Hi, ❶I dropped my car off this morning. Have you checked my tires yet?

🇦🇺 M Yes. ❷Our mechanic checked the tires on your car. Unfortunately, the front tires do need to be replaced. The mechanic noticed that they're wearing out.

🇬🇧 W Oh, I didn't realize they were that worn out. Can I still get my car back this afternoon?

🇦🇺 M I'm sorry, ❸we won't have the tires available until tomorrow.

🇬🇧 W But, ❹I have a client meeting tomorrow, and I'll have no way to get there.

🇦🇺 M Oh, ❺we can offer you a loaner car. You can use it until your car is ready.

問題35-37は次の会話に関するものです。

こんにちは、今朝車を置いていった者です。私のタイヤはもう検査していただけましたか。

はい。当店の整備工があなたの車のタイヤを検査しました。あいにく、フロントタイヤは交換する必要があります。整備工は、それらが摩耗しているのに気付きました。

ああ、そんなに摩耗していたとは気付きませんでした。それでも、私は今日の午後に車を返してもらうことはできますか。

申し訳ございません、当店はそのタイヤを明日まで入手できないのです。

でも、私は明日顧客との会合があるので、そこへ行く手段がなくなってしまいます。

ああ、当店が代車をあなたにご提供できます。ご自身のお車の用意ができるまで、あなたはそれをお使いいただけます。

---

35 Where does the man most likely work?

(A) At an auto repair shop
(B) At a construction site
(C) At a factory
(D) At an airport

男性はどこで働いていると考えられますか。

(A) 自動車修理店
(B) 建設現場
(C) 工場
(D) 空港

正解 **A** 女性は男性に❶で、今朝置いていった車のタイヤ検査が済んだか尋ねている。それに対し、男性は❷「当店の整備工があなたの車のタイヤを検査した」と伝えているので、男性は自動車修理店で働いていると考えられる。auto「自動車の」、repair「修理」。
(B) construction「建設」、site「現場、場所」。

---

36 What does the woman say she needs to do tomorrow?

(A) Conduct an inspection
(B) Meet a client
(C) Reserve a parking space
(D) Make a payment

女性は、明日何をする必要があると言っていますか。

(A) 検査を行う
(B) 顧客と会う
(C) 駐車スペースを予約する
(D) 支払いをする

正解 **B** 男性から❸で、交換に必要なタイヤが明日まで入手できないと聞いた女性は、❹「私は明日顧客との会合があるので、そこへ行く手段がなくなる」と述べている。
(A) conduct「～を行う」、inspection「検査」。
(C) reserve「～を予約する」、parking space「駐車スペース」。
(D) make a payment「支払いをする」。

---

37 What does the man offer the woman?

(A) Some safety glasses
(B) Express delivery
(C) Another vehicle
(D) An alternate date

男性は女性に何を提供しますか。

(A) 保護眼鏡
(B) 速達便
(C) 別の車
(D) 代替日

正解 **C** ❹で、女性が顧客との会合に車を必要としていると知った男性は、❺「当店が代車をあなたに提供できる」と女性に申し出ている。a loaner carをanother vehicleと表している(C)が正解。vehicle「車」。
(A) safety glasses「保護眼鏡」。
(B) express delivery「速達便」。
(D) alternate「代替の」、date「日取り」。

Words & Phrases

drop off ～ ～を置いていく　tire タイヤ　mechanic 整備工　unfortunately あいにく
front 前面の　replace ～を交換する　notice ～に気付く　wear out すり減る　realize (that)～ ～だと気付く
worn out すり切れた　still それでもなお　get back ～ ～を取り戻す、～を返す　available 入手できる　client 顧客
way 手段　offer ～ … ～に…を提供する　loaner car 代車　ready 用意のできた

Questions 38 through 40 refer to the following conversation with three speakers.

問題38-40は3人の話し手による次の会話に関するものです。

🇺🇸 W Excuse me. Do you work at this museum?

すみません。あなたはこの美術館で働いている方ですか。

🇨🇦 M Yes. How can I help you two?

はい。お二人はどのようなご用件でしょうか。

🇺🇸 W Well, my friend and I were planning to see the sculpture exhibit, but ❶there's such a long line of people waiting to get in.

ええと、友人と私は彫刻展を見るつもりだったのですが、入場を待つ人々でこんなに長い行列ができています。

🇬🇧 W Yeah, ❷we're really surprised. There's usually no line at all. ❸Is there a special event today?

そうなんです、私たちは本当に驚いています。普段は行列が全くないですから。今日は特別なイベントがあるのですか。

🇨🇦 M Yes, ❹there's a free tour for children at noon, so a lot of families are here for that. In fact, ❺the museum's going to be very crowded for the next hour or so.

はい、正午に子ども向けの無料ツアーがありまして、そのために多くのご家族がこちらにいらしています。実のところ、当美術館はこれから1時間ほど非常に混み合うことになります。

🇺🇸 W Hmm… OK. ❻Nadia, why don't we grab lunch at McSally's and come back later?

うーん…なるほど。Nadia、私たちはMcSally'sで昼食を手早く取って、後で戻ってくるのはどう?

🇬🇧 W ❼Good idea! I've been wanting to try that place!

いい考えね! 私はあの店に行ってみたいと思っていたのよ。

---

38 What are the women surprised about?

(A) A line is long.
(B) An exhibit is closed.
(C) A sign is missing.
(D) A speaker is delayed.

女性たちは何について驚いていますか。

(A) 行列が長い。
(B) 展示が終了している。
(C) 看板がなくなっている。
(D) 講演者が遅れている。

正解 A 美術館スタッフの男性に用件を尋ねられた1人目の女性は、❶「入場を待つ人々でこんなに長い行列ができている」と述べている。また2人目の女性は、❷「私たちは本当に驚いている。普段は行列が全くない」と入場を待つ行列の長さについて驚きを伝えている。
(B) closed「終了した」。
(C) sign「看板、掲示」、missing「紛失した」。
(D) speaker「講演者」、delay「～を遅らせる」。

---

39 According to the man, what will take place at noon?

(A) A lecture
(B) A tour
(C) A concert
(D) An art sale

男性によると、正午に何が行われますか。

(A) 講演
(B) ツアー
(C) コンサート
(D) 美術品の販売

正解 B 2人目の女性に❸「今日は特別なイベントがあるのか」と尋ねられた男性は、❹「正午に子ども向けの無料ツアーがある」と答えているので、(B)が正解。according to ～「～によると」。
(A) lecture「講演」。
(D) art「美術の、美術品の」。

---

40 Where will the women probably go next?

(A) To a park
(B) To a theater
(C) To a restaurant
(D) To a school

女性たちはおそらく次にどこへ行きますか。

(A) 公園
(B) 劇場
(C) レストラン
(D) 学校

正解 C 男性から❺で、今後1時間は美術館が大混雑すると聞いた1人目の女性は、❻「Nadia、私たちはMcSally'sで昼食を手早く取って、後で戻ってくるのはどうか」と、2人目の女性に提案している。それを受けた2人目の女性は、❼「いい考えだ。私はあの店に行ってみたかった」と賛同している。McSally'sとはレストランの店名で、女性たちは次にそこへ昼食を食べに行くと考えられる。probably「おそらく」。

Words & Phrases

plan to *do* ～するつもりである　sculpture 彫刻　exhibit 展覧会、展示　line 行列、列　surprised 驚いた　usually 普段は　free 無料の　in fact 実際は　crowded 混み合った　～ or so ～かそのくらい　why don't we ～ ～しませんか　grab ～を素早く食べる、～を不意につかむ　later 後で　place 店

Questions 41 through 43 refer to the following conversation.

🇬🇧 W Hello, **❶Technical Support. This is Maria Diaz.**

🇦🇺 M Hi, Maria. **❷I'm having trouble signing onto my work computer. The computer doesn't seem to recognize my password.**

🇬🇧 W OK, I should be able to help you with that. I just need to get some basic information. **❸What's your computer's identification number?** You'll find that on the side of the computer.

🇦🇺 M Let's see. It's A45HR2. And **❹just so you know, I'm presenting at a meeting in 30 minutes.**

🇬🇧 W OK. In that case, let me give you a temporary password. You'll be able to log in, and you can change it later.

問題41-43は次の会話に関するものです。

もしもし、技術サポート窓口です。こちらはMaria Diazです。

こんにちは、Maria。私の仕事用のコンピューターにサインオンするのに苦労しています。コンピューターが私のパスワードを認証しないようなのです。

分かりました、それなら手助けできるはずです。私は、基本情報だけもらう必要があります。あなたのコンピューターの識別番号は何ですか。それはコンピューターの側面で見つけられますよ。

ええと。A45HR2です。それから、一応お伝えしておきますと、私は30分後に会議で発表することになっているのです。

なるほど。そういうことであれば、あなたに臨時パスワードを発行しましょう。あなたはログインできるようになりますし、後でそれを変更できますよ。

41 Why is the man calling?

(A) To check the status of an order
(B) To report a computer problem
(C) To propose a policy change
(D) To discuss a software installation

男性はなぜ電話しているのですか。

(A) 注文状況を確認するため
(B) コンピューターの問題を伝えるため
(C) 方針の変更を提案するため
(D) ソフトウエアのインストールについて話し合うため

正解 B ❶で、技術サポート窓口だと応答する女性に対し、男性は❷「私の仕事用のコンピューターにサインオンするのに苦労している。コンピューターが私のパスワードを認証しないようだ」とコンピューターに生じている問題を伝えている。
(A) status「状況」、order「注文」。
(C) propose「～を提案する」、policy「方針」。
(D) installation「(ソフトなどの)インストール」。

42 What information does the woman request?

(A) A username
(B) A call-back number
(C) An office location
(D) An identification number

女性はどんな情報を求めていますか。

(A) ユーザー名
(B) 折り返しのための電話番号
(C) 会社所在地
(D) 識別番号

正解 D 男性のコンピューターの問題を手助けできると応じた女性は、❸「あなたのコンピューターの識別番号は何か」と尋ねて、その番号の記載場所を伝えている。
(B) call-back「折り返しの電話の」。

43 Why does the man say, "I'm presenting at a meeting in 30 minutes"?

(A) To express urgency
(B) To decline an invitation
(C) To correct a misunderstanding
(D) To request a deadline extension

男性はなぜ "I'm presenting at a meeting in 30 minutes" と言っていますか。

(A) 緊急性を表すため
(B) 招待を断るため
(C) 誤解を正すため
(D) 締め切りの延長を頼むため

正解 A 自分のコンピューターの問題の手助けを求めた男性は、❹「一応伝えておくと」と述べてから、下線部で「私は30分後に会議で発表する」と差し迫った予定を伝えている。よって、男性はこのコンピューターの問題解決の必要の緊急性を示すために、この発言をしていると判断できる。express「～を表す」、urgency「緊急性」。
(B) decline「～を断る」、invitation「招待」。
(C) correct「～を正す」、misunderstanding「誤解」。
(D) deadline「締め切り」、extension「延長」。

Words & Phrases

Technical Support 技術サポート(部)　　have trouble *doing* ～するのに苦労する
sign onto ～ ～にサインオンする、～にログインする　　recognize ～を認識する　　password パスワード
be able to *do* ～することができる　　help ～ with … ～の…を手伝う　　basic 基本的な　　information 情報
identification number 識別番号　　side 側面　　just so you know 一応言っておきますが　　present (～を)発表する
in that case その場合には　　temporary 臨時の　　log in ログインする

TEST1 PART 3

Questions 44 through 46 refer to the following conversation.

M Hi, Mary. ❶I've heard from some of the library patrons that our upstairs reading room is getting too crowded. There are not enough places to sit and read.

W Well, ❷we do have some open space in the back of that room. Let's order some chairs to put back there.

M ❸That's a great idea. Have we gotten any advertisements from furniture stores lately?

W Actually, ❹a couple of furniture store catalogs came in last week. ❺I think I saw them on the counter in the supply room. I'll go look for them.

問題44-46は次の会話に関するものです。

こんにちは、Mary。一部の図書館利用者から、当館2階の閲覧室が非常に混み合ってきていると聞きました。座って読書をするのに十分な数の席がないのです。

それなら、あの部屋の奥に空きスペースがあります。椅子を数脚注文して、奥のあそこに置きましょう。

それは素晴らしい思いつきです。最近私たちは家具店から広告を受け取りましたか。

実は先週、家具店のカタログが数冊届きました。それらを備品室のカウンターの上で見かけたと思います。私が探しに行ってきますよ。

44 Where do the speakers work?

(A) At an art gallery
(B) At a library
(C) At a cafeteria
(D) At a bus station

話し手たちはどこで働いていますか。

(A) 画廊
(B) 図書館
(C) カフェテリア
(D) バスターミナル

正解 B 男性は女性に対し、❶「一部の図書館利用者から、当館2階の閲覧室が非常に混み合ってきていると聞いた」と述べている。その後も図書館の席の不足を解消するための話を続けているので、話し手たちが働いているのは図書館と分かる。
(A) art gallery「画廊、美術館」。
(D) bus station「バスターミナル」。

45 What do the speakers plan to purchase?

(A) Some furniture
(B) Laptop computers
(C) Additional lighting
(D) Some artwork

話し手たちは何を購入することを計画していますか。

(A) 家具
(B) ノートパソコン
(C) 追加の照明装置
(D) 美術品

正解 A ❷で、椅子を数脚注文して閲覧室の奥にある空きスペースに置くことを提案する女性に対し、男性は❸で賛同し、その後も2人は家具店の広告やカタログについて話を続けている。購入する椅子数脚をsome furniture「家具」と表している(A)が正解。purchase「〜を購入する」。
(B) laptop computer「ノートパソコン」。
(C) additional「追加の」、lighting「照明装置」。

46 Where will the woman go next?

(A) To a budget meeting
(B) To a training session
(C) To a department store
(D) To a supply room

女性は次にどこへ行きますか。

(A) 予算会議
(B) 研修会
(C) 百貨店
(D) 備品室

正解 D 男性から、最近家具店の広告を受け取ったかと尋ねられた女性は、❹で先週カタログが数冊届いたと伝え、続けて❺「それらを備品室のカウンターの上で見かけたと思う。私が探しに行ってくる」と述べている。themは❹のfurniture store catalogsを指すので、女性は次にカタログを探しに備品室へ行くと考えられる。
(A) budget「予算」。
(B) training「研修」、session「会、集まり」。
(C) department store「百貨店」。

Words & Phrases
patron （図書館など施設の）利用者、常連客　upstairs 2階の　reading room 閲覧室、図書室　crowded 混み合った　place 席、場所　open space 空きスペース　back 奥(の)　order 〜を注文する　advertisement 広告　furniture 家具　lately 最近　actually 実は　a couple of 〜 2、3の〜　come in 入ってくる、到着する　supply 備品　look for 〜 〜を探す

18

Questions 47 through 49 refer to the following conversation with three speakers.

🏴 w Good afternoon. How can I help you?

🏴 м Hi. ❶I checked in yesterday. My room key card was working just fine then, but when I tried it just now, I couldn't get in.

🏴 w Hmm, sometimes the magnetic strip on the key card stops working. ❷Let me get my manager. She'll be able to help you.

🏴 w ❸Hi, I'm Isabel. ❹I understand your room key isn't working. I just need your room number to provide you with a replacement.

🏴 м I'm in room 639.

🏴 w All right... ❺Now this new key should work for you. And ❻for the inconvenience, please accept this coupon for the hotel restaurant. You'll receive ten percent off a meal there.

問題47-49は3人の話し手による次の会話に関するものです。

こんにちは。どのようなご用件でしょうか。

どうも。私は昨日チェックインしました。その時は私のルームカードキーは全く問題なく機能していたのですが、たった今試してみたところ、私は入室できなかったのです。

ええと、時々カードキーの磁気ストリップが機能しなくなることがございまして。主任を呼んでまいります。彼女ならお客さまのお力になれるでしょう。

こんにちは、Isabelと申します。お客さまのルームキーが機能していないと伺いました。代わりの物をご提供するのにお客さまの部屋番号だけ頂きたいのです。

私は639号室にいます。

分かりました…。はい、この新しいキーでしたら、うまくいくはずです。それから、ご不便をお掛けいたしましたので、当ホテルレストラン用のこのクーポンをお受け取りください。そちらでのお食事に対し、お客さまは10パーセント引きが受けられます。

 TEST 1 PART 3

---

47 Where do the women most likely work?

(A) At a hotel
(B) At an airport
(C) At a car rental service
(D) At a travel agency

女性たちはどこで働いていると考えられますか。

(A) ホテル
(B) 空港
(C) レンタカー会社
(D) 旅行代理店

> 正解 A　男性が❶で、昨日のチェックイン時には機能したルームカードキーが現在使えないと問題を伝えており、それを受けた1人目の女性は❷で、主任を呼ぶと応じている。主任である2人目の女性は❹・❺で、男性に部屋番号を尋ねて、新しいキーを差し出している。よって、女性たちが働いているのはホテルと考えられる。
> (D) travel agency「旅行代理店」。

---

48 What problem does the man mention?

(A) He cannot connect to the Internet.
(B) He cannot make a reservation.
(C) A key is not working properly.
(D) A restaurant is closed.

男性はどんな問題について述べていますか。

(A) 彼はインターネットに接続できない。
(B) 彼は予約をすることができない。
(C) キーが正常に機能していない。
(D) レストランが閉まっている。

> 正解 C　男性は❶で「私は昨日チェックインした。その時は私のルームカードキーは全く問題なく機能していたが、たった今試してみたところ、私は入室できなかった」と問題を述べている。properly「正常に、適切に」。
> (A) connect to ~「~に接続する」。
> (B) make a reservation「予約をする」。
> (D) 2人目の女性がレストラン用のクーポンに言及しているだけ。

---

49 What does Isabel give the man?

(A) A discount coupon
(B) A free upgrade
(C) A brochure
(D) A souvenir

Isabelは男性に何を差し出していますか。

(A) 割引クーポン
(B) 無料のアップグレード
(C) パンフレット
(D) 記念品

> 正解 A　❸でIsabelと名乗った主任の女性は、❺で新しいキーを男性に渡した後、❻「不便を掛けたので、当ホテルレストラン用のこのクーポンを受け取ってください。そこでの食事に対し、お客さまは10パーセント引きが受けられる」とクーポンを差し出している。
> (B) upgrade「アップグレード」。
> (C) brochure「パンフレット」。
> (D) souvenir「記念品、土産」。

Words & Phrases

check in　チェックインする　　key card　カードキー　　work　作動する
magnetic strip　磁気ストリップ　　manager　主任、支配人　　be able to do　~することができる
provide ~ with …　~に…を提供する　　replacement　代わりのもの、取り換え品　　inconvenience　不便
accept　~を受け取る　　coupon　クーポン　　receive　~を受ける　　meal　食事

Questions 50 through 52 refer to the following conversation.

M **So** ❶what did I miss from the staff meeting?

W Well, ❷they're finally repaving the parking lot here at the office next week. **So we won't be able to park there.**

M But ❸where are we supposed to park while the work is being done?

W Well, ❹since most of the employees have laptops now, the company's encouraging us to work from home while the repaving's being done.

M OK. But ❺I don't have a work laptop yet. What should I do?

W ❻You can go ask the office manager to lend you one.

問題50-52は次の会話に関するものです。

それで、私がそのスタッフ会議で聞き損なったことは何ですか。

そうですね、来週、ここの事務所の駐車場をついに再舗装するそうです。ですから、私たちはそこには駐車できなくなります。

でも、その作業が行われている間、私たちはどこに駐車することになっているのですか。

ええと、今や従業員の大半がノートパソコンを持っているので、再舗装が行われている間、会社は私たちに在宅勤務をするよう奨励しています。

なるほど。でも、私はまだ仕事用のノートパソコンを持っていません。どうすればいいですか。

1台貸与してくれるよう、あなたは総務責任者に頼みに行くことができますよ。

---

50 According to the woman, what will the company do next week?

(A) Repave a parking area
(B) Hold an annual staff meeting
(C) Update a vacation policy
(D) Have an anniversary celebration

女性によると、会社は来週何をしますか。

(A) 駐車場を再舗装する
(B) 年次スタッフ会議を開催する
(C) 休暇方針を改訂する
(D) 記念祝賀会を開く

正解 A ❶で、自分が欠席した会議の内容に関して情報を求める男性に対し、女性は❷「来週、ここの事務所の駐車場をついに再舗装するそうだ」と伝えている。theyは会社を指しているので、(A)が正解。
(B) hold「～を開催する」、annual「年次の」。
(C) update「～を改訂する」、policy「方針」。
(D) anniversary「記念」、celebration「祝賀会」。

51 What are employees encouraged to do?

(A) Sign up for additional tasks
(B) Complete a questionnaire
(C) Apply for a business course
(D) Work from home

従業員は何をするよう奨励されていますか。

(A) 追加の職務に署名して参加する
(B) アンケートに全て記入する
(C) ビジネス講座に申し込む
(D) 在宅勤務をする

正解 D ❸で、再舗装期間中の駐車場所について尋ねる男性に対し、女性は❹「今や従業員の大半がノートパソコンを持っているので、再舗装が行われている間、会社は私たちに在宅勤務をするよう奨励している」と述べている。
(A) sign up for ～「（署名して）～に参加する」、additional「追加の」、task「職務、仕事」。
(B) complete「～に全て記入する」、questionnaire「アンケート」。
(C) apply for ～「～に申し込む」、course「講座」。

52 Who will the man most likely talk to?

(A) A building contractor
(B) An office manager
(C) A training coordinator
(D) A computer salesperson

男性は誰と話をすると考えられますか。

(A) 建築請負業者
(B) 総務責任者
(C) 研修の調整者
(D) コンピューターの営業担当者

正解 B 男性が❺で、仕事用のノートパソコンを所有していない自分は、どうすべきか尋ねているのに対し、女性は❻「1台貸与してくれるよう、あなたは総務責任者に頼みに行くことができる」と、総務責任者の所に貸与の依頼に行くように勧めているので、(B)が正解。
(A) contractor「請負業者」。
(C) coordinator「調整者、まとめ役」。
(D) salesperson「営業担当者」。

Words & Phrases

miss ～を聞き損なう、～を逃す　finally ついに　repave ～を再舗装する　parking lot 駐車場
be supposed to *do* ～することになっている　laptop ノートパソコン　encourage ～ to *do* ～に…するよう奨励する
work from home 在宅勤務する　ask ～ to *do* ～に…するよう頼む　lend ～ … ～に…を貸与する

Questions 53 through 55 refer to the following conversation.

🇺🇸 W ❶This is the Centerville Department of Transportation. How can I help you?

🇨🇦 M Hello. ❷I'm calling about the survey the city is conducting, about extending the bus routes? ❸I'd love to have a bus stop near my apartment, so I've been trying to respond to the survey online. ❹It doesn't seem to be working for me, though.

🇺🇸 W Oh yes, I'm sorry. ❺Our survey Web page has been down for several hours. I've been getting a lot of calls about it. We expect it to be back up and running by eight o'clock this evening.

🇨🇦 M Thanks—I'll try it again later tonight.

問題53-55は次の会話に関するものです。

こちらはセンタービル市運輸交通局です。どのようなご用件でしょうか。

もしもし。市が実施中のアンケート調査の件で電話しています、バス路線拡大の件ですよね。私のアパートの近くにバス停がぜひ欲しいので、オンラインでアンケート調査に回答しようと試み続けています。でも、私にはうまくいかないようなのです。

ああ、はい、申し訳ございません。当局のアンケート調査用ウェブページは、数時間ダウンしております。その件でたくさんのお電話を頂いております。今夜8時までには、それが元通り順調に稼働するようになると見込んでおります。

ありがとうございます——今夜、後でもう一度試してみます。

53 Which city department does the woman work for?

(A) Health
(B) Housing
(C) Finance
(D) Transportation

女性はどの市局で働いていますか。

(A) 保健局
(B) 住宅局
(C) 財務局
(D) 運輸交通局

正解 D 女性は❶「こちらはセンタービル市運輸交通局だ」と電話に応答し、用件を尋ねているので、(D)が正解。
(A) health「保健、衛生」。
(B) housing「住宅」。
(C) finance「財務」。

54 What does the man say he has been trying to do?

(A) Renew a lease
(B) Respond to a survey
(C) Buy a monthly pass
(D) Find a map

男性は何をしようと試み続けていると言っていますか。

(A) 賃貸借契約を更新する
(B) アンケート調査に回答する
(C) 月間パスを購入する
(D) 地図を探し出す

正解 B ❷で、電話の用件をバス路線拡大に関するアンケート調査の件と伝えた男性は、❸「私のアパートの近くにバス停がぜひ欲しいので、オンラインでアンケート調査に回答しようと試み続けている」と言っている。
(A) renew「～を更新する」、lease「賃貸借契約」。
(C) monthly「月間の」、pass「パス、定期券」。

55 Why does the woman apologize?

(A) A payment method has been declined.
(B) A remodeling project must be postponed.
(C) A Web page is not working.
(D) A street has been closed.

女性はなぜ謝罪しているのですか。

(A) 支払い方法が拒否されているから。
(B) 改築計画が延期される必要があるから。
(C) ウェブページが稼働していないから。
(D) 通りが閉鎖されているから。

正解 C 男性は❸・❹で、オンラインのアンケート調査に回答する試みがうまくいっていないことを伝えている。それに対し女性は謝罪後、❺「当局のアンケート調査用ウェブページは、数時間ダウンしている」とウェブページの不具合が原因と説明している。このことをis not workingを用いて表している(C)が正解。apologize「謝罪する」。
(A) payment「支払い」、method「方法」、decline「～を拒否する、～を断る」。
(B) remodeling「改築」、postpone「～を延期する」。

Words & Phrases

department 局　transportation 運輸、交通　survey アンケート調査　conduct ～を実施する、～を行う　extend ～を拡大する　route 路線　bus stop バス停　apartment アパート　try to do ～しようと試みる　respond to ～ ～に回答する　online オンラインで　though でも、けれども　down （コンピューターなどが）ダウンして、故障して　several 幾つかの　call 電話　expect ~ to do ～が…すると見込む　back （状態が）元へ　up and running （コンピューターなどが）順調に作動して　later 後で

21

Questions 56 through 58 refer to the following conversation.　問題56-58は次の会話に関するものです。

M ❶Did you hear about the Fontana Theater? A real estate developer just bought it.

Fontana劇場について聞きましたか。ある不動産開発業者がちょうどそこを買い取ったところです。

W That place has been for sale for quite a while.

あの建物は、かなり長い間売りに出されていましたよね。

M Well, ❷the exterior of the building has to be preserved because it's a historic landmark. That's probably why it took so long to sell.

そうですね、あれは歴史的建造物なので、建物の外観を保存する必要があります。それがおそらく、売却にとても時間がかかった理由でしょう。

W ❸Yeah, most developers don't like to deal with the regulations protecting historic buildings.

ええ、たいていの開発業者は歴史的建築物を保護する規制に対応したがりませんからね。

M I heard they're going to renovate the theater and build a high-rise hotel on top of it. ❹There are even plans for a rooftop terrace that'll be open to the public.

劇場を改装し、その上に高層ホテルを建設する予定だと僕は聞きました。一般の人が利用できる屋上テラスの計画さえあるようですよ。

W ❺I bet it would have fantastic views of the city! That's something I'd look forward to seeing.

きっと素晴らしい市の景色を眺められるでしょうね! それは見るのが楽しみです。

---

56 Why does the woman say, "That place has been for sale for quite a while"?

(A) She is disappointed by a decision.
(B) She will visit a location soon.
(C) She is surprised at some news.
(D) She plans to make an offer.

女性はなぜ "That place has been for sale for quite a while" と言っていますか。

(A) 彼女は決定に失望しているから。
(B) 彼女は間もなく所在地を訪れるつもりだから。
(C) 彼女は知らせに驚いているから。
(D) 彼女は売り込みをする予定だから。

正解 C 下線部の発言は、男性が❶で、開発業者がFontana劇場を買い取ったと知らせているのに対するもの。❷・❸で、男性も女性も劇場が歴史的建造物であるため保護規制があり、開発業者が購入したがらないと考えていたことが分かる。よって、女性は買い取りの知らせに驚きを示していると考えられる。be surprised at ～「～に驚いている」。
(A) be disappointed by ～「～に失望している」。
(D) offer「売り込み」。

57 What is special about the Fontana Theater?

(A) It is close to the city center.
(B) It is a historic landmark.
(C) It is near public transportation.
(D) It is owned by a celebrity.

Fontana劇場について何が特別ですか。

(A) それは市の中心部に近い。
(B) それは歴史的建造物である。
(C) それは公共交通機関の近くにある。
(D) それは著名人に所有されている。

正解 B 不動産開発業者に買い取られたというFontana劇場について、男性は❷「あれは歴史的建造物なので、建物の外観を保存する必要がある」と述べている。
(A) close to ～「～の近くに」。
(C) public transportation「公共交通機関」。
(D) own「～を所有する」、celebrity「著名人」。

58 What does the woman say she would look forward to seeing?

(A) A historic tour of the city
(B) The draft of a contract
(C) A theater production
(D) The view from a rooftop

女性は何を見ることを楽しみにしていると言っていますか。

(A) 市の歴史のツアー
(B) 契約書の草案
(C) 演劇作品
(D) 屋上からの眺め

正解 D 売却された劇場の上に建設予定の高層ホテルについて、❹「一般の人が利用できる屋上テラスの計画さえある」と述べる男性に対し、女性は❺「きっと素晴らしい市の景色を眺められるだろう。それは見るのが楽しみだ」と屋上からの眺望を楽しみにしていると言っている。
(B) draft「草案」、contract「契約書」。
(C) production「作品」。

Words & Phrases

real estate　不動産　developer　開発業者　for sale　売りに出した
for quite a while　かなり長い間　exterior　外観　preserve　～を保存する　historic landmark　歴史的建造物
deal with ～　～に対処する　regulation　規制　protect　～を保護する　renovate　～を改装する　high-rise　高層の
rooftop　屋上　be open to ～　～が利用できる　the public　一般の人々　I bet ～　きっと～だと思う　★~には節が入る
fantastic　素晴らしい　view　眺め　look forward to *doing*　～することを楽しみにする

Questions 59 through 61 refer to the following conversation.

🇺🇸 W Hello, this is the International Arts Festival information line, how can I help you?

🇦🇺 M Hi. My name's Alexi Solokov. ❶I'd like to apply for a permit to take pictures at this year's festival for my magazine.

🇺🇸 W Thanks for your interest. There's a link on our Web site where you can apply for a permit.

🇦🇺 M OK. ❷What information will I need to apply?

🇺🇸 W ❸We just ask that you upload a letter from your current supervisor.

🇦🇺 M Sure. I can do that.

🇺🇸 W Great. And ❹once you're approved for a permit, contact the Help Desk. They'll make sure you get complimentary tickets to the performances you want to attend.

問題59-61は次の会話に関するものです。

もしもし、国際芸術フェスティバル情報電話サービスです、どのようなご用件でしょうか。

こんにちは。Alexi Solokovと申します。うちの雑誌のために、今年のフェスティバルでの写真撮影許可証を申請したいのですが。

ご関心をお持ちいただきありがとうございます。私どものウェブサイトにリンクがあり、そちらから許可証の申請ができます。

分かりました。申請するにはどのような情報が必要でしょうか。

あなたの現監督者からの書状をアップロードしていただくことだけをお願いしております。

もちろん。それは可能です。

良かったです。それから、許可証が承認されましたら、ヘルプデスクにご連絡ください。そちらで必ず、あなたが入場をなさりたい公演の招待券を入手できるように手配いたしますので。

---

59 Who most likely is the man?

(A) A musician
(B) A radio announcer
(C) A film critic
(D) A photographer

男性は誰だと考えられますか。

(A) 音楽家
(B) ラジオアナウンサー
(C) 映画評論家
(D) 写真家

正解 D 電話をかけてきた男性は、❶「うちの雑誌のために、今年のフェスティバルでの写真撮影許可証を申請したい」と用件を伝えている。よって、男性は写真家だと考えられる。photographer「写真家」。
(B) announcer「アナウンサー」。
(C) critic「評論家」。

---

60 According to the woman, what will the man have to do to get a permit?

(A) Pay a processing fee
(B) Submit a work sample
(C) Attend an orientation session
(D) Provide a letter from an employer

女性によると、男性は許可証を取得するために何をする必要がありますか。

(A) 手数料を支払う
(B) 作品見本を提出する
(C) 説明会に出席する
(D) 雇用先からの書状を提供する

正解 D 男性は❷で、ウェブサイトのリンクを通じて写真撮影許可証を申請するために必要な情報を尋ねている。それに対し、女性は❸「あなたの現監督者からの書状をアップロードしてもらうことだけをお願いしている」と雇用先からの書状を求めているので(D)が正解。provide「～を提供する」、employer「雇用先、雇用者」。
(A) processing fee「手数料」。
(B) submit「～を提出する、～を投稿する」、work「作品」、sample「見本」。
(C) orientation session「説明会」。

---

61 Why should the man contact the Help Desk?

(A) To buy recordings of previous events
(B) To pick up free tickets to shows
(C) To get advice on planning local trips
(D) To schedule interviews with performers

男性はなぜヘルプデスクに連絡すべきなのですか。

(A) 以前のイベントの記録物を購入するため
(B) ショーの無料券を受け取るため
(C) 現地旅行の計画に関する助言を得るため
(D) 出演者へのインタビューの予定を組むため

正解 B 女性は❹で、許可証が承認された後はヘルプデスクに連絡するよう男性に伝え、男性が入場を希望する公演の招待券をヘルプデスクが手配すると説明している。complimentary ticketsをfree ticketsと表している(B)が正解。pick up ～「～を受け取る」、show「ショー、出し物」。
(A) recording「(映像などの)記録物」、previous「前の」。
(C) plan「～を計画する」、local「現地の、地元の」。
(D) performer「出演者」。

Words & Phrases

apply for ～　～を申請する　　permit　許可証　　current　現在の　　supervisor　監督者
once　いったん～すると　　approve　～を承認する　　contact　～に連絡する　　make sure (that) ～　必ず～ということをする
complimentary　招待の、無料の　　performance　公演　　attend　～に出席する

TEST1 PART 3

23

Questions 62 through 64 refer to the following conversation and schedule.

問題62-64は次の会話と予定表に関するものです。

🇬🇧 w Hi, ❶I'm interested in taking a pottery class. I've only taken one class before.

こんにちは、陶芸講座を受けたいと思っています。私は以前に1講座だけ受けたことがあります。

🇨🇦 M Here's the schedule for our spring and summer offerings. ❷We still have openings in all the classes.

こちらが、当センターの春期および夏期講座の予定表です。まだ、全ての講座に空きがあります。

🇬🇧 w I'll be traveling for business in June, so ❸the Level 3 class won't work. I suppose another level is a possibility, but I don't want it to be too easy.

私は6月に出張する予定なので、レベル3の講座は都合に合いませんね。別のレベルが候補かと思うのですが、私は易し過ぎるものは望んでいません。

🇨🇦 M Well, ❹the class given in May would probably be good for you, then. It should be at the right level, and the teacher is great.

そうですね、でしたら、5月に開設される講座がおそらくあなたに合うでしょう。こちらはぴったりのレベルでしょうし、講師が素晴らしいです。

🇬🇧 w Good, thanks. ❺Should I pay now?

良かった、ありがとうございます。私は今支払った方がいいですか。

🇨🇦 M Yes, please. ❻If you can't attend, it's refundable. Just let us know two weeks before the class starts.

はい、お願いいたします。ご出席になれない場合、そちらは払い戻し可能です。講座が始まる2週間前までに当センターにお知らせいただくだけです。

Art Center Pottery Classes	
Class	Dates
Level 1	April 1- April 30
Level 2	May 1 – May 31
Level 3	June 1 – June 30
Level 4	July 1 – July 31

芸術センター陶芸講座	
講座	期間
レベル1	4月1日～4月30日
レベル2	5月1日～5月31日
レベル3	6月1日～6月30日
レベル4	7月1日～7月31日

62 What does the man say about all of the classes?

(A) They include free materials.
(B) They take place in the morning.
(C) They can be repeated.
(D) They are still available.

男性は全ての講座について何と言っていますか。

(A) それらには無料の材料が含まれる。
(B) それらは午前中に行われる。
(C) それらは再受講可能である。
(D) それらはまだ受講可能である。

63 Look at the graphic. Which class level will the woman most likely choose?

(A) Level 1
(B) Level 2
(C) Level 3
(D) Level 4

図を見てください。女性はどのレベルの講座を選ぶと考えられますか。

(A) レベル1
(B) レベル2
(C) レベル3
(D) レベル4

64 What does the man say about a payment?

(A) It can be paid in installments.
(B) It must be paid by credit card.
(C) It is refundable.
(D) It will be collected on the first day of class.

男性は支払いについて何と言っていますか。

(A) それは分割払いで支払える。
(B) それはクレジットカードで支払われる必要がある。
(C) それは払い戻し可能である。
(D) それは講座の初日に徴収されることになっている。

Words & Phrases		

schedule 予定表　　be interested in *doing* ～したいと思っている　　pottery class 陶芸講座　　offering 講座、講義科目

opening 空き、欠員　　suppose ～だと思う　　possibility 候補、実行できる手段　　right ぴったりの　　pay 支払う

attend 出席する　　refundable 払い戻し可能な

予定表 dates 期間

Questions 65 through 67 refer to the following conversation and map.

M Hi, ❶this is Gerard Travers. I'm calling about a furniture delivery for Dorum Incorporated. ❷I'm the office manager here.

W Yes, Mr. Travers. That delivery is on the schedule for this afternoon.

M Oh, good. And ❸your driver should know that the usual delivery entrance—the one on Clarks Road—is not accessible today. That street's closed for repairs.

W OK. ❹Which door should he use then?

M ❺The Linden Drive entrance would be good. There's room for a truck to park alongside the road.

W OK, ❻I'll let the driver know. Your phone number is on the delivery paperwork. ❼He'll call you when he arrives.

問題65-67は次の会話と地図に関するものです。

もしもし、Gerard Traversです。Dorum社への家具配達の件でお電話しています。私は同社の総務責任者です。

はい、Travers様。その配達は本日午後に予定されております。

ああ、良かった。それで、通常の搬入口が——クラークス通りに面しているものですが——本日利用できないことを、御社の運転手の方が知っておく方がいいと思いまして。その通りが補修作業で閉鎖されているのです。

分かりました。それでは、彼はどの出入り口を利用すればいいですか。

リンデン大通りの入り口が良いでしょう。道路沿いにトラック1台が駐車できるスペースがあります。

分かりました、私が運転手に知らせておきます。御社の電話番号は配達書類に記載されております。到着時に、彼の方からあなたにお電話を差し上げるようにします。

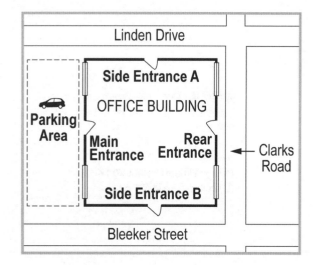

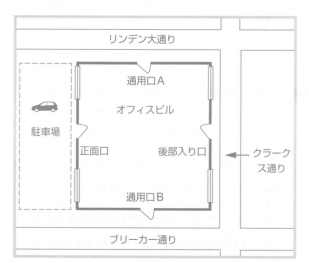

65 Who is the man?

    (A) A construction worker
    (B) A repair technician
    (C) A security guard
    (D) An office manager

男性は誰ですか。

    (A) 建設作業員
    (B) 補修技術者
    (C) 警備員
    (D) 総務責任者

正解 D	男性は❶で自分の名前を名乗り、家具の配達先の会社から電話をしていることを伝えてから、❷「私は同社の総務責任者だ」と述べている。 (A) construction「建設」。 (B) 補修作業に言及しているが、自分が技術者だとは述べていない。technician「技術者」。 (C) security guard「警備員」。

66 Look at the graphic. Where will a delivery be made?

    (A) At side entrance A
    (B) At the rear entrance
    (C) At side entrance B
    (D) At the main entrance

図を見てください。どこに配達されますか。

    (A) 通用口A
    (B) 後部入り口
    (C) 通用口B
    (D) 正面口

正解 A	男性から❸で、本日はクラークス通りに面した搬入口が利用できないと伝えられた女性は❹で、配達の運転手がどの出入り口を利用すればよいか尋ねている。それに対し、男性は❺「リンデン大通りの入り口が良いだろう」と答えている。図を見ると、リンデン大通りに面している入り口は通用口Aなので、(A)が正解。make a delivery「配達する」。 (B) クラークス通り沿いの通常の搬入口は、本日利用できないと述べられている。図より、それは後部入り口のことなので、ここには配達できない。

67 What does the woman say the driver will do?

    (A) Provide an invoice
    (B) Install some equipment
    (C) Make a phone call
    (D) Show identification

女性は、運転手が何をすると言っていますか。

    (A) 請求書を渡す
    (B) 機器を設置する
    (C) 電話をかける
    (D) 身元証明書を提示する

正解 C	女性は❻で運転手に利用すべき入り口を知らせると言い、男性の会社の電話番号が配達書類に記載されていると述べている。さらに、❼「到着時に、彼の方からあなたに電話を入れるようにする」と続けている。この「彼」は❻のthe driverを指すので、運転手本人から男性に電話をかけるようにすると言っていることが分かる。make a phone call「電話をかける」。 (A) invoice「請求書、送り状」。 (B) install「～を設置する」、equipment「機器」。 (C) identification「身元証明書」。

Words & Phrases

furniture　家具　　delivery　配達　　～ incorporated　～社　★会社名の後に付けて使用する　　usual　通常の
entrance　入り口　　accessible　利用可能な　　repairs　補修作業　　door　出入り口　　～ Drive　(道路名で)～大通り
room　スペース　　truck　トラック　　park　駐車する　　alongside　～に沿って、～のそばに　　paperwork　書類
arrive　到着する

地図　parking area　駐車場　　side entrance　脇の入り口　　main entrance　正面口　　rear entrance　後部口

Questions 68 through 70 refer to the following conversation and Web page.

問題68-70は次の会話とウェブページに関するものです。

🇨🇦 M Hi, Simone. ❶I heard you'll be attending the National Edutech Convention. ❷They definitely chose the right person to present teaching strategies to elementary school instructors.

こんにちは、Simone。あなたが全国教育工学協議会に出席すると聞きました。彼らは間違いなく、小学校教師に教授戦略を提示するのに適任の人物を選びましたね。

🇬🇧 W Thanks! Actually ❸I'm searching for plane tickets right now, but I can't find any at a reasonable price. ❹I'm hoping to bring expenses down, so I don't want tickets that cost too much.

ありがとう。実は、ちょうど今航空券を検索しているのですが、私はほどほどの価格のものを全く見つけられません。経費を抑えたいと思っているので、私は費用がかかり過ぎる航空券は欲しくないのです。

🇨🇦 M ❺Have you checked Alabaster Airlines? Their ticket prices are usually good.

あなたは、Alabaster航空を調べてみましたか。あそこの航空券の価格は、たいてい妥当ですよ。

🇬🇧 W Let's see. Oh, you're right! ❻There's a flight for 50 dollars, and it's nonstop too. That's perfect.

どれどれ。ああ、あなたの言う通りですね！ 50ドルの便があります、しかも直行便です。これなら完璧ですね。

---

www.alabasterair.com/tickets

Alabaster Airlines ✈

Destination	Details	Price
Boston	Nonstop	$50
Los Angeles	One connection	$236
Chicago	Nonstop	$189
Philadelphia	One connection	$74

www.alabasterair.com/tickets

Alabaster航空 ✈

目的地	詳細	価格
ボストン	直行便	50ドル
ロサンゼルス	乗り継ぎ1回	236ドル
シカゴ	直行便	189ドル
フィラデルフィア	乗り継ぎ1回	74ドル

68 What field does the woman most likely work in?

(A) Hospitality
(B) Finance
(C) Education
(D) Transportation

女性はどの分野で働いていると考えられますか。

(A) 接客サービス
(B) 金融
(C) 教育
(D) 運輸

---

69 What does the woman say she is hoping to do?

(A) Publish an article
(B) Reduce expenses
(C) Change a date
(D) Increase membership

女性は何をすることを望んでいると言っていますか。

(A) 論文を発表する
(B) 経費を削減する
(C) 日にちを変更する
(D) 会員数を増やす

---

70 Look at the graphic. What is the woman's travel destination?

(A) Boston
(B) Los Angeles
(C) Chicago
(D) Philadelphia

図を見てください。女性の旅の目的地はどこですか。

(A) ボストン
(B) ロサンゼルス
(C) シカゴ
(D) フィラデルフィア

Words & Phrases

attend　～に出席する　　national　全国的な　　edutech　教育工学　★educational technologyの略　　convention　協議会
definitely　間違いなく　　choose　～を選ぶ　　person　人　　present　～を提示する　　teaching strategy　教授戦略
elementary school　小学校　　instructor　教師　　search for ～　～を検索する　　reasonable　（値段が）ほどほどの、手頃な
hope to do　～することを望む　　bring down ～　～を下げる　　expense　経費　　cost　～の費用がかかる
airline　航空会社　★社名の場合には通例複数形　　flight　（航空機の）便、フライト　　nonstop　直行便の　　perfect　完璧な

ウェブページ　destination　目的地　　details　詳細　　connection　乗り継ぎ

Questions 71 through 73 refer to the following advertisement.　問題71-73は次の広告に関するものです。

🇺🇸 W

Do you work in downtown Vancouver? ❶Do you want to live close to where you work? Then Bora Park Tower is the place for you! ❷This ultramodern apartment building is in the center of Vancouver with spacious rental units and excellent facilities. ❸But what you'll appreciate the most is the fact that we're just a short walk away from a train station, a hospital, and a shopping district. Still not convinced? Then ❹check out the videos on our Web site, and listen to what our current residents are saying about Bora Park Tower!

バンクーバーの中心街で働いているのですか？職場の近くに住みたいですか？でしたら、Boraパークタワーがあなたにぴったりの場所です。この超現代的な集合住宅はバンクーバーの中心部にあり、広々とした賃貸住戸と素晴らしい設備を備えています。しかし、皆さまに最も高く評価いただけるであろう点は、鉄道駅、病院、商店街から歩いてすぐの距離にあるという事実です。これでもまだ納得なさいませんか？でしたら、私どものウェブサイトにある動画をご覧になり、現在お住まいの方々がBoraパークタワーについて何と言っているかお聞きください。

---

71 What is being advertised?

(A) A convention center
(B) A shopping mall
(C) An apartment building
(D) An amusement park

何が宣伝されていますか。
(A) コンベンションセンター
(B) ショッピングモール
(C) 集合住宅
(D) 遊園地

正解 C 話し手は、❶で「職場の近くに住みたいなら、Boraパークタワーがあなたにぴったりの場所だ」と言い、❷「この超現代的な集合住宅はバンクーバーの中心部にあり、広々とした賃貸住戸と素晴らしい設備を備えている」と、その集合住宅の特長を述べている。advertise「～を宣伝する」。
(A) convention center「コンベンションセンター（会議や博覧会のための大型建物）」。
(B) 商店街に言及があるが、店の宣伝はしていない。
(D) amusement park「遊園地」。

---

72 What will the listeners appreciate the most about Bora Park Tower?

(A) The convenient location
(B) The low prices
(C) The free parking
(D) The fast Internet access

聞き手はBoraパークタワーについて、何を最も高く評価するでしょうか。
(A) 便利な立地
(B) 低価格
(C) 無料の駐車場
(D) 高速のインターネット接続

正解 A 話し手は❷で、Boraパークタワーが町の中心部にあることやその設備について述べた後、❸「しかし、皆さんに最も高く評価いただけるであろう点は、鉄道駅、病院、商店街から歩いてすぐの距離にあるという事実だ」と便利な場所にあることを強調している。convenient「近くて便利な、手近な」、location「立地」。
(B) low price「低価格」。
(C) parking「駐車場」。
(D) fast「速い」、access「接続」。

---

73 What does the speaker suggest the listeners do online?

(A) Download discount coupons
(B) Watch some videos
(C) Apply for a job
(D) Schedule a visit

話し手は聞き手に、オンラインで何をすることを提案していますか。
(A) 割引クーポンをダウンロードする
(B) 動画を閲覧する
(C) 職に応募する
(D) 訪問の予定を組む

正解 B 話し手はBoraパークタワーの特長を並べてから、まだ納得がいかないかと問いかけ、❹「私たちのウェブサイトにある動画を見て、現在住んでいる人々がBoraパークタワーについて何と言っているか聞いてください」と、オンラインで動画を見るよう勧めている。online「オンラインで」。
(A) download「～をダウンロードする」、discount「割引」。
(C) apply for ～「～に応募する」。
(D) schedule「～の予定を組む」。

Words & Phrases

advertisement 広告　　downtown 中心街　　ultramodern 超現代的な
apartment building 集合住宅　　center 中心　　spacious 広々とした　　rental 賃貸の　　unit 集合住宅の1戸
excellent 素晴らしい、優良な　　facility 設備、施設　　appreciate ～を高く評価する　　fact 事実　　walk 歩行距離
shopping district 商店街　　convince ～を納得させる　　check out ～ ～を調べる　　video 動画　　current 現在の
resident 居住者

Questions 74 through 76 refer to the following announcement.

🇨🇦 M

Can I have your attention, please, everyone. ❶We will begin producing the next generation of our best-selling car model next quarter. ❷We have already received all the parts we need, so we can start the assembly process in July. ❸As supervisors, you'll have to reassign some tasks for your workers on the factory floor. ❹I'll be e-mailing you information on production targets and timelines to help you do that. Thank you for your cooperation.

問題74-76は次のお知らせに関するものです。

注目してもらえますか、皆さん。私たちは次の四半期、当社のベストセラーの自動車モデルの次世代版の生産を開始します。私たちはすでに必要な部品は全て受け取っているので、7月に組み立て工程を開始できます。皆さんは監督者として、工場内の生産現場の工具に対し、仕事をあらためて割り当てる必要があります。それを皆さんが行うのに役立つよう、私は生産の目標と日程に関する情報をEメールで送ります。皆さんのご協力に感謝します。

74 What does the company make?

(A) Furniture
(B) Electronics
(C) Cars
(D) Toys

この会社は何を製造していますか。

(A) 家具
(B) 電子機器
(C) 自動車
(D) 玩具

正解 C 話し手は、聞き手全員に注目を促してから、❶「私たちは次の四半期、当社のベストセラーの自動車モデルの次世代版の生産を開始する」と知らせている。よって、話し手と聞き手の会社は自動車を製造していると分かる。
(A) furniture「家具」。
(B) electronics「電子機器」。
(D) toy「玩具」。

75 According to the speaker, what will happen next quarter?

(A) Factory machinery will be upgraded.
(B) Assembly of a new product will begin.
(C) New-hire training will take place.
(D) A vacation policy will be updated.

話し手によると、次の四半期に何が起こりますか。

(A) 工場の機械がアップグレードされる。
(B) 新製品の組み立てが始まる。
(C) 新人研修が行われる。
(D) 休暇方針が改訂される。

正解 B 話し手は❶で、次の四半期に、既存の自動車モデルの次世代版の生産を開始すると知らせてから、❷「私たちはすでに必要な部品は全て受け取っているので、7月に組み立て工程を開始できる」と補足している。product「製品」。
(A) machinery「機械(類)」、upgrade「～をアップグレードする」。
(C) new-hire「新人の」、take place「行われる」。
(D) vacation policy「休暇方針」、update「～を改訂して最新のものにする」。

76 What are the listeners asked to do?

(A) Reassign some work
(B) Draft a cost estimate
(C) Prepare a safety manual
(D) Conduct an inventory

聞き手は何をするよう求められていますか。

(A) 作業をあらためて割り当てる
(B) 費用見積書の草案を書く
(C) 安全マニュアルを準備する
(D) 棚卸しをする

正解 A 話し手は❷で、7月からの次世代自動車モデルの組み立て工程の開始を伝え、❸「皆さんは監督者として、工場内の生産現場の工具に対し、仕事をあらためて割り当てる必要がある」と述べている。さらに❹でも、聞き手がその割り当てを行えるよう、生産の目標と日程に関するEメールを送ると続けている。
(B) draft「～の草案を書く」、cost estimate「費用見積書」。
(C) prepare「～を準備する」、safety「安全」。
(D) conduct「～を行う」、inventory「棚卸し」。

TEST1 PART 4

Words & Phrases

announcement お知らせ　　attention 注目　　produce ～を生産する
next generation 次世代　　best-selling ベストセラーの　　quarter 四半期　　receive ～を受け取る　　part 部品
assembly 組み立て　　process 工程　　supervisor 監督者　　reassign ～を割り当て直す　　task 仕事、任務
worker 工具、作業員　　factory floor 工場内の生産現場　　e-mail ～ … ～に…をEメールで送る　　production 生産
target 目標　　timeline 日程　　help ~ do ～が…するのに役立つ、～が…するのを助ける　　cooperation 協力

Questions 77 through 79 refer to the following tour information. 問題77-79は次のツアー案内に関するものです。

M

❶Now that you've seen the studio where Fernando Ortiz worked on designs for some of the most iconic, celebrated buildings in Spain, ❷let's move on to the extensive gardens, where Ortiz found inspiration for his designs in nature. But ❸first, let's take a break. ❹Feel free to purchase some food and drinks from our café. ❺We do have a dining area indoors, but there are tables and chairs on the patio overlooking the rose garden, and as you can see, the sun is shining. Let's meet by the fountain in the garden in twenty minutes to continue our tour.

さて、皆さんは今、Fernando Ortizがスペインで最も象徴的かつ名高い建物群の設計に取り組んだ仕事場をご覧になりましたので、広大な庭園へ移りましょう。その場所でOrtizは、自然界から設計のインスピレーションを得ました。ですが、まずは休憩しましょう。どうぞご自由に当館のカフェで飲み物を購入してください。屋内にも食事エリアはあるのですが、バラ園を見渡せるテラスにテーブルと椅子がありますよ。それにご覧の通り、太陽が輝いていますし。20分後に庭園内にある噴水のそばに集合し、ツアーを続けましょう。

77 Who most likely is Fernando Ortiz?
(A) An actor
(B) A chef
(C) A gardener
(D) An architect

Fernando Ortizとは誰だと考えられますか。
(A) 俳優
(B) シェフ
(C) 造園家
(D) 建築家

正解 D 話し手は❶で、Fernando Ortizがスペインで最も象徴的かつ名高い建物群の設計に取り組んだ仕事場を見終えたと述べている。さらに❷で、次に行く庭園について、Ortizが自然界から設計のインスピレーションを得た場所だと説明しているので、Fernando Ortizとは建築家だと考えられる。
(A) actor「俳優」。
(C) Ortizは庭園で設計のインスピレーションを得たと言っているだけで、造園家だという言及はない。

78 According to the speaker, what can the listeners purchase during the break?
(A) Maps
(B) Souvenirs
(C) Refreshments
(D) Transportation passes

話し手によると、聞き手は休憩中に何を購入することができますか。
(A) 地図
(B) 記念品
(C) 軽食
(D) 交通機関の乗車パス

正解 C 話し手は❸で、休憩することを提案してから、❹「自由に当館のカフェで飲食物を購入してください」と聞き手にカフェの提供物を利用するよう勧めている。some food and drinksをrefreshments「軽食」と表している(C)が正解。
(B) souvenir「記念品」。
(D) transportation「交通機関」、pass「通行証、パス」。

79 Why does the speaker say, "the sun is shining"?
(A) To make a recommendation
(B) To disagree with a weather report
(C) To ask for assistance
(D) To explain why an itinerary has changed

話し手はなぜ "the sun is shining" と言っていますか。
(A) 推薦をするため
(B) 天気予報に異を唱えるため
(C) 援助を求めるため
(D) 旅程が変更になった理由を説明するため

正解 A ❹で、休憩中にカフェを利用するよう促した話し手は、❺「屋内にも食事エリアはあるが、バラ園を見渡せるテラスにテーブルと椅子がある」と聞き手に案内してから、下線部で「太陽が輝いているし」と天気の良さを強調している。よって、話し手はカフェの屋外にあるテラス席の利用を勧めるために、この発言をしていると判断できる。make a recommendation「推薦をする」。
(B) disagree with ～「～に反対する」、weather report「天気予報」。
(C) ask for ～「～を求める」、assistance「援助」。
(D) itinerary「旅程、旅行計画」。

Words & Phrases
information 案内　now that ～ 今や～なので　studio 仕事場、アトリエ
work on ～ ～に取り組む　design 設計　iconic 象徴的な　celebrated 名高い　move on to ～ ～へ移る
extensive 広大な　inspiration インスピレーション、創造的刺激　nature 自然界、自然　take a break 休憩する
feel free to do 自由に～する、遠慮なく～する　purchase ～を購入する　dining 食事　indoors 屋内に
patio テラス　★屋外での食事などに使う　overlook ～を見渡す　shine 輝く、照る　fountain 噴水　continue ～を続ける

Questions 80 through 82 refer to the following excerpt from a meeting.

問題80-82は次の会議の抜粋に関するものです。

🇬🇧 W

Starting next month, ❶we'll be implementing a new security measure at our facility. ❷To protect the items people store in here, we'll be installing scanners at the main gate. ❸All customers will have to swipe an access card at the gate in order to get to their storage units. ❹This system has the added benefit of keeping a record of everyone who comes and goes through the main gate. In fact, we'll all need to obtain access cards in order to enter and leave. ❺As employees, your cards will have your photos on them. Please see Hao Nan to get your picture taken.

来月から、当施設では新しい安全対策を実施します。人々がここに保管する品物を保護するため、メインゲートにスキャナーを設置します。顧客は全員、自分の保管場所に行くために、ゲートで通行カードを読み取り機に通さなくてはならなくなります。このシステムには、メインゲートを出入りする全ての人の記録を取るという付加的な利点があります。実際、私たちは皆、出入りするのに通行カードを取得する必要があります。従業員として、皆さんのカードにはご自分の写真が載ることになります。写真を撮ってもらうためにHao Nanの所に行ってください。

80 Where does the talk most likely take place?

(A) At a bank
(B) At a storage facility
(C) At a hardware store
(D) At a real estate office

この話はどこで行われていると考えられますか。

(A) 銀行
(B) 保管施設
(C) 金物店
(D) 不動産会社

正解 B 話し手は❶で、当施設で新しい安全対策を実施する予定だと伝えた後、❷「人々がここに保管する品物を保護するため、メインゲートにスキャナーを設置する」と述べている。さらに❸「顧客は全員、自分の保管場所に行くために、ゲートで通行カードを読み取り機に通さなくてはならなくなる」と説明していることから、この話は保管施設で行われていると考えられる。
(C) hardware store「金物店」。
(D) real estate「不動産」。

81 What added benefit of a system does the speaker mention?

(A) It records all visitors.
(B) It turns off automatically.
(C) It is easy to upgrade.
(D) It is portable.

話し手は、システムのどんな付加的な利点について述べていますか。

(A) それは全訪問者を記録する。
(B) それは自動的に電源が切れる。
(C) それはアップグレードをするのが簡単である。
(D) それは持ち運び可能である。

正解 A 話し手は❷で、新しい安全対策としてメインゲートにスキャナーを設置すると伝えてから、❹「このシステムには、メインゲートを出入りする全ての人の記録を取るという付加的な利点がある」と言っている。record「～を記録する」。
(B) turn off「(電源などが)切れる」、automatically「自動的に」。
(C) upgrade「～をアップグレードする」。
(D) portable「持ち運び可能な」。

82 Why are employees asked to see Hao Nan?

(A) To get a parking pass
(B) To sign up for training
(C) To update payroll information
(D) To have a photograph taken

従業員はなぜ、Hao Nanの所に行くよう求められているのですか。

(A) 駐車証を取得するため
(B) 研修の参加登録をするため
(C) 給与台帳情報を更新するため
(D) 写真を撮ってもらうため

正解 D 話し手は❺で、従業員用の通行カードには各自の写真が載ると伝えてから、写真を撮ってもらうためにHao Nanの所に行くよう依頼している。have ～ done「～を…してもらう」。
(A) pass「通行証、無料入場券」。
(B) sign up for ～「～の参加登録をする」。
(C) update「～を更新する」、payroll「給与台帳」。

TEST1 PART 4

Words & Phrases

excerpt 抜粋　　implement ～を実施する　　security 安全　　measure 対策　　facility 施設
protect ～を保護する　　item 品物　　store ～を保管する　　install ～を設置する　　scanner スキャナー
main gate メインゲート　　customer 顧客　　swipe ～(磁気カードなど)を読み取り装置に通す、～をスワイプする
access 通行　　in order to do ～するために　　get to ～ ～に到着する　　storage 保管　　unit ユニット、設備
system システム　　added 付加的な　　benefit 利点　　keep a record of ～ ～の記録を取る　　in fact 実際に
obtain ～を取得する　　enter 入る　　leave 退出する　　employee 従業員

Questions 83 through 85 refer to the following speech.

問題83-85は次の講演に関するものです。

🍁 M

❶I'm Alberto Giordano, the owner of Alberto's Pasta Sauces, and I'm honored to be a speaker at this year's Artisanal Foods Conference. Like all of us here, I faced many challenges when I decided to start my business three years ago. ❷Back then I used to sell my products only from my home, ❸but now I'm very proud to say that Alberto's Pasta Sauces are sold in supermarkets throughout the country—a remarkable achievement. ❹No matter how much my company grows in the future, I will continue to honor my grandmother's traditional recipes through my commitment to using traditional techniques. After all, I believe that has been the key to the brand's success.

私はAlberto'sパスタソース社のオーナー、Alberto Giordano です。今年の職人的食品大会の講演者を務めることができて光栄です。ここにいらっしゃる皆さまと同様に、私は3年前に起業すると決意したとき、多くの課題に直面しました。その当時、私は自宅からのみ製品を販売しておりました。しかし今では、Alberto'sパスタソースが全国のスーパーマーケットで販売されているとお伝えできることを私は大変誇りに思います——これは目覚ましい業績です。今後、私の会社がどんなに成長しようとも、伝統的技術を用いることへのこだわりを通じて、祖母の伝統的なレシピに敬意を表し続けます。つまるところ、これこそが私のブランドの成功への鍵であったのだと思っています。

---

83 What type of product does the speaker sell?

(A) Food
(B) Clothing
(C) Kitchen appliances
(D) Cookbooks

話し手はどのような製品を販売していますか。

(A) 食品
(B) 衣類
(C) 台所用家電
(D) 料理の本

正解 A 話し手は❶「私はAlberto'sパスタソース社のオーナー、Alberto Giordanoで、今年の職人的食品大会の講演者を務めることができて光栄だ」と自己紹介している。さらに❸で、Alberto'sパスタソースは全国のスーパーマーケットで販売されていると述べているので、(A)が正解。
(B) clothing「衣類」。
(C) kitchen appliance「台所用家電」。
(D) cookbook「料理の本」。

---

84 What achievement is the speaker proud of?

(A) His products broke a sales record.
(B) His products have become widely available.
(C) His products were featured in a news article.
(D) His products won an industry award.

話し手は、どんな業績を誇りに思っていますか。

(A) 彼の製品は販売記録を更新した。
(B) 彼の製品は広く入手可能である。
(C) 彼の製品はニュース記事で特集された。
(D) 彼の製品は業界の賞を獲得した。

正解 B 話し手は❷で、起業当時は自宅からしか製品を販売していなかったと述べてから、❸「しかし今では、Alberto'sパスタソースが全国のスーパーマーケットで販売されているとお伝えできることを私は大変誇りに思う——これは目覚ましい業績だ」と続けているので(B)が正解。be proud of ~「~を誇りに思う」。widely「広く」、available「入手可能な」。
(A) break a record「記録を更新する」。
(C) feature「~を特集する」、article「記事」。
(D) win an award「賞を獲得する」、industry「業界」。

---

85 What does the speaker say he will do in the future?

(A) Work with local farms
(B) Raise funds for charities
(C) Continue using traditional techniques
(D) Try different business models

話し手は今後、何をすると言っていますか。

(A) 地元農家と連携する
(B) 慈善団体のために資金を集める
(C) 伝統的な技術を使用し続ける
(D) さまざまなビジネスモデルを試してみる

正解 C 話し手は❹「今後、私の会社がどんなに成長しようとも、伝統的技術を用いることへのこだわりを通じて、祖母の伝統的なレシピに敬意を表し続ける」と抱負を語っている。continue doing「~し続ける」。
(A) local「地元の」。
(B) raise「~(資金など)を集める」、fund「資金」、charity「慈善団体」。

Words & Phrases

be honored to do ~することを光栄に思う　artisanal 職人の　conference 大会、協議会　face ~に直面する　challenge 課題　decide to do ~することを決意する　start one's business 起業する　back then その当時は　used to do 以前は~していた　product 製品　be proud to do ~することを誇りに思う　throughout ~中、~の至る所に　remarkable 素晴らしい、注目に値する　achievement 業績　grow 成長する　in the future 今後　continue to do ~し続ける　honor ~に敬意を表す　traditional 伝統的な　recipe レシピ　commitment 献身、積極的関与　technique 技術　after all 結局　brand ブランド　success 成功

Questions 86 through 88 refer to the following instructions.

🇦🇺 M

問題86-88は次の説明に関するものです。

❶Welcome to the Bransford Public Library's workshop on digital photo editing. ❷Today you'll learn how to use the basic features of a well-known photo editing program. Before we start, a few reminders. ❸Please refrain from eating in the classroom, and keep drinks away from the computers. They were a generous donation, and we'd like to have the computers for future classes. Also, ❹don't forget there's a special summer discount available if you'd like to purchase a copy of the software for your home computer. You can find more information on it by clicking the "Partners" link on the library Web site.

Bransford公立図書館による、デジタル写真編集の講習会へようこそ。皆さんは本日、よく知られている写真編集プログラムの基本機能の使い方を学びます。始める前に、幾つかご留意いただきたい点があります。教室内での食事はご遠慮ください、また飲み物はコンピューターから遠ざけておいてください。これらはご厚意による寄贈品で、当館は今後の講座のためにコンピューターを保有しておきたいと思っています。それから、皆さんのご自宅のコンピューター用にソフトウエアをご購入希望の場合、夏の特別割引が利用可能であることをお忘れなく。当図書館のウェブサイトにある『パートナー業者』のリンクをクリックすると、それに関する詳細をご覧になれます。

86 What is the main topic of the workshop?

(A) Photo editing
(B) Cooking
(C) Computer repair
(D) Nutrition

講習会のテーマは何ですか。

(A) 写真編集
(B) 料理
(C) コンピューターの修理
(D) 栄養学

正解 **A** 話し手は❶「Bransford公立図書館による、デジタル写真編集の講習会へようこそ」と聞き手を歓迎してから、❷「皆さんは本日、よく知られている写真編集プログラムの基本機能の使い方を学ぶ」と伝えている。よって、写真編集プログラムの使い方が講習会のテーマだと分かる。topic「テーマ、トピック」。
(C) コンピューターに言及しているが、修理が講習会のテーマだとは述べていない。repair「修理」。
(D) nutrition「栄養、栄養学」。

87 What does the speaker mean when he says, "we'd like to have the computers for future classes"?

(A) The speaker is requesting donations.
(B) The speaker wants to renew a contract.
(C) The listeners should be careful.
(D) The listeners should complete a questionnaire.

話し手は "we'd like to have the computers for future classes" という発言で、何を意味していますか。

(A) 話し手は寄付を要請している。
(B) 話し手は契約を更新したいと思っている。
(C) 聞き手は気を付けるべきである。
(D) 聞き手はアンケートに全て記入すべきである。

正解 **C** 話し手は講習会開始前の留意点として❸で、教室内での食事を控え、飲料をコンピューターから遠ざけるよう頼んでいる。さらに、コンピューターは寄贈品だと述べてから、下線部の発言をしているので、話し手は今後の講座にも使用する教室内の貴重なコンピューターの取り扱いに関して注意喚起していると考えられる。careful「気を付ける」。
(B) renew「～を更新する」、contract「契約」。
(D) complete「～に全て記入する」、questionnaire「アンケート」。

88 What does the speaker say is discounted?

(A) A software program
(B) A library membership
(C) A magazine subscription
(D) A workshop registration

話し手は何が割引になっていると言っていますか。

(A) ソフトウエアプログラム
(B) 図書館の会員資格
(C) 雑誌の購読
(D) 講習会への登録

正解 **A** 話し手は、講習会での飲食上の留意点に続けて、❹「皆さんの自宅のコンピューター用にソフトウエアを購入希望の場合、夏の特別割引が利用可能であることを忘れないでください」とソフトウエアの割引について案内している。
(B) membership「会員資格」。
(C) subscription「購読」。
(D) registration「登録」。

Words & Phrases

instructions 説明、指示　public 公立の　workshop 講習会　digital photo デジタル写真　editing 編集　feature 機能、特徴　well-known よく知られた　reminder 注意、思い出させるもの　refrain from *doing* ～することを控える　keep ～ away from … ～を…から遠ざけておく　generous 思いやりのある、気前のよい　donation 寄贈品、寄付　future 今後の　discount 割引　available 利用可能な　purchase ～を購入する　a copy of ～ ～（ソフトウエア・CD・本など）の1点、～の1枚　click ～をクリックする　partner パートナー、共同事業者　link リンク

Questions 89 through 91 refer to the following excerpt from a meeting.

問題89-91は次の会議の抜粋に関するものです。

🇺🇸 W

Good morning, everyone. ❶I've analyzed the results from our latest sales report, and it's obvious we need a change in strategy. ❷Sales of our smart speakers in the European markets have fallen in the last quarter. This may be because of the way we advertise there. ❸Research has shown online advertisements in Europe are more effective than television ads. So, we've decided to stop our television ad campaign there… which could also save us money, as TV ads are expensive to produce. ❹We'll use the extra money to hire more people with expertise in social media advertising. Job openings will be posted soon.

おはようございます、皆さん。私が最新の売上報告書の結果を分析したところ、当社が戦略の変更を必要とするのは明らかです。前四半期に、ヨーロッパ市場における当社のスマートスピーカーの売り上げは落ち込みました。これは、現地での宣伝の仕方に原因がある可能性があります。調査では、ヨーロッパではオンライン広告の方がテレビ広告よりも効果的であると示されています。そのため、当社は現地でのテレビ広告キャンペーンの廃止を決定しました…これにより資金を節約することもできるでしょう、テレビ広告は制作に費用がかかりますから。当社は、その余剰資金をソーシャルメディア広告に関する専門的知識を持つ人々をさらに雇うのに充てるつもりです。求人は間もなく掲示されます。

---

89 According to the speaker, why is a change in strategy needed?

(A) Sales results have been disappointing.
(B) Competition in the technology field has increased.
(C) An overseas office has recently opened.
(D) A manufacturing process has changed.

話し手によると、なぜ戦略の変更が必要なのですか。

(A) 売上実績が期待外れなものになっているから。
(B) テクノロジー分野の競争が増しているから。
(C) 最近、海外事務所が開設されたから。
(D) 製造工程が変更になったから。

正解 A 話し手は❶で、売上報告書の結果分析により、戦略の変更が必要と述べ、❷「前四半期に、ヨーロッパ市場における当社のスマートスピーカーの売り上げは落ち込んだ」と続けている。よって、売上実績が期待外れなため戦略の変更が必要と分かる。disappointing「失望させるような」。
(B) competition「競争」、increase「増す」。
(C) overseas「海外の」、recently「最近」。
(D) manufacturing「製造（の）」、process「工程」。

90 According to the speaker, what has research indicated?

(A) Television sets are decreasing in price.
(B) Online advertising is successful.
(C) Customers prefer to pay with credit cards.
(D) Most consumers own several mobile devices.

話し手によると、調査は何を示していますか。

(A) テレビは価格が低下している。
(B) オンライン広告は好結果をもたらす。
(C) 顧客はクレジットカードでの支払いを好む。
(D) 大多数の消費者は、複数の携帯機器を所有している。

正解 B 話し手は、売り上げの低下が宣伝方法に起因する可能性に言及してから、❸「調査では、ヨーロッパではオンライン広告の方がテレビ広告よりも効果的であると示されている」と伝えている。successful「好結果の」。
(A) decrease「低下する、減少する」。
(C) prefer to do「～する方を好む」。
(D) consumer「消費者」、own「～を所有する」、several「幾つかの」、mobile device「携帯機器」。

91 What is the company planning to do?

(A) Upgrade its computer system
(B) Merge with another company
(C) Conduct a customer survey
(D) Hire specialized employees

会社は何をすることを計画していますか。

(A) 自社のコンピューターシステムをアップグレードする
(B) 別の会社と合併する
(C) 顧客調査を実施する
(D) 専門分野に特化した従業員を雇用する

正解 D 話し手は、ヨーロッパでのテレビ広告キャンペーンの廃止決定を伝えてから、その結果生じる余剰資金について、❹「当社は、その余剰資金をソーシャルメディア広告に関する専門的知識を持つ人々をさらに雇うのに充てるつもりだ」と述べている。people with expertiseをspecialized employeesと表している(D)が正解。specialized「専門分野に特化した」。
(B) merge with ～「～と合併する」。
(C) conduct「～を実施する」、survey「調査」。

Words & Phrases

analyze ～を分析する　result 結果、実績　latest 最新の　sales report 売上報告書　obvious 明らかな　strategy 戦略　smart speaker （AI機能搭載の）スマートスピーカー　market 市場　fall 落ち込む　quarter 四半期　because of ～ ～ゆえに　advertise 宣伝する　research 調査　advertisement 広告 ★省略形はad　effective 効果的な　campaign キャンペーン　save ～ … ～の…を節約する　expensive 高価な　produce ～を制作する　extra 余分な、臨時の　hire ～を雇用する　expertise 専門的知識　social media ソーシャルメディア　advertising 広告、宣伝　job opening 求人　post ～を掲示する

Questions 92 through 94 refer to the following news report.

🇬🇧 w

Thanks for listening to Radio 101, Ashton's local news station. ❶Tonight's featured story is the town's plan to renovate the old railroad line that runs alongside Dorset Avenue. **The line has been out of service for over 40 years and the tracks are now rusted.** ❷The line will be converted into a beautiful walking path and new community garden. ❸Several designs have been proposed, and digital images are available on the town's Web site. ❹Residents are encouraged to view the designs and vote on their favorite. ❺Just keep in mind that <u>construction will begin in two months</u>.

問題92-94は次のニュース報道に関するものです。

Ashtonの地方ニュース放送局、ラジオ101をお聞きくださりありがとうございます。今夜の特集ニュースは、ドーセット大通りに沿って走る老朽化した鉄道線路を刷新するという町の計画です。この線路は40年以上使用されておらず、レールは現在さび付いています。線路は、美しい遊歩道と新たな地域庭園に転用されることになっています。幾つかのデザインが提案されており、デジタル画像が町のウェブサイトで閲覧できます。住民はそのデザインを見て、自分の好きなものに投票するよう奨励されています。建設作業は2カ月後に開始するということだけ覚えておいてください。

---

92 What project is being discussed?

(A) The opening of a town library
(B) The construction of a new bus station
(C) The conversion of a railroad line
(D) The demolition of a historic building

どんなプロジェクトについて述べられていますか。

(A) 町立図書館の開設
(B) 新しいバスターミナルの建設
(C) 鉄道線路の転用
(D) 歴史的建造物の取り壊し

正解 **C** 話し手はラジオ放送局名に続けて、❶「今夜の特集ニュースは、ドーセット大通りに沿って走る老朽化した鉄道線路を刷新するという町の計画だ」と述べている。その後も、❷「線路は、美しい遊歩道と新たな地域庭園に転用されることになる」と説明している。conversion「転換」。
(B) bus station「バスターミナル」。
(D) demolition「取り壊し」、historic「歴史的な」。

---

93 According to the speaker, what can the listeners view on the town's Web site?

(A) A map
(B) Some images
(C) The annual budget
(D) A list of upcoming events

話し手によると、聞き手は町のウェブサイトで何を見ることができますか。

(A) 地図
(B) 画像
(C) 年度予算
(D) 今度のイベントのリスト

正解 **B** 話し手は、❷で老朽化した線路を遊歩道と庭園に転用する計画について説明した後、❸「幾つかのデザインが提案されており、デジタル画像が町のウェブサイトで閲覧できる」と聞き手に伝えている。
(C) annual「年間の」、budget「予算」。
(D) upcoming「今度の」。

---

94 What does the speaker imply when she says, "construction will begin in two months"?

(A) Some work is on schedule.
(B) Noise in an area will likely increase.
(C) The listeners might experience traffic delays.
(D) The listeners should make a choice soon.

話し手は "construction will begin in two months" という発言で、何を示唆していますか。

(A) 作業が予定通りに進んでいる。
(B) ある地域における騒音がおそらく増すだろう。
(C) 聞き手は交通の遅れを経験するかもしれない。
(D) 聞き手はすぐに選択をすべきである。

正解 **D** 話し手は❸で、線路転用後のデザインがウェブサイトで閲覧できると伝え、❹「住民はそのデザインを見て、自分の好きなものに投票するよう奨励されている」と述べている。さらに、❺で注意喚起してから、下線部の発言を続けているので、建設開始が2カ月後と間近なことを強調して、早く投票するよう聞き手を促していると考えられる。choice「選択」。
(A) on schedule「予定通りに」。
(B) noise「騒音」、increase「増す」。
(C) experience「〜を経験する」、traffic「交通(の)」、delay「遅れ、遅延」。

Words & Phrases

local 地方の　　station 放送局　　featured 特集の　　renovate 〜を刷新する
railroad 鉄道　　line 線路　　alongside 〜に沿って　　〜 Avenue (道路名で)〜大通り
out of service 使用中止になって　　track レール、線路　　rust 〜をさび付かせる　　convert 〜 into … 〜を…に転換する
walking path 遊歩道　　community 地域　　design デザイン、図案　　propose 〜を提案する　　digital デジタルの
image 画像　　available 利用可能な　　resident 住民　　encourage 〜 to do 〜に…するよう奨励する　　view 〜を見る
vote on 〜 〜に投票する　　keep in mind that 〜 〜ということを覚えておく　　construction 建設作業、建設

TEST1 PART 4

Questions 95 through 97 refer to the following telephone message and room layouts.

問題95-97は次の電話のメッセージと室内レイアウトに関するものです。

🍁 M

❶Hello, Dr. Chung. I'm organizing the upcoming physicians' convention. ❷We're especially happy about the topic you've selected—holistic healthcare. ❸I sent you an e-mail with various room arrangements. In your proposal ❹you said the attendees will be taking notes, so I'd suggest the one with two rows of tables with all participants facing the same way. ❺I also need an updated professional biography for our program booklet. Please e-mail it to me before the end of the month. Thank you.

もしもし、Chung先生。私は今度の医師協議会の準備をしています。私たちは、あなたが選択なさった題目——ホリスティック医療——をとりわけ気に入っています。さまざまな室内配置を添付したEメールをあなたに送りました。ご提案書であなたは、出席者がメモを取るだろうと書いておられたので、テーブルが2列で全参加者が同じ方向に向く配置を提案いたします。また、プログラム小冊子用に最新の職業上の経歴が必要です。月末までにそれを私宛てにEメールでお送りください。よろしくお願いいたします。

Conference Room Arrangements

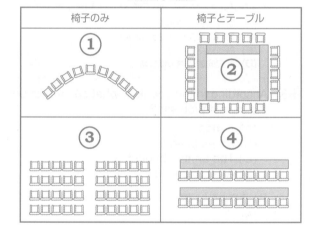

会議室内の配置

95 What is the caller pleased about?

    (A) A high attendance rate
    (B) An award nomination
    (C) A convention location
    (D) A presentation topic

電話をかけた人は何について満足していますか。

    (A) 高い出席率
    (B) 賞への候補者として推薦されること
    (C) 協議会の開催地
    (D) 発表題目

正解 D

電話をかけた話し手は❶で、聞き手のChung医師に対し、今度の医師協議会の準備をしていると述べた後、❷「私たちは、あなたが選択した題目——ホリスティック医療——をとりわけ気に入っている」と伝えている。よって、聞き手が選んだ発表題目について満足していると判断できる。caller「電話の発信者」、be pleased about ～「～に満足している」。presentation「発表」。
(A) attendance「出席」、rate「率、割合」。
(B) award「賞」、nomination「候補として推薦を受けること、ノミネート」。
(C) location「場所、所在地」。

---

96 Look at the graphic. Which room arrangement does the caller recommend?

    (A) Arrangement 1
    (B) Arrangement 2
    (C) Arrangement 3
    (D) Arrangement 4

図を見てください。電話をかけた人はどの室内配置を勧めていますか。

    (A) 配置1
    (B) 配置2
    (C) 配置3
    (D) 配置4

正解 D

話し手は、❸でさまざまな室内配置を添付したEメールを聞き手に送ったと伝えてから、❹「あなたは、出席者がメモを取るだろうと書いていたので、テーブルが2列で、全参加者が同じ方向に向く配置を提案する」と勧めている。図を見ると、テーブルが2列用意され、かつ着席者が皆同じ方向に向く配置は4。よって、(D)が正解。recommend「～を勧める」。

---

97 What needs to be updated in the program booklet?

    (A) Some agenda items
    (B) A registration deadline
    (C) A biography
    (D) A city map

プログラム小冊子の中で、何が最新のものにされる必要がありますか。

    (A) 議題項目
    (B) 登録の締め切り
    (C) 経歴
    (D) 市内地図

正解 C

医師協議会の準備役の話し手は、❸・❹でChung医師に対し、発表の手配のための連絡をしている。さらに❺「また、プログラム小冊子用に最新の職業上の経歴が必要だ」と述べ、最新の経歴を送るよう聞き手に頼んでいる。
(A) agenda item「議題項目」。
(B) registration「登録」、deadline「締め切り」。

Words & Phrases

layout レイアウト、配置　　organize ～の準備をする、～を企画する　　upcoming 今度の　　physician 医師、内科医
convention 協議会　　especially 特に　　topic 題目、トピック　　select ～を選ぶ
holistic ホリスティックの、全体観的治療の　　healthcare 医療　　various さまざまな　　arrangement 配置
proposal 提案、提案書　　attendee 出席者　　take notes メモを取る
I'd suggest ～　～をご提案します　★このI'dはI wouldの略で丁寧さを表す　　row 列　　participant 参加者
face ～の方向に向く　　update ～を最新のものにする　　professional 職業上の　　biography 経歴　　booklet 小冊子

レイアウト　conference room　会議室

39

Questions 98 through 100 refer to the following excerpt from a meeting and fund-raising flyer.

🇺🇸 W

As you all know, ❶our software company started a fund-raiser to launch a summer camp for kids who want to become computer programmers. We've already raised a nice amount of money. In fact, ❷we've run out of thank-you gifts for the ten-dollar donation level. So ❸now, anyone who makes a donation of ten dollars will receive a baseball hat instead. Also ❹please remember to check your e-mail for a link to the fund-raiser survey. ❺Completing this survey will help us to make informed decisions about what kinds of youth programs to run in the future.

問題 98-100 は次の会議の抜粋と資金集め用のチラシに関するものです。

皆さんご存じのように、当ソフトウエア会社は、コンピュータープログラマーになりたい子ども向けのサマーキャンプを始めるために、資金集めイベントを開始しました。すでに私たちは、かなりの金額を集めております。実際、10ドルの寄付層に対する返礼品はなくなってしまいました。そのため今後は、10ドルの寄付をしてくださる方は皆、代わりに野球帽を受け取ることになります。また、資金集めイベントのアンケート調査へのリンクが載っていますので、ご自分のEメールを忘れずに確認してください。このアンケート調査に全て入力していただくことは、今後どのような若者向けプログラムを提供するべきか、当社が情報に基づいた決定を下すのに役立つでしょう。

Company Fund-raiser!

Receive a free...	*with your donation of...*
Key chain	$5.00
Tote bag	$10.00
Water bottle	$25.00
Company T-shirt	$50.00

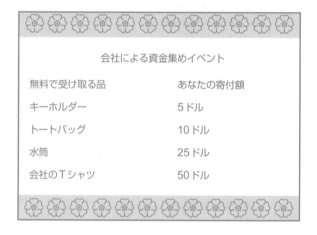

会社による資金集めイベント

無料で受け取る品	あなたの寄付額
キーホルダー	5ドル
トートバッグ	10ドル
水筒	25ドル
会社のTシャツ	50ドル

98 What is the company raising money for?

(A) A mobile health clinic
(B) A music school
(C) A summer camp program
(D) A library computer room

会社は何のために資金を集めていますか。

(A) 移動式診療所
(B) 音楽学校
(C) サマーキャンプ・プログラム
(D) 図書館のコンピューター室

正解 **C** 話し手は❶「当ソフトウエア会社は、コンピュータープログラマーになりたい子ども向けのサマーキャンプを始めるために、資金集めイベントを開始した」と述べているので、(C)が正解。
(A) mobile「移動式の」、health clinic「診療所」。
(D) コンピュータープログラマー志望者に言及しているが、コンピューター室用の資金とは言っていない。

---

99 Look at the graphic. Which thank-you gift has the company run out of?

(A) Key chains
(B) Tote bags
(C) Water bottles
(D) Company T-shirts

図を見てください。会社はどの返礼品を切らしていますか。

(A) キーホルダー
(B) トートバッグ
(C) 水筒
(D) 会社のTシャツ

正解 **B** 話し手は、資金集めイベントにて、すでにかなりの金額を集めたと伝えてから、❷「10ドルの寄付層に対する返礼品はなくなってしまった」と述べ、続けて❸「今後は、10ドルの寄付をする人は皆、代わりに野球帽を受け取る」と伝えている。図を見ると、寄付額が10ドルの場合に受け取る品はトートバッグなので、(B)が正解。

---

100 What does the speaker ask the listeners to do?

(A) Order more supplies
(B) Choose a design
(C) Complete a survey
(D) Run a report

話し手は、聞き手に何をするよう求めていますか。

(A) 備品をさらに注文する
(B) デザインを選ぶ
(C) アンケート調査に全て入力する
(D) リポート作成プログラムを実行する

正解 **C** 話し手は、❹で、アンケート調査へのリンクを記載したEメールを確認するよう聞き手に伝え、続けて❺「このアンケート調査に全て入力してもらうことは、今後どのような若者向けプログラムを提供するべきか、当社が情報に基づいた決定を下すのに役立つだろう」と、アンケート調査に全て入力するよう聞き手に求めている。
(A) supplies「備品」。
(D) run「～（コンピューターのプログラム）を実行する」。

Words & Phrases

fund-raising 資金集めの　flyer チラシ　fund-raiser 資金集めイベント　launch ～を始める、～を立ち上げる
summer camp サマーキャンプ　kid 子ども　raise ～(資金など)を集める　amount 金額　in fact 実際
run out of ～ ～がなくなる、～を切らす　thank-you お礼の　gift 景品　donation 寄付、寄付金　level 階層、水準
receive ～を受け取る　baseball hat 野球帽　instead 代わりに　remember to do 忘れずに～する　link リンク
survey アンケート調査　complete ～に全て記入する　make a decision 決定を下す　informed 情報に基づく
youth 若者　run ～(講座など)を提供する、～を運営する
チラシ　free 無料の　key chain キーホルダー　tote bag トートバッグ　water bottle 水筒

101 All FFP employees are encouraged to participate ------- in community programs.

(A) regularly
(B) regular
(C) regulation
(D) regularity

FFP社の従業員は皆、地域活動プログラムに定期的に参加するよう奨励されています。

(A) 定期的に
(B) 定期的な
(C) 規則
(D) 規則正しさ

正解 **A** 文の述語動詞はare encouragedで、その後ろはtoにparticipate in ～「～に参加する」が続いたto不定詞。「従業員は皆、地域活動プログラムに参加するよう奨励されている」と、空所に何も入れなくても文が成立するので、空所には副詞が入る。よって、空所前後のparticipate in ～を修飾する副詞の(A) regularly「定期的に」が適切。encourage ～ to do「～に…するよう奨励する」、community「地域社会」、program「プログラム、事業計画」。
(B) 形容詞。(C) (D) 名詞。participateが他動詞の場合、名詞を続けられるが、文意に合わない。

102 Please inspect the contents of the package and contact us with any -------.

(A) questionable
(B) questioning
(C) questioned
(D) questions

小包の中身を点検していただき、どのようなご質問でも私どもにご連絡ください。

(A) 疑わしい
(B) 質問すること
(C) 質問された
(D) 質問

正解 **D** Please ～で始まる命令文。空所の前にwith anyとあり、後ろに何も続いていないので、空所には形容詞anyによって修飾される名詞が入る。小包の中身の点検を促しているという文意から、名詞question「質問」の複数形の(D)が適切。inspect「～を点検する」、content「中身」、package「小包」、contact「～に連絡する」。
(A) 形容詞。(B) 名詞だとしても、「質問をすること、尋問」の意味となり、文意に合わない。
(C) 動詞「～に質問する」の過去分詞。

103 The training instructors will stay at the ------- renovated guest house.

(A) newly
(B) enough
(C) directly
(D) exactly

研修の講師陣は、最近改装されたゲストハウスに宿泊します。

(A) 最近
(B) 十分に
(C) 直接に
(D) 正確に

正解 **A** 選択肢は全て副詞の働きを持つ語。研修の講師陣の宿泊場所を伝える文であり、空所直後のrenovated「改装された」を修飾して文意に合うのは(A) newly「最近」。training「研修」、instructor「講師」、guest house「ゲストハウス（施設に付属した来客用宿舎）」。
(B) 副詞として使う場合、enoughは形容詞の後ろに置くので不適切。
(C) (D) 文意に合わない。

104 Sunnyville Public Library is ------- today because of a problem with the electrical system.

    (A) certain
    (B) closed
    (C) returned
    (D) simple

Sunnyville公立図書館は、電気系統の障害のため本日は閉まっています。

    (A) 確信して
    (B) 閉まった
    (C) 返却された
    (D) 簡素な

> 正解 **B** 選択肢は全て形容詞の働きを持つ語。空所の後ろに because of a problem with the electrical system「電気系統の障害のため」と理由が示されているので、(B) closed「閉まった」を入れて、図書館が本日休館であることと、その理由を伝える内容にすると文意が通る。because of ~「~のため、~のゆえに」、problem「障害、支障」、electrical system「電気系統」。

105 Ms. Suzuki ------- as a leader in the Asian financial services industry.

    (A) recognizes
    (B) recognizing
    (C) is recognized
    (D) has recognized

Suzukiさんは、アジアの金融サービス業界で第一人者として認められています。

＊選択肢の訳は省略

> 正解 **C** 動詞recognize「~を認める」の適切な形を選ぶ。この文には述語動詞がないため、空所に必要。recognizeは他動詞で目的語が必要だが、目的語となる名詞(句)がないので、空所には受動態の (C) is recognizedが適切。recognize ~ as …「~を…として認める」、leader「先導者」、financial services「金融サービス」、industry「業界」。
> (A) 三人称単数現在形、(D) 現在完了形。どちらも後ろに目的語が必要。
> (B) 現在分詞。単独では述語動詞にならない。

106 Before meeting with the board, Mr. Ortiz practiced his ------- several times.

    (A) presentation
    (B) leader
    (C) setting
    (D) education

重役との会議の前に、Ortizさんは数回自分のプレゼンテーションの練習をしました。

    (A) プレゼンテーション
    (B) 先導者
    (C) 環境
    (D) 教育

> 正解 **A** 選択肢は全て名詞の働きを持つ語。空所には代名詞hisによって修飾され、動詞practicedの目的語となる名詞が入る。カンマの前にBefore meeting with the board「重役との会議の前に」とあるので、大事な会議の前に練習したものとして文意に合うのは、(A) presentation「プレゼンテーション」。meet with~「~と面談する、~と会談する」、board「重役、取締役会」。

TEST1 PART 5

107 The firm's ------- strategy is quite different from that of its competitors.

    (A) hired
    (B) to hire
    (C) hires
    (D) hiring

その会社の採用戦略は、競合各社のものとはかなり異なっています。

＊選択肢の訳は省略

正解 D 選択肢は全て動詞hire「～を雇う」の変化した形。文の述語動詞はis、主語はThe firm's ------- strategyで、firm'sは所有格だと判断できる。空所には後ろのstrategyと共に名詞句を作り、The firm'sに修飾される語が入る。動名詞(D) hiringを入れてhiring strategyとすれば、The firm'sと合わせて「その会社の採用戦略」となる。thatはhiring strategyを、itsはthe firm'sを指す。firm「会社」、be different from ～「～と異なる」、quite「かなり」、competitor「競合会社、競争相手」。
(A) 過去分詞。名詞を修飾できるが、文意に合わない。
(B) to不定詞。(C) 三人称単数現在形。

108 Before the cafeteria's expansion, a limited number of employees could ------- the seating area at one time.

    (A) access
    (B) accessibly
    (C) accessing
    (D) to access

カフェテリアの拡張以前は、限られた数の従業員しか座席のあるエリアを一度に利用できませんでした。

    (A) ～を利用する
    (B) 行きやすく
    (C) 利用している
    (D) ～を利用するために

正解 A 選択肢は動詞access「～を利用する」と、その変化した形や派生語。カンマ以降では空所の前に、文の主語のa limited number of employees「限られた数の従業員」と助動詞couldがあるが、動詞がない。couldに続くことができる動詞の原形の(A) accessが適切。cafeteria「セルフサービスの食堂」、expansion「拡張」、limited「限られた、わずかな」、seating「座席」、at one time「一度に」。
(B) 副詞。(C) 現在分詞。(D) to不定詞。

109 The proposal from ------- development team was met with great enthusiasm.

    (A) us
    (B) we
    (C) ours
    (D) our

われわれの開発チームからの提案は、非常に強い関心を持って迎えられました。

    (A) われわれを
    (B) われわれは
    (C) われわれのもの
    (D) われわれの

正解 D 選択肢は全て一人称複数の人称代名詞。空所の前に前置詞fromがあり、後ろにはdevelopment team「開発チーム」が続いている。これを修飾してfromの目的語となる名詞句を作る所有格の(D) our「われわれの」が適切。proposal「提案」、development「開発」、be met with ～「（提案などが）～で迎えられる」、enthusiasm「強い関心、熱狂」。
(A) 目的格。(B) 主格。(C) 所有代名詞。

110 At Triton Bank, new employees have 30 days to ------- in the company's benefits program.

    (A) credit
    (B) renew
    (C) commit
    (D) enroll

Triton銀行では、新規従業員は会社の福利厚生プログラムに登録するための期間が30日あります。

    (A) 〜を信用する
    (B) 〜を更新する
    (C) 誓約する
    (D) 登録する

正解 D 選択肢は全て動詞の働きを持つ語。主語がnew employees「新規従業員」で、その後ろにはhave 30 days to ------- in「〜に-------するための期間が30日ある」と続いている。enroll in 〜で「〜に登録する」という意味になる(D) enrollが適切。入社後に福利厚生プログラムに登録可能な期間を伝える内容となり、文意が通る。benefits「給付金、手当」。

---

111 Epiquick Production Services hired a ------- speaker to boost employee morale.

    (A) motivational
    (B) motivate
    (C) to motivate
    (D) motivates

Epiquick制作サービス社は、やる気を起こさせるような講演者を雇って従業員の士気を高めてもらいました。

    (A) やる気を起こさせる
    (B) 〜にやる気を起こさせる
    (C) 〜にやる気を起こさせるための
    (D) 〜にやる気を起こさせる

正解 A 空所の前に冠詞aがあり、後ろには名詞speaker「講演者」が続いているので、空所には名詞を修飾する語が入る。名詞の前に置くと「やる気を起こさせる」を意味する、形容詞の(A) motivationalが適切。production「制作」、hire「〜を雇う」、boost「〜を高める」、morale「士気」。
(B) 動詞「〜にやる気を起こさせる」の原形。
(C) to不定詞。
(D) 三人称単数現在形。

---

112 The branch office in Riyadh will be closed on Thursday and Friday ------- a national holiday.

    (A) at
    (B) of
    (C) for
    (D) with

リヤドにある支店は国民の祝日のため、木曜日と金曜日に休業します。

    (A) 〜に
    (B) 〜の
    (C) 〜のために
    (D) 〜で

正解 C 選択肢は全て前置詞の働きを持つ語。今度の木曜と金曜にリヤド支店が休業することを知らせる文。空所の後ろに名詞句a national holiday「国民の祝日」があり、これがリヤド支店が休業する理由だと考えられるので、理由や原因を表す(C) for「〜のために」が文意に合う。branch office「支店」。

113 Ms. Patel ------- offered to share the results of her research with the planning board.

(A) generosity
(B) most generous
(C) generously
(D) generous

Patelさんは寛大にも、自らの調査結果を計画委員会と共有することを申し出ました。

(A) 寛大さ
(B) 最も寛大な
(C) 寛大にも
(D) 寛大な

正解 C 文の主語はMs. Patel、述語動詞はofferedでその直前に空所がある。動詞offeredを修飾できる副詞の(C) generously「寛大にも」が適切。offer to do「～することを申し出る」、share ～ with …「～を…と共有する」、result「結果」、research「調査」、planning「計画立案」、board「委員会」。
(A) 名詞。
(B) 形容詞の最上級。(D) 形容詞の原級。

114 The training session will begin fifteen minutes late ------- Ms. Stumpff is still in a meeting.

(A) as
(B) then
(C) or
(D) but

Stumpffさんがまだ会議中のため、研修会は15分遅れで開始します。

(A) ～なので
(B) そのとき
(C) あるいは
(D) しかし

正解 A 空所の前後は共に〈主語＋動詞〉の形を含む文なので、空所には両方の文をつなぐ接続詞が入る。空所の後ろは「Stumpffさんがまだ会議中である」という意味で、空所の前のThe training session will begin fifteen minutes late「研修会は15分遅れで開始する」の理由となる。理由や原因を表す(A) as「～なので」が適切。training session「研修会」。
(B) 副詞。
(C) 選択を示す接続詞、(D) 逆接を表す接続詞。どちらも文意に合わない。

115 Skyspan Airlines compensated passengers whose flights ------- due to crew shortage.

(A) cancel
(B) to be canceled
(C) were canceled
(D) canceling

Skyspan航空会社は、乗務員不足のためにキャンセルされた便の乗客に補償しました。

＊選択肢の訳は省略

正解 C 動詞cancel「～をキャンセルする」の適切な形を選ぶ。whose以降の関係代名詞節には、他動詞cancelの目的語がなく、節の主語flights「便」はキャンセルされる対象なので、受動態となる。キャンセルは過去の事象であることから、過去形の(C) were canceledが適切。airline「航空会社」、compensate「～に補償する」、passenger「乗客」、flight「（航空機の）便、フライト」、due to ～「～のために」、crew「乗務員」、shortage「不足」。
(A) 原形。(B) to不定詞の受動態。「キャンセルされる予定の」という未来の意味になり、不適切。(D) 現在分詞。

116 Over the past six months, there has been a tremendous ------- for Hudson's motorized bicycles.

(A) amount
(B) demand
(C) speed
(D) service

過去6カ月にわたって、Hudson社のモーター付き自転車にはとてつもない需要がありました。

(A) 量
(B) 需要
(C) 速度
(D) サービス

正解 **B** 選択肢は全て名詞の働きを持つ語。カンマの後ろは「Hudson社のモーター付き自転車にはとてつもない-------があった」という意味。Over the past six months「過去6カ月にわたって」と期間が示されているので、その期間中に製品に対し継続して存在したものとして文意に合うのは (B) demand「需要」。tremendous「とてつもない、莫大な」、motorized「モーター付きの」。

117 The marketing director is ------- in the latest Web site design than in the previous ones.

(A) more interested
(B) most interested
(C) too interested
(D) interested

マーケティング部長は、以前のウェブサイトのデザインよりも最新のものに興味を持っています。

(A) より興味を持った
(B) 最も興味を持った
(C) 興味を持ち過ぎた
(D) 興味を持った

正解 **A** 文末に than in the previous ones「以前のものよりも」とあり、ウェブサイトの最新のデザインを以前のものと比較しているので、比較級の (A) more interested が適切。文末の ones は、Web site designs を指している。be interested in ～「～に興味を持っている」。marketing「マーケティング(の)」、director「責任者」、latest「最新の」、previous「以前の」。
(B) 形容詞の最上級。

118 November's sales figures were ------- high given the poor weather conditions during that month.

(A) primarily
(B) surprisingly
(C) separately
(D) accurately

11月の売上高は、同月中の悪天候を考えれば驚くほど高いものでした。

(A) 主に
(B) 驚くほど
(C) 別々に
(D) 正確に

正解 **B** 選択肢は全て副詞。空所の後ろは given ～「～を考えれば」の形で前提条件を示し、「同月中の悪天候を考えれば」と条件が良くなかったことを表している。一方、文頭から空所の後ろの high までは、「11月の売上高は高かった」と好結果を伝えている。空所は形容詞 high を修飾する副詞なので、文意に合うのは意外性を表す (B) surprisingly「驚くほど」。sales figures「売上高」、poor「(天候が)悪い、不順の」、weather conditions「天候状況」。

119 Camico Broadband Services earned excellent ratings for ------- on the latest consumer survey.

(A) reliable
(B) reliability
(C) reliably
(D) rely

Camicoブロードバンド・サービス社は最新の消費者調査で、信頼性について素晴らしい評価を得ました。

(A) 信頼できる
(B) 信頼性
(C) 信頼すべき筋から
(D) 信頼する

> 正解 **B** 　空所の前に前置詞forがあり、後ろは前置詞句on the latest consumer survey「最新の消費者調査で」が続いているので、空所には名詞が入る。(B) reliability「信頼性」が適切。broadband「ブロードバンド(の)」、earn「～を得る」、excellent「素晴らしい」、rating「評価」、latest「最新の」、consumer survey「消費者調査」。
> (A) 形容詞。後ろに名詞が必要。(C) 副詞。
> (D) 動詞「信頼する」の原形。rely on ～で「～を頼りにする」だが、原形ではforに続けることはできない。

---

120 ------- volunteered to complete the report, so Ms. Hughes assigned it to Mr. Nakamura.

(A) Have not
(B) Having nobody
(C) No one
(D) No

誰も、その報告書を完成させようと進んで申し出なかったので、HughesさんはそれをNakamuraさんに割り当てました。

＊選択肢の訳は省略

> 正解 **C** 　カンマの後ろに結果を表す接続詞so「そのため」があるので、カンマ前後は共に〈主語＋動詞〉の形を含み、因果関係を表す文と考えられる。空所直後は述語動詞volunteeredで、カンマまでに主語がないため空所に主語が必要。不定代名詞の(C) No one「誰も～ない」が文意にも合い適切。volunteer to do「～しようと進んで申し出る」、complete「～を完成させる」、assign ～ to …「～を…に割り当てる」。
> (B) 後ろに2つの文をつなぐ接続詞soがあるので、カンマの前は分詞構文にはならない。
> (D) 形容詞で「1人も～ない」という意味にするには、後ろに名詞が必要。

---

121 ------- the guidance of a talented coach, Belfast's chess team has made great progress.

(A) Under
(B) Along
(C) Toward
(D) Among

才能のあるコーチの指導の下、ベルファストのチェスチームは大きな進歩を遂げました。

(A) ～の下に
(B) ～に沿って
(C) ～に向かって
(D) ～の間で

> 正解 **A** 　選択肢は全て前置詞の働きを持つ語。空所の後ろからカンマまでのthe guidance of a talented coach「才能のあるコーチの指導」を目的語として続けて適切なのは、under the guidance of ～で「～の指導の下に」という意味になる(A) Under。カンマの後ろの「ベルファストのチェスチームは大きな進歩を遂げた」という文意にも合う。guidance「指導」、talented「才能のある」、make progress「進歩する」。

122 Mr. Lukas e-mailed his staff to ask whether ------- would be available to cover the front desk from noon to 1 P.M.

(A) other
(B) himself
(C) few
(D) anyone

誰か正午から午後 1 時まで受付を担当することができるかどうか尋ねるため、Lukas さんは自身のスタッフに E メールを送りました。

(A) 他の人
(B) 彼自身
(C) 少数（ほとんど〜ない）
(D) 誰か

正解 **D** 　選択肢は全て代名詞の働きを持つ語。whether から文末までは動詞 ask の目的語となる名詞節だが、節内には主語がないので空所に必要。(D) anyone「誰か」を入れると、whether 節は「誰か正午から午後 1 時まで受付を担当することができるかどうか」となり、Lukas さんが部下であるスタッフに E メールで尋ねた内容として文意が通る。staff「スタッフ」、available to *do*「〜する都合がつく」、cover「〜（ある地域・分野）を担当する」、front desk「受付」。

---

123 Bluing, Inc., combined its two warehouses in order to ------- the efficiency of its operations.

(A) collapse
(B) maximize
(C) astonish
(D) resemble

Bluing 社は業務の効率を最大化するために、自社の 2 つの倉庫を統合しました。

(A) 〜を崩壊させる
(B) 〜を最大化する
(C) 〜を驚かせる
(D) 〜に似ている

正解 **B** 　選択肢は全て動詞の働きを持つ語。空所とその直前は目的を表す in order to ------- 「------- するために」で、その前に「Bluing 社は自社の 2 つの倉庫を統合した」とあるので、空所以降では倉庫を統合した目的が述べられていると考えられる。(B) maximize「〜を最大化する」を入れると、in 以降が「同社の業務の効率を最大化するために」となり、文意が通る。Inc. は incorporated の略で「〜社」を表す。combine「〜を統合する」、warehouse「倉庫」、in order to *do*「〜するために」、efficiency「効率」、operation「業務」。

---

124 ------- he is scheduled for a promotion, Anton Shaqua plans to leave the law firm soon.

(A) Although
(B) Prior to
(C) From
(D) Perhaps

昇進が予定されているにもかかわらず、Anton Shaqua は間もなく、その法律事務所を辞めるつもりです。

(A) 〜にもかかわらず
(B) 〜の前に
(C) 〜から
(D) もしかすると

正解 **A** 　カンマの前後は共に〈主語＋動詞〉の形を含む文なので、空所には両方の文をつなぐ接続詞が入る。空所直後の he は後ろの Anton Shaqua を指し、カンマの前の「彼は昇進が予定されている」に対し、後ろは「Anton Shaqua はその法律事務所を辞めるつもりだ」と意味が転じている。接続詞の (A) Although「〜にもかかわらず」が文意に合い適切。be scheduled for 〜「〜が予定されている」、promotion「昇進」、plan to *do*「〜するつもりである」、law firm「法律事務所」。
(B) 前置詞句、(C) 前置詞。どちらも節は続かない。
(D) 副詞。文を修飾できるが、2 つの文をつなぐことはできない。

125 Margolex' survey results were ------- analyzed using state-of-the-art software.

(A) brightly
(B) thickly
(C) boastfully
(D) effortlessly

Margolex社の調査結果は、最先端のソフトウエアを使用して難なく分析されました。

(A) 賢く
(B) 厚く
(C) 自慢そうに
(D) 難なく

正解 **D** 選択肢は全て副詞。空所の前後にある述語動詞 were analyzedを修飾するのに適切な語を選ぶ。文末でusing state-of-the-art software「最先端のソフトウエアを使用して」と手段を述べているので、(D) effortlessly「難なく」を入れると、最新のソフトウエアによって調査結果が難なく分析された、となり文意が通る。survey「調査」、result「結果」、analyze「〜を分析する」、state-of-the-art「最先端の」。

126 ------- Zamlo toys are sold primarily in Australia, they are manufactured in Malaysia.

(A) Despite
(B) Even
(C) While
(D) That

Zamlo社の玩具は主にオーストラリアで販売されていますが、それらはマレーシアで製造されています。

(A) 〜にもかかわらず
(B) 〜でさえ
(C) 〜ではあるが
(D) 〜ということ

正解 **C** カンマの後ろが主節で、空所を含むカンマまでが主節を修飾する副詞節になっていると考えられる。譲歩や対比を表す接続詞(C) While「〜ではあるが、〜の一方で」を入れると、販売先はオーストラリアである一方、製造はマレーシアで行われる、と玩具の主要販売先と製造元の国が異なることを述べる一文になり、文意が通る。toy「玩具」、primarily「主に」、manufacture「〜を製造する」。
(A) 前置詞。(B) 副詞。2つの節をつなぐことはできない。
(D) 接続詞。空所にThatを入れても、文が成り立たない。

127 Ms. Cho asked her secretary to compile a list of caterers ------- menus include vegetarian options.

(A) who
(B) whom
(C) whose
(D) whoever

Choさんは自分の秘書に、メニューの中にベジタリアン向けの選択肢があるケータリング業者のリストを作成するように頼みました。

(A) 〜する(人)
(B) 〜するところの(人)
(C) その〜が…する
(D) 〜する人は誰でも

正解 **C** 空所の前後は共に〈主語＋動詞〉の形を含む文なので、空所には両方の文をつなぐ関係代名詞が入る。空所の前の名詞は「人」であるcaterers。これを先行詞として受け、後ろの関係代名詞節の主語のmenusを修飾できる所有格の関係代名詞(C) whoseが適切。compile a list「リストを作る」、caterer「ケータリング業者」、include「〜を含む」、vegetarian「ベジタリアン（向けの）」、option「選択肢」。
(A)「人」を表す関係代名詞の主格または目的格。(B) 目的格。
(A) (B) 後ろの文とつながらない。
(D) 複合関係代名詞。先行詞なしで用いるので不適切。

128 The customer who called to complain had received an ------- tracking number.

(A) unheard
(B) absent
(C) inaccurate
(D) opposite

苦情を言うために電話をかけたその顧客は、不正確な追跡番号を受け取っていました。

(A) 聞こえない
(B) 不在の
(C) 不正確な
(D) 逆の

正解 C 選択肢は全て形容詞の働きを持つ語。主語はThe customerで、whoからcomplainまでの関係代名詞節がcustomerを説明している。この文の述語動詞は過去完了のhad receivedなので、顧客は苦情の電話をかける前にtracking number「追跡番号」を受け取っていたと分かる。空所に(C) inaccurate「不正確な」を入れると、追跡番号が誤っていたことが顧客が苦情の電話をかけた理由となり、文意が通る。customer「顧客」、complain「苦情を言う」。

129 After 25 years of use, Burl Business Solutions has decided to ------- its well-known logo.

(A) approach
(B) retire
(C) reduce
(D) appoint

25年の使用の後、Burlビジネス・ソリューションズ社は、同社のよく知られたロゴの使用をやめることを決定しました。

(A) ～に近づく
(B) ～を使うのをやめる
(C) ～を減らす
(D) ～を任命する

正解 B 選択肢は全て動詞の働きを持つ語。文頭から空所までの部分は、「25年の使用の後、Burlビジネス・ソリューションズ社は、-------すると決定した」という意味。空所の後ろのits well-known logo「同社のよく知られたロゴ」を目的語として続けて文意に合うのは、(B) retire「～を使うのをやめる、～を引退させる」。use「使用」、well-known「よく知られた、なじみ深い」、logo「ロゴ」。

130 Any ------- to the company's work-from-home policy must be approved by the Human Resources Department.

(A) inspection
(B) exception
(C) acquisition
(D) correlation

会社の在宅勤務方針に対するいかなる例外も、人事部による許可を受ける必要があります。

(A) 点検
(B) 例外
(C) 獲得
(D) 相関関係

正解 B 選択肢は全て名詞。must be approved by the Human Resources Departmentは、「人事部による許可を受ける必要がある」という意味。Any ------- to the company's work-from-home policyが文の主語。在宅勤務方針に関連し、人事部による許可を得なければならないものとして文意に合うのは(B) exception「例外」。work-from-home「在宅勤務の」、policy「方針」、approve「～を許可する」、Human Resources Department「人事部」。
(C) acquisition to ～で「～への追加物」の意味。文意に合わない。

PART 6

Questions 131-134 refer to the following instructions.

Residential Garbage and Recycling Disposal

❶ Garbage and recycling are picked up on ------- days, depending on your address. Check our
131.
Web site to find your designated pickup day. All residents receive a large blue container for

regular household garbage and a large green container for material to be recycled. -------. For
132.
recyclables, do not include plastic bags. ------- may get caught in the sorting machinery at the
133.
processing plant. Please also try to reduce the number of items you throw away. -------, old
134.
furniture or clothing that is still usable can be donated to one of our many local charity

organizations or secondhand shops.

問題131-134は次の指示書に関するものです。

一般家庭ごみとリサイクル資源の処分

ごみとリサイクル資源はお住まいの住所に応じて、異なる曜日に収集されます。指定収集日を知るには、当方のウェブサイトをご確認ください。全住民の方が、通常の家庭ごみ用の青色の大型容器と、リサイクルされる資材用の緑色の大型容器を1つ受け取ります。*それらは最初は無料ですが、取替品には料金がかかります。リサイクル可能な資源にはビニール袋を含めないでください。これらは処理工場の分別装置に挟まってしまうことがあります。また、捨てる物の数を減らすよう努めてください。例えば、まだ使える古い家具や衣類は、当地域に数多くある慈善団体もしくはリサイクルショップの1つに寄付することが可能です。

*問題132の挿入文の訳

131

(A) strict
(B) different
(C) recent
(D) direct

(A) 厳格な
(B) 異なる
(C) 最近の
(D) 直接的な

正解 **B** 選択肢は全て形容詞の働きを持つ語。空所を含む文は「ごみとリサイクル資源はあなたの住所に応じて、------日に収集される」という意味で、空所に入る語は後ろの名詞daysを修飾している。直後の文でCheck our Web site to find your designated pickup day.「あなたの指定収集日を知るには、当方のウェブサイトを確認してください」と読み手の地区の指定収集日を確かめる方法が説明されている。空所に(B) different「異なる」を入れて、ごみの収集が行われる曜日が住所によって違うことを知らせる内容にすると文意が通る。

132

(A) If there are any problems with the payment, you will be notified.
(B) The calendar is updated regularly.
(C) They are free initially, but there is a fee for replacements.
(D) By all accounts, the program was a success.

(A) 支払いに関して問題があった場合には、お知らせします。
(B) 予定表は定期的に更新されます。
(C) それらは最初は無料ですが、取替品には料金がかかります。
(D) 誰に聞いても、プログラムは成功でした。

正解 **C** 見出しと❶1～2行目より、この指示書は一般家庭ごみとリサイクル資源の処分に関する方針を説明したものだと分かる。空所直前の文では、通常の家庭ごみ用の青色の大型容器と、リサイクル資材用の緑色の大型容器が1つずつ全住民に配布されると述べられている。(C)を入れるとTheyが配布される2つの容器を指し、住民は初回は容器を無料で受け取れるが、取替品を求める場合には料金が発生するという留意点が続くこととなり、流れとして自然。free「無料の」、initially「最初は」、fee「料金」、replacement「取替品」。
(A) payment「支払い」、notify「～に知らせる」。
(B) calendar「予定表」、update「～を更新する」、regularly「定期的に」。
(D) by all accounts「誰に聞いても」、success「成功」。

133

(A) What
(B) These
(C) Theirs
(D) Either

(A) ～すること
(B) これら
(C) それらのもの
(D) どちらか

正解 **B** 空所を含む文は「------は処理工場の分別装置に挟まってしまうことがある」という意味で、空所が文の主語になっている。空所直前ではFor recyclables, do not include plastic bags.「リサイクル可能な資源にはビニール袋を含めないでください」と述べられているので、名詞の複数形のplastic bagsを指すことのできる(B) These「これら」を入れると、ビニール袋をリサイクル可能な資源に含めてはいけない理由を示す文になり適切。
(A) 先行詞を含む関係代名詞。
(C) 所有代名詞。
(D) 代名詞。

134

(A) Otherwise
(B) Nevertheless
(C) Instead
(D) For example

(A) さもなければ
(B) それにもかかわらず
(C) その代わりに
(D) 例えば

正解 **D** 空所直前の文では、捨てるごみの数を減らすよう呼びかけており、空所の後ろでは「まだ使える古い家具や衣類は、当地域に数多くある慈善団体もしくはリサイクルショップの1つに寄付することが可能だ」と、ごみを減らす具体的な方策の一例を述べているので、具体例を挙げる時に使う(D) For exampleが適切。
(A) (B) (C) 前後の話の内容が論理的につながらない。

Questions 135-138 refer to the following e-mail.

To: <hiddenlist>
From: events@estoncity.gov
Date: July 1
Subject: Scavenger hunt

Dear Residents,

❶ This year's Eston City Scavenger Hunt (ECSH) is coming soon! Now in its seventh year, the ECSH has become a ------- for local residents. Gather clues, solve challenges, and uncover
135.
hidden details about historical sites throughout the city.

❷ The ECSH starts in Founders Park at 10:00 A.M. on July 20. ------- takes two to four hours to
136.
complete, and a smartphone is required. -------. All of the sites are within walking distance of
137.
the park. -------, join your neighbors to celebrate with refreshments and music in the park.
138.
Register online at www.estoncity.gov/ecsh by July 18 or in person on the day of the event.

❸ We hope to see you there!

Eston City Events Office

問題135-138は次のEメールに関するものです。

受信者：＜非公開リスト＞
送信者：events@estoncity.gov
日付：7月1日
件名：スカベンジャー・ハント

住民の皆さま

今年のエストン市スカベンジャー・ハント（ECSH）が間もなくやって来ます！ 今や7年目を迎えたECSHは、地元住民にとって慣例となっています。手掛かりを集めて難問を解き、当市の至る所にある史跡に関する隠された詳細な事実を見つけ出してください。

ECSHは7月20日午前10時に、Founders公園で始まります。終えるのに2時間から4時間かかり、スマートフォン1台が必要です。＊チームにつき1台のみ端末が必要です。史跡は全て同公園の徒歩圏内にあります。その後は、公園内で近隣住民の方々と一緒に軽食と音楽で盛り上がってください。7月18日までにwww.estoncity.gov/ecshにてオンラインで、あるいはイベント当日に直接、登録してください。

現地で皆さんにお会いできることを願っております。

エストン市イベント局

＊問題137の挿入文の訳

135 (A) tradition
(B) traditional
(C) traditions
(D) traditionally

(A) 慣例
(B) 慣例となった
(C) 慣例
(D) 慣例的に

正解 **A** 空所の前に冠詞aがあり、後ろには前置詞句for local residents「地元住民にとって」が続いているので、空所には名詞の単数形が入る。よって、(A) tradition「慣例、伝統」が適切。
(B) 形容詞。冠詞aに続けることはできるが、後ろに名詞の単数形が必要。
(C) 名詞の複数形。空所の前にaがあるので複数形は不適切。
(D) 副詞。後ろに動詞などの修飾されるものがないので不適切。

---

136 (A) Another
(B) Each
(C) Mine
(D) It

(A) もう1つ
(B) それぞれ
(C) 私のもの
(D) （形式主語）

正解 **D** このEメールはECSHというイベントの概要を説明して、その参加を促すもの。空所の前ではイベントの開始日時が示されており、後ろにはtakes two to four hours to complete「終えるのに2時間から4時間かかる」とある。空所に(D) Itを入れて、It takes ～ to doという所要時間を表す文にすると、文意が通る。it takes ～ to do「…するのに（時間が）～かかる」。

---

137 (A) The park map is very detailed.
(B) City hall was built 75 years ago.
(C) You will need only one device per team.
(D) Feedback from participants would be helpful.

(A) 公園の地図は非常に詳細なものです。
(B) 市役所は75年前に建てられました。
(C) チームにつき1台のみ端末が必要です。
(D) 参加者からの感想は役立つでしょう。

正解 **C** 空所の直前の文では、イベントへの参加条件としてスマートフォンが1台必要だと述べられている。(C)を空所に入れると、one deviceが前文にあるa smartphoneを指し、必要なスマートフォンの台数はチーム単位で1台だけだと補足する内容になるので、流れとして自然。device「端末」、per「～につき」。
(A) detailed「詳細な」。
(B) city hall「市役所」。
(D) feedback「感想、フィードバック」、participant「参加者」、helpful「役立つ」。

---

138 (A) Afterward
(B) However
(C) Similarly
(D) Rather

(A) その後で
(B) しかしながら
(C) 同様に
(D) むしろ

正解 **A** 選択肢は全て副詞の働きを持つ語。空所の前では、イベントの概要とその開始から終了までの一連の流れが説明されており、後ろには「公園内で近隣住民の方々と一緒に軽食と音楽で盛り上がってください」と続いている。よって、空所を含む文ではイベント終了後の催しについて知らせていると考えられるので、(A) Afterward「その後で」が適切。
(B) (C) (D) 前後の話の内容が論理的につながらない。

Words & Phrases

scavenger hunt　スカベンジャー・ハント　★指定されたさまざまな物を見つけてくるゲーム　　resident　住民
❶ local　地元の　　gather　～を集める　　clue　手掛かり　　solve　～を解く　　challenge　難問　　uncover　～を発見する
hidden　隠された　　details　詳細、詳しい情報　　historical　歴史に関する　　site　跡、場所　　throughout　～の至る所に
❷ complete　（を）終える　　require　～を必要とする　　within walking distance of ～　～の徒歩圏内で　　join　～に加わる
neighbor　近隣住民　　celebrate　祝杯を挙げる、陽気に騒ぐ　　refreshments　軽食　　register　登録する
online　オンラインで　　in person　直接、自分で

Expressions

～ be coming soon　「～が間もなくやって来る」（❶ 1行目）
　It seems the rainy season is coming soon to this region.
　この地域に間もなく雨季が来るようです。

Questions 139-142 refer to the following letter.

Matisson Tire Supply
37 Fieldcrest Pike
Milwaukee, WI 53205

January 15

Dear Valued Customer,

① You may have heard recent news reports about a ------- of the raw materials needed to make
139.

our products. -------, we purchase our materials three months in advance and will not need to
140.

increase our prices at this time. However, given the increase in our costs, we anticipate a

slight price increase of 5 percent beginning on May 1. -------.
141.

② We ------- your business and look forward to your continued patronage. If you have any
142.

questions or concerns, please feel free to contact me.

③ Sincerely,

Hugh Toussaint
Wholesale Manager, Matisson Tire Supply

問題139-142は次の手紙に関するものです。

Matisson タイヤ供給会社
フィールドクレスト通り37番地
ミルウォーキー、WI 53205

1月15日

大切な顧客の皆さま

当社の製品作りに必要な原材料の不足に関する最近のニュース報道はお聞きになっているかもしれません。幸いなことに、当社は原料を3カ月前に購入いたしますので、現時点では値上げを行う必要はございません。しかしながら、原価の上昇を考慮して、5月1日より5パーセントのわずかな値上げを見越しております。*状況が変わった場合は、お客さまにお知らせします。

当社はお客さまからのお引き立てを大切にしており、引き続きのご愛顧をお待ち申し上げます。ご質問やご懸念がございましたら、どうぞご遠慮なく私にご連絡ください。

敬具

Hugh Toussaint
卸売マネージャー、Matisson タイヤ供給会社

*問題141の挿入文の訳

139
(A) short
(B) shortage
(C) shortly
(D) shortening

(A) 短い
(B) 不足
(C) 間もなく
(D) 短縮

正解 B 空所の前に冠詞aがあり、後ろに前置詞句of the raw materials「原材料の」が続いているので、名詞が入る。(B) shortage「不足」を入れて原材料不足について言及する文にすると、❶3行目のHoweverで始まる文で値上げを見越していることを知らせる流れにも合う。
(A) 形容詞。同形の名詞「短編映画、(電気の)ショート」は、文意に合わない。
(C) 副詞。冠詞aに続けることはできない。
(D) 名詞。文意に合わない。

140
(A) Unexpectedly
(B) Besides
(C) Fortunately
(D) Likewise

(A) 意外なことに
(B) その上
(C) 幸いなことに
(D) 同様に

正解 C 選択肢は全て副詞の働きを持つ語。空所直前の文では、製品作りに必要な原材料の不足という不安要因に言及がある一方、空所の後ろではwe purchase our materials three months in advance and will not need to increase our prices at this time「当社は原料を3カ月前に購入するので、現時点では値上げを行う必要はない」と即座の値上げを否定する説明が続いている。よって、不利な状況に反することを表す(C) Fortunately「幸いなことに」が適切。
(A) (B) (D) 前後の話の内容が論理的につながらない。

141
(A) These materials are sourced underground.
(B) We will let you know if the situation changes.
(C) We guarantee all of our tires for one year.
(D) Our products are the best on the market.

(A) これらの原料は地中から取れます。
(B) 状況が変わった場合は、お客さまにお知らせします。
(C) 当社は全てのタイヤを1年間保証いたします。
(D) 当社製品は市場に出ている中で最良のものです。

正解 B この手紙はMatissonタイヤ供給会社が、顧客に対し製品価格について知らせるもの。空所の2つ前の文で目下値上げの必要はないと現状を説明した後、続く空所直前の文では、5月1日から製品を5パーセント値上げするという今後の予定が述べられている。よって、この予定の状況が変わった場合について言及している(B)を入れると、流れとして自然。
(A) source「～を(ある供給源から)手に入れる」、underground「地下で」。
(C) guarantee「～を保証する」。
(D) on the market「市場に出て」。

142
(A) values
(B) valuation
(C) valuing
(D) value

(A) ～を評価する
(B) 評価
(C) ～を評価している
(D) ～を評価する

正解 D 選択肢は動詞value「～を評価する、～を大切にする」とその変化した形や派生語。空所には、文の主語であるWeに続き、後ろのyour business「あなたの引き立て」を目的語に取る動詞が必要。よって、動詞の(D) valueが適切。この文はWeを主語として、value your businessとlook forward to your continued patronageが、接続詞andを挟んで並列されている。
(A) 動詞の三人称単数現在形。主語が一人称複数を表すWeなので、不適切。
(B) 名詞。
(C) 現在分詞。単独では述語動詞にならないので不適切。

Words & Phrases

tire タイヤ　supply 供給　value ～を大切にする、～を重んじる　❶ recent 最近の　report 報道
raw material 原材料　product 製品　purchase ～を購入する　material 原料　in advance 前もって
increase ～を増やす　at this time 現時点では　given ～を考慮すれば　increase 上昇、増加　cost 原価、費用
anticipate ～を見越す、～を予期する　slight わずかな　❷ business 商取引、引き立て
look forward to ～ ～を心待ちにする　continued 継続した　patronage 愛顧　concern 懸念
contact ～に連絡する　❸ wholesale 卸売

Expressions

feel free to *do* 「遠慮なく～する、気軽に～する」(❷ 2行目)

Please feel free to visit us if you come to Japan.
もし日本に来られることがありましたら、どうぞお気軽に私たちをお訪ねください。

Questions 143-146 refer to the following article.

❶ Heswall Natural Foods (HNF), a Liverpool-based food retailer, announced yesterday that it has appointed Sven Larsen as vice president. ------- **143.**. Larsen has twenty years of experience in the food industry and will be ------- **144.** for the company's York facility. He will report directly to CEO Wilma Collins. "We are delighted to welcome Mr. Larsen to head our York operations," said Collins. "His ------- **145.** in the natural and organic food business is legendary."

❷ Prior to accepting the position at HNF, Larsen worked for Simcox Foods, where he rose through the ranks to become senior director of marketing. ------- **146.** working at Simcox, Larsen designed magazine advertisements for the food industry.

問題143-146は次の記事に関するものです。

リバプールに拠点を置く食品小売業のHeswall自然食品社（HNF）は昨日、Sven Larsenを副社長に任命したと発表した。*彼は、退職するJudith Middletonの後任となる。Larsenは食品業界で20年の経験があり、同社のヨークにある施設の責任を担うことになる。彼は、最高経営責任者のWilma Collinsに直属する。「私たちは喜んで、Larsen氏を当社のヨーク事業統括者に迎えます」とCollinsは述べた。「自然食品・有機農産物事業における彼の統率力は非常に有名です」。

HNF社での職を受諾する前、LarsenはSimcox食品社に勤務しており、そこで彼は出世街道を歩んでマーケティング担当取締役になった。Simcox社に勤める以前は、Larsenは食品業界の雑誌広告を企画していた。

*問題143の挿入文の訳

143
(A) He is replacing Judith Middleton, who is retiring.
(B) HNF entered the Canadian market last year.
(C) Simcox Foods is engaged in merger talks with a former competitor.
(D) Collins has been CEO for more than a decade.

(A) 彼は、退職する Judith Middleton の後任となる。
(B) HNF 社は昨年、カナダ市場に参入した。
(C) Simcox 食品社は、かつての競合社との合併協議に取り組んでいる。
(D) Collins は 10 年以上、最高経営責任者を務めている。

正解 A 空所の直前の文で、Sven Larsen という人物が HNF 社副社長に任命されたことが伝えられ、直後の文では、同氏の経歴と副社長就任後の職務内容が述べられている。誰の後任となるか説明している (A) を空所に入れると、He が Larsen さんを指すことになり、HNF 社の新しい副社長の決定を知らせる記事として自然な流れになる。replace「～の後任となる、～に取って代わる」、retire「退職する」。
(B) enter the market「市場に参入する」。
(C) be engaged in ～「～に携わっている」、merger「合併」、talks「協議、会談」、former「かつての、以前の」、competitor「競合会社」。
(D) 最高経営責任者である Collins さんについては、この 2 つ後の文で初めて言及しており、空所前後は Larsen さんに関する説明なので、文脈に合わない。decade「10 年」。

144
(A) responsibility
(B) responsibly
(C) responsibleness
(D) responsible

(A) 責任
(B) 責任を持って
(C) 責任があること
(D) 責任がある

正解 D 選択肢は全て形容詞 responsible「責任がある」の派生語。空所を含む文の文頭から and までは、Larsen さんのこれまでの経験を述べている。続く and 以降では、Larsen さんについて未来を表す文で will be ------- for the company's York facility.「Larsen は同社のヨークにある施設の ------- になる」と述べているので、空所は Larsen さんの今後の職務に関する説明をしていると考えられる。be responsible for ～で「～に監督責任のある」という意味になる、形容詞の (D) responsible が適切。
(A) (C) 名詞。文意に合わない。
(B) 副詞。

145
(A) purpose
(B) observation
(C) leadership
(D) calculation

(A) 目的
(B) 観察
(C) 統率力
(D) 計算

正解 C 選択肢は全て名詞。空所を含む文は、「自然食品・有機農産物事業における彼の ------- は非常に有名だ」という意味で、直前の「私たちは喜んで、Larsen 氏を当社のヨーク事業統括者に迎える」という、最高経営責任者の Collins さんによる発言の続きである。(C) leadership「統率力」を入れると、Larsen さんを副社長に任命してヨーク事業統括者に迎え入れる根拠としてふさわしく、適切。

146
(A) Until
(B) Without
(C) Near
(D) Before

(A) ～まで
(B) ～なしに
(C) ～の近くで
(D) ～以前は

正解 D 選択肢は全て前置詞の働きを持つ語。空所を含む文は、「Simcox 社に勤める -------、Larsen は食品業界の雑誌広告を企画していた」という Larsen さんの経歴について述べているもの。❷ 1 行目にも「HNF 社での職を受諾する前、Larsen は Simcox 食品社に勤務していた」とあり、これは Larsen さんの直近の経歴を述べたものなので、空所を含む文で述べられている雑誌広告の企画の仕事は、Larsen さんがそれ以前に携わっていたものだと考えられる。(D) Before「～以前は」が適切。

PART 7

Questions 147-148 refer to the following sign.

Attention All Zandpro Technology Employees and Visitors

1 Welcome to our Product Innovation Factory.

2 • To safeguard our designs, no cameras or audio- and video-recording devices are permitted on the factory floor.

3 • Please leave all such devices, including mobile phones, in the safe in room 332.

問題147-148は次の掲示に関するものです。

Zandpro テクノロジー社の従業員および来訪者の皆さまへのお知らせ

当社の製品イノベーション工場へようこそ。

・当社の製品設計を保護するため、作業現場へのカメラや録音・録画機器類の持ち込みは認められておりません。

・携帯電話を含め、そのような機器類は全て332号室の金庫に預けていただくようお願いいたします。

147 According to the sign, why most likely are recording devices prohibited on the factory floor?

(A) To ensure privacy for factory floor workers
(B) To minimize distractions for factory floor workers
(C) To avoid interference with assembly line equipment
(D) To protect unreleased product information

掲示によると、記録機器類はなぜ作業現場で禁止されていると考えられますか。

(A) 作業現場の労働者のプライバシーを確保するため
(B) 作業現場の労働者の注意をそらす要因を最小限にするため
(C) 組み立てライン装置への電波障害を防ぐため
(D) 未発表の製品情報を保護するため

> **正解 D** ❷に To safeguard our designs, no cameras or audio- and video-recording devices are permitted on the factory floor.「当社の製品設計を保護するため、作業現場へのカメラや録音・録画機器類の持ち込みは認められていない」とある。よって、会社が発表前の製品情報を保護するために、作業現場への記録機器類の持ち込みを禁止していると考えられるので、(D)が正解。prohibit「～を禁止する」。protect「～を保護する」、unreleased「未発表の、未発売の」。
> (A) ensure「～を確保する」、privacy「プライバシー」。
> (B) minimize「～を最小限にする」、distraction「注意をそらすもの」。
> (C) avoid「～を防ぐ」、interference「障害、妨害」、assembly line「組み立てライン」、equipment「装置、機器」。

---

148 What is suggested about room 332?

(A) It has no Internet access.
(B) It contains a secure storage location.
(C) It is available to employees only.
(D) It is used for large meetings.

332号室について何が分かりますか。

(A) その部屋ではインターネットに接続できない。
(B) その部屋には安全な保管場所がある。
(C) その部屋は従業員だけが利用できる。
(D) その部屋は大規模な会議に使用される。

> **正解 B** ❸で、カメラや録音・録画機器類について、Please leave all such devices, including mobile phones, in the safe in room 332.「携帯電話を含め、そのような機器類は全て 332 号室の金庫に預けてください」と依頼している。よって、332 号室には記録機器類を保管できる場所があると分かるので、(B)が正解。(B)では、the safe を a secure storage location と表している。contain「～を含む」、secure「安全な」、storage「保管」、location「場所」。
> (A) インターネットの接続状況については述べられていない。access「接続、アクセス」。
> (C) 見出しから、この掲示は従業員と来訪者の両方に向けられたものだと分かるので、332 号室は従業員専用の部屋ではない。available「利用可能な」。
> (D) 332号室が会議で使用されるとは述べられていない。

Expressions

be permitted 「認められている、許可されている」（❷2行目）
Smoking is not permitted on the premises of this factory.
喫煙は、この工場の敷地内では許可されていません。

Questions 149-150 refer to the following form.

Arstonia, Inc.
ID Request Form

① Please complete the top portion of this form and bring it with you on your first day of work. You will be escorted to Corporate Security, where you will submit the form and obtain your employee identification badge.

② Name: **Martin McGuigan**

Department: **Research & Development**

Supervisor: **Lakeisha Washington**

License plate: **G98 MDL**

Badge number: **59756**

Date of hire: **June 1**

- -

③ Approved by: Nancy Arusyak　　　　Date: June 1

問題149-150は次の用紙に関するものです。

Arstonia社
ID申請用紙

本用紙の上部に全て記入し、出勤初日にご持参ください。あなたは保安部に案内され、そこでこの用紙を提出して、ご自身の従業員用IDバッジを受け取ることになっています。

氏名：Martin McGuigan
部署：研究開発部
上司：Lakeisha Washington
ナンバープレート：G98 MDL
バッジ番号：59756
雇用日：6月1日

- -

承認者：Nancy Arusyak　　　　　　　　日付：6月1日

149 What does the form indicate about Mr. McGuigan?　用紙はMcGuiganさんについて何を示していますか。

(A) He reports to Ms. Washington.　(A) 彼はWashingtonさんの部下である。
(B) He comes to work by bus.　(B) 彼はバスで通勤する。
(C) He started a special project in June.　(C) 彼は6月に特別なプロジェクトを開始した。
(D) He has worked at Arstonia for many years.　(D) 彼は長年の間Arstonia社で働いている。

正解 A　見出しと❶より、この用紙は新入社員が従業員用IDバッジを受け取るための申請用紙だと分かる。❷1行目のName「氏名」欄にMcGuiganさんの名前があり、同3行目のSupervisor「上司」の欄にWashingtonさんの名前が記入されているので、McGuiganさんはこの用紙の申請者で、Washingtonさんがその上司だと分かる。つまりMcGuiganさんはWashingtonさんに直属する部下なので、(A)が正解。report to ～「～の部下である、～の監督下にある」。
(B) ❷4行目にMcGuiganさんの自動車ナンバーの記載があるが、通勤手段については言及がない。
(C) ❷6行目の「雇用日」と❸の「日付」欄に6月1日とあるが、特別なプロジェクトに関する言及はない。
(D) ❶より、この申請用紙は出勤初日に持参する必要があると分かるので、McGuiganさんは入社したばかりだと考えられる。

150 What department will most likely process the form?　どの部署がこの用紙を処理すると考えられますか。

(A) Personnel　(A) 人事部
(B) Corporate Security　(B) 保安部
(C) Legal　(C) 法務部
(D) Facilities Management　(D) 設備管理部

正解 B　❶2～3行目に、You will be escorted to Corporate Security, where you will submit the form and obtain your employee identification badge.「あなたは保安部に案内され、そこでこの用紙を提出して、ご自身の従業員用IDバッジを受け取ることになっている」とあるので、この用紙を処理するのは保安部だと考えられる。よって、(B)が正解。process「～を処理する」。
(A) personnel「人事部」。
(C) legal「法務の、法律の」。
(D) facility「設備、施設」、management「管理」。

Questions 151-152 refer to the following e-mail.

From:	Customer Service <customerservice@coldmountaingear.ie>
To:	Joy Hsaio <hsaioj@zellmail.ie>
Subject:	Order number 94166
Date:	11 July

Dear Ms. Hsaio,

❶ Thank you for your order. The Xtreme Hiking Jacket in gray, women's size Medium, is currently out of stock. We expect to receive more inventory in about two weeks.

❷ To compensate you for the delay, we will send your order by overnight shipping at no extra charge as soon as it becomes available. We will inform you when processing is complete.

Yours sincerely,

Cold Mountain Gear Customer Service

問題151-152は次のEメールに関するものです。

送信者：顧客サービス部 <customerservice@coldmountaingear.ie>
受信者：Joy Hsaio <hsaioj@zellmail.ie>
件名：ご注文番号94166
日付：7月11日

Hsaio様

ご注文いただきありがとうございます。Xtremeハイキングジャケットの灰色、女性用のMサイズは、現在在庫を切らしております。当社では約2週間後に追加在庫を受け取る見込みです。

お客さまには、この遅延のおわびといたしまして、ご注文品が入荷次第、追加料金なしで翌日配送にてお送りします。処理が完了しましたら、お客さまにお知らせいたします。

敬具

Cold登山用品社　顧客サービス部

Words & Phrases

customer service 顧客サービス　　order 注文、注文品　　❶ hiking ハイキング　　jacket ジャケット、上着　　gray 灰色
medium Mサイズ、中間のもの　　currently 現在　　out of stock 在庫切れで　　receive ～を受け取る
inventory 在庫品　　❷ compensate ～ for … ～に…の償いをする　　delay 遅延　　overnight 翌日配達の
shipping 輸送　　extra 追加の　　charge 料金　　as soon as ～ ～するとすぐに　　available 入手できる、在庫の
inform ～に知らせる　　processing 処理　　complete 完了した　　gear 用具一式

151 What is indicated about Ms. Hsaio's order?

    (A) It will arrive later than expected.

    (B) It was sent to the wrong address.

    (C) It was damaged during shipping.

    (D) It is an unusual color.

Hsaioさんの注文品について何が示されていますか。

    (A) それは想定より遅れて届く。

    (B) それは間違った住所に送られた。

    (C) それは配送中に損傷した。

    (D) それは珍しい色である。

正解 A Hsaioさんの注文品について、❶1〜2行目に、「Xtremeハイキングジャケットの灰色、女性用のMサイズは、現在在庫を切らしている」とあり、続く2行目で、We expect to receive more inventory in about two weeks.「当社では約2週間後に追加在庫を受け取る見込みだ」と述べられている。つまり、Hsaioさんの元へ注文品が届くのは約2週間後以降。また、❷で商品発送の遅延に対するおわびとして配送の特別対応の申し出があることからも、注文品は想定より遅れてHsaioさんに届くと分かる。(A)が正解。

(B) wrong「間違った」。

(C) ❷1行目に翌日配送とあるが、配送中の損傷には言及していない。damage「〜に損傷を与える」。

(D) ❶1行目に注文品は灰色とあるが、珍しい色だとは述べられていない。unusual「珍しい」。

---

152 What does Cold Mountain Gear offer Ms. Hsaio?

    (A) A replacement item

    (B) A frequent-customer membership

    (C) A discount on her next order

    (D) A shipping service upgrade

Cold登山用品社はHsaioさんに何を提供しますか。

    (A) 代替品

    (B) 常連客向けの会員資格

    (C) 次回注文時の割引

    (D) 配送サービスの格上げ

正解 D Eメールの文末から、Cold登山用品社とは、このメールの送信元だと分かる。❷1〜2行目で、To compensate you for the delay, we will send your order by overnight shipping at no extra charge as soon as it becomes available.「あなたには、この遅延のおわびとして、注文品が入荷次第、追加料金なしで翌日配送にて送る」と伝えている。よって、Cold登山用品社は商品発送の遅延に対するおわびとして、通常であれば追加料金がかかる翌日配送サービスをHsaioさんに無料提供すると分かるので、(D)が正解。upgrade「ランクを上げること、サービスなどの向上」。

(A) replacement「代替（の）」、item「商品」。

(B) frequent「常連の」、membership「会員資格、会員権」。

(C) discount「割引」。

Expressions

expect to *do* 「〜する見込みである、〜する予定である」(❶2行目)
I expect to arrive at Narita Airport by five.
私は5時までに成田空港に着く見込みです。

Questions 153-154 refer to the following online chat discussion.

①	**Rex Martinez [10:16 A.M.]**	Hello, Tzu-Tsu. Could you please assist me with regard to my paycheck?
②	**Tzu-Tsu Yeh [10:18 A.M.]**	Of course. Was it scheduled to arrive before today?
③	**Rex Martinez [10:19 A.M.]**	It was supposed to—yes.
④	**Tzu-Tsu Yeh [10:20 A.M.]**	Let me check to make sure that all of your paperwork is on file.
⑤	**Tzu-Tsu Yeh [10:33 A.M.]**	The Employee Agreement was not signed by the director until yesterday even though you filled it out last week. The payment was sent out this morning and you should receive it tomorrow.
⑥	**Rex Martinez [10:34 A.M.]**	OK. Thank you very much for your help.

問題153-154は次のオンラインチャットの話し合いに関するものです。

Rex Martinez［午前10時16分］	こんにちは、Tzu-Tsuさん。私の給与支払小切手のことで助けていただけますか。
Tzu-Tsu Yeh［午前10時18分］	もちろんです。それは今日より前に届く予定だったのですか。
Rex Martinez［午前10時19分］	そのはずでした──はい。
Tzu-Tsu Yeh［午前10時20分］	あなたの事務書類が全てファイルに保管されているか確認させてください。
Tzu-Tsu Yeh［午前10時33分］	従業員契約書が昨日になってようやく部長に署名されたのですよ、あなたは先週それを記入していたのに。支払いは今朝発送されたので、あなたは明日それを受け取るはずです。
Rex Martinez［午前10時34分］	分かりました。助けていただいてどうもありがとうございました。

66

153 At 10:19 A.M., what does Mr. Martinez most likely mean when he writes, "It was supposed to"?

    (A) His paperwork should have been completed sooner.

    (B) He received a different amount of money than he agreed to.

    (C) His bank account should have been set up last week.

    (D) He expected to have already received a payment.

午前10時19分に、Martinezさんは "It was supposed to" という発言で、何を意味していると考えられますか。

    (A) 彼の事務書類はもっと早く記入完了されるべきだった。

    (B) 彼は同意していたものとは異なる額のお金を受け取った。

    (C) 彼の銀行口座は先週に開設されているはずだった。

    (D) 彼はすでに支払いを受け取っている予定であった。

正解 D ❶の給与支払小切手のことで助けてほしいというMartinezさんからの依頼に対し、Yehさんは❷で快諾し、続けてWas it scheduled to arrive before today?「それは今日より前に届く予定だったのか」と尋ねている。それに対しMartinezさんは下線部の発言をした後、yesと肯定している。itはその前の❶で述べられているmy paycheck「私の給与支払小切手」を指しているので、Martinezさんは、自分が給与支払小切手をもっと前に受け取る予定だったと伝えていると考えられる。expect to *do*「～する予定である、～する見込みである」。
(A) 事務書類への言及は下線部の発言の後なので、不適切。complete「～に全て記入する」。
(B) agree to ～「～に同意する」。
(C) bank account「銀行口座」に関する言及はない。set up ～「～を開設する」。

154 In what department does Ms. Yeh most likely work?

    (A) Sales

    (B) Advertising

    (C) Payroll

    (D) Customer Relations

Yehさんはどんな部署で働いていると考えられますか。

    (A) 営業部

    (B) 宣伝部

    (C) 給与部

    (D) 顧客窓口

正解 C Yehさんは、Martinezさんが給与支払小切手のことで手助けを求めたのに対し❷で快諾し、❹で事務書類の保管状況を確認すると申し出ている。さらに❺で、従業員契約書が昨日ようやく部長に署名された、と給与支払いの遅延理由を説明し、「支払いは今朝発送されたので、あなたは明日それを受け取るはずだ」と、Martinezさんが給与支払い小切手を受け取る予定日を伝えている。よって、Yehさんは給与支払いを担当する部署で働いていると考えられる。payroll「給与支払業務」。
(B) advertising「広告すること、広告」。
(D) customer relations「顧客窓口」。

Words & Phrases

❶ assist ～を助ける、～を手伝う   with regard to ～ ～に関して   paycheck 給与支払小切手、給与
❷ be scheduled to *do* ～する予定である   ❸ be supposed to *do* ～するはずである、～することになっている
❹ paperwork 事務書類   on file ファイルに保管されて、整理されて   ❺ employee agreement 従業員契約書
not ～ until … …になってようやく～する、…まで～ない   sign ～に署名する   director 部長
even though ～ ～ではあるが、～にもかかわらず   fill out ～ ～に記入する   payment 支払い、支払金
send out ～ ～を発送する、～を送る

Expressions

make sure (that) ～ 「～ということを確かめる」（❹）
First, please make sure that your computer is connected to the Internet.
まず、コンピューターがインターネットに接続されていることを確かめてください。

Questions 155-157 refer to the following letter.

Lavenham Management Services
5 Bennett Park
Ipswich IP1 2AL
01632 960862 (phone)
01632 960863 (fax)
info@lavenhamservices.co.uk

❶ 10 August

Ruby S. Brown
67 Cloch Road
Peterborough
PE1 1XQ

Dear Ms. Brown,

❷ We are pleased to announce the move of our headquarters. Since launching our consulting practice five years ago, we have rapidly expanded our customer base, and our staff has grown accordingly. As a result, our current facility is no longer adequate for our needs, and we have <u>spent</u> the last six months in search of a new home.

❸ Our staff will officially move to Colchester on 10 September. From that date on, please address all correspondence to our new address listed on the enclosed card. Our phone and fax numbers will also change at that time. All other contact information will stay the same. Mail sent to our Ipswich address will be forwarded for two months following the move.

❹ We look forward to serving you from our new and improved headquarters.

Sincerely,

Lavenham Management Services

Enclosure

問題155-157は次の手紙に関するものです。

Lavenhamマネジメントサービス社
ベネットパーク5番地
イプスウィッチ IP1 2AL
01632 960862（電話）
01632 960863（ファクス）
info@lavenhamservices.co.uk

8月10日

Ruby S. Brown様
クロック通り67番地
ピーターバラ
PE1 1XQ

Brown様

弊社は、謹んで私どもの本社の移転をお知らせいたします。5年前にコンサルティング業務を開始して以来、弊社は顧客基盤を急速に拡大し、スタッフもそれに応じて増加いたしました。結果として、現在の施設はもはや私どものニーズに見合わなくなっており、新しい本拠地を探してこの6カ月間を費やしてまいりました。

弊社スタッフは9月10日に正式にコルチェスターに転居いたします。その日以降、全ての郵便物は同封のカードに記載された弊社の新しい住所宛てにお出しください。私どもの電話番号とファクス番号もその際に変わります。他の全ての連絡先は同じままです。イプスウィッチの弊社の住所へ送付された郵便物は、移転後2カ月間は転送されることになっています。

快適になった新本社より、皆さまのお役に立てることを心待ちにしております。

敬具

Lavenhamマネジメントサービス社

同封物あり

155 What does the letter suggest about Lavenham's new headquarters facility?

(A) It will be in the same city as the current one.
(B) It will offer additional parking spaces for visitors.
(C) It will feature state-of-the-art technology.
(D) It will be larger than the current one.

手紙は、Lavenham社の新しい本社施設について何を示唆していますか。

(A) それは現在のものと同じ市にある。
(B) それは訪問者用に追加の駐車スペースを提供する。
(C) それは最先端技術を特長とする。
(D) それは現在のものよりも広い。

正解 D ❷1行目に本社の移転に言及があり、同1～3行目に、「5年前にコンサルティング業務を開始して以来、弊社は顧客基盤を急速に拡大し、スタッフもそれに応じて増加した」とある。続く3～4行目で「結果として、現在の施設はもはや私どものニーズに見合わなくなった」と移転理由が説明されている。

よって、新しい本社施設は現在のものより多くの人数を収容可能な、より広い所だと考えられるので、(D)が正解。
(B) additional「追加の」、parking space「駐車スペース」。
(C) feature「～を特長とする」、state-of-the-art technology「最先端技術」。

156 The word "spent" in paragraph 1, line 4, is closest in meaning to

(A) paid
(B) gone
(C) used
(D) wasted

第1段落・4行目にある "spent" に最も意味が近いのは

(A) ～を支払った
(B) 行った
(C) ～を使った
(D) ～を無駄にした

正解 C ❷1～4行目で、会社の顧客基盤の拡大に伴いスタッフが増加したため、現施設がもはやニーズに合わなくなったことが述べられている。それに続く該当の語を含む文は、「弊社は新しい本拠地を探してこの6カ月間を-------」という意味の現在完了形の文。spentは新施設を探すのに費やした期間を表

していると考えられるので、use「～を使う」の過去分詞の(C) usedが適切。
(A) pay「～を支払う」の過去分詞。(B) go「行く」の過去分詞。
(D) waste「～を無駄にする」の過去分詞。❷1行目と❸1行目より、移転先は見つかったと分かるので不適切。

157 When will the move take place?

(A) In one week
(B) In one month
(C) In two months
(D) In six months

移転はいつ行われますか。

(A) 1週間後
(B) 1カ月後
(C) 2カ月後
(D) 6カ月後

正解 B ❸1行目に、Our staff will officially move to Colchester on 10 September. 「弊社スタッフは9月10日に正式にコルチェスターに転居する」とある。❶より、この手紙が書かれたのは8月10日で、移転はこの手紙を送付した1

カ月後に行われる予定と分かる。よって、(B)が正解。take place「行われる」。
(C) two monthsは❸4～5行目に、移転前の本社宛ての郵便物が移転後の本社に転送される期間として記載されているだけ。

Words & Phrases

❷ be pleased to *do* ～してうれしい　　announce ～を知らせる　　move 〈名詞で〉移転、〈動詞で〉移転する
headquarters 本社　　launch ～を開始する　　consulting コンサルタント(の)　　practice (弁護士・医師などの)業務
rapidly 急速に　　expand ～を拡大する　　customer base 顧客基盤　　staff スタッフ、人員　　grow 増大する
accordingly それに応じて　　as a result 結果として　　current 現在の　　facility 施設、設備
adequate for ～ ～に適した、～に十分な　　needs 必要(なもの)、ニーズ　　in search of ～ ～を探して
❸ officially 正式に　　address ～ to … ～を…宛てに出す　　correspondence 書状、手紙　　list ～を記載する
enclose ～を同封する　　contact information 連絡先情報　　stay the same 同じ状態のままである　　mail 郵便物
forward ～を転送する　　following ～の後に　　❹ look forward to *doing* ～することを心待ちにする
serve ～のために働く　　improved 改善された　　enclosure 同封物

Expressions

no longer ～ 「もはや～でない」（❷3～4行目）
This credit card is no longer usable since it has expired.
期限が切れているので、このクレジットカードはもはや使用できません。

Questions 158-160 refer to the following article.

① KINGSTON (1 July)—On a street corner in downtown Kingston, the noise of hammers, drills, and saws can be heard from behind a large blue tarp. Above the tarp hangs a banner announcing the future home of the first Taco Park franchise in Kingston, Jamaica.

② According to its marketing plan, Taco Park will launch the restaurant next month, just in time for the Independence Day holiday. The construction is expected to be finished by the end of this month.

③ "Few people here are familiar with Taco Park, since this is the first one in the city," explained Darryl Grange, general manager of Taco Park Jamaica. "We hope that by placing friendly greeters outside for the grand opening and offering samples from our regular menu we can create a new generation of Taco Park fans right here in Kingston."

④ The new restaurant will hire more than 50 employees, including cooks, servers, and cashiers. Interested candidates can apply at www.tacopark.com.jm. They must indicate their job skills, work experience, and provide a brief explanation of why they want to work at Taco Park. Applicants who are invited to interview for a position must provide two references from former places of employment.

問題158-160は次の記事に関するものです。

キングストン（7月1日）——キングストンの中心街の街角で、金づち、ドリル、のこぎりの音が大きなブルーシートの背後から聞こえてくる。ブルーシートの上方には、ジャマイカのキングストン市におけるTaco Parkのフランチャイズ第1号店の予定地を知らせる横断幕が掛かっている。

同社のマーケティング計画によると、Taco Parkはちょうど独立記念日の祝日に間に合う来月、このレストランを開店する。建設は今月末までに終わる見込みだ。

「Taco Parkをよく知っている人はこの地にはほとんどいません、これが市で最初のものですから」と、Taco Parkジャマイカ社の統括責任者であるDarryl Grangeは説明した。「当社は、グランドオープンには親しみやすい案内係を店外に配置し、通常メニューから試食品を提供することによって、まさにここキングストンに新世代のTaco Parkファンを生み出せればと願っています」。

この新しいレストランは料理人、接客係、レジ係を含め50名を上回る従業員を雇う予定だ。関心のある志望者はwww.tacopark.com.jmで申し込みが可能だ。志望者は自身の仕事の技能や職歴を記し、またTaco Parkで働きたい理由を簡潔に説明する必要がある。職の面接に招かれた応募者は、過去の雇用先からの推薦状を2通提出しなければならない。

Words & Phrases

❶ street corner 街角　downtown 中心街の、繁華街の　hammer 金づち　drill ドリル　saw のこぎり　tarp 防水シート ★tarpaulinの略　hang 掛かる　banner 横断幕　announce ～を知らせる　franchise フランチャイズ店　❷ according to ～ ～によると　marketing マーケティング　launch ～を開始する　in time for ～ ～に間に合って　Independence Day 独立記念日　construction 建設　be expected to do ～する見込みである　❸ explain ～と説明する　general manager 統括責任者　place ～を配置する　friendly 親しみのある　greeter 案内係、出迎える人　grand opening グランドオープン、開店記念　offer ～を提供する　sample 試食品　regular 通常の　create ～を生み出す、～を作り出す　generation 世代　❹ hire ～を雇う　more than ～ ～を上回る　employee 従業員　including ～を含めて　server 接客係　cashier レジ係　candidate 志望者、候補者　apply 申し込む、志願する　indicate ～を示す　skill 技能、スキル　work experience 職歴　provide an explanation 説明をする　brief 簡潔な　applicant 応募者　interview for～ ～（職）の面接を受ける　position 職　reference 推薦状　former 過去の、以前の　employment 雇用、勤務

Expressions

be familiar with ～ 「～をよく知っている」（❸1～2行目）
Ms. Chen is familiar with the subject of sustainable products.
Chenさんは持続可能な製品というテーマに精通しています。

158 What is the article mainly about?

(A) A new trend in the construction industry

(B) The reorganization of a company's marketing department

(C) A proposed solution to a neighborhood's noise issue

(D) The opening of a new business

記事は主に何についてですか。

(A) 建設業界における新しい傾向

(B) 会社のマーケティング部門の再編成

(C) 近隣の騒音問題に対して提案された解決策

(D) 新しい店の開業

正解 D ❶4～7行目に、Above the tarp hangs a banner announcing the future home of the first Taco Park franchise in Kingston, Jamaica. 「ブルーシートの上方には、ジャマイカのキングストン市におけるTaco Parkのフランチャイズ第1号店の予定地を知らせる横断幕が掛かっている」とあり、❷1～2行目にTaco Park will launch the restaurant next month「Taco Parkは来月、このレストランを開店する」と書かれている。以降では、同ジャマイカ社の統括責任者による開店に

向けた計画や、新規従業員の募集について述べられているので、(D)が正解。opening「開業」、business「店、会社」。

(A) trend「傾向」、industry「業界」。

(B) ❷1行目でマーケティング計画に言及はあるが、マーケティング部門の再編成は述べられていない。reorganization「再編成」、department「部門」。

(C) proposed「提案された」、solution「解決策」、neighborhood「近隣」、issue「問題」。

---

159 According to the article, what most likely will happen by the end of July?

(A) A city ordinance will be revised.

(B) A menu will be updated for the holiday.

(C) A construction project will be completed.

(D) An employee training program will begin.

記事によると、7月末までに何が起こると考えられますか。

(A) 市の条例が改正される。

(B) メニューが祝日用に新しくなる。

(C) 建設プロジェクトが完了する。

(D) 従業員研修プログラムが始まる。

正解 C ❷4～5行目に、The construction is expected to be finished by the end of this month. 「建設は今月末までに終わる見込みだ」と述べられている。❶1行目の日付から、この記事は7月1日付のものだと分かるので、今月末とは7月末を指し、建設作業は7月末までに完了すると考えられる。よって、(C)が正解。complete「～を完了する」。

(A) ordinance「条例」、revise「～を改正する」。

(B) ❷1～4行目に、祝日に間に合うよう店を開業するとあるが、メニューの改訂に言及はない。update「～を新しくする」。

(D) ❹3～10行目で、新規従業員の募集に言及はあるが、研修については述べられていない。training「研修」。

---

160 What does the article indicate must be included with the online application?

(A) Areas of expertise

(B) Proof of residency

(C) A copy of a current driver's license

(D) A preference for full-time or part-time employment

記事は、オンラインでの応募には何が含まれていなければならないと示していますか。

(A) 専門分野

(B) 居住証明

(C) 有効な運転免許証のコピー

(D) フルタイムとパートタイム雇用のどちらを希望するか

正解 A ❹1～3行目では、新しいレストランの従業員雇用予定が述べられ、続く3～4行目に応募はオンライン経由で可能とある。さらに同4～7行目に、「志望者は自身の仕事の技能や職歴を記し、またTaco Parkで働きたい理由を簡潔に説明する必要がある」と述べられている。つまり、オンラインでの応募時に自身の専門技能と経験を記載する必要があるので、(A)が正解。include「～を含める」。area「分野」、expertise「専門」。

(B) proof「証明」、residency「居住」。

(C) current「(免許などが)有効な」、driver's license「運転免許証」。

(D) ❹7～10行目に、面接に臨む応募者は過去の雇用先からの推薦状が必要とあるが、希望する雇用形態の記載に言及はない。preference「希望、好み」、full-time「フルタイムの、常勤の」、part-time「パートタイムの、時間制の」。

Questions 161-163 refer to the following memo.

To: All employees
From: Patricia Ogdencort, CEO
Date: 22 June
Subject: Company-wide discussion

1 Here at Ogdencort, we believe in partnering with our employees to make positive changes. — [1] —. As such, we would like one representative from each department to participate in company-wide discussions on reducing costs.

2 Employees interested in serving as a representative must have worked at Ogdencort for a minimum of one year. — [2] —. Also, they must have received positive performance reviews and must be able to attend four meetings during one calendar year. Department heads are asked to withhold from serving as representatives. Please submit your name for consideration to your department head no later than 20 August. — [3] —. Successful applicants will be notified within one week of the deadline.

3 We will also be creating a suggestion box. — [4] —. Further information will be provided soon.

問題161-163は次のメモに関するものです。

宛先：従業員各位
差出人：Patricia Ogdencort、最高経営責任者
日付：6月22日
件名：全社討議

当Ogdencort社では、従業員と連携して積極的な改善を図っていくことを信条としています。そこで、各部門から代表者1名に、経費削減に関する全社討議への参加をお願いします。

代表者を務めることに興味がある従業員は、最低限1年間Ogdencort社で勤務していなければなりません。また、その人物たちは肯定的な勤務評定を受けている必要があり、1年間に4回開かれる会議に出席できる必要もあります。部門長は、代表者を務めることを控えるようお願いします。検討のために、8月20日までに所属の部門長に氏名を提出してください。*各部門長が最終決定を下します。選出者は提出期限から1週間以内に通知されます。

提案箱も新設することになっています。より詳しい情報については近日中にお知らせします。

*問題163の挿入文の訳

Words & Phrases

CEO 最高経営責任者   company-wide 全社的な   discussion 討議   **1** believe in ～ ～を信条とする、～の価値を信じる   partner with ～ ～と提携する   make a change 変化をもたらす   positive 積極的な、肯定的な   as such それゆえに、だから   representative 代表者   department 部署   participate in ～ ～に参加する   reduce ～を減らす   cost 費用   **2** serve as ～ ～を務める   minimum 最低限   performance review 勤務評定   be able to do ～することができる   attend ～に出席する   calendar year 1年間、暦年   head 長、責任者   withhold from ～ ～を差し控える   submit ～を提出する   consideration 検討   successful 成功した   applicant 応募者   notify ～に通知する   deadline 締め切り期限   **3** create ～を作り出す   suggestion box 提案箱   provide ～を提供する

161 What is the purpose of the memo?

    (A) To request ideas for reducing costs

    (B) To announce a company initiative

    (C) To offer training for future leaders

    (D) To collect data on employee performance reviews

メモの目的は何ですか。

    (A) 経費削減のための案を求めること

    (B) 会社の新たな取り組みを告知すること

    (C) 将来のリーダーのための研修を提供すること

    (D) 従業員の勤務評定に関するデータを収集すること

正解 B ❶2～4行目で、経費削減に関する全社討議のために各部門から代表者1名を出すことが求められており、❷では代表者の要件と決定手順が説明されている。さらに❸では、新たに提案箱を設置することが伝えられている。よって、メモの目的は会社のこれらの新たな取り組みについて全従業員に告知することだと分かる。announce「～を告知する」、initiative「新しい試み、新規行動計画」。
(A) ❶2～4行目に経費削減に言及があるが、メモではその案を求められてはいない。

---

162 What is NOT a requirement for participation?

    (A) A leadership position

    (B) One year of employment at the company

    (C) A positive performance review

    (D) Availability to attend four meetings

参加の要件ではないものは何ですか。

    (A) 指導者の役職

    (B) 会社での1年の勤務歴

    (C) 肯定的な勤務評定

    (D) 4回の会議に出席できること

正解 A 代表者として全社討議に参加するための要件については❷で説明されている。同4～5行目に「部門長は、代表者を務めることを控えるようお願いする」とあり、指導者の役職にある者は応募しないよう求められている。よって参加の要件でないのは(A)。(B)については同1～2行目で、最低1年間の同社勤務歴が、(C)については同2～3行目で、肯定的な勤務評定を受けていることが、(D)については同3～4行目で、年間4回の会議への出席が、それぞれ参加条件として述べられている。requirement「必要条件」、participation「参加」。leadership「指導者の地位」、position「職、地位」。
(B) employment「勤務、雇用」。
(D) availability「都合がつくこと、利用できること」。

---

163 In which of the positions marked [1], [2], [3], and [4] does the following sentence best belong?

"Each department head will make the final decision."

    (A) [1]

    (B) [2]

    (C) [3]

    (D) [4]

[1]、[2]、[3]、[4]と記載された箇所のうち、次の文が入るのに最もふさわしいのはどれですか。

「各部門長が最終決定を下します」

正解 C 挿入文は最終決定を行う人物を伝えるもの。❷の後半で全社討議に参加する各部門の代表者の決定手順が述べられている。同5～6行目に、Please submit your name for consideration to your department head「検討のために、所属の部門長に氏名を提出してください」と応募手順の説明があり、その後ろに「選出者は提出期限から1週間以内に通知される」と決定結果の通知時期が案内されている。よって、この間の(C) [3]に挿入文を入れると、代表者の応募、決定とその結果発表までの一連の流れを説明することになり、適切。make a decision「決定を下す」、final「最終的な」。

Expressions

no later than ～ 「～までに、～より遅くなることなく」(❷6行目)
You should arrive at the office no later than 10:00 A.M.
あなたは午前10時までに出社すべきです。

Questions 164-167 refer to the following Web page.

---

https://www.lkjsportswear.com.br/about/founders ▼

Company Founders

❶ Matheus Mori was a standout business student at Lowell University in Toronto, Canada. After graduating, he received funding from a regional business organisation to launch a travel software business. — [1] —. Four years later, he realised that he wanted to do more than just make money. He wanted to pursue his interests and dreams. So he sold his business and entered into a period of travel and cycling.

❷ — [2] —. While at a sports conference in Brazil, Mr. Mori attended a presentation by Gustavo Santana, who had recently developed three-dimensional body-scanning software to create custom athletic wear. After the presentation, Mr. Mori introduced himself to Mr. Santana, and the two got into an in-depth conversation. — [3] —. In subsequent months, more exchanges between the two men followed, ultimately leading them to create LKJ Sportswear. Mr. Mori's travels had helped him formulate crucial ideas for revamping cycling apparel, which he was able to realise in collaboration with Mr. Santana, using Mr. Santana's software. — [4] —. Today, after 25 years in business, LKJ Sportswear continues to be a leader in sports apparel in Brazil and throughout South America, while sales of its products, most notably the cycling and tennis lines, continue to grow in Europe.

問題164-167は次のウェブページに関するものです。

https://www.lkjsportswear.com.br/about/founders

会社の創業者たち

Matheus Moriは、カナダのトロントにあるローウェル大学で傑出したビジネス専攻の学生でした。卒業後、彼は地域の事業組合から資金提供を受けて旅行関連のソフトウエア事業を立ち上げました。4年後に、彼は自分がただお金を稼ぐだけではないことをしたいと気付きました。彼は自分の関心事と夢を追求したかったのです。そこで彼は事業を売却して、旅とサイクリングの時期に入りました。

ブラジルでのスポーツ協議会に参加している間、Mori氏はGustavo Santanaによるプレゼンテーションに出席しました。その人物は少し前に特注の競技用ウエアを作るための3Dボディー・スキャニングソフトを開発していました。プレゼンテーションの後、Mori氏はSantana氏に自己紹介して、2人は踏み込んだ会話を始めました。*彼らは、自分たちが高性能スポーツウエアへの関心を共に持っていることを知りました。その後数カ月間、2人の間ではさらにやりとりが続き、最終的に彼らはLKJスポーツウエア社を設立するに至りました。Mori氏の旅は、サイクリング用衣料を改良するための重要なアイデアを自ら考案するのに役立ちましたが、それを彼はSantana氏と共同でSantana氏開発のソフトウエアを使用することで実現できました。今日、創業25年を経て、LKJスポーツウエア社はブラジルと南米全域におけるスポーツ衣料のトップ企業であり続ける一方、同社の製品、とりわけサイクリングとテニスの製品ラインの売り上げはヨーロッパで成長し続けています。

*問題167の挿入文の訳

Words & Phrases

founder 創業者　❶ standout 傑出した　funding 資金　regional 地域の
organisation 組織 ★米国表記はorganization　launch ～を開始する　realise ～に気付く ★米国表記はrealize
pursue ～を追求する　interest 関心　enter into ～ ～に入る、～に従事する　period 時期　cycling サイクリング
❷ conference 協議会、会議　attend ～に出席する　three-dimensional 3Dの、三次元の
body-scanning ボディー・スキャニング　custom 特注の　athletic 運動競技の　get into ～ ～(議論など)を始める
in-depth 詳細な、徹底的な　subsequent 後の、続いて起こる　exchange やりとり　ultimately 最終的に
formulate ～を考案する　crucial 重大な　revamp ～を改良する　apparel 衣料、衣類　realise ～を実現する
in collaboration with ～ ～と共同で　in business 営業して　continue to do ～し続ける　notably とりわけ
line 商品ライン

Expressions

lead ~ to do 「～を…するよう導く」(❷5行目)
　The flyers led the residents to participate in the forum.
　そのチラシが住民を討論会に参加するように導きました。

164 According to the Web page, why did Mr. Mori sell his first business?

(A) To pay some debts
(B) To return to his studies
(C) To spend time traveling
(D) To establish a new business

ウェブページによると、Moriさんはなぜ自身の最初の事業を売却したのですか。

(A) 借金を支払うため
(B) 研究活動に戻るため
(C) 旅をして時間を過ごすため
(D) 新たな事業を立ち上げるため

| 正解 C | ❶ 2〜3行目に、Moriさんが大学卒業後に旅行関連のソフトウエア事業を立ち上げたとあるが、同4行目では、Moriさんは自分の関心事と夢を追求したかったと説明されている。続けてSo he sold his business and entered into a period of travel and cycling.「そこで彼は事業を売却して、旅とサイクリングの時期に入った」とあるので、旅とサイクリングが |

Moriさんの関心事と夢で、これを追求するために事業を売却したと分かる。よって、(C)が正解。spend time *doing*「〜して時間を過ごす」。
(A) debt「借金」。
(D) ❷より、Moriさんが新たな事業を立ち上げたのは前の事業を売却してからしばらく後だと分かる。establish「〜を設立する」。

165 Where did LKJ Sportswear's founders meet?

(A) At a university
(B) At a conference
(C) At a cycling race
(D) At a sportswear store

LKJスポーツウエア社の創業者たちはどこで出会いましたか。

(A) 大学
(B) 協議会
(C) 自転車レース
(D) スポーツウエア店

| 正解 B | ❷ 1〜2行目に While at a sports conference in Brazil, Mr. Mori attended a presentation by Gustavo Santana「ブラジルでのスポーツ協議会に参加している間、Mori氏はGustavo Santanaによるプレゼンテーションに出席した」とあり、同3〜4行目で2人が知り合った経緯が述べられ |

ている。さらに同5行目で、「最終的に彼らはLKJスポーツウエア社を設立するに至った」とあることから、LKJスポーツウエア社の創業者たちとはMoriさんとSantanaさんであることが分かり、2人が出会ったのはブラジルで開催された協議会なので、(B)が正解。

166 What is indicated about LKJ Sportswear?

(A) It sells its products in multiple countries.
(B) It now makes only cycling apparel.
(C) Its products are often sold at a discount.
(D) Its founders are both from Canada.

LKJスポーツウエア社について何が示されていますか。

(A) 同社は複数の国で製品を販売している。
(B) 同社は現在、サイクリング用衣料のみを製造している。
(C) 同社の製品は頻繁に、割引価格で販売されている。
(D) 同社の創業者は両者ともカナダ出身である。

| 正解 A | LKJスポーツウエア社の現在の状況について、❷ 8〜10行目に、LKJ Sportswear continues to be a leader in sports apparel in Brazil and throughout South America「LKJスポーツウエア社はブラジルと南米全域におけるスポーツ衣料のトップ企業であり続ける」とあり、さらに sales of its products ...... continue to grow in Europe「同社の製品の売り上 |

げはヨーロッパで成長し続けている」と述べられているので、LKJスポーツウエア社が南米やヨーロッパの複数の国で製品を販売していることが分かる。よって、(A)が正解。multiple「複数の」。
(C) at a discount「割引価格で」。
(D) ❶ 1行目にMoriさんがカナダの大学を卒業したとあるが、創業者の出身地についての言及はない。

167 In which of the positions marked [1], [2], [3], and [4] does the following sentence best belong?

"They discovered that they shared an interest in high-performance sportswear."

(A) [1]　　　　(C) [3]
(B) [2]　　　　(D) [4]

[1]、[2]、[3]、[4]と記載された箇所のうち、次の文が入るのに最もふさわしいのはどれですか。

「彼らは、自分たちが高性能スポーツウエアへの関心を共に持っていることを知りました」

| 正解 C | 挿入文は複数の人物を示すtheyがあるので、複数の人物に関する記述の後ろに入ると考えられる。❷ 1〜5行目で、MoriさんとSantanaさんが出会ってから会社を立ち上げるまでの経緯が述べられている。同4行目のthe two got into an in-depth conversation「2人は踏み込んだ会話を始めた」の直後の(C) [3]に挿入文を入れると、挿入文中のtheyがMoriさんとSantanaさんを指すことになる。踏み込んだ会話で共通の関心事があると分かった結果、2人のやりとりが続き、最終的にLKJスポーツウエア社を設立するに至った、と会社設立の経緯を説明する流れとなり、適切。discover that 〜「〜ということを知る」、share「〜を共に持つ」。 |

Questions 168-171 refer to the following online chat discussion.

Gail Oneta (1:20 P.M.) Hi, Mary. Can you send me a copy of the client questionnaire you mentioned during our meeting yesterday?

Mary Huang (1:21 P.M.) Sure. I will e-mail you the link to it right now.

Gail Oneta (1:22 P.M.) OK. Got it. But I can't edit the document for some reason.

Mary Huang (1:23 P.M.) Let me check with Brian Becker. Brian, I just sent Gail a link to the client questionnaire, but she cannot edit it.

Brian Becker (1:24 P.M.) It's probably because Gail has not been approved as an editor. Gail, I'll enter your name in the system now.

Gail Oneta (1:25 P.M.) OK. Thanks. I'm able to edit now. Would it be OK for me to add a few more questions to the document?

Brian Becker (1:26 P.M.) That's fine. But I would limit it to two or three at most. We promised the client that the questionnaire will take only ten minutes to complete.

Gail Oneta (1:27 P.M.) OK, understood. I'll keep that in mind.

Mary Huang (1:28 P.M.) So Brian, we will see you next on Tuesday at the Querol Health Services Center for the meeting with their team. It will be our first meeting with them, so it's important for us all to be there.

Brian Becker (1:29 P.M.)
Right. Thanks for reminding me. I'll put it on my calendar.

問題168-171は次のオンラインチャットの話し合いに関するものです。

Gail Oneta（午後1時20分）　　こんにちは、Mary。昨日会議中にあなたが言っていた顧客アンケートを1部、私に送ってもらえますか。

Mary Huang（午後1時21分）　　いいですよ。今すぐそのリンクをEメールで送ります。

Gail Oneta（午後1時22分）　　はい。受け取りました。でも、どういうわけか、私はこの文書を編集することができないのです。

Mary Huang（午後1時23分）　　Brian Beckerに確認してみますね。Brian、私はたった今Gailに顧客アンケートへのリンクを送信したのですが、彼女がそれを編集できないのです。

Brian Becker（午後1時24分）　　それはおそらく、Gailが編集者として承認されていないからでしょう。Gail、僕が今システムにあなたの名前を入力しますよ。

Gail Oneta（午後1時25分）　　了解。ありがとう。これで編集できるようになりました。文書にあと幾つか質問を加えてもいいですか。

Brian Becker（午後1時26分）　　構いませんよ。でも僕なら、多くてもそれを2つか3つに限定するでしょうね。当社は顧客に、アンケートに全て記入するのに10分しかかからないと約束したのです。

Gail Oneta（午後1時27分）　　なるほど、分かりました。そのことを心にとどめておきます。

Mary Huang（午後1時28分）　　それではBrian、次は火曜日にQuerol医療サービスセンターで、先方チームとの会合で会いましょう。それが先方との初会合になるので、その場に私たち全員がいることが大切です。

Brian Becker（午後1時29分）　　そうですね。思い出させてくれてありがとう。それを僕の予定表に入れておきます。

Words & Phrases

❶ a copy of ～　～の1部　　questionnaire　アンケート　　mention　～のことを言う　　❸ edit　～を編集する
document　文書（ファイル）　　for some reason　どういうわけか　　❹ check with ～　～に確認する
❺ approve　～を承認する　　editor　編集者　　❻ add ～ to …　～を…に加える　　❼ limit ～ to …　～を…に制限する
at most　多くても　　complete　～に全て記入する　　❽ keep ～ in mind　～を覚えておく　　❿ remind　～に念を押す
calendar　予定表

168 What problem does Ms. Oneta have?

  (A) Meeting notes have been misplaced.
  (B) An important meeting was canceled.
  (C) She is unable to update a document.
  (D) She has accidentally deleted an electronic file.

Onetaさんはどんな問題を抱えていますか。

  (A) 会議のメモが間違った場所に置かれた。
  (B) 重要な会議が中止になった。
  (C) 彼女は文書を更新することができない。
  (D) 彼女は誤って電子ファイルを削除してしまった。

正解 **C** ❶で顧客アンケートを1部送るよう頼んだOnetaさんは、❸でアンケートへのリンクをEメールで受け取った後、I can't edit the document for some reason.「どういうわけか、私はこの文書を編集することができない」と述べている。(C)が正解。be unable to *do*「～することができない」、update「～を更新する」。
(A) misplace「～を置き間違える」。
(D) Onetaさんは顧客アンケートの文書ファイルを編集できないと伝えているだけで、削除したとは述べていない。accidentally「誤って、偶然に」、delete「～を削除する」。

169 At 1:27 P.M., what does Ms. Oneta mean when she writes, "I'll keep that in mind"?

  (A) She must ask permission to access a report.
  (B) She will limit the number of changes she makes to a questionnaire.
  (C) She will remember the password to open a document.
  (D) She has been given a strict deadline to complete a task.

午後1時27分に、Onetaさんは "I'll keep that in mind" という発言で、何を意味していますか。

  (A) 彼女は、報告書にアクセスするための許可を求めなければならない。
  (B) 彼女は、アンケートに加える変更の数を限定するつもりである。
  (C) 彼女は、文書を開くためのパスワードを覚えておくつもりである。
  (D) 彼女は、作業を完了するのに厳守すべき締め切りを課されている。

正解 **B** ❻でOnetaさんが文書に質問を加えてもよいかと尋ねているのに対し、Beckerさんは❼で、構わないと述べながらも、「でも僕なら、多くてもそれを2つか3つに限定するだろう」と伝え、アンケート記入にかかる時間について顧客に10分と約束した、とその理由を説明している。それを受けたOnetaさんはOK, understood.とBeckerさんの助言を受け入れてから下線部の発言をしている。よってBeckerさんの助言に従って、約束した時間内に顧客がアンケートを完了できるよう、加える質問数を限定するつもりだと考えられる。(B)が正解。
(A) permission「許可」、access「～にアクセスする」。
(D) strict「厳密な」、task「作業」。

170 How long should it take to complete the questionnaire?

  (A) Two minutes
  (B) Three minutes
  (C) Five minutes
  (D) Ten minutes

アンケートに全て記入するには、どのくらいの時間がかかるはずですか。

  (A) 2分
  (B) 3分
  (C) 5分
  (D) 10分

正解 **D** ❼でBeckerさんが、We promised the client that the questionnaire will take only ten minutes to complete.「当社は顧客に、アンケートに全て記入するのに10分しかかからないと約束した」と述べている。(D)が正解。
(A) (B) ❼のtwo or threeは加える質問数であって、記入時間ではない。

171 What is Mr. Becker going to note on his calendar?

  (A) A team review of a document
  (B) An appointment with a new client
  (C) A celebration of a new contract
  (D) A consultation with a medical professional

Beckerさんは自分の予定表に何を書き留めるつもりですか。

  (A) チームでの文書の見直し
  (B) 新規顧客と会う約束
  (C) 新規契約の祝賀会
  (D) 医療専門家との相談

正解 **B** ❾でHuangさんはBeckerさんに対し、「次は火曜日にQuerol医療サービスセンターで、先方チームとの会合で会おう」と言い、それは初会合なので自分たち全員の参加が大切だ、と伝えている。Beckerさんは、それに答えて❿で、I'll put it on my calendar.「それを僕の予定表に入れておく」と述べている。よって、新規顧客との初会合を自分の予定表に書き留めるつもりだと分かる。note「～を書き留める」。appointment「会う約束」。
(A) review「見直し、再検討」。
(C) celebration「祝賀会」、contract「契約」。
(D) consultation「相談」、professional「専門家」。

Questions 172-175 refer to the following press release.

FOR IMMEDIATE RELEASE   **Contact:** Carla Guerra 512-555-0172, c_guerra@dupontcamera.com

Dupont Camera Store Hosts Its Tenth Annual Photography Equipment Swap and Sell

❶ (Monday, June 12)—Dupont Camera Store is once again hosting its photography equipment Swap and Sell event. On Friday, June 16, the store's showroom will be packed with tables of new and used photography gear from various vendors and hobbyists. Entry is $6 cash. Doors open at 10:00 A.M., and the event lasts until 5:00 P.M.

❷ "This is an event people look forward to all year," said Dupont Camera Store's marketing manager Don Bergner. "Every time we've hosted it, a line has started forming about an hour before we even open the doors."

❸ Professional dealers and camera companies can rent tables for $250 as an official vendor. Tables are 6 meters by 2 meters and include clear plastic clips for attaching a company banner or poster. Hobby photographers wanting to sell or trade a few handheld items can pay an entry fee of $50 and bring crates or camera bags of gear to set up in a designated area on the floor.

❹ "I went to the event last year and definitely plan to go again," said Jonathan McDougall. "I didn't have anything to sell, but I got to meet some interesting people. I also ended up finding some accessories for my outdated camera model that I hadn't been able to find online."

問題172-175は次のプレスリリースに関するものです。

即日解禁

連絡先：Carla Guerra 512-555-0172、
c_guerra@dupontcamera.com

Dupontカメラストア社が、毎年恒例の写真撮影機材の交換・販売会の第10回を開催

（6月12日、月曜日）——Dupontカメラストア社は再び、写真撮影機材の交換・販売のイベントを開催します。6月16日金曜日に、当社のショールームは、各種販売業者と愛好家からの新品および中古の写真撮影機材のテーブルでいっぱいになるでしょう。入場料は6ドルの現金払いです。開場は午前10時で、イベントは午後5時まで続きます。

「これは、人々が一年通じて楽しみにしているイベントです」とDupontカメラストア社のマーケティング部長であるDon Bergnerは述べました。「当社がこれを開催するたびに、開場する1時間くらい前にはもう列が出来始めるのです」。

専門取扱業者やカメラ会社は公式販売業者として、250ドルでテーブルを借りることができます。テーブルは幅6メートル、奥行2メートルで、会社の横断幕やポスターを取り付けるための透明なプラスチック製クリップが含まれます。数点の小型製品を販売または交換したい写真愛好家の方々は、入場料50ドルを支払って、機材が入った箱やカメラバッグを持ち込み、会場の指定場所に並べることができます。

「私は昨年このイベントに足を運んだのですが、絶対にまた行くつもりです」とJonathan McDougallは語りました。「私は売るものは何もありませんでしたが、興味深い人々に出会う機会を得ました。また、オンラインでは見つけることができなかった自分の旧型のカメラの付属品をついに見つけることにもなったのです」。

172 What does Mr. Bergner imply about the event?

(A) Tickets sell out within a few days.

(B) Attendees start arriving before 10:00 A.M.

(C) It is hosted by a different camera company each year.

(D) Store staff will unload the vendors' items.

Bergnerさんはイベントについて何を示唆していますか。

(A) チケットは数日以内に売り切れる。

(B) 参加者は午前10時よりも前に到着し始める。

(C) それは毎年異なるカメラ会社によって主催される。

(D) 店舗スタッフが販売業者の商品の荷降ろしをする。

正解 **B**	❷ 1～2行目より、BergnerさんとはDupontカメラストア社のマーケティング部長。Bergnerさんは同2～3行目で、毎年恒例の写真撮影機材の交換・販売のイベントについて、Every time we've hosted it, a line has started forming about an hour before we even open the doors.「当社がこれを開催するたびに、開場する1時間くらい前にはもう列が出来始める」と述べている。❶ 4行目に、今年のイベントの開催について、「開場は午前10時」と示されているので、Bergnerさんは、開場時刻である午前10時よりも前に参加者が会場に到着し始めることを示唆していると考えられる。attendee「参加者」。

(A) sell out「売り切れる」。
(D) unload「～を降ろす」。

---

173 According to the press release, what is the purpose of the table clips?

(A) To display marketing materials

(B) To promote the Dupont logo

(C) To hold gift bags together

(D) To keep the tablecloths in place

プレスリリースによると、テーブルのクリップの目的は何ですか。

(A) 宣伝用の資材を展示すること

(B) Dupont社のロゴを宣伝すること

(C) 贈答用の袋をまとめておくこと

(D) テーブルクロスを所定の位置に留めておくこと

正解 **A**	❸ 2～3行目で、イベントの出展業者に貸し出されるテーブルについて、Tables ...... include clear plastic clips for attaching a company banner or poster.「テーブルには、会社の横断幕やポスターを取り付けるための透明なプラスチック製クリップが含まれる」と述べられている。出展業者にとって、自社の横断幕やポスターは宣伝用の資材に当たるので、(A)が正解。display「～を展示する」、material「資材」。

(B) promote「～を宣伝する」、logo「ロゴ」。
(C) hold ～ together「～をまとめる」。
(D) in place「あるべき場所に」。

Words & Phrases

immediate release 即日解禁 ★プレスリリースの情報の指定で使う　host ～を主催する　annual 年に一度の、毎年恒例の
photography 写真撮影　equipment 機材　swap 交換　❶ showroom ショールーム
packed with ～ ～でいっぱいの　used 中古の　gear 用具、装置　various 各種の　vendor 販売業者
hobbyist 愛好家　entry 入場(権)　cash 現金払い、現金　last 続く　❷ look forward to ～ ～を心待ちにする
every time ～ ～するたびに　line 列、行列　form 形成する　❸ professional 職業上の、専門的な　dealer 取扱業者
rent ～を借りる　official 公式の　clear 透明な　clip クリップ、書類ばさみ　attach ～を取り付ける
banner 横断幕、バナー　poster ポスター　trade ～を交換する　handheld 小型の　fee 料金
crate 運搬用の木箱　set up 並べる　designated 指定された　❹ definitely 間違いなく
get to *do* ～する機会を得る　accessories 付属品　outdated 旧式の、時代遅れの　online オンラインで

174 What is suggested about hobby photographers?

 (A) They will not be provided with a table.
 (B) They can sell only certain items.
 (C) They pay the same entry fee as the public.
 (D) They have to sign up online.

写真愛好家について、何が分かりますか。

 (A) 彼らにはテーブルが提供されない。
 (B) 彼らは特定の品物しか販売できない。
 (C) 彼らは一般の人々と同額の入場料を支払う。
 (D) 彼らはオンラインで参加登録をしなければならない。

正解 A ❸ 3～5 行目に Hobby photographers wanting to sell or trade a few handheld items can ...... bring crates or camera bags of gear to set up in a designated area on the floor.「数点の小型製品を販売または交換したい写真愛好家は、機材が入った箱やカメラバッグを持ち込み、会場の指定場所に並べることができる」とある。テーブルの貸し出しについては同 1～3 行目に、商用の業者に対する貸し出しが説明されているだけで、写真愛好家に対する貸し出しの記載はない。よって、出展する写真愛好家には、テーブルの貸し出しはないと分かる。provide ～ with …「～に…を提供する」。
(B) ❸ 3～5 行目に「数点の小型製品」とあるが、写真愛好家が販売可能な品を限定する記述はない。
(C) ❶ 3 行目より、一般入場料は 6 ドルだが、❸ 3～4 行目より、写真愛好家が出展するための入場料は 50 ドルで、一般入場料と同額ではない。the public「一般の人々」。
(D) sign up「参加登録をする」。

---

175 What does Mr. McDougall mention about his experience at the event last year?

 (A) He was representing his employer.
 (B) He learned about new online camera stores.
 (C) He found some rare items he wanted.
 (D) He sold an old camera and bag.

McDougall さんは、昨年のイベントでの経験について何を述べていますか。

 (A) 彼は自身の雇用先を代表して参加していた。
 (B) 彼は、新しいオンラインのカメラ店について知った。
 (C) 彼は欲しかった希少品を見つけた。
 (D) 彼は古いカメラとバッグを売った。

正解 C McDougall さんは❹で、昨年のイベントに参加したときの経験について語っている。同 2～4 行目で、I also ended up finding some accessories for my outdated camera model that I hadn't been able to find online.「また、オンラインでは見つけることができなかった自分の旧型のカメラの付属品をついに見つけることにもなった」と述べているので、探していた希少な品を昨年のイベントの会場で発見できたと考えられる。よって、(C)が正解。rare「希少な、まれな」。
(A) represent「～の代表として出ている」、employer「雇用企業、雇用者」。
(D) ❹ 2 行目で、私は売るものは何もなかった、と述べているので不適切。

Expressions

end up *doing* 「ついには～することになる、結局～になる」（❹ 2～3 行目）
Because of the typhoon, we ended up staying another night at a hotel.
台風のために、私たちは結局もう一晩ホテルに泊まることになりました。

Questions 176-180 refer to the following e-mail and schedule.

1 Eメール

To:	alee@terratasker.com
From:	jaznar@dynaston.com
Date:	5 March
Subject:	Order number 329XSU

Dear Ms. Lee,

I have been in communication with the shipping company, Marsantis, over the past week about your order of trucks. Apparently, the earliest we can get the TC73 trucks to you is 8 May, which puts us three days behind our estimated delivery date. Unfortunately, the only other ship departing from Valencia in April with enough <u>clearance</u> for the TC73 trucks was cancelled. Only certain ships can transport these trucks because of their height of 4.5 metres. In any case, I apologise for the inconvenience. I will work with our team on waiving some of your transport fees on this order.

Best regards,

Javier Aznar
Assistant Sales Director, Dynaston

2 スケジュール表

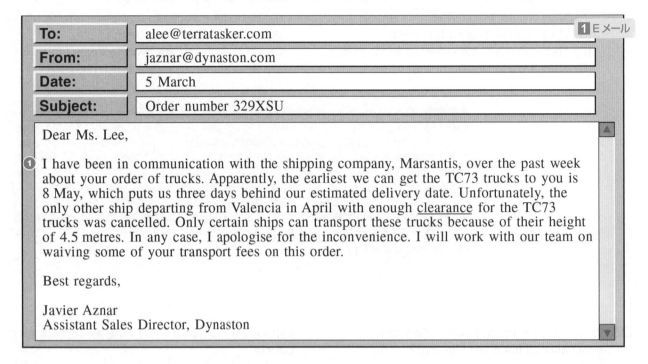

Marsantis Shipping
Valencia to Toyohashi Service
Spring Schedule

Voyage Number	Ship Name	Maximum Cargo Height	Valencia (Spain)	Halifax (Canada)	Veracruz (Mexico)	San Diego (USA)	Toyohashi (Japan)
22	Olympia	5 metres	16 March	25 March	30 March	—	17 April
48	Pegasus	4 metres	2 April	9 April	—	cancelled	5 May
33	Karenga IV	5 metres	13 April	20 April	27 April	cancelled	16 May
57	Yoshimo	5 metres	14 April	cancelled	30 April	8 May	19 May

問題176-180は次のEメールとスケジュール表に関するものです。

受信者：alee@terratasker.com
送信者：jaznar@dynaston.com
日付：3月5日
件名：注文番号329XSU

Lee様

私はこの1週間、あなたのトラックのご注文に関して、海運会社のMarsantis社と連絡を取っておりました。どうやら、TC73トラックをお届けできる最短日程は5月8日で、当社が見積もった納期より3日遅れるということになります。残念ながら、4月にバレンシアを出港し、TC73トラックのための十分な隙間を持つ、別の唯一の船は寄港中止になりました。このトラックは4.5メートルという車高のため、特定の船でのみ輸送可能です。いずれにせよ、ご迷惑をお掛けすることをおわび申し上げます。このご注文の輸送費の一部を差し控えるよう、当社のチームと連携いたします。

敬具

Javier Aznar
営業部長補佐、Dynaston社

Marsantis 海運社 バレンシア ～ 豊橋 便 春期スケジュール表							
航海番号	船名	積荷の最大の高さ	バレンシア（スペイン）	ハリファクス（カナダ）	ベラクルス（メキシコ）	サンディエゴ（アメリカ）	豊橋（日本）
22	Olympia号	5メートル	3月16日	3月25日	3月30日	—	4月17日
48	Pegasus号	4メートル	4月2日	4月9日	—	中止	5月5日
33	Karenga IV号	5メートル	4月13日	4月20日	4月27日	中止	5月16日
57	Yoshimo号	5メートル	4月14日	中止	4月30日	5月8日	5月19日

176 Why did Mr. Aznar most likely write the e-mail?

(A) To explain a delay
(B) To request a shipment
(C) To offer a discount
(D) To clarify a policy

AznarさんはなぜEメールを書いたと考えられますか。

(A) 遅延を説明するため
(B) 出荷を依頼するため
(C) 割引を提供するため
(D) 方針を明確にするため

正解 A ❶のEメールの一番下の送信者氏名の肩書から、Aznarさんは営業業務を担当していると分かる。AznarさんはLeeさんに宛てて、同❶ 2〜3行目で、Leeさんが注文したトラックについて、Apparently, the earliest we can get the TC73 trucks to you is 8 May, which puts us three days behind our estimated delivery date.「どうやら、TC73 トラックを届けることができる最短日程は5月8日で、当社が見積もった納期より3日遅れるということになる」とトラックの納期の遅延について伝えている。以降でその理由や謝罪を述べていることからも、(A)が正解。delay「遅延」。
(B) shipment「出荷、配送」。
(D) clarify「〜を明確にする」。

---

177 In the e-mail, the word "clearance" in paragraph 1, line 4, is closest in meaning to

(A) removal
(B) permission
(C) experience
(D) space

Eメールの第1段落・4行目にある "clearance" に最も意味が近いのは

(A) 除去
(B) 許可
(C) 経験
(D) 空き

正解 D ❶の❶ 3〜4行目のclearanceを含む文では、Leeさんが注文したトラックの到着が遅れる理由として、「4月にバレンシアを出港し、TC73 トラックのための十分な------- を持つ、別の唯一の船は寄港中止になった」と述べている。さらに、同5〜6行目で、Only certain ships can transport these trucks because of their height of 4.5 metres.「このトラックは4.5メートルという車高のため、特定の船でのみ輸送可能だ」と説明を加えているので、車高が高いTC73 トラックを輸送する船には十分な空間的余裕が必要になると判断できる。よって、(D) space「空き、スペース」が正解。clearanceには車両と壁・天井などの間のゆとり、という意味がある。

---

178 What is the shipping destination for the TC73 trucks?

(A) Canada
(B) Mexico
(C) United States
(D) Japan

TC73トラックの輸送目的地はどこですか。

(A) カナダ
(B) メキシコ
(C) アメリカ
(D) 日本

正解 C ❶の❶ 1〜2行目で、Leeさんが注文したトラックについて、Aznarさんは海運会社のMarsantis社と連絡を取っていたとあり、続く同2〜3行目で、TC73 トラックが輸送先である注文主のLeeさんの元に到着可能な日程は最短で5月8日と伝えている。❷のMarsantis海運社の船便のスケジュール表を見ると、同❹のYoshimo号という船が5月8日にアメリカのサンディエゴに寄港する予定だと分かるので、(C)が正解。destination「目的地」。

179 When is the Olympia scheduled to arrive at its final destination?

    (A) On March 16
    (B) On April 17
    (C) On May 16
    (D) On May 19

Olympia号はいつ最終目的地に到着する予定ですか。

    (A) 3月16日
    (B) 4月17日
    (C) 5月16日
    (D) 5月19日

> **正解 B** ❷は、バレンシアから豊橋に向かう船便のスケジュール表。同❶ Olympia号の行を見ると、同号の最終目的地である豊橋への到着予定は4月17日と分かる。be scheduled to *do*「〜する予定である」。
> (A) ❷の❶より、Olympia号がバレンシアに到着する予定日。
> (C) ❷の❸より、Karenga IV号が豊橋に到着する予定日。
> (D) ❷の❹より、Yoshimo号が豊橋に到着する予定日。

180 According to the schedule, what ship will travel directly from Canada to Japan?

    (A) The Olympia
    (B) The Pegasus
    (C) The Karenga IV
    (D) The Yoshimo

スケジュール表によると、どの船がカナダから日本へ直行しますか。

    (A) Olympia号
    (B) Pegasus号
    (C) Karenga IV号
    (D) Yoshimo号

> **正解 B** ❷のスケジュール表で、カナダのハリファクスと日本の豊橋の間にある欄を見ると、同❷よりPegasus号はベラクルスの欄には日付の記載がなく、サンディエゴの欄にはcancelled「中止」とある。よって同号は、ベラクルスにもサンディエゴにも寄港せず、カナダから日本に直行すると分かるので(B)が正解。directly「直接、真っすぐに」。
> (A) (C) (D) いずれもメキシコのベラクルスに寄港するので直行ではない。

Words & Phrases

❶ Eメール   ❶ in communication with ~ 　~と連絡を取って　shipping 海運業、輸送　past 過去の　truck トラック　put ~ …　~を…の状態にさせる　~ days behind …　…に~日遅れで　estimated 推定の　delivery date 納期、配達日　unfortunately 残念ながら　depart 出発する　enough ~ for …　…に十分な~　cancel ~を中止する　certain 特定の　transport ~を運ぶ　because of ~　~のために　height 高さ　metre メートル　★米国表記は meter　in any case いずれにせよ　apologise for ~　~を謝罪する　★米国表記は apologize for ~　inconvenience 迷惑、不便　waive ~を差し控える、~を放棄する　fee 料金

❷ スケジュール表   voyage 航海　maximum 最大限の　cargo 積荷、貨物

Expressions

Apparently, ~ 　「どうやら~らしい」（❶の❷ 2~3行目）

Apparently, the product review for that new detergent was not truthful.
どうやら、その新しい洗剤の商品レビューは事実に即していなかったようです。

Questions 181-185 refer to the following advertisement and letter.

KELLER ATTIRE

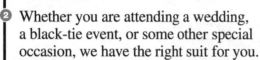

❶ Renting a suit from Keller Attire has never been easier! We now have an expanded range of men's formal wear in sizes XS to XXL, all available to rent online.

❷ Whether you are attending a wedding, a black-tie event, or some other special occasion, we have the right suit for you. Visit our Web site at www.kellerattire.com to see our full range of styles, colors, and fabrics. One of our style experts is ready to chat with you about your choices and walk you through our super accurate online Measuring Wizard. We will help you find a great suit that fits you perfectly!

❸ Our <u>standard</u> delivery service will get your order to you in three to five days. For faster service, we offer overnight delivery for an additional charge of $50.

Antonio Varela
808 Avenue K, Apt. 5B
Dallas, TX 75246

October 14

Joanne Ford, President
Keller Attire, Inc.
2200 East Fourth Street
Chicago, IL 60611

Dear Ms. Ford,

❶ I recently ordered a suit from Keller Attire to wear to an important client dinner in New York. I chose your overnight delivery service and provided a New York address for delivery. However, the suit was delivered to my home address in Dallas instead—I was already on my way to New York at the time.

❷ Your customer service team handled the problem with spotless professionalism. As there was not enough time to send a replacement, they arranged for a local rental company to deliver a similar suit to my hotel at no additional cost to me.

❸ I am extremely grateful for your team's superior customer service. I will certainly use Keller Attire again in the future.

Yours sincerely,

Antonio Varela

Antonio Varela

問題 181-185 は次の広告と手紙に関するものです。

Keller衣装社

Keller衣装社からスーツを借りるのが、これまでにないほど簡単になりました。現在、男性用フォーマルウエアがXSからXXLまでの幅広いサイズ展開となり、全てオンラインでお借りいただけます。

結婚式、準正装のイベント、あるいはその他の特別な行事のいずれにご出席であれ、当社はあなたにぴったりのスーツをご用意しております。当社ウェブサイトのwww.kellerattire.comにアクセスして、幅広いスタイル、色、そして生地をご覧ください。当社のスタイリング専門家の一人がいつでもあなたが選んだ品についてチャットでお話しし、当社の極めて精密なオンラインの採寸ウィザードの使い方を一つ一つ丁寧にご説明します。あなたがご自身にぴったり合う素晴らしいスーツを見つけられるよう、私たちがお手伝いをいたします。

当社の標準配送サービスは、ご注文品を3～5日でお手元にお届けします。より早いサービスとして、追加料金50ドルで翌日配送をご提供しております。

Antonio Varela
K大通り808番地、アパート5B号室
ダラス、TX 75246

10月14日

Joanne Ford 社長
Keller衣装社
東4番通り2200番地
シカゴ、IL 60611

Ford様

私は先日、ニューヨークでの顧客との大事な夕食会に着るためのスーツをKeller衣装社で注文しました。私は貴社の翌日配送サービスを選択し、ニューヨークのある住所を配送先として伝えました。しかしながら、そこではなく、ダラスの私の自宅住所にスーツが届けられたのです——私はそのときにはすでにニューヨークへ向かう途中でした。

貴社の顧客サービスチームは、非の打ちどころのないプロ意識を持ってその問題に対処してくれました。代替品を送るのに十分な時間がなかったため、彼らは私に追加の費用を求めることなく、現地のレンタル会社が類似のスーツを私のホテルに届けるよう手配してくれたのです。

貴社のチームの優れた顧客サービスに非常に感謝しています。私は将来、必ずまたKeller衣装社を利用するつもりです。

敬具
Antonio Varela（署名）
Antonio Varela

181 What would NOT be available to customers who visit Keller Attire's Web site?

(A) Shoes to match a suit
(B) Professional advice
(C) Images of clothes
(D) A way to find correct sizes

Keller衣装社のウェブサイトにアクセスする顧客が利用できないのは何ですか。

(A) スーツに合う靴
(B) 専門的な助言
(C) 服の画像
(D) 適切なサイズを見つける方法

> **正解 A** Keller衣装社の広告である**1**の**①**に、同社ではオンラインで男性用スーツが借りられるとあり、**②**には、同社ウェブサイトで利用可能なサービスの記載がある。(C)は、同4〜5行目に「当社ウェブサイトのwww.kellerattire.comにアクセスして、幅広いスタイル、色、そして生地を見てください」とあるので、閲覧可能と分かる。また(B)と(D)についても、同5〜8行目で「当社のスタイリング専門家の一人がいつでもあなたが選んだ品についてチャットで話し、当社の極めて精密なオンラインの採寸ウィザードの使い方を一つ一つ丁寧に説明する。あなたが自身にぴったり合う素晴らしいスーツを見つけられるよう、私たちが手伝う」とあることから、いずれも利用可能と分かる。(A)「スーツに合う靴」に関する言及はないので、(A)が正解。match「〜に合う」。
> (B) professional「専門的な」。
> (C) image「画像」。
> (D) correct「適切な」。

182 In the advertisement, the word "standard" in paragraph 3, line 1, is closest in meaning to

(A) basic
(B) valuable
(C) average
(D) affordable

広告の第3段落・1行目にある "standard" に最も意味が近いのは

(A) 基本的な
(B) 価値のある
(C) 平均的な
(D) 手頃な

> **正解 A** **1**の**③**では、Keller衣装社が提供している2種類の配送サービスについて説明されている。同1〜2行目の該当の語を含む文では、配送サービスで3〜5日で注文品が届くとあり、さらに同2〜3行目では、For faster service, we offer overnight delivery for an additional charge of $50.「より早いサービスとして、追加料金50ドルで翌日配送を提供している」と付け加えている。後者の翌日配送は、別途料金のかかる特別な速配サービスであるのに対し、前者は通常の基本的な配送サービスであると考えられるので、(A) basic「基本的な」が正解。

183 Why did Mr. Varela write to Ms. Ford?

(A) To report a mistake in an advertisement
(B) To express his concern about a policy
(C) To invite her to meet his clients
(D) To praise her company's customer service

VarelaさんはなぜFordさんに手紙を書いたのですか。

(A) 広告の誤りを報告するため
(B) 方針についての彼の懸念を表すため
(C) 彼自身の担当顧客と会うよう彼女を招くため
(D) 彼女の会社の顧客サービスを称賛するため

> **正解 D** Keller衣装社社長のFordさんに宛てた手紙である**2**の**①**で、Varelaさんは注文したスーツが指定先とは違う宛先に配送されたと伝え、同**②**1行目で「貴社の顧客サービスチームは、非の打ちどころのないプロ意識を持ってその問題に対処してくれた」と同社の顧客対応を褒めている。さらに同**③**1行目で、I am extremely grateful for your team's superior customer service.「貴社のチームの優れた顧客サービスに非常に感謝している」とその対応への感謝を述べているので、VarelaさんはFordさんの会社の顧客サービスを称賛するために手紙を書いたと考えられる。praise「〜を称賛する」。
> (B) express「〜を表す」、concern「懸念」、policy「方針」。
> (C) invite 〜 to do「〜に…するよう招く」。

184 What is suggested about Mr. Varela?

(A) He lives in New York.
(B) He is dissatisfied with a service.
(C) He was unable to attend a dinner.
(D) He paid $50 for delivery.

Varelaさんについて何が分かりますか。

(A) 彼はニューヨークに住んでいる。
(B) 彼はサービスに不満を感じている。
(C) 彼は夕食会に出席することができなかった。
(D) 彼は配送のために50ドルを支払った。

正解 D Varelaさんは、❷の❶2～3行目で、I chose your overnight delivery service and provided a New York address for delivery.「私は貴社の翌日配送サービスを選択し、ニューヨークのある住所を配送先として伝えた」と述べている。❶の広告の❸2～3行目に、we offer overnight delivery for an additional charge of $50「追加料金50ドルで翌日配送を提供している」とあるので、Varelaさんは翌日配送を選択して、そのための追加料金50ドルを支払ったと分かる。
(A) ❷の冒頭の差出人住所より、住んでいるのはダラスであり、ニューヨークではない。
(B) ❷で、顧客対応を褒めているので不適切。be dissatisfied with ～「～に不満を感じている」。
(C) be unable to *do*「～することができない」。

---

185 What problem did Mr. Varela have with the suit he ordered?

(A) It did not fit.
(B) It was the wrong color.
(C) It was delivered to the wrong address.
(D) It arrived late.

Varelaさんは、注文したスーツに関してどんな問題がありましたか。

(A) それは大きさが合わなかった。
(B) それは間違った色だった。
(C) それは間違った住所に届けられた。
(D) それは遅れて届いた。

正解 C ❷の❶1～3行目で、Varelaさんはニューヨークでの夕食会のためにスーツを注文し、I …… provided a New York address for delivery「私はニューヨークのある住所を配送先として伝えた」と述べている。続く同3～4行目で、the suit was delivered to my home address in Dallas instead「そこではなく、ダラスの私の自宅住所にスーツが届けられた」と、指定先とは違う住所にスーツが届けられたことを伝えている。よって、(C)が正解。

Words & Phrases

1 広告 attire 衣装　❶ rent ～を賃借りする　suit スーツ　expand ～を拡大する　range 範囲
formal wear 礼服　available 利用可能な　online オンラインで、インターネットで　❷ attend ～に出席する
wedding 結婚式　black-tie 準正装の　occasion 特別な行事　full range of ～ 幅広い～　fabric 生地、布
expert 専門家　be ready to *do* いつでも～できる、喜んで～する　chat チャットする、おしゃべりする
choice 選んだもの、選択　super 非常に　accurate 精密な　measure 採寸する
wizard ウィザード　★操作などを補助する対話型のプログラム　fit ～に合う、大きさが合う　perfectly 完璧に
❸ delivery 配送　order 〈名詞で〉注文品、〈動詞で〉注文する　overnight 翌日配送の　additional 追加の
charge 料金

2 手紙 apt. アパート　★apartmentの略　❶ recently 最近　provide ～を提供する　deliver ～を届ける
instead そうではなく、その代わりに　on *one's* way to ～ ～に向かう途中で　❷ customer service 顧客サービス
handle ～に対処する　spotless 非の打ちどころのない　professionalism プロ意識
replacement 代替品、交換品　arrange for ～ to *do* ～が…するように手配する　local 現地の、地元の
similar 類似の　❸ extremely 非常に　grateful 感謝する　superior 優れた　certainly 間違いなく

Expressions

walk ～ through … 「～に…の方法を丹念に一つずつ教える」（**1**の❷6～7行目）
Could you walk me through how to use the tools to set up this online meeting?
このオンライン会議を設定するために、ツールの使い方を私に一つずつ教えていただけますか。

Questions 186-190 refer to the following agenda and e-mails.

Hendriks Chemicals Corporate Sales Meeting
Amsterdam Centre Hotel
12–14 May
Day 1 Agenda—Conference Room C

Time	Subject/Activity	Facilitator
8:30 A.M.	*Using the Sales Process to Win*	Anika De Vries
10:00 A.M.	Break	
10:30 A.M.	*Preparing to Call on the Customer*	Hasen Alghamdi
12:30 P.M.	Lunch	
1:30 P.M.	*Planning to Win the Contract*	Lucas Bakker
3:00 P.M.	Break	
3:30 P.M.	*Best Practices Discussion*	Sofie Meijer
5:30 P.M.	End of Day 1	
7:00 P.M.	Dinner—Old Canal Restaurant	

To:	Thomas Visser
From:	Emma Jansen
Date:	23 April
Subject:	Sales meeting agenda—Day 1

Thomas:

Gerritt Smit has put together a proposed agenda for Day 1 of the corporate sales meeting next month. After looking it over, I would like to switch the 10:30 A.M. and 1:30 P.M. sessions, so the order makes more sense.

Gerritt has made a reservation for a group dinner that night at a well-known restaurant in Amsterdam. The plan is to have another group dinner on the second night, and everyone is free to make his or her own dinner plans on the third night.

I still do not have the agendas for Days 2 and 3. Gerritt indicated that he is waiting on confirmation from at least one facilitator before sending them out.

Regards,

Emma Jansen
Regional Sales Manager

To:	Emma Jansen
From:	Thomas Visser
Date:	23 April
Subject:	RE: Sales meeting agenda—Day 1

Emma:

I agree with your proposed change to the agenda for Day 1. Please note that Anika De Vries is no longer able to facilitate her session, but she still plans to participate in the meeting via videoconferencing. Sofie Meijer will now lead Anika's session. She has done it before, so I do not anticipate any issues with this. However, I would like to take a few minutes at the beginning of the day to give a short introduction to the sales process before turning the session over to Ms. Meijer.

Please forward the agendas for Day 2 and Day 3 to me when you receive them.

Best,

Thomas Visser
Vice President of Sales

問題186-190は次の進行表と２通のＥメールに関するものです。

Hendriks化学製品社　全社営業会議
アムステルダムセンターホテル
5月12日～14日
1日目の進行表──会議室Ｃ

時間	テーマ／アクティビティー	進行役
午前8時30分	「成功するための営業プロセスの活用」	Anika De Vries
午前10時	休憩	
午前10時30分	「顧客訪問の準備」	Hasen Alghamdi
午後12時30分	昼食	
午後1時30分	「契約を獲得するための計画の立案」	Lucas Bakker
午後3時	休憩	
午後3時30分	「成功事例についての議論」	Sofie Meijer
午後5時30分	1日目終了	
午後7時	夕食──Old Canalレストラン	

受信者：Thomas Visser
送信者：Emma Jansen
日付：4月23日
件名：営業会議の進行表──1日目

Thomasさん

Gerritt Smitが来月の全社営業会議1日目の進行表の案をまとめました。私はそれに目を通しまして、順番がより理にかなうものになるよう、午前10時30分と午後1時30分のセッションを入れ替えたいと思います。

Gerrittは、その晩はアムステルダムの有名なレストランでの団体夕食会を予約しました。予定では、2日目の夜にももう一回団体での夕食会を設け、3日目の夜は皆が自由に各自の夕食の予定を立てることができます。

私はまだ2日目と3日目の進行表をもらっていません。Gerrittは、それらを送付する前に少なくとも1名の進行役からの確認を待っているとのことでした。

敬具

Emma Jansen
地域担当営業部長

受信者：Emma Jansen
送信者：Thomas Visser
日付：4月23日
件名：RE：営業会議の進行表──1日目

Emmaさん

私は1日目の進行表を変更するというあなたの提案に賛成します。Anika De Vriesは、もうセッションの進行役を務められないことにご留意ください。それでも彼女はオンラインシステムを通じて会議に参加する予定です。そこで、Sofie MeijerがAnikaのセッションを主導することになります。彼女は以前それを行ったことがあるので、これに関して私は何の問題もないと考えています。しかし、私が1日目の冒頭で数分取って営業プロセスへの簡単な概論を述べてから、Meijerさんにセッションを引き継ぎたいと思います。

2日目と3日目の進行表を受け取ったら、私に転送してください。

よろしくお願いします。

Thomas Visser
営業担当役員

186 What session does Ms. Jansen want to move to the 1:30 P.M. time slot?

(A) *Using the Sales Process to Win*
(B) *Preparing to Call on the Customer*
(C) *Planning to Win the Contract*
(D) *Best Practices Discussion*

Jansenさんは、どのセッションを午後1時30分の時間枠に移したいと思っていますか。

(A)「成功するための営業プロセスの活用」
(B)「顧客訪問の準備」
(C)「契約を獲得するための計画の立案」
(D)「成功事例についての議論」

正解 **B** 2の1通目のEメールは、JansenさんがVisserさん宛てに送信したもので、同❶2〜3行目に、全社営業会議1日目の進行表案について、I would like to switch the 10:30 A.M. and 1:30 P.M. sessions「午前10時30分と午後1時30分のセッションを入れ替えたいと思う」とある。1の会議1日目の進行表を見ると、午前10時30分から始まるセッションは(B)。time slot「時間枠」。

---

187 According to the first e-mail, what is the plan for dinner on Day 3?

(A) It will be held at the Old Canal Restaurant.
(B) It will be served at 7:00 P.M.
(C) Participants will make their own arrangements.
(D) Mr. Smit will reserve a table at the hotel dining room.

1通目のEメールによると、3日目の夕食の予定はどのようなものですか。

(A) それはOld Canalレストランで開かれる。
(B) それは午後7時に食事が出される。
(C) 参加者が自分で手配をする。
(D) Smitさんがホテルのレストランの席を予約する。

正解 **C** 1通目のEメールである2の❷2〜3行目に、everyone is free to make his or her own dinner plans on the third night「3日目の夜は皆が自由に各自の夕食の予定を立てることができる」とある。よって(C)が正解。participant「参加者」、make an arrangement「手配をする」。
(A) 1の会議1日目の進行表の❶最下行より、Old Canalレストランは1日目の夕食会が開かれる場所。
(B) 2の❷2〜3行目に、3日目の夕食は各自の自由とあるので、夕食の時刻は決まっていない。serve「〜（飲食物など）を出す」。
(D) reserve a table「席を予約する」、dining room「食堂、ダイニングルーム」。

---

188 What does the first e-mail mention about the agendas for Day 2 and Day 3?

(A) Mr. Visser wants to add an activity to both of them.
(B) Ms. Jansen has already seen them.
(C) Lunch will not be included.
(D) The facilitators have not been finalized.

1通目のEメールは、2日目と3日目の進行表について何を述べていますか。

(A) Visserさんは、両日にアクティビティーを追加したいと思っている。
(B) Jansenさんはすでにそれらを見た。
(C) 昼食は含まれない。
(D) 進行役が確定していない。

正解 **D** 2の❸1行目に、「私はまだ2日目と3日目の進行表をもらっていない」とあり、続けて同1〜2行目で、進行表をまとめているGerritt Smitさんについて、Gerritt indicated that he is waiting on confirmation from at least one facilitator before sending them out.「Gerrittは、それらを送付する前に少なくとも1名の進行役からの確認を待っているとのことだった」とある。ここでのthemとは2日目と3日目の進行表を指すので、両日の進行役がまだ確定していない状況だと分かる。finalize「〜を最終決定する」。
(A) add 〜 to …「〜を…に加える」。
(B) 2の❸1行目に、「私はまだ2日目と3日目の進行表をもらっていない」とあり、このEメールを書いたJansenさんは進行表をまだ見てはいない。
(C) include「〜を含む」。

189 What does the second e-mail indicate about Ms. De Vries?

(A) She recently started working at Hendriks Chemicals.

(B) She has never led a sales session before.

(C) She will give a brief overview before the first session begins.

(D) She will not attend the meeting in person.

2通目のEメールは、De Vriesさんについて何を示していますか。

(A) 彼女は最近、Hendriks化学製品社で働き始めた。

(B) 彼女は以前に、営業のセッションを主導したことがない。

(C) 彼女は最初のセッションが始まる前に概要を述べる。

(D) 彼女は会議に直接は出席しない。

正解 D 2通目のEメールである**3**の**❶** 1～3行目で、De Vriesさんについて、Please note that Anika De Vries is no longer able to facilitate her session, but she still plans to participate in the meeting via videoconferencing.「Anika De Vriesは、もうセッションの進行役を務められないことに留意してください。それでも彼女はオンラインシステムを通じて会議に参加する予定だ」と述べている。つまり、De Vriesさんは会議の場には来ず、オンラインシステムを通じて会議に参加すると分かるので、(D)が正解。in person「直接に、じかに」。
(C) **3**の**❶** 4～6行目より、1日目の冒頭で簡単な概論を述べるのは、2通目のEメールの送信者であるVisserさん。brief overview「概要」。

190 Who will lead the *Using the Sales Process to Win* session?

(A) Ms. De Vries
(B) Mr. Alghamdi
(C) Ms. Meijer
(D) Mr. Bakker

「成功するための営業プロセスの活用」のセッションを誰が主導しますか。

(A) De Vriesさん
(B) Alghamdiさん
(C) Meijerさん
(D) Bakkerさん

正解 C 会議の進行表である**1**の午前8時30分の欄より、「成功するための営業プロセスの活用」の進行役はAnika De Vries。しかし**3**の**❶** 1～2行目で、Please note that Anika De Vries is no longer able to facilitate her session「Anika De Vriesは、もうセッションの進行役を務められないことに留意してください」と述べられ、同3行目に、Sofie Meijer will now lead Anika's session.「そこで、Sofie MeijerがAnikaのセッションを主導することになる」とある。よって、Anika De Vriesに代わって「成功するための営業プロセスの活用」を主導するのは、(C)のMeijerさん。

Words & Phrases

1 進行表 agenda 議題、予定表
chemical 化学製品　　corporate 団体に所属する　　sales 営業(の)、販売活動(の)　　conference 会議
❶ subject 議題　　activity アクティビティー、活動　　facilitator 進行役　　process プロセス、過程
break 休憩　　call on ～ ～を訪問する　　contract 契約　　best practice 成功事例　　discussion 議論
2 Eメール **❶** put together ～ ～をまとめる　　proposed 提案された　　switch ～を取り替える　　session セッション、会合
order 順番　　make sense 理にかなう　　**❷** make a reservation 予約をする　　well-known 有名な
be free to *do* 自由に～できる　　**❸** wait on ～ ～を待つ　　confirmation 確認　　at least 少なくとも
send out ～ ～を送付する　　regional 地域の　　manager マネージャー、管理者
3 Eメール **❶** agree with ～ ～に賛成する　　note ～に留意する　　no longer ～ もはや～ない
facilitate ～の進行役を務める、～を円滑に進める　　participate in ～ ～に参加する　　via ～を通して
videoconferencing オンライン会議(システム)　　lead ～を主導する　　anticipate ～を予期する　　issue 問題
beginning 冒頭　　introduction 概論、導入　　turn ～ over to … ～を…に引き継ぐ　　**❷** forward ～を転送する
vice president 役員、副社長

Expressions

look over ～ 「～に目を通す」(**2**の**❶** 2行目)
Would you look over my presentation slides before we visit the new client?
新規顧客を訪問する前に、私のプレゼンのスライドに目を通していただけますか。

Questions 191-195 refer to the following advertisement, article, and report.

Fairview Bicycle Share (FBS): *Become a Rider!*

① Get an FBS pass to ride to work, school, or around the city. Then select a bicycle from one of our 40 FBS stations in the city and return it to any station by the end of the day.

②
- ■ **Yearly pass**—$800/year—Commuters' top choice.
- ■ **Three-month pass**—$200—Available only to students over the summer.
- ■ **Weekly pass**—$18/week—Tourists love this option.
- ■ **Pay-per-ride**—$2/ride—Affordable option for occasional users.

1 広告

Fairview Daily News
Happy Birthday to FBS

2 記事

① December 17 (FAIRVIEW)—The Fairview Bicycle Share program (FBS) turns one today, and yesterday Mayor Mahdasian provided her thoughts on the program's success.

② "Before we got started, we proposed the idea for the FBS program to Fairview residents at a planning meeting. Critics said a program like FBS would work only in big cities, such as New York and San Francisco. They thought that a small city like ours would not have enough riders to cover the costs," said the mayor, who has made the launch of FBS a priority since starting her second term in office. She noted that she herself uses a Pay-per-ride card.

③ The city's Office of Transport conducted random polling this month to measure the success of FBS. Our journalists are compiling the information, and the full findings will be released tomorrow.

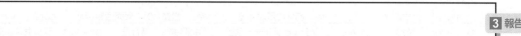

3 報告書

December 18

Report on Year One of Fairview Bicycle Share

① The following statistics were gathered to help capture and analyze the role of FBS one year after its launch.

②
- Individuals who have used FBS since it began: 2,638
- Estimated number of users who report now using FBS more than their cars: 310
- Percent of users who report that FBS has reduced their commute time: 12 percent
- Percent of Fairview University students who report using FBS at least once a week: 19 percent
- Summary of types of passes sold over the first year:
  —Weekly pass: 7 percent
  —Three-month pass: 24 percent
  —Annual pass: 30 percent
  —Pay-per-ride card: 39 percent

問題191-195は次の広告、記事、報告書に関するものです。

フェアビュー自転車シェア（FBS）：自転車利用者になりましょう！

通勤や通学、あるいは市内を回るのにFBSパスを手に入れてください。そして、市内40カ所のFBS拠点の1つで自転車を選び、その日の終わりまでにいずれかの拠点へ返却してください。

■ 年間パス──1年につき800ドル──通勤通学者に一番の選択肢。
■ 3カ月パス──200ドル──夏季の間、学生のみ購入可能。
■ 週間パス──1週間につき18ドル──観光客に大好評の選択肢。
■ 利用ごと払い──1回の利用につき2ドル──不定期利用者向けのお手頃な選択肢。

フェアビュー・デイリーニュース
FBS創設記念日を祝う

12月17日（フェアビュー）──フェアビュー自転車シェアプログラム（FBS）は今日で1年を迎えるが、Mahdasian市長が昨日、プログラムの成功について自らの考えを述べた。

「開始する前に、私たちは企画会議でFBSプログラムのアイデアをフェアビュー市の住民に提案しました。批判していた方々は、FBSのようなプログラムはニューヨークやサンフランシスコなどの大都市でしかうまくいかないだろうと言っていました。彼らは、当市のような小さな市には費用を賄うのに足りるだけの自転車利用者がいないだろうと思っていたのです」と市長は述べた。彼女は2期目を開始以来、FBSの立ち上げを一つの優先課題としてきた。彼女は自身も利用ごと払いカードを使っていると言及した。

市の運輸局は今月、FBSの成功度を評価するために無作為抽出の世論調査を行った。当紙の記者がその情報をまとめており、詳細な調査結果は明日公表される予定だ。

12月18日

フェアビュー自転車シェアの1年目に関する報告書

次の統計は、開始後1年間のFBSの役割を把握して分析する一助とするために収集された。

・開始以来、FBSを利用した個人：2,638
・現在、自家用車よりもFBSを利用していると報告する利用者の推定数：310
・FBSが自分の通勤通学時間を減少させたと報告する利用者の割合：12パーセント
・少なくとも週に1回FBSを利用していると報告するフェアビュー大学の学生の割合：19パーセント
・初年度に販売されたパスの種類の概要：
　　──週間パス：7パーセント
　　──3カ月パス：24パーセント
　　──年間パス：30パーセント
　　──利用ごと払いカード：39パーセント

191 What does the advertisement indicate about FBS bicycles?

(A) They cannot be kept overnight.
(B) They are mostly used by tourists.
(C) They are stored in one location.
(D) They are not available in different sizes.

広告はFBSの自転車について何を示していますか。

(A) それらは次の朝まで保有することはできない。
(B) それらは多くが観光客に利用されている。
(C) それらは1つの場所に保管されている。
(D) それらはさまざまなサイズでは用意されていない。

> **正解 A** フェアビュー自転車シェア（FBS）の広告である**1**の**①** 2行目に、提供している自転車について、return it to any station by the end of the day「その日の終わりまでにいずれかの拠点へ返却してください」とある。つまり当日中に返却する必要があり、日をまたいで借り続けることはできないので、(A)が正解。overnight「一晩中」。
> (B) **1**の**②**より、パスの種類によって主要利用者は異なる。mostly「多くは、大部分は」。
> (C) **1**の**①** 2行目に「市内40カ所のFBS拠点」とあり、保管場所は1つではない。
> (D) different「さまざまな」。

192 According to the article, why did some local residents think FBS would not succeed?

(A) The planning team was not experienced.
(B) The market was too competitive.
(C) The city was not large enough.
(D) The advertising budget was too low.

記事によると、一部の地域住民はなぜFBSが成功しないだろうと考えたのですか。

(A) 企画チームが経験豊富ではなかったから。
(B) 市場が競争過多だったから。
(C) 市が十分に大きくなかったから。
(D) 広告予算が低過ぎたから。

> **正解 C** FBSの1周年を伝える記事である**2**の**②** 3～5行目に、Critics said a program like FBS would work only in big cities「批判していた人々は、FBSのようなプログラムは大都市でしかうまくいかないだろうと言った」とあり、同**②** 5～7行目で、They thought that a small city like ours would not have enough riders to cover the costs「彼らは、当市のような小さな市には費用を賄うのに足りるだけの自転車利用者がいないだろうと思っていた」とその理由が説明されている。よって、(C)が正解。
> (A) experienced「経験豊富な」。
> (B) market「市場」、competitive「競争の激しい」。
> (D) advertising「広告」、budget「予算」。

193 What is suggested about Mayor Mahdasian?

(A) She recently celebrated her birthday.
(B) She occasionally uses an FBS bicycle.
(C) She is in her first term as mayor.
(D) She has visited San Francisco.

Mahdasian市長について何が分かりますか。

(A) 彼女は最近、自分の誕生日を祝った。
(B) 彼女は時折、FBSの自転車を利用する。
(C) 彼女は市長として最初の任期を務めている。
(D) 彼女はサンフランシスコを訪問したことがある。

> **正解 B** **2**の**②** 10～11行目に、Mahdasian市長について、She noted that she herself uses a Pay-per-ride card.「彼女は自身も利用ごと払いカードを使っていると言及した」とある。利用ごと払いについては、**1**の**②**の最後の行にフェアビュー自転車シェア（FBS）が提供するパスの一つの種類として記載があり、Affordable option for occasional users.「不定期利用者向けの手頃な選択肢」と書かれている。よって、市長は時折FBSの自転車を利用すると分かる。occasionally「時折」。
> (A) **2**の見出しは、市長ではなく、FBSプログラムの創設記念日を祝うもの。celebrate「～を祝う」。
> (C) **2**の**②** 8～10行目より、Mahdasian市長の任期は少なくとも2期目。

194 What is implied in the report?

(A) Some people are using their car less frequently.

(B) Students are attending more classes.

(C) Commuters are saving money on public transportation.

(D) Some workers are getting to work early.

報告書では何が示唆されていますか。

(A) 一部の人々は自家用車を使用する頻度が減っている。

(B) 学生がより多くの授業に出席している。

(C) 通勤通学者は公共交通機関にかかるお金を節約している。

(D) 一部の勤労者は職場に早く着いている。

> **正解 A** FBS開始後1年間の利用者に関する世論調査結果の報告書である **3** の **❷** 2行目に、Estimated number of users who report now using FBS more than their cars: 310「現在、自家用車よりもFBSを利用していると報告する利用者の推定数：310」とあるので、(A)が正解。frequently「頻繁に」。
> (B) attend「〜に出席する」。
> (C) public transportation「公共交通機関」。
> (D) get to work「職場に着く」。

---

195 What is suggested about 24 percent of FBS passes?

(A) The passes were sold to tourists.

(B) The passes were sold to students.

(C) The passes were sold during the first half of the year.

(D) The passes were sold to people who live outside of Fairview.

FBSパスの24パーセント分について何が分かりますか。

(A) それらのパスは観光客に販売された。

(B) それらのパスは学生に販売された。

(C) それらのパスは1年の上半期の間、販売された。

(D) それらのパスはフェアビュー市の外に住む人々に販売された。

> **正解 B** **3** の **❷** 6行目Summary of types of passes sold over the first year「初年度に販売されたパスの種類の概要」の2項目目に、Three-month pass: 24 percent「3カ月パス：24パーセント」とある。この「3カ月パス」については、**1** の **❷** 2行目に、Available only to students over the summer.「夏季の間、学生のみ購入可能」と書かれているので、FBSパスの24パーセント分は学生に販売されたと分かる。
> (C) the first half of the year「1年の上半期」。
> (D) outside of 〜「〜の外に」。

Words & Phrases

1 広告　share 共有　rider 乗り手　❶ pass 乗車券、定期券　select 〜を選ぶ　station 拠点　❷ yearly 年間の　commuter 通勤通学者　choice 選択肢　available 利用できる、求めに応じられる　weekly 週単位の　option 選択肢　pay-per-ride 乗る都度支払う　affordable 手頃な価格の　occasional 不定期の、時折の

2 記事　❶ turn 〜になる　mayor 市長　thoughts on 〜 〜についての考え　❷ get started 始める　propose 〜を提案する　resident 住民　planning meeting 企画会議　critic 批判する人　work うまくいく　cover 〜（費用など）を賄う　cost 費用　launch 開始　priority 優先事項、優先　term 任期　in office 在任して　note 〜に言及する　❸ Office of Transport 運輸局　conduct 〜を行う　random 無作為の　polling 世論調査　measure 〜を評価する、〜を測る　journalist 記者　compile 〜をまとめる　full 詳細な、完全な　findings 調査結果　release 〜を公表する

3 報告書　❶ statistics 統計　gather 〜を集める　capture 〜を捉える　analyze 〜を分析する　role 役割　❷ individual 個人　estimated 推定の　reduce 〜を減少させる　commute time 通勤通学時間　summary 概要　annual 1年間の

Expressions

such as 〜　「例えば〜など、〜のような」（**2** の **❷** 4〜5行目）
XYZ company exports a lot of fruits, such as lemons, oranges, and apples.
XYZ社はレモン、オレンジ、りんごなどの果物をたくさん輸出しています。

Questions 196-200 refer to the following e-mails and schedule.

To:	Won Ho Kang
From:	Ayaz Naseem
Date:	2 February
Subject:	Introduction to Korean market

Dear Won Ho,

I recently joined Hample Asset Managers in Sydney as an emerging business analyst with a particular focus on software technology companies. I would like to research some of the new related small businesses in Korea and have a couple of questions for you. In your opinion, what brokerage firm runs the best technology conference there? And are there any software startups that you know of that I should focus on?

I look forward to hearing from you.

Many thanks,

Ayaz Naseem
Analyst, Hample Asset Managers

To:	Ayaz Naseem
From:	Won Ho Kang
Date:	3 February
Subject:	Re: Introduction to Korean market

Hi, Ayaz,

It is a pleasure to make your acquaintance. My work is also focused on software technology. To respond to your questions, WR Asiana's conference is definitely the best and is scheduled to take place in Seoul next May. I will be attending the conference with a few colleagues, and I highly recommend that you join us. If you would like, I could forward contact information to you for the salesperson that covers our sector, and you can make your reservations through her.

It would be great to meet you in person if you are able to come. Also, feel free to reach out if you need help finding your way around the city.

Best,

Won Ho Kang
Senior Analyst, Hample Asset Managers

WR Asiana Technology Conference, Thursday, 8 May
Afternoon schedule, continued
Concurrent Business Sessions—2:00 to 3:00 P.M.

	1	2	3	4
Sector	Internet	Software	Hardware	Mobile Phones
Company	Wingbae Tech	Kedia	Namhaejin Max	Vindoh
Room	Petunia Room	Rose Hall	Lily Suite	Tulip Salon

問題196-200は次の2通のEメールと予定表に関するものです。

受信者：Won Ho Kang
送信者：Ayaz Naseem
日付：2月2日
件名：韓国市場へのご紹介

Won Hoさん

私は、ソフトウエアテクノロジー企業に特に重点を置く新興ビジネスのアナリストとして、シドニーのHample資産管理会社に最近入社いたしました。韓国の関連する新規中小企業の幾つかを調査したいと思っており、あなたに2点伺いたいことがあります。あなたのお考えでは、韓国でどの仲介業者が最良のテクノロジー協議会を運営していますか。また、ご存じのソフトウエア新興企業で、私が重点を置くべき企業はありますか。

ご連絡をお待ちしております。

よろしくお願いいたします。

Ayaz Naseem
アナリスト、Hample資産管理会社

受信者：Ayaz Naseem
送信者：Won Ho Kang
日付：2月3日
件名：Re：韓国市場へのご紹介

Ayazさん

あなたとお知り合いになれてうれしく思います。私の仕事もソフトウエアテクノロジーに重点を置いています。ご質問にお答えしますと、WR Asiana社の協議会が間違いなく最良で、この5月にソウルで開催される予定です。私は数名の同僚とその協議会に出席することにしており、あなたも参加されることをぜひお勧めします。もしよろしければ、私たちの分野を担当する営業員の方の連絡先をあなたにお送りしますので、彼女を通してご自身の予約をすることが可能です。

あなたがおいでになるなら、直接お会いできると大変うれしく思います。また、市内を回るのに手助けが必要でしたらお気兼ねなくご連絡ください。

敬具

Won Ho Kang
上級アナリスト、Hample資産管理会社

WR Asiana社テクノロジー協議会、5月8日木曜日
午後の予定表、続き
同時進行となるビジネスセッション──午後2時から3時まで

	1	2	3	4
分野	インターネット	ソフトウエア	ハードウエア	携帯電話
企業	Wingbae Tech社	Kedia社	Namhaejin Max社	Vindoh社
部屋	ペチュニア・ルーム	バラ・ホール	ユリ・スイート	チューリップ・サロン

196 What is indicated about Mr. Naseem?

(A) He is a new employee at Hample Asset Managers.
(B) He used to work closely with Mr. Kang.
(C) He has worked as an analyst for many years.
(D) He recently moved to Sydney.

Naseemさんについて何が示されていますか。

(A) 彼はHample資産管理会社の新しい従業員である。
(B) 彼は以前は、Kangさんと密に協力して働いていた。
(C) 彼は長年アナリストとして働いている。
(D) 彼は最近シドニーに引っ越した。

> **正解 A** 1通目のEメールである**1**は、NaseemさんがKangさん宛てに送信したもので、同**❶**1行目に、I recently joined Hample Asset Managers「私は、Hample資産管理会社に最近入社した」とある。よって、(A)が正解。employee「従業員」。
> (B) used to *do*「以前は～していた」、closely「密接に、親しく」。
> (C) Naseemさんはアナリストとして入社したが、経歴の長さについては言及がない。
> (D) **1**の**❶**1行目からNaseemさんの勤務先はシドニーにあると分かるが、Naseemさんが最近シドニーに引っ越したという記載はない。

197 Why did Mr. Naseem write the first e-mail?

(A) To ask for directions to a meeting
(B) To request information on companies
(C) To offer investment advice
(D) To learn more about Mr. Kang's job

Naseemさんはなぜ1通目のEメールを書いたのですか。

(A) 会議への行き方を尋ねるため
(B) 企業に関する情報を求めるため
(C) 投資の助言を与えるため
(D) Kangさんの仕事についてもっと知るため

> **正解 B** 1通目のEメールである**1**の**❶**2～3行目で、NaseemさんはKangさんに宛てて「韓国の関連する新規中小企業の幾つかを調査したいと思っており、あなたに2点伺いたい」と述べている。質問は同3～5行目のIn your opinion, what brokerage firm runs the best technology conference there?「あなたのお考えでは、韓国でどの仲介業者が最良のテクノロジー協議会を運営しているか」と、are there any software startups that you know of that I should focus on?「ご存じのソフトウエア新興企業で、私が重点を置くべき企業はあるか」という、企業に関する2つの情報を求めるもの。よって、(B)が正解。request「～を求める、～を要請する」。
> (A) ask for ～「～を尋ねる」、directions「道順」。
> (C) investment「投資」。

198 According to Mr. Kang, how should Mr. Naseem arrange his attendance at a conference?

(A) By calling a customer service department
(B) By speaking with a travel agent
(C) By contacting a salesperson
(D) By visiting WR Asiana's Web site

Kangさんによると、Naseemさんは自身の協議会への出席をどのように手配すべきですか。

(A) 顧客サービス部門に電話することによって
(B) 旅行業者と話をすることによって
(C) 営業員に連絡することによって
(D) WR Asiana社のウェブサイトにアクセスすることによって

> **正解 C** 2通目のEメールである**2**は、Kangさんが**1**のNaseemさんからのEメールに返信したもの。**2**の**❶**3～4行目でKangさんは、NaseemさんにWR Asiana社の協議会への参加を勧め、続けて同**❶**4～6行目でIf you would like, I could forward contact information to you for the salesperson that covers our sector, and you can make your reservations through her.「もしよければ、私たちの分野を担当する営業員の連絡先をあなたに送るので、彼女を通して自身の予約をすることが可能だ」と述べている。つまり、WR Asiana社の営業員をNaseemさんに紹介するので、自身で直接その営業員に連絡して協議会への出席予約をするよう説明している。よって、(C)が正解。arrange「～を手配する」、attendance「出席」。
> (B) travel agent「旅行業者、旅行代理店従業員」。

199 What is suggested about Mr. Kang?

  (A) He travels regularly to Sydney.

  (B) He does not like attending professional conferences.

  (C) He lives outside of Seoul.

  (D) He forgot to answer all of Mr. Naseem's questions.

Kangさんについて何が分かりますか。

  (A) 彼は定期的にシドニーへ旅行する。

  (B) 彼は専門的な協議会に出席することを好まない。

  (C) 彼はソウルの外に住んでいる。

  (D) 彼はNaseemさんの質問の全てに答えるのを忘れた。

正解 D Naseemさんは、Kangさん宛てのEメールである**1**の**❶** 3～5行目で、「あなたの考えでは、韓国でどの仲介業者が最良のテクノロジー協議会を運営しているか」と「ソフトウエア新興企業で、私が重点を置くべき企業はあるか」という2つの質問をしている。それに対しKangさんは、**2**の**❶** 2～3行目で、To respond to your questions, WR Asiana's conference is definitely the best and is scheduled to take place in Seoul next May. 「質問に答えると、WR Asiana社の協議会が間違いなく最良で、この5月にソウルで開催される予定だ」と1つ目の質問に答えている。しかしその後、2つ目の質問である、重点を置くべきソフトウエア新興企業については答えていない。よって、(D)が正解。forget to *do*「～するのを忘れる」。

(A) regularly「定期的に」。(B) professional「専門的な」。(C) outside of ～「～の外に」。

---

200 What session will Mr. Kang most likely attend at 2 P.M. on May 8?

  (A) Wingbae Tech's session

  (B) Kedia's session

  (C) Namhaejin Max's session

  (D) Vindoh's session

Kangさんは5月8日午後2時に、どのセッションに出席すると考えられますか。

  (A) Wingbae Tech社のセッション

  (B) Kedia社のセッション

  (C) Namhaejin Max社のセッション

  (D) Vindoh社のセッション

正解 B **3**は、5月8日に開かれるWR Asiana社のテクノロジー協議会の予定表であり、午後2時から3時の間に同時進行するセッションが示されている。Kangさんは、**2**の**❶** 1～2行目で、「私の仕事もソフトウエアテクノロジーに重点を置いている」と述べている。**3**の**❶**のソフトウエアの列を見ると、すぐ下の企業名にKediaとあるので、Kangさんは自身が重点を置く分野の(B)「Kedia社のセッション」に出席すると考えられる。

Expressions

in *one's* opinion 「～の考えでは」（**1**の**❶** 3～4行目）

In my opinion, building a personal Web site is necessary for your career.

私の考えでは、個人のウェブサイトを構築することがあなたのキャリアに必要です。

TEST 2 の正解一覧

リスニングセクション

問題番号	正解
Part 1	
1	B
2	A
3	B
4	C
5	B
6	D
Part 2	
7	B
8	A
9	B
10	A
11	C
12	B
13	A
14	A
15	C
16	A
17	C
18	A
19	A
20	B
21	B
22	C
23	A
24	B
25	B
26	B
27	A
28	A
29	B
30	A
31	A
Part 3	
32	C
33	A
34	C
35	A
36	C
37	B
38	D
39	B
40	C
41	D
42	C
43	B
44	D
45	A
46	B
47	C
48	A
49	B
50	D

問題番号	正解
51	B
52	B
53	C
54	B
55	C
56	B
57	C
58	A
59	D
60	C
61	A
62	C
63	A
64	B
65	B
66	D
67	A
68	C
69	C
70	B
Part 4	
71	D
72	C
73	D
74	D
75	B
76	A
77	A
78	B
79	C
80	B
81	C
82	A
83	A
84	B
85	D
86	A
87	D
88	A
89	A
90	D
91	B
92	A
93	B
94	B
95	C
96	D
97	A
98	A
99	B
100	D

リーディングセクション

問題番号	正解
Part 5	
101	A
102	A
103	D
104	A
105	B
106	D
107	C
108	B
109	B
110	A
111	B
112	A
113	C
114	D
115	C
116	B
117	A
118	D
119	B
120	C
121	D
122	D
123	A
124	C
125	D
126	B
127	C
128	D
129	D
130	C
Part 6	
131	A
132	D
133	C
134	B
135	C
136	B
137	D
138	B
139	A
140	D
141	C
142	B
143	B
144	C
145	B
146	A
Part 7	
147	D
148	B
149	B
150	C

問題番号	正解
151	D
152	D
153	B
154	A
155	B
156	A
157	D
158	D
159	C
160	D
161	C
162	B
163	D
164	A
165	A
166	D
167	A
168	C
169	D
170	C
171	B
172	C
173	A
174	D
175	C
176	C
177	B
178	A
179	C
180	D
181	B
182	D
183	A
184	C
185	A
186	D
187	A
188	B
189	D
190	A
191	C
192	A
193	B
194	D
195	B
196	D
197	C
198	A
199	B
200	D

1

2

3

---

1 🇬🇧 W

(A) She's opening some lockers.
(B) She's stacking some chairs.
(C) She's picking up a wooden box.
(D) She's adjusting her safety vest.

(A) 彼女はロッカーを開けている。
(B) 彼女は椅子を積み重ねている。
(C) 彼女は木箱を持ち上げている。
(D) 彼女は安全ベストを調節している。

> **正解 B** 重ねられた椅子の上に、女性がさらに1
> 脚椅子を積み重ねようとしている。
> stack「〜を積み重ねる、〜を積み上げる」。
> (A) 複数のlocker「ロッカー」が写っているが、女性
> はそれらを開けているところではない。
> (C) pick up 〜「〜を持ち上げる」、wooden box「木
> 箱」。
> (D) 女性はsafety vest「安全ベスト」を着ているが、
> それを調節してはいない。adjust「〜を調節する」。

---

2 🇺🇸 W

(A) He's standing in front of a sink.
(B) He's putting some dishes in a cupboard.
(C) He's installing a faucet in the kitchen.
(D) He's pouring water into a bottle.

(A) 彼はシンクの前に立っている。
(B) 彼は食器棚に数枚の皿を入れている。
(C) 彼はキッチンに蛇口を取り付けている。
(D) 彼はボトルの中に水を注いでいる。

> **正解 A** 男性はシンクの前に立って作業をしてい
> る。sink「シンク、流し」。
> (B) cupboard「食器棚」。
> (C) faucet「蛇口」は写っているが、男性がそれをキ
> ッチンに取り付けているところではない。install「〜
> を取り付ける」。
> (D) 蛇口から水が流れているが、男性は水をbottle
> 「ボトル」の中に注いではいない。pour 〜 into …「〜
> を…の中に注ぐ」。

---

3 🇦🇺 M

(A) A man is reading a notice on a bulletin board.
(B) A woman is placing a bag on a bench.
(C) They are shaking hands.
(D) They are walking through a doorway.

(A) 男性が掲示板のお知らせを読んでいる。
(B) 女性がバッグをベンチの上に置いている。
(C) 彼らは握手している。
(D) 彼らは出入り口を歩いて通り抜けている。

> **正解 B** 女性が右手に持ったバッグをベンチの
> 上に置いている。place「〜を置く」、
> bench「ベンチ」。
> (A) notice「お知らせ」、bulletin board「掲示板」。
> (C) 男性は女性から離れて座っており、2人は握手
> していない。shake hands「握手する」。
> (D) through「〜を通り抜けて」、doorway「出入り
> 口」。

4

5

6

---

4 🇨🇦 M

(A) He's removing a coat from a rack.
(B) He's arranging some merchandise in a display.
(C) He's trying on a hat in a store.
(D) He's selecting a pair of gloves from a basket.

(A) 彼はラックからコートを取り外している。
(B) 彼はディスプレーに商品を並べている。
(C) 彼は店で帽子を試着している。
(D) 彼はかごから1組の手袋を選び出している。

正解 **C** 男性は商品が陳列された店のような場所で、帽子をかぶろうとしている。try on ～「～を試着する」。
(A) 男性はコートを着用しており、それをラックから取り外してはいない。remove「～を取り外す、～を取り去る」、rack「ラック、棚」。
(B) arrange「～をきちんと並べる」、merchandise「商品」、display「ディスプレー、陳列」。
(D) select「～を選び出す」、a pair of ～「1組の～」、basket「かご」。

---

5 🇬🇧 W

(A) She's organizing items in a cabinet.
(B) She's reaching for an item on a shelf.
(C) She's turning on a ceiling fan.
(D) She's storing a package beneath a counter.

(A) 彼女は戸棚の中の品物を整理している。
(B) 彼女は棚の上の品物を取ろうと手を伸ばしている。
(C) 彼女はシーリングファンの電源を入れている。
(D) 彼女は小包をカウンターの下に収納しているところである。

正解 **B** 女性は手を伸ばしてshelf「棚」の物を取ろうとしている。reach for ～「～を取ろうと手を伸ばす」、item「品物」。
(A) 女性の前にcabinet「戸棚（扉付きの棚）」はない。organize「～を整理する」。
(C) ceiling fan「シーリングファン、天井扇風機」は写っていない。
(D) 女性の右手にカウンターはあるが、package「小包」を収納しているところではない。store「～を収納する」、beneath「～の真下に」。

---

6 🇦🇺 M

(A) A screen is mounted on a wall.
(B) A cup has been left on top of some books.
(C) A plastic stool has been pushed under a desk.
(D) A workstation is next to a window.

(A) スクリーンが壁に取り付けられている。
(B) カップが数冊の本の上に置かれたままである。
(C) プラスチック製の腰掛けが机の下に押しやられている。
(D) 仕事場所が窓のそばにある。

正解 **D** 窓際にworkstation「（個人用の）仕事場所、作業机」がある。next to ～「～の隣に」。
(A) mount「～を取り付ける」。
(B) カップは写っているが、本の上に置かれてはいない。〈have[has] been＋過去分詞〉で「～された状態である」という意味。
(C) plastic「プラスチック製の」、stool「（背もたれのない）腰掛け」、push「～を押して動かす」。

PART 2

7 🇺🇸 W Who's in charge of stocking the supply cabinet?

🇦🇺 M (A) Typically once a month or so.

(B) Jae-Min does that.

(C) Next to So-Hee's office.

誰が、備品用戸棚への補充を担当していますか。

(A) 通例、1カ月に1度くらいです。

(B) Jae-Minがそれをします。

(C) So-Heeの執務室の隣です。

正解 **B** Who ～?で備品用戸棚への補充を担当している人物を尋ねているのに対し、「Jae-Minがそれをする」と担当者名を伝えている(B)が正解。in charge of ～「～を担当して」、stock「～に補充する」、supply「備品」、cabinet「戸棚」。

(A) 頻度は尋ねられていない。typically「通例」。

(C) 場所は尋ねられていない。

---

8 🇨🇦 M Where are you holding the company anniversary dinner?

🇬🇧 W (A) At the Riverside Café.

(B) Yes, it was very good.

(C) Five years now.

会社の記念日の夕食会をどこで開催するのですか。

(A) Riversideカフェです。

(B) はい、それは非常に良かったです。

(C) 今や5年です。

正解 **A** Where ～?で会社の記念日の夕食会を開催する場所を尋ねているのに対し、「Riversideカフェだ」と店の名前を伝えている(A)が正解。hold「～を開催する」、anniversary「記念日」。

(B) 場所を尋ねられているので、Yes、Noでは応答にならない。

(C) 期間は尋ねられていない。

---

9 🇦🇺 M Did you hire a new store manager?

🇺🇸 W (A) A little higher up, please.

(B) Yes, she starts on Monday.

(C) We're open until ten P.M. every day.

あなたは新しい店長を雇いましたか。

(A) もう少し高く上げてください。

(B) はい、彼女は月曜日に勤務を始めます。

(C) 当店は毎日午後10時まで営業しております。

正解 **B** 新しい店長を雇用したのか尋ねているのに対し、Yesと肯定した上で、「彼女は月曜日に勤務を始める」とその人物の勤務開始予定日を知らせている(B)が正解。hire「～を雇用する」。

(A) 質問にあるhireと同じ音の形容詞higherに注意。

(C) 店の営業時間は尋ねられていない。

---

10 🇬🇧 W Why is everyone leaving early today?

🇦🇺 M (A) Because there's a conference this afternoon.

(B) Make a left turn on the next street.

(C) A little bit later.

なぜ今日は皆、早く出て行くのですか。

(A) 今日の午後に協議会があるからです。

(B) 次の通りを左折してください。

(C) もう少し後です。

正解 **A** Why ～?で皆が早く出て行く理由を尋ねているのに対し、Because ～を用いて、「今日の午後に協議会があるからだ」と理由を伝えている(A)が正解。leave「出発する、去る」、early「(予定・定刻などより)早く」。conference「協議会、会議」。

(B) make a left turn「左折する」。

(C) later「後で」。

---

11 🇨🇦 M When are you meeting the client from India?

🇺🇸 W (A) Yes, I know that area well.

(B) The new pamphlets.

(C) At nine A.M. on Tuesday.

あなたはいつそのインドからの顧客と会うのですか。

(A) はい、私はその地域をよく知っています。

(B) 新しいパンフレットです。

(C) 火曜日の午前9時です。

正解 **C** When ～?でインドからの顧客といつ会う予定か尋ねているのに対し、「火曜日の午前9時だ」と具体的な曜日と時刻を伝えている(C)が正解。client「顧客」。

(A) 時期を尋ねられているので、Yes、Noでは応答にならない。

(B) pamphlet「パンフレット」。

12 M Would you like to get some lunch now?

M (A) A cooking class at night.
(B) Sure, I'm hungry.
(C) Two days ago.

今から昼食を取りませんか。

(A) 夜間の料理教室です。
(B) いいですね、私はおなかがすいています。
(C) 2日前です。

正解 **B** Would you like to do ～?は「～しませんか」という勧誘の表現。今から昼食を取ろうと誘っているのに対し、Sureと承諾し、「私はおなかがすいている」と昼食への賛同を表している(B)が正解。
(A) 質問にある名詞lunchと関連するcookingが含まれるが、応答になっていない。
(C) 時期は尋ねられていない。

13 W Do you like the new office chairs?

M (A) They're not worth the expense.
(B) From an advertisement in the newspaper.
(C) He's the president of the company.

その新しい事務用椅子をあなたは気に入っていますか。

(A) それらは費用に見合う価値がありません。
(B) 新聞広告からです。
(C) 彼はその会社の社長です。

正解 **A** 新しい事務用椅子を気に入っているかと感想を尋ねているのに対し、「それらは費用に見合う価値がない」と否定的な評価を述べている(A)が正解。Theyは質問にあるthe new office chairsを指す。worth「～の価値がある」、expense「費用」。
(B) advertisement「広告」。
(C) Heが誰を指すのか不明。president「社長」。

14 W What are you working on today?

W (A) The next marketing plan.
(B) From eight A.M. to five P.M.
(C) Yes, walking through the park.

あなたは今日、何に取り組んでいるのですか。

(A) 次のマーケティング計画です。
(B) 午前8時から午後5時です。
(C) はい、公園を歩いて通り抜けます。

正解 **A** 今日取り組んでいる業務を尋ねているのに対し、「次のマーケティング計画だ」と業務内容を伝えている(A)が正解。work on ～「～に取り組む」。
(B) 時間帯は尋ねられていない。
(C) 何に取り組むか尋ねられているので、Yes、Noでは応答にならない。質問にあるworkingと似た音のwalkingに注意。

15 M How do I order more paper?

W (A) Yes, the files were in order.
(B) The candy is in a paper bag.
(C) There's some in the cabinet.

どのように追加の用紙を注文すればいいのですか。

(A) はい、ファイルはきちんと整っていました。
(B) 菓子は紙袋に入っています。
(C) 戸棚に幾らかありますよ。

正解 **C** How ～?で、用紙を追加注文する方法を尋ねているのに対し、「戸棚に幾らかある」と伝え、用紙を注文する必要がないことを示唆している(C)が正解。someは質問にあるpaperを指す。order「～を注文する」。
(A) 質問にあるorderが含まれるが、応答になっていない。in order「きちんと整って」。
(B) 質問にあるpaperが含まれるが、candy「(あめ・チョコレートなどの)砂糖菓子」については尋ねられていない。paper bag「紙袋」。

16 M The new mobile phone is being launched today, isn't it?

W (A) No, not until next week.
(B) Extended battery life.
(C) My telephone extension is 56.

新しい携帯電話は今日、発売されるのですよね?

(A) いいえ、来週まではされません。
(B) 長くなった電池寿命です。
(C) 私の電話の内線番号は56です。

正解 **A** 肯定文の文末に ～, isn't it?を付けて「～ですよね」と、新しい携帯電話が発売されるのが今日なのか確認している。これに対し、Noと否定して、来週までは発売されないことを伝えている(A)が正解。launch「～を発売する、～を開始する」。not until ～「～(ある時点)まで…ない」。
(B) 質問にあるmobile phoneと関連するbattery life「電池寿命」が含まれるが、新しい電話の特長などは尋ねられていない。extended「延長された」。
(C) extension「内線番号、内線」。

17 W　Why don't you apply for that position in Sales?

　　🇨🇦 M　(A) Did you make that deposit in the bank?
　　　　(B) On a spreadsheet, please.
　　　　(C) Yes, I think I'll do that.

営業部のその職に応募してはいかがですか。
(A) あなたは銀行にその預金をしましたか。
(B) スプレッドシートにお願いします。
(C) はい、そうしようと思います。

正解 **C**　Why don't you ~?「~したらどうか」で、営業部の職への応募を提案しているのに対し、Yesと肯定して、「そうしようと思う」と応募の意思を伝えている(C)が正解。do thatは、営業部の職に応募することを指す。apply for ~「~に応募する」、position「職」、sales「営業部門」。
(A) make a deposit「預金をする」。
(B) spreadsheet「スプレッドシート、表計算シート」。

18 🇦🇺 M　How many copies of the application should I make?

　　🇺🇸 W　(A) About 30.
　　　　(B) Just one coffee, please.
　　　　(C) I already made the cake.

私は申請書を何部コピーすべきですか。
(A) 30部ぐらいです。
(B) コーヒーを1杯だけお願いします。
(C) 私はすでにケーキを作りました。

正解 **A**　How many ~?で用意すべき申請書のコピー部数を尋ねているのに対し、「30部ぐらいだ」とおおよその数量を伝えている(A)が正解。make a copy「コピーを取る」、application「申請書」。
(B) 質問にあるcopiesと似た音のcoffeeに注意。
(C) ケーキについては尋ねられていない。

19 🇬🇧 W　Are you able to stay late tonight to help set up?

　　🇦🇺 M　(A) Yes, for an extra hour or two.
　　　　(B) Try that large display in the front.
　　　　(C) An expensive rate.

今夜、遅くまで残って準備するのを手伝ってもらうことはできますか。
(A) はい、追加で1、2時間なら。
(B) 前方にあるその大型ディスプレーを試してみてください。
(C) 高額な料金です。

正解 **A**　今夜、残業して準備を手伝ってくれるか尋ねているのに対し、Yesと肯定して、「追加で1、2時間なら」と条件を足している(A)が正解。be able to do「~することができる」、stay late「遅くまで残る」、set up「準備する」。
(B) front「前方」。
(C) 質問にあるlateと似た音のrate「料金、割合」に注意。expensive「高額な」。

20 🇦🇺 M　Who will be presenting at the technology conference?

　　🇺🇸 W　(A) Is it a popular film?
　　　　(B) I haven't looked at the program book yet.
　　　　(C) Buying a new phone every year.

誰がテクノロジー協議会で発表するのですか。
(A) それは有名な映画ですか。
(B) 私はまだプログラムの冊子を見ていません。
(C) 毎年新しい電話機を購入することです。

正解 **B**　Who ~?でテクノロジー協議会で発表する予定の人物を尋ねているのに対し、「私はまだプログラムの冊子を見ていない」と、誰が発表することになっているか知らないことを示唆している(B)が正解。present「(~を)発表する」、technology「テクノロジー、技術」、conference「協議会」。
(A) itが何を指すか不明であり、film「映画」については尋ねられていない。

21 🇦🇺 M　Can you give me a ride, or should I wait for the bus?

　　🇬🇧 W　(A) A few minutes ago.
　　　　(B) I'll be happy to take you.
　　　　(C) On the next corner.

私を車に乗せてもらえますか、それとも私はバスを待った方がよいですか。
(A) 数分前です。
(B) 喜んであなたをお連れしますよ。
(C) 次の角です。

正解 **B**　A or B?の形で、相手の車に乗せてもらえるか、バスを待った方がよいか尋ねているのに対し、「喜んであなたを連れて行く」と依頼を快諾している(B)が正解。give ~ a ride「~を車に乗せる」。be happy to do「喜んで~する」、take「~を連れて行く」。
(A) 時は尋ねられていない。
(C) 場所は尋ねられていない。

22 🇨🇦 M The accounting department is on the fifth floor, right?

🇬🇧 W (A) Please check your departure time.
(B) She gave the presentation twice.
(C) I just started working here.

経理部は5階ですよね？
(A) あなたの出発時間を確認してください。
(B) 彼女はそのプレゼンテーションを2回行いました。
(C) 私はここで働き始めたばかりなのです。

正解 C 肯定文の文末に ～, right? を付けて「～ですよね」と、経理部が5階にあるのか確認している。これに対し、「私はここで働き始めたばかりだ」と答え、経理部があるフロアを知らないことを示唆している(C)が正解。accounting「経理、会計」、department「部署」。
(A) 質問にあるdepartmentと似た音のdeparture「出発」に注意。
(B) Sheが誰を指すのか不明。give a presentation「プレゼンテーションを行う」。

23 🇺🇸 W We have an employee appreciation dinner every quarter.

🇨🇦 M (A) When is the next one?
(B) I just bought new dishes.
(C) That position has been filled.

当社は四半期ごとに、従業員慰労夕食会を行っています。
(A) 次のものはいつですか。
(B) 私はちょうど、新しい皿を購入したところです。
(C) その職の空きは埋まりました。

正解 A 「当社は四半期ごとに、従業員慰労夕食会を行う」という説明に対し、「次のものはいつか」と次回の開催時期を尋ねている(A)が正解。oneは、説明にある employee appreciation dinner を指す。appreciation「感謝、称賛」、quarter「四半期」。
(B) 説明にあるdinnerと関連する名詞dishesが含まれるが、かみ合わない応答。dish「皿、料理」。
(C) fill「～を補充する、～を満たす」。

24 🇬🇧 W Weren't the safety inspectors supposed to be here by now?

🇦🇺 M (A) The bank down the street, I believe.
(B) I'm sure they'll be here soon.
(C) You should accept the new job.

今頃はもう、ここに安全検査官たちが来ているはずではありませんでしたか。
(A) その通りの先の銀行だと思います。
(B) きっと、彼らは間もなくここに来るでしょう。
(C) あなたはその新しい仕事を受けるべきです。

正解 B 否定疑問文で、安全検査官たちが来ているはずではなかったか、と到着予定を確認しているのに対し、「きっと、彼らは間もなくここに来るだろう」と伝えている(B)が正解。theyは質問にある the safety inspectorsを指す。safety inspector「安全検査官」、be supposed to do「～するはずである、～することになっている」。
(C) accept「～を受諾する」。

25 🇺🇸 W Did you travel to England for business, or was it a vacation?

🇨🇦 M (A) I reserved a table for two.
(B) We went on a family holiday.
(C) A direct flight, please.

あなたはイングランドまで仕事で旅行したのですか、それともそれは休暇だったのですか。
(A) 私は2名用の席を予約しました。
(B) 私たちは家族での休暇に出掛けました。
(C) 直行便をお願いします。

正解 B A or B? の形で、イングランドへの旅行の目的は仕事と私的な休暇のどちらだったのか尋ねている。vacationをholidayで言い換えて、「私たちは家族での休暇に出掛けた」と伝えている(B)が正解。business「仕事」、vacation「休暇」。go on a holiday「休暇に出掛ける」。
(A) reserve「～を予約する」。
(C) 飛行機の経路は尋ねられていない。direct flight「(飛行機の)直行便」。

26 🇦🇺 M What documents should I bring to the meeting?

🇬🇧 W (A) Tomorrow at three o'clock.
(B) You'll just be watching a presentation.
(C) She prefers a vegetarian dish.

私は会議にどんな書類を持参すべきですか。
(A) 明日の3時です。
(B) あなたはプレゼンテーションを見るだけです。
(C) 彼女はベジタリアン向けの料理を好みます。

正解 B 会議にどのような書類を持参すべきか尋ねているのに対し、「あなたはプレゼンテーションを見るだけだ」と述べ、書類を持参する必要がないことを示唆している(B)が正解。document「書類」。
(A) 日時は尋ねられていない。
(C) Sheが誰を指すのか不明。prefer「～の方を好む」、vegetarian「ベジタリアン(の)、菜食主義(の)」。

27 🇺🇸 W What time is the workshop on effective communication?

🇦🇺 M (A) I thought it was canceled.

(B) Yes, I called yesterday.

(C) Several interesting presenters.

効果的なコミュニケーションに関する講習会は何時ですか。

(A) それは中止されたと思っていました。

(B) はい、私は昨日電話しました。

(C) 数名の興味深い講演者です。

正解 **A** What time ～?で講習会の時刻を尋ねているのに対し、「それは中止されたと思っていた」と講習会についての自分の認識を伝えている(A)が正解。itは質問にあるthe workshopを指す。effective「効果的な」。

(B) 時刻を尋ねられているので、Yes、Noでは応答にならない。

(C) presenter「講演者」。

28 🇬🇧 W Why's the current vacation policy being changed?

🇨🇦 M (A) I guess you didn't see Ms. Garcia's e-mail.

(B) Starting next Monday.

(C) Yes, the parking meter accepts change.

現在の休暇方針はなぜ変更されるのですか。

(A) あなたはGarciaさんのEメールを見なかったようですね。

(B) 今度の月曜日からです。

(C) はい、パーキングメーターは小銭が使えます。

正解 **A** Why ～?で休暇方針が変更される理由を尋ねているのに対し、「あなたはGarciaさんのEメールを見なかったようだ」と述べ、変更理由はGarciaさんからのEメールに書いてあったことを示唆している(A)が正解。Why'sはWhy isの短縮形。current「現在の」、policy「方針」。

(B) 開始時期は尋ねられていない。

(C) parking meter「パーキングメーター(駐車料金計)」、accept「～を受け付ける」、change「小銭」。

29 🇦🇺 M Where is the new printer being installed?

🇺🇸 W (A) Twenty color copies, please.

(B) The manager didn't approve that purchase.

(C) I already downloaded the program.

新しいプリンターはどこに設置されるのですか。

(A) カラーコピーを20部、お願いします。

(B) 管理者がその購入を承認しませんでした。

(C) 私はすでにプログラムをダウンロードしました。

正解 **B** Where ～?で新しいプリンターの設置予定場所を尋ねているのに対し、「管理者がその購入を承認しなかった」と伝えて、新しいプリンターの購入と設置が取りやめになったことを示唆している(B)が正解。install「～を設置する」。approve「～を承認する」、purchase「購入」。

(A) 質問にあるprinterに関連するcolor copiesが含まれるが、応答になっていない。

30 🇬🇧 W Why don't we meet in the lobby at eleven thirty?

🇨🇦 M (A) Noon would work better for me.

(B) They're going to lunch.

(C) I saw him at the main entrance.

11時30分にロビーで待ち合わせませんか。

(A) 正午の方が私は都合が良いのですが。

(B) 彼らは昼食に行くところです。

(C) 私は、正面玄関で彼を見かけました。

正解 **A** Why don't we ～?は「～しませんか」と提案する表現。11時30分にロビーで待ち合わせないかという提案に対し、「正午の方が私は都合が良いのだが」と希望する待ち合わせ時刻を控えめに伝えている(A)が正解。lobby「ロビー」。work for ～「～に都合が良い」。

(B) theyが誰を指すのか不明。

(C) 待ち合わせ場所になりそうなmain entrance「正面玄関」に注意。

31 🇨🇦 M I just received my auditor certification.

🇺🇸 W (A) We'll need someone with that experience.

(B) Yes, they'll be there.

(C) A six-month course.

私はちょうど、会計監査人の資格認定を受けたところです。

(A) 私たちは、その知識を持つ人を必要とするでしょう。

(B) はい、彼らはそこにいるでしょう。

(C) 6カ月間の講座です。

正解 **A** 「私はちょうど、会計監査人の資格認定を受けたところだ」という発言に対し、「私たちは、その知識を持つ人を必要とするだろう」と述べ、会計監査の資格は今後に生かせると伝えている(A)が正解。receive「～を受ける」、auditor「会計監査人」、certification「資格の認定」。experience「(経験によって得た)知識、技能」。

(B) theyが誰を、thereがどこを指すのか不明。

PART 3

Questions 32 through 34 refer to the following conversation.

問題32-34は次の会話に関するものです。

🏴 W Welcome to Sullivan Technology Store.

Sullivanテクノロジーストアへようこそ。

🍁 M Hi. I'm looking to buy a laptop. ❶I'm a travel photographer. And I want to be able to edit my photos while I'm on location.

こんにちは。ノートパソコンを購入しようとしています。私は旅行写真家で、野外撮影中に自分の写真の編集ができたらいいなと思っています。

🏴 W OK. Any other requirements?

分かりました。その他のご要望は？

🍁 M ❷Since I'll be traveling a lot with it, I need a laptop that's really light.

私はそれを携帯して頻繁に旅行するつもりなので、とても軽いノートパソコンが必要です。

🏴 W ❸We do sell several laptops that aren't too heavy. But ❹before we look at those, you might be more interested in buying a tablet computer instead. ❺They're much lighter than any laptop we sell.

当店ではもちろん、あまり重くないノートパソコンを何種類か販売しております。ですが、そちらをご覧になる前に、お客さまはむしろタブレットコンピューターを購入したいとお思いになるかもしれません。これらは、当店が販売しているどのノートパソコンよりもはるかに軽いですよ。

---

32 What is the man's job?

(A) Computer programmer
(B) Travel agent
(C) Photographer
(D) Product tester

男性の職業は何ですか。

(A) コンピュータープログラマー
(B) 旅行代理店員
(C) 写真家
(D) 製品検査官

正解 C Sullivanテクノロジーストアへようこそ、と店員に声をかけられた男性は、来店の目的をノートパソコンの購入だと述べてから、❶「私は旅行写真家だ」と職業を伝えている。
(A) ノートパソコンやタブレットコンピューターに言及はあるが、男性はコンピュータープログラマーだとは述べていない。
(B) agent「代理業者」。
(D) product「製品」、tester「検査人」。

33 What product feature is most important to the man?

(A) Weight
(B) Color
(C) Battery life
(D) Reliability

男性にとって、製品のどのような特徴が最も重要ですか。

(A) 重量
(B) 色
(C) 電池寿命
(D) 信頼性

正解 A 購入を検討中のノートパソコンに対する要望を尋ねられた男性は、❷「私はそれを携帯して頻繁に旅行するつもりなので、とても軽いノートパソコンが必要だ」と伝えている。よって、男性にとって最も重要な特徴は、重量と判断できる。feature「特徴」。weight「重さ」。
(C) battery「電池」、life「寿命」。
(D) reliability「信頼性」。

34 What does the woman suggest that the man do?

(A) Talk to her colleague
(B) Use a coupon code
(C) Consider a different product
(D) Purchase an extended warranty

女性は、男性が何をすることを提案していますか。

(A) 彼女の同僚と話す
(B) クーポンコードを使う
(C) 別の製品を検討する
(D) 長期保証を購入する

正解 C 女性は男性に❸で、店にはあまり重くないノートパソコンがあると言っているが、❹で「そちらを見る前に、あなたはむしろタブレットコンピューターを購入したいと思うかもしれない」と代わりにタブレットコンピューターの検討を提案し、❺で、これらはパソコンより軽量だと述べている。a tablet computerをa different productと表している(C)が正解。consider「～を検討する」。
(A) colleague「同僚」。
(B) coupon code「クーポンコード」。
(D) extended「長期の」、warranty「保証」。

Words & Phrases

technology テクノロジー、技術　look to *do* ～しようとする、～することを目指す
laptop ノートパソコン　photographer 写真家　be able to *do* ～することができる　edit ～を編集する
on location 野外撮影で　requirement 要求　light 軽い　several 幾つかの　heavy 重い
be interested in *doing* ～したいと思っている　tablet computer タブレットコンピューター　instead むしろ
much 〈比較級を強調して〉はるかに、ずっと

Questions 35 through 37 refer to the following conversation.

M　Zoya, ❶did you photocopy the documents for the staff meeting?

W　Oh, ❷you mean the ones about the new security policy? Yes—they're right here.

M　Thanks— ❸it's important that all staff get this, because starting next week, they'll need to follow some new rules at work, like wearing their ID badges at all times.

W　I noticed that—I think it's a good idea. By the way, ❹Taro said that he wouldn't be able to make it to the meeting.

M　OK, ❺can you please put a copy on his desk, then?

問題35-37は次の会話に関するものです。

Zoya、スタッフ会議用の資料をコピーしましたか。

ああ、新しいセキュリティー方針に関する資料のことですか。はい——ちょうどここにあります。

ありがとう——これが全スタッフの手に渡ることが重要です。というのも来週から皆が、IDバッジの常時着用といった、職場での新しいルールに従う必要がありますからね。

それには気付いていました——良い考えだと思います。ところで、Taroが会議には出席できそうにないと言っていました。

分かりました、では彼の机の上に1部置いておいてもらえますか。

---

35 What are the speakers preparing for?

(A) A staff meeting
(B) A company picnic
(C) A business trip
(D) A product demonstration

話し手たちは何の準備をしていますか。

(A) スタッフ会議
(B) 会社のピクニック
(C) 出張
(D) 製品の実演

正解 A　男性が、❶「スタッフ会議用の資料をコピーしたか」と尋ねているのに対し、女性は❷で、セキュリティー方針の資料ならばここにある、とスタッフ会議で必要な資料の準備ができていることを伝えている。prepare for ～「～の準備をする」。
(B) picnic「ピクニック」。
(C) business trip「出張」。
(D) demonstration「実演、デモ」。

---

36 What will happen next week?

(A) A photocopier will be replaced.
(B) An office will be renovated.
(C) A company policy will change.
(D) A client will visit.

来週に何が起こりますか。

(A) コピー機が交換される。
(B) オフィスが改装される。
(C) 会社の方針が変わる。
(D) 顧客が訪れる。

正解 C　女性は❷で、新しいセキュリティー方針に関する資料の準備ができていると伝えている。それに対し男性は❸で、「資料が全スタッフの手に渡ることが重要だ」と言い、続けて「来週から皆が、職場での新しいルールに従う必要があるので」と、その理由を述べている。来週にセキュリティー方針が変わると判断できるので(C)が正解。
(A) photocopier「コピー機」。
(B) renovate「～を改装する」。

---

37 What does the man ask the woman to do?

(A) Visit an event location
(B) Leave documents for a coworker
(C) Set up a display
(D) Check a reservation

男性は女性に何をするよう求めていますか。

(A) イベント会場を訪問する
(B) 同僚のために資料を置いておく
(C) 展示品を設置する
(D) 予約を確認する

正解 B　女性が❹で、Taroという同僚が会議に出席できそうにないと伝えたのに対し、男性は❺「では彼の机の上に1部置いておいてもらえるか」と、会議資料をTaroの机の上に置いておくよう頼んでいる。Taroを a coworker と表している(B)が正解。leave「～を置いていく」、coworker「同僚」。
(A) location「場所」。
(C) set up ～「～を設置する」、display「展示品」。
(D) reservation「予約」。

Words & Phrases

photocopy　～をコピーする　　document　資料、書類　　security　セキュリティー、安全性
policy　方針　　follow　～に従う　　at work　職場で　　ID　身元証明書　★identificationの略　　badge　バッジ
at all times　常に　　notice　～に気付く　　by the way　ところで　　make it to ～　～に出席できる、～に都合がつく
copy　1部

TEST 2　PART 3

Questions 38 through 40 refer to the following conversation.

🇨🇦 M Emily, ❶did you hear that a new pharmacy's opening on West Avenue?

🇬🇧 W No, but that's great news. ❷I usually go to Paxton's Drug Store on Main Street. It has a very friendly staff, ❸but the parking downtown is so inconvenient. There's never anywhere to park there!

🇨🇦 M I agree! Plus ❹the article I read about the pharmacy on West Avenue said it's supposed to have wellness classes every week. ❺It'll be great to learn more about them.

問題38-40は次の会話に関するものです。

Emily、ウェスト大通りに新しい薬局が開業することを聞きましたか？

いいえ、でも素晴らしいニュースですね。私は普段、メイン通りにあるPaxton'sドラッグストアに行きます。そこはとても親切なスタッフがいますが、中心街の駐車場はとても不便です。あそこには駐車できる場所がどこにもあったためしがありませんから。

同感です。それに、ウェスト大通りの薬局について僕が読んだ記事には、そこが毎週、健康推進講座を開催することになっていると書いてありましたよ。それらについて、もっと知ることができたらいいですよね。

---

38 What news does the man share?

(A) A delivery will be delayed.
(B) A store has extended its hours.
(C) A parking garage is being built.
(D) A new business will open.

男性はどんな知らせを共有していますか。

(A) 配達が遅延する。
(B) 店が営業時間を延長した。
(C) 駐車場が建設中である。
(D) 新しい店が開業する。

正解 D 男性は❶「ウェスト大通りに新しい薬局が開業することを聞いたか」と女性に尋ねている。a new pharmacyをa new businessと表している(D)が正解。❶のpharmacy's openingは pharmacy is opening の短縮形で近い未来の予定を表している。share「～を共有する」。business「店、事業」。
(A) delivery「配達」、delay「～を遅らせる」。
(B) extend「～を延長する」、hours「営業時間」。
(C) parking garage「駐車場」。

---

39 Why does the woman dislike shopping at Paxton's Drug Store?

(A) Its prices are high.
(B) It is difficult to find parking.
(C) It has poor customer service.
(D) It has a small selection of products.

女性はなぜ、Paxton'sドラッグストアでの買い物が嫌なのですか。

(A) 同店の品物価格が高いから。
(B) 駐車スペースを見つけることが困難だから。
(C) 同店は顧客サービスが悪いから。
(D) 同店は製品の品ぞろえが少ないから。

正解 B 女性は❷で、普段利用するPaxton'sドラッグストアには、とても親切なスタッフがいると述べてから、❸「でも中心街の駐車場はとても不便だ。あそこには駐車できる場所がどこにもあったためしがない」と同店での買い物に不満を述べている。dislike doing「～するのが嫌である」。
(A) price「価格」。
(C) 女性は同店のスタッフは親切だと褒めている。poor「(品質の)劣った」、customer service「顧客サービス」。
(D) selection「品ぞろえ、選択」。

---

40 What does the man want to learn more about?

(A) Some journalists
(B) A bus schedule
(C) Some classes
(D) A medication

男性は何についてもっと知りたいと思っていますか。

(A) ジャーナリスト
(B) バスの時刻表
(C) 講座
(D) 薬物治療

正解 C 男性は❹「ウェスト大通りの薬局について僕が読んだ記事には、そこが毎週、健康推進講座を開催することになっていると書いてあった」と言った後、❺「それらについて、もっと知ることができたらいい」と述べている。themは、前文のwellness classes「健康推進講座」を指すので(C)が正解。
(A) journalist「ジャーナリスト」。
(B) schedule「時刻表、予定表」。
(D) medication「薬物治療、投薬」。

Words & Phrases

pharmacy 薬局　open 開業する、開店する　friendly 親切な　parking 駐車場　downtown 中心街の　inconvenient 不便な　anywhere 〈否定文で〉どこにも～ない　park 駐車する　agree 同意する　plus それに、加えて　article 記事　be supposed to do ～することになっている　wellness 健康推進、心身が健康な状態

112

Questions 41 through 43 refer to the following conversation with three speakers.

🇺🇸 W ❶I need to extend my reservation, please. I'm in room five-ten.

🇨🇦 M ❷How many extra nights do you need?

🇺🇸 W ❸Just one. I was supposed to interview someone for an article, but it's been postponed until tomorrow.

🇨🇦 M I'll make that change now. Oh, wait. ❹Mr. Aziz, could you check this? The new checkout date isn't showing up in the system.

🇦🇺 M Sure. Just hit this button. ❺Can we help you with anything else?

🇺🇸 W Actually, ❻I'm interested in the show at Ravendale Theater. Have you heard anything about it?

🇦🇺 M I definitely recommend it. In fact, ❼there are several guests going on a shuttle bus from the hotel. It leaves at six P.M. this evening if you're interested.

問題41-43は3人の話し手による次の会話に関するものです。

私は予約を延長する必要があるのでお願いできますか。510号室に滞在しています。

追加で何泊される必要がございますか。

1泊だけです。記事のために、ある人にインタビューすることになっていたのですが、明日まで延期されたのです。

今すぐ、その変更を行います。ああ、ちょっと。Azizさん、これを確認してもらえませんか。新しいチェックアウト日がシステムに表示されません。

いいですよ。このボタンを押すだけです。お客さま、何か他に私どもがお手伝いできることはございますか。

実は、Ravendale劇場でのショーに興味があるのです。それについて何か聞いていますか。

そちらは間違いなくお薦めいたしますよ。実は、当ホテルからシャトルバスで向かうお客さまが数名いらっしゃいます。もし、ご希望でしたら、今晩午後6時に出発いたします。

---

41 Where most likely are the speakers?

(A) At an art museum
(B) At an employment agency
(C) At an airport
(D) At a hotel

話し手たちはどこにいると考えられますか。

(A) 美術館
(B) 人材派遣会社
(C) 空港
(D) ホテル

正解 D 女性は❶で、予約の延長を依頼し、自分の部屋番号を伝えている。それに対し、1人目の男性は❷「追加で何泊する必要があるか」と尋ね、システムで変更の入力を行っている。よって、ホテルの宿泊客の女性が、受付で従業員の男性と話していると考えられる。
(B) employment agency「人材派遣会社」。

---

42 Why is a change requested?

(A) A space is unavailable.
(B) Some employees are on vacation.
(C) An appointment was rescheduled.
(D) An announcement was postponed.

なぜ変更が求められているのですか。

(A) スペースが利用できないから。
(B) 何人かの従業員が休暇中だから。
(C) 約束の日時が変更されたから。
(D) 発表が延期されたから。

正解 C 延泊日数を尋ねられた女性は❸で、「1泊だけだ」と伝え、「記事のために、ある人にインタビューすることになっていたが、明日まで延期された」と理由を述べている。appointment「(面会の)約束」、reschedule「〜の日時を変更する」。
(A) unavailable「利用できない」。
(B) employee「従業員」、on vacation「休暇中で」。
(D) announcement「発表」。

---

43 What does Mr. Aziz tell the woman about?

(A) A pamphlet
(B) Transportation
(C) Computer access
(D) A voucher

Azizさんは女性に、何について伝えていますか。

(A) パンフレット
(B) 交通手段
(C) コンピューターへのアクセス
(D) 引換券

正解 B ❹で、Azizさんと呼び掛けられた2人目の男性は、❺で宿泊客の女性に他に用件はないか尋ねている。❻でRavendale劇場のショーの情報を求める女性に対し、それを薦めたAzizさんは、❼「当ホテルからシャトルバスで向かう客が数名いる」と述べ、劇場へのシャトルバスの出発時刻を伝えている。transportation「交通手段」。
(D) voucher「(商品・サービスの)引換券、割引券」。

Words & Phrases

extend 〜を延長する　reservation 予約　extra 追加の　interview 〜にインタビューする
postpone 〜を延期する　checkout チェックアウト　show up 表示される、現れる　hit 〜(ボタンなど)を押す
button ボタン　help 〜 with … …のことで〜を手伝う　actually 実は　be interested in 〜 〜に興味がある
theater 劇場　definitely 断然、全く　recommend 〜を薦める　in fact 事実、実際に　several 幾つかの
guest 宿泊客　shuttle bus シャトルバス　leave 出発する

Questions 44 through 46 refer to the following conversation.

問題44-46は次の会話に関するものです。

🇨🇦 M Lena, ❶I wanted to talk to you about the script you submitted for our upcoming radio commercial, the one advertising our electric stoves.

Lena、あなたが今度のラジオコマーシャル用に提出した台本について、あなたと話したかったのです。当社製電気コンロを宣伝するものですよ。

🇬🇧 W Oh, yes. ❷I wasn't sure about including the slogan—the one that goes, "You can count on Plymouth Appliances. We'll make your kitchen our priority."

ああ、はい。あのキャッチフレーズを含めるべきかどうかには、確信が持てませんでした――『Plymouth電気器具社にお任せください。当社はあなたのキッチンを大切に考えています』というものです。

🇨🇦 M You're right. ❸I think we'll have to take that out. We only have 30 seconds of audio, so we'll have to shorten the script.

もっともです。それを削除する必要があると思います。たった30秒の音声なので、台本を短くする必要があるでしょう。

🇬🇧 W Well, ❹I'm worried about our deadline. The script has to be ready by the end of the week. We've already reserved time in the recording studio.

ええと、私は締め切りを心配しています。台本は今週末までに用意ができていなければなりません。すでに録音スタジオの時間を予約してありますから。

---

44 What products does the company sell?

(A) Furniture
(B) Electronics
(C) Automobiles
(D) Appliances

会社はどんな製品を販売していますか。

(A) 家具
(B) 電子機器
(C) 自動車
(D) 電気器具

正解 D 男性は❶で、女性が提出した自社製電気コンロのコマーシャル用の台本について話したかったと述べ、女性は❷で「Plymouth電気器具社にお任せください。当社はあなたのキッチンを大切に考えています」と、自社のキャッチフレーズに言及している。よって、設問の会社とは話し手たちの勤務先で、電気器具を扱う会社と分かる。
(A) furniture「家具」。
(B) electronics「電子機器」。
(C) automobile「自動車」。

---

45 What does the man want to change?

(A) A script
(B) A contract
(C) A product name
(D) A company logo

男性は何を変更したいと思っていますか。

(A) 台本
(B) 契約書
(C) 製品名
(D) 会社のロゴ

正解 A ❷で、自社製品のコマーシャル用台本にキャッチフレーズを含めるべきか確信が持てなかったと言う女性に対し、男性は同調して、❸「それを削除する必要があると思う。たった30秒の音声なので、台本を短くする必要がある」と、台本を変更する必要性を伝えている。
(B) contract「契約書」。
(C) 製品のコマーシャルに関する会話だが、その品名の変更は述べられていない。
(D) logo「ロゴ」。

---

46 What concern does the woman have?

(A) A budget is too small.
(B) A deadline is approaching.
(C) Some actors are not available.
(D) Some equipment is not working.

女性はどんな心配を抱いていますか。

(A) 予算が少な過ぎる。
(B) 締め切りが近づいている。
(C) 一部の俳優の都合がつかない。
(D) 一部の機器が作動していない。

正解 B ❸で、コマーシャルの台本を短くする必要があると言う男性に対し、女性は❹「私は締め切りを心配している。台本は今週末までに用意ができていなくてはならない」と、締め切りが近づいていることを心配している。concern「心配」。approach「近づく」。
(A) budget「予算」。
(C) available「都合がつく、利用できる」。
(D) equipment「機器」。

Words & Phrases		
script 台本　submit ～を提出する　upcoming 今度の　commercial コマーシャル		
advertise ～を宣伝する　electric stove 電気コンロ　sure 確信があって　include ～を含める		
slogan キャッチフレーズ　count on ～ ～を頼りにする　appliance 電気器具　priority 優先事項		
take out ～ ～を削除する、～を外す　second 秒　shorten ～を短くする　be worried about ～ ～を心配している		
deadline 締め切り　ready 用意ができた　reserve ～を予約する、～を確保する　recording studio 録音スタジオ		

Questions 47 through 49 refer to the following conversation.

🇺🇸 W Hi. ❶You've reached R&W Plumbing.

🇨🇦 M Hi, ❷I'm calling about the water at my business. The pressure is really weak; I think there must be something wrong with the pipes.

🇺🇸 W OK. ❸Can I take your name and phone number and get back to you about making a service appointment? ❹Our schedule is pretty full right now.

🇨🇦 M Well... I run a car wash.

🇺🇸 W Oh, I see. ❺Let me transfer your call to someone who can help right away.

問題47-49は次の会話に関するものです。

はい。こちらはR&W配管工事社です。

もしもし、私の店の給水について電話しています。水圧が非常に弱いのです。思うに、水道管に何か問題があるに違いありません。

なるほど。お名前とお電話番号を頂戴して、修理点検サービスのご予約についてお客さまに折り返しご連絡させていただくことはできますか。ただ今、私どものスケジュールはかなり詰まっておりまして。

ええと…私は洗車場を経営しているのです。

ああ、承知しました。今すぐ、お手伝いできる者にお電話を転送いたします。

---

47 Where does the woman work?

(A) At a cleaning service
(B) At an advertising agency
(C) At a plumbing company
(D) At a property management company

女性はどこで働いていますか。

(A) 清掃サービス会社
(B) 広告代理店
(C) 配管工事会社
(D) 不動産管理会社

正解 **C** ❶「こちらはR&W配管工事社」と電話に応答した女性に対し、男性は❷で、電話の用件を自分の店の給水についてだと述べ、問題点を説明している。よって、女性は配管工事会社で働いていると分かる。
(B) advertising「広告」、agency「代理店」。
(D) property「不動産」、management「管理」。

---

48 What does the man imply when he says, "I run a car wash"?

(A) His problem is urgent.
(B) He is correcting some misinformation.
(C) He needs to hire more workers.
(D) He is too busy to help.

男性は "I run a car wash" という発言で、何を示唆していますか。

(A) 彼の問題は急を要する。
(B) 彼は間違った情報を訂正している。
(C) 彼は作業員をもっと雇用する必要がある。
(D) 彼は忙し過ぎて手助けができない。

正解 **A** 女性は❸で、水道管の修理点検サービスの予約について男性に折り返し連絡してよいか尋ね、❹で「今、私どものスケジュールはかなり詰まっている」と即時対応が困難な状況を伝えている。それに対し、男性は下線部の発言で、自分の店は洗車場だと述べている。これは、給水の問題が事業に関わる緊急性の高いものだと示唆していると考えられる。urgent「急を要する、緊急の」。
(B) correct「～を訂正する」、misinformation「間違った情報、誤報」。
(C) hire「～を雇用する」。

---

49 What will the woman do next?

(A) Conduct a training
(B) Transfer a call
(C) Prepare an invoice
(D) Update a Web site

女性は次に何をしますか。

(A) 研修を実施する
(B) 電話を転送する
(C) 請求書を準備する
(D) ウェブサイトを更新する

正解 **B** 男性の状況が緊急であると理解した女性は、❺「今すぐ、お手伝いできる者に電話を転送する」と申し出ているので、女性は次に、男性の問題に即時に対応できる担当者に電話を転送すると考えられる。
(A) conduct「～を実施する」、training「研修」。
(C) prepare「～を準備する」、invoice「請求書」。
(D) update「～を更新する」。

TEST 2 PART 3

Words & Phrases

reach ～と連絡を取る　plumbing 配管工事　water 給水　business 店、会社
pressure 圧力　weak 弱い　There is something wrong with ～ ～に何か問題がある　pipe 管、パイプ
get back to ～ ～に折り返し連絡する　make an appointment 予約を取る　service 修理点検サービス　pretty かなり
full ぎっしり詰まった　run ～を経営する　car wash 洗車場　transfer ～を転送する　right away 今すぐ

Questions 50 through 52 refer to the following conversation with three speakers.

問題50-52は3人の話し手による次の会話に関するものです。

🇬🇧 W ❶We've learned a lot about your background and qualifications, Jerome. ❷Any more questions for us before we finish up?

あなたの経歴や資格に関して、我々は多くを知ることができました、Jerome。終わりにする前に、他に我々へのご質問はおありですか。

🇦🇺 M Yes… just one. ❸You mentioned the benefits package. I'm wondering about time off. What's the policy?

はい…1つだけ。福利厚生を話に出されましたよね。休暇について知りたいと思っています。方針はどのようなものですか。

🇬🇧 W Noriko can answer that.

それには Noriko がお答えします。

🇺🇸 W Sure. It's a generous arrangement. ❹If hired, you'd start with three weeks per year, plus some additional personal days. After two years of service, the time increases by a week.

はい。手厚い制度です。雇用されたら、1年につき3週間、プラス数日の特別な私用休暇で始めることになります。勤続年数が2年を超えると、期間は1週間単位で増えます。

🇦🇺 M That's great to know. Thank you.

それは伺って良かったです。ありがとうございます。

🇬🇧 W Well, it's been a pleasure, Jerome. Thank you for coming in. ❺Please do remember to submit that additional work sample we discussed.

それでは、お話しできて良かったです、Jerome。ご来社いただきありがとうございました。話に出た、例の追加のお仕事サンプルを提出するのをどうかお忘れなく。

---

50 What type of meeting is taking place?

(A) A midyear performance review
(B) A policy planning meeting
(C) A training session
(D) A job interview

どんな種類の会合が行われていますか。

(A) 中間勤務評定
(B) 方策立案会議
(C) 研修会
(D) 就職面接

正解 D　1人目の女性は、❶「あなたの経歴や資格に関して、我々は多くを知ることができた」と言っている。また、❸で休暇方針について質問した男性に対し、2人目の女性が❹で「雇用されたら」と前置きした上で、休暇制度の説明をしていることからも、男性に対する就職面接が行われていると分かる。job interview「就職面接」。

(A) midyear「1年の中頃の」、performance review「勤務評定」。

51 What does the man ask about?

(A) A salary increase
(B) A vacation policy
(C) A security guideline
(D) A telecommuting arrangement

男性は何について尋ねていますか。

(A) 昇給
(B) 休暇方針
(C) 安全ガイドライン
(D) 在宅勤務の制度

正解 B　❷で、他に聞きたいことがあるかと確認する1人目の女性に対し、男性は❸で、福利厚生に関連して休暇方針がどのようなものであるか尋ねている。time off を vacation と表している(B)が正解。

(A) salary「給与」、increase「増加」。
(C) security「安全」、guideline「ガイドライン、指針」。
(D) telecommuting「(コンピューター通信による)在宅勤務」。

52 What is the man reminded to submit?

(A) A time sheet
(B) A work sample
(C) An authorization request
(D) A project timeline

男性は何を提出するよう念を押されていますか。

(A) タイムシート
(B) 仕事のサンプル
(C) 承認依頼書
(D) プロジェクトの日程表

正解 B　1人目の女性は、男性に来社への謝意を伝えて会話を締めくくりながら、❺で、話に出た、仕事のサンプルを追加で提出するのを忘れないようにと念を押している。remind ~ to do「~に…するよう念を押す」。

(A) time sheet「タイムシート、勤務記録用紙」。
(C) authorization「承認」、request「依頼書」。
(D) timeline「日程表」。

Words & Phrases

background 経歴　qualification 資格、適性　finish up 終わりにする
mention ~を話に出す　benefits package 福利厚生　wonder about ~ ~について知りたいと思う　time off 休暇
generous 寛大な、十分な　arrangement 制度　hire ~を雇用する　per ~につき　additional 特別な、追加の
personal day (病欠などでない)個人都合による休暇　service 勤務　increase 増える　pleasure 喜び
remember to do 忘れずに~する　submit ~を提出する　sample サンプル、見本　discuss ~を話題にする

Questions 53 through 55 refer to the following conversation.

問題53-55は次の会話に関するものです。

🇦🇺 M Thanks for listening to *Weekend Science*! I'm your host, Paul Farooq. ❶My guest today is Dr. Helen Yu. ❷She's part of a team working on the Z9 telescope, which is used to look at distant stars. Dr. Yu, can you tell us more about the project?

『週末の科学』をお聞きくださり、ありがとうございます。私が司会者のPaul Farooqです。本日のゲストはHelen Yu博士です。博士はZ9望遠鏡に取り組んでいるチームの一員で、その望遠鏡は遠く離れた星を観測するのに使用されています。Yu博士、そのプロジェクトについて詳しく教えていただけますか。

🇬🇧 W Sure. ❸The Z9 telescope is located in one of the driest deserts on Earth. We chose that spot so there'd be very little interference from rain or clouds… so you get a very clear image.

もちろんです。Z9望遠鏡は、地球上で最も乾燥した砂漠の1つに設置されています。我々がその地点を選んだのは、雨や雲による干渉がほとんどないからです。…ですから、非常に鮮明な画像が得られるのです。

🇦🇺 M And ❹has your team made any interesting discoveries?

そして、あなた方のチームは何か興味深い発見をなさいましたか。

🇬🇧 W ❺It has! Tomorrow I'll be presenting our findings at a research conference in Sydney. And I can share some of the highlights with you now.

しました。私は明日、シドニーの研究会議で我々の研究成果を発表することになっています。それで今から、その最も重要な部分をいくつか皆さんにお話しします。

---

53 What most likely is the woman's occupation?

(A) Weather forecaster
(B) Computer programmer
(C) Scientist
(D) Photographer

女性の職業は何だと考えられますか。

(A) 気象予報士
(B) コンピュータープログラマー
(C) 科学者
(D) 写真家

正解 **C**　*Weekend Science*という番組名の後に男性は、❶「本日のゲストはHelen Yu博士だ」と述べ、❷「博士はZ9望遠鏡に取り組んでいるチームの一員だ」と女性を紹介している。以降で女性は、望遠鏡の設置地点と、自分たちの研究成果の発表について話しているので、科学者だと考えられる。occupation「職業」。scientist「科学者」。
(A) weather forecaster「気象予報士」。
(D) 画像に言及があるだけ。

---

54 What does the woman say is beneficial about a location?

(A) It is near the ocean.
(B) It has a dry climate.
(C) It is accessible using public transportation.
(D) It has a renewable energy source.

女性はある選定地について、何が利点だと言っていますか。

(A) そこは海に近い。
(B) そこは気候が乾燥している。
(C) そこは公共交通機関を利用して行きやすい。
(D) そこには再生可能なエネルギー源がある。

正解 **B**　女性は、❸「Z9望遠鏡は、地球上で最も乾燥した砂漠の1つに設置されている。我々がその地点を選んだのは、雨や雲による干渉がほとんどないからだ」と言っている。つまり、選択した地点は、気候が乾燥していることが利点と分かる。beneficial「利益となる」、location「選定地、場所」。climate「気候」。
(A) ocean「海」。
(C) accessible「到達できる」。
(D) renewable「再生可能な」、source「源」。

---

55 What will the woman do tomorrow?

(A) Edit some images
(B) Start a new project
(C) Present at a conference
(D) Install some software

女性は明日、何をしますか。

(A) 画像を編集する
(B) 新しいプロジェクトを開始する
(C) 会議で発表する
(D) ソフトウエアをインストールする

正解 **C**　❹で、プロジェクトチームが興味深い発見をしたか尋ねる男性に対し、❺で女性は肯定し、続けて「私は明日、シドニーの研究会議で我々の研究成果を発表することになっている」と明日の会議の予定を伝えている。
(A) edit「～を編集する」。
(D) install「～をインストールする」。

Words & Phrases

science 科学　host 司会者　part 一員　work on ～ ～に取り組む　telescope 望遠鏡
distant 遠く離れた　locate ～を設置する、～を配置する　dry 乾燥した　desert 砂漠　choose ～を選ぶ
spot 地点、場所　interference 干渉、妨害　cloud 雲　clear 鮮明な　image 画像　discovery 発見
findings 研究成果　conference 会議、協議会　share ～ with … ～を…に話す　highlight 最も重要な部分、ハイライト

Questions 56 through 58 refer to the following conversation.

🇺🇸 W Hey, William. ❶Have you heard from Dolores at the Saint Petersburg factory yet? ❷We need feedback on the new electroplating machines. Our goal this month is 1,000 trumpets, which isn't going to happen if those machines aren't working well.

🇦🇺 M I haven't heard from her this morning, so I'm planning to call her right after lunch.

🇺🇸 W OK. ❸Speaking of lunch, a couple of us are headed to the noodle shop downstairs. ❹Do you want to come?

🇦🇺 M I'm working on a financial report.

🇺🇸 W I understand. Well, ❺let me know what Dolores says. ❻Those machines were a major investment for us and I'm worried that they won't be efficient enough to warrant the expense.

問題56-58は次の会話に関するものです。

ねえ、William。サンクトペテルブルグ工場にいるDoloresから、もう連絡をもらいましたか。私たちは、新しい電気めっき装置についての意見が必要です。当社の今月の目標はトランペット1,000本ですが、それは、あの装置がうまく機能しないと実現しないでしょう。

今日の午前中は彼女から連絡をもらっていないので、昼食の後すぐに、彼女に電話するつもりです。

分かりました。昼食と言えば、私たち数名で階下の麺類屋へ向かいます。あなたも来ますか。

私は会計報告書に取り組んでいるところなのです。

分かりました。では、Doloresが何と言っているか、私に知らせてください。あの装置は当社にとって大きな投資でしたので、その費用を正当化できるほど効率的でなかったらと気をもんでいます。

---

56 What type of business do the speakers probably work for?

(A) A music school
(B) A manufacturing company
(C) A construction firm
(D) A travel agency

話し手たちはおそらく、どのような事業所で働いていますか。

(A) 音楽学校
(B) 製造会社
(C) 建設会社
(D) 旅行代理店

正解 **B** 男性に対し❶で、サンクトペテルブルグ工場から連絡をもらったか尋ねた女性は、❷「私たちは、新しい電気めっき装置についての意見が必要だ」と述べ、「当社の今月の目標はトランペット1,000本だが、それは、あの装置がうまく機能しないと実現しないだろう」と言っている。よって、話し手たちが働くのはトランペットの製造会社と考えられる。manufacturing company「製造会社」。
(A) トランペットに言及があるだけ。
(C) construction「建設」、firm「会社」。

57 Why does the man say, "I'm working on a financial report"?

(A) To offer help
(B) To share an accomplishment
(C) To decline an invitation
(D) To make a request

男性はなぜ "I'm working on a financial report"? と言っていますか。

(A) 手伝いを申し出るため
(B) 達成を伝えるため
(C) 誘いを断るため
(D) 頼み事をするため

正解 **C** 女性は❸「昼食と言えば、私たち数名で階下の麺類屋へ向かう」と述べ、❹「あなたも来るか」と、男性を昼食に誘っている。それに対し、男性は下線部の発言で会計報告書に取り組んでいる最中であると伝えているので、男性は昼食への誘いを断るために、この発言をしていると考えられる。decline「~を断る」、invitation「誘い」。
(B) accomplishment「達成、業績」。
(D) request「頼み事、依頼」。

58 What is the woman worried about?

(A) Whether an investment is worth the cost
(B) Whether a job applicant is qualified
(C) Whether a flight will arrive on time
(D) Whether a customer will complain

女性は何について心配していますか。

(A) 投資が費用に見合った価値があるかどうか
(B) 職への応募者が適任かどうか
(C) 航空機の便が予定通りに到着するかどうか
(D) 顧客が苦情を言うかどうか

正解 **A** 女性は❺で、新しい装置に関するDoloresの意見を知らせるよう男性に頼んだ後、❻「あの装置は当社にとって大きな投資だったので、その費用を正当化できるほど効率的でなかったらと気をもんでいる」と懸念を述べている。warrant the expenseをworth the costと表している(A)が正解。worth「~の価値がある」、cost「費用」。
(B) applicant「応募者」、qualified「適任な」。
(C) on time「予定通りに」。
(D) customer「顧客」、complain「苦情を言う」。

Words & Phrases

hear from ~ ~から連絡をもらう　feedback 意見、フィードバック　electroplating 電気めっき
trumpet トランペット　speaking of ~ ~と言えば　a couple of ~ 2、3の~　be headed to ~ ~に向かっている
downstairs 階下の　work on ~ ~に取り組む　financial report 会計報告書　major 大規模な、主要な
investment 投資　worried 心配して　efficient 効率的な　~ enough to do …するに足りるだけ~
warrant ~を正当化する、~を保証する　expense 費用

Questions 59 through 61 refer to the following conversation.

🇬🇧 W Prashant, we're showing a film tomorrow evening in the courtyard outside the library. ❶Will you or someone else from IT be able to stay to make sure the projector and audio equipment work properly?

🇨🇦 M ❷I can't stay, but Karima will be here. I've already given her the instructions about when and where to set up the equipment. That reminds me, ❸there's a 50 percent chance of rain in the forecast. ❹What are your contingency plans? Do you think you'll reschedule or…?

🇬🇧 W ❺We'll just move the event inside—into the library's community room. ❻I'll go find Karima now and give her a set of keys for that room, just in case she needs them. Thanks.

問題59-61は次の会話に関するものです。

Prashant、私たちは明日の晩、図書館の外の中庭で映画を上映することになっています。あなたか情報技術部の他の誰かが残って、プロジェクターと音響機器がきちんと作動するようにしてもらうことは可能ですか。

私は残れませんが、Karimaにここにいてもらいます。すでに彼女には、いつどこに機器を設置すべきか指示を出してあります。それで思い出したのですが、天気予報では降水確率が50パーセントです。万一の場合の計画はどのようなものですか。日時を変更することを考えていますか、それとも…?

イベントを屋内に移すだけです――図書館のコミュニティールーム内に。私が今からKarimaを探しに行って、その部屋の鍵一式を彼女が必要とする場合に備えて渡しておきます。ありがとうございます。

---

59 What department does the man most likely work in?

(A) Groundskeeping
(B) Human Resources
(C) Transportation
(D) Information Technology

男性はどんな部署で働いていると考えられますか。

(A) 用地管理部
(B) 人事部
(C) 運輸部
(D) 情報技術部

正解 D　男性は、明晩に開催する映画上映イベントについて、❶「あなたか情報技術部の他の誰かが残って、プロジェクターと音響機器がきちんと作動するようにするのは可能か」と女性から依頼を受けている。男性は❷で居残り予定のKarimaに自分が機器設置の指示を出したと言っていることからも、情報技術部で働いていると考えられる。
(A) groundskeeping「用地管理」。
(B) human resources「人事部、人的資源」。
(C) transportation「運輸」。

---

60 What does the man ask about?

(A) How much some equipment will cost
(B) What time a colleague will arrive
(C) What will happen if it rains
(D) Why a repair is being delayed

男性は何について尋ねていますか。

(A) 機器が幾らかかるのか
(B) 同僚が何時に到着するのか
(C) 雨が降ったらどうなるのか
(D) 修理作業がなぜ遅れているのか

正解 C　男性は❸「天気予報では降水確率が50パーセントだ」と述べ、続けて❹「万一の場合の計画はどのようなものか」と、雨天時の計画について女性に尋ねている。
(A) 機器の設置について話しているが、その費用に関しては言及していない。
(B) colleague「同僚」。
(D) repair「修理作業」、delay「～を遅らせる」。

---

61 What is the woman going to give to Karima?

(A) Some keys
(B) A receipt
(C) A book order
(D) Some money

女性はKarimaに何を渡すつもりですか。

(A) 鍵
(B) 領収書
(C) 本の注文
(D) 金銭

正解 A　映画上映イベントについて、❺で雨天時には開催場所を屋内のコミュニティールームに移すことを伝えた女性は、❻「私が今からKarimaを探しに行って、その部屋の鍵一式を彼女が必要とする場合に備えて渡しておく」と述べている。a set of keysをsome keysと言い換えた(A)が正解。
(B) receipt「領収書」。
(C) order「注文、注文品」。

Words & Phrases

courtyard 中庭　　IT 情報技術(部)　★information technologyの略
be able to do ～することができる　　make sure (that) ～ 必ず～ということをする　　equipment 機器
properly きちんと　　instructions 指示、説明　　set up ～ ～を設置する　　That reminds me それで思い出したのですが
chance 確率　　forecast 天気予報、予報　　contingency plan 緊急対策　　reschedule ～の日時を変更する
move ～を移す　　community 共用、共同体　　a set of ～ ～一式　　key 鍵　　just in case ～ ～の場合に備えて

Questions 62 through 64 refer to the following conversation and directory.

M Carol, ❶did you see the sales report from last quarter?

W I did... and ❷I'm surprised. Our paper products really aren't selling well.

M I noticed that too. ❸How about moving some of the products there to other locations? For example, we could put facial tissues in the beauty supplies aisle.

W Hm, ❹good idea. We should put them next to the face lotions.

M OK. ❺I'll keep that in mind when the next shipment comes in on Thursday.

問題62-64は次の会話と案内板に関するものです。

Carol、前四半期の売上報告書を見ましたか。

見ました…そして驚いています。当店の紙製品は、売れ行きが実に良くありません。

私もそれに気付きました。あそこの一部の製品を別の場所に移してはどうでしょうか。例えば、ティッシュペーパーを美容用品売り場に置くことができるかもしれません。

ああ、いい考えですね。化粧水の隣にそれらを置いたらきっといいでしょう。

なるほど。次の配送品が木曜日に入荷するときに、そのことを覚えておくようにします。

Store Directory	
Aisle 1 –Beauty supplies	**Aisle 2** –Paper products
Aisle 3 –Cleaning supplies	**Aisle 4** –Pet food

店舗案内板	
通路1 — 美容用品	通路2 — 紙製品
通路3 — 清掃用品	通路4 — ペットフード

62 Why is the woman surprised?

(A) Customers have complained about a brand.
(B) An inspection will take place soon.
(C) Some merchandise is not selling well.
(D) A supplier has gone out of business.

女性はなぜ驚いているのですか。

(A) 顧客がある銘柄について苦情を言っているから。
(B) 間もなく点検が行われるから。
(C) ある商品の売れ行きが良くないから。
(D) 納入業者が廃業したから。

正解 **C** ❶で前四半期の売上報告書を見たかと尋ねる男性に対し、女性は❷で自分は驚いていると伝えて、「当店の紙製品は、売れ行きが実に良くない」とその理由を述べている。our paper productsをsome merchandiseと表している(C)が正解。merchandise「商品」。
(A) complain about 〜「〜について苦情を言う」、brand「銘柄、ブランド」。
(B) inspection「点検」。
(D) supplier「納入業者、供給会社」、go out of business「廃業する」。

---

63 Look at the graphic. Which aisle will some products be moved to?

(A) Aisle 1
(B) Aisle 2
(C) Aisle 3
(D) Aisle 4

図を見てください。一部の製品はどの通路へ移されますか。

(A) 通路1
(B) 通路2
(C) 通路3
(D) 通路4

正解 **A** 紙製品の売れ行きが良くないと述べる女性に対し、男性は❸「あそこの一部の製品を別の場所に移してはどうか。例えば、ティッシュペーパーを美容品売り場に置くことができるかもしれない」と提案している。女性はそれに対し❹で賛同し、移動先として化粧水の隣の位置を薦めている。図を見ると、美容用品が置かれているのは通路1なので、(A)が正解。
(B) 移動させようとしているティッシュペーパーが現在置かれている場所。

---

64 What is scheduled to happen on Thursday?

(A) A training will be held.
(B) A shipment will arrive.
(C) A promotional event will begin.
(D) A budget report will be updated.

木曜日に何が起こる予定ですか。

(A) 研修が行われる。
(B) 配送品が到着する。
(C) 販売促進イベントが始まる。
(D) 予算報告書が更新される。

正解 **B** ❹でティッシュペーパーは化粧水の隣に置くとよいと提案する女性に対し、男性は❺「次の配送品が木曜日に入荷するときに、そのことを覚えておくようにする」と言っているので、木曜日にはティッシュペーパーを含む配送品が店舗に到着すると考えられる。be scheduled to do「〜する予定である」。
(C) promotional「販売促進用の」。
(D) budget「予算」、update「〜を更新する」。

TEST 2 PART 3

Words & Phrases

directory （ビルなどの）案内板　　sales 売り上げ　　quarter 四半期　　sell well 売れ行きが良い　　notice 〜に気付く

location 場所、位置　　for example 例えば　　facial tissue ティッシュペーパー　　beauty supplies 美容用品

aisle （店舗内の商品陳列棚間の）通路　　next to 〜 〜の隣に　　face lotion 化粧水　　keep 〜 in mind 〜を覚えておく

shipment 配送品、積み荷　　come in 入荷する、到着する

案内板 cleaning supplies 清掃用品　　pet food ペットフード

Questions 65 through 67 refer to the following conversation and map.

問題65-67は次の会話と地図に関するものです。

M Hi, So-Hee? ❶This is Axel from the car service. I'm waiting outside to pick you up.

もしもし、So-Heeさんですか。こちらはお車サービス会社のAxelです。あなたを車にお乗せするため、外でお待ちしています。

W Hmm… I don't see your car. Do you have the right address?

ええと…私には、そちらの車が見えません。正しい住所をお持ちですか。

M ❷1080 Bergen Street West, right?

バーゲン通り西1080番地ですよね？

W Oh, ❸it's actually 1080 Bergen Street East.

ああ、実は、バーゲン通り東1080番地なのです。

M Oops. I hope you won't be late for your flight.

しまった。お乗りになる飛行機の便に遅れないといいのですが。

W Don't worry. ❹If you head east, my building is across from the big supermarket.

ご心配なく。東へ進んだら、うちの建物は大型スーパーマーケットの向かいにありますよ。

M OK. Let me enter the new address in my GPS… Oh, ❺what a relief. It says it'll only take five minutes to get to your location.

分かりました。新しい住所をGPSに入力させてください…ああ、安心しました。それには、あなたの場所に到着するのに5分しかかからないと表示されています。

W Great! And ❻do you have water in your car, or should I bring some?

良かった！ところで、そちらの車に水はありますか、それとも少し持っていった方がいいでしょうか。

M ❼No, I have some water—no need to bring your own.

いいえ、こちらに水は用意してあります——ご自身のものをお持ちいただく必要はありません。

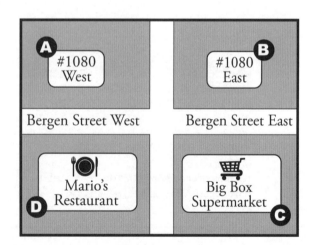

65 Look at the graphic. Where will the man pick the woman up?

    (A) At location A
    (B) At location B
    (C) At location C
    (D) At location D

図を見てください。男性はどこで女性を車に乗せますか。

    (A) 場所A
    (B) 場所B
    (C) 場所C
    (D) 場所D

正解 B ❶で、女性を車で送迎するため外で待機していると言う男性は、❷で女性の居場所がバーゲン通り西1080番地で合っているか確認している。それに対し、女性は❸「実は、バーゲン通り東1080番地だ」と住所の誤りを正してから、❹「東へ進むと、うちの建物は大型スーパーマーケットの向かいにある」と自分の居場所を説明している。図を見ると、バーゲン通り東に面し、かつスーパーマーケットの向かいにある建物の場所はB。よって、(B)が正解。
(A) 誤って男性が女性を乗せると思っていた場所。

---

66 Why is the man relieved?

    (A) A colleague will take over an assignment.
    (B) A parking spot is available.
    (C) A business is already open.
    (D) A drive will be short.

男性はなぜほっとしたのですか。

    (A) 同僚が業務を引き継ぐだろうから。
    (B) 駐車場所が空いているから。
    (C) 店がすでに営業しているから。
    (D) 車の走行時間が短いだろうから。

正解 D 女性の居場所の正しい住所をGPSに入力した男性は、❺で「安心した。それには、あなたの場所に到着するのに5分しかかからないと表示されている」とGPSの表示を伝えている。よって、男性は自分の現在地から女性の居場所までの車での所要時間が短いと分かり、ほっとしたと判断できる。relieved「ほっとした」。drive「(自動車で行く)道のり」。
(A) colleague「同僚」、take over ~「~を引き継ぐ」、assignment「業務、割り当て」。
(B) parking spot「駐車場所」、available「利用できる」。
(C) business「店、会社」。

---

67 What does the man say he will provide?

    (A) Some water
    (B) Some coupons
    (C) An umbrella
    (D) A phone charger

男性は何を提供すると言っていますか。

    (A) 水
    (B) クーポン
    (C) 1本の傘
    (D) 電話の充電器1台

正解 A ❻「そちらの車に水はあるか、それとも少し持っていった方がよいか」と尋ねる女性に対し、男性は❼で「こちらに水は用意してある——自身のものを持ってくる必要はない」と車内で水を提供していることを伝えている。provide「~を提供する」。
(C) umbrella「傘」。
(D) charger「充電器」。

Words & Phrases

pick up ~ ～を車に乗せる、～を車で迎えに行く   right 正しい   address 住所   oops しまった、おっと

be late for ~ ～に遅れる   flight (航空機の)便、フライト   head 進む   enter ～を入力する

GPS GPS、全地球測位システム ★Global Positioning Systemの略   what a relief やれやれ安心した

get to ~ ～に到着する   location 場所、位置   own 自分のもの

Questions 68 through 70 refer to the following conversation and table.

問題68-70は次の会話と表に関するものです。

M ❶The ovens are working, and the health inspector has given us the go-ahead!

オーブンは正常に作動しているし、衛生検査官が私たちに開始許可をくれましたよ。

W Great! ❷I'm sure our cakes and pastries will sell quickly when our shop opens next month.

良かった！うちの店が来月開業したら、私たちのケーキや焼き菓子類は瞬く間に売れると確信しています。

M I've also found an online service that could create our Web site. It's called Bixter. Here are their options.

それに、私たちのウェブサイトを制作できそうなオンラインサービス業者を見つけました。Bixterというところです。これが、そこの選択肢ですよ。

W Let's see… Well, ❸budget-wise, we shouldn't go higher than 30 dollars a month.

どれどれ…そうですね、予算に関しては、月に30ドルより高くならないことが望ましいですね。

M OK. And ❹we don't need their tech support option, since your brother can help with that.

了解です。それに、私たちには同社の技術サポートは不要ですね、それに関してはあなたのお兄さんが手伝ってくれますから。

W Agreed! Oh, um, one other thing… ❺we do definitely need to be able to upload videos to show people how our breads are made.

賛成です！ああ、ええと、もう1つ…私たちのパンがどのように作られるかを人々に見せるために、動画をアップロードできることが絶対に必要です。

M Well, ❻that's settled then. I'll give them a call after lunch.

ええと、ではその件は決まりですね。昼食後、彼らに電話します。

Bixter Web Site Builder				
	Design Tools	Unlimited Storage Capacity	Video Capable	Tech Support
Package 1 $10/month	✔			
Package 2 $15/month	✔	✔		
Package 3 $20/month	✔	✔	✔	
Package 4 $35/month	✔	✔	✔	✔

Bixterウェブサイト制作会社				
	デザインツール	無制限のストレージ容量	動画対応	技術サポート
パッケージ1 10ドル／月	✔			
パッケージ2 15ドル／月	✔	✔		
パッケージ3 20ドル／月	✔	✔	✔	
パッケージ4 35ドル／月	✔	✔	✔	✔

68 What type of business do the speakers most likely own?

(A) A computer repair store
(B) An online newspaper
(C) A bakery
(D) A medical supply company

話し手たちは、どのような事業を所有していると考えられますか。

(A) コンピューター修理店
(B) オンライン新聞社
(C) パン屋
(D) 医療用品会社

正解 C 男性は❶「オーブンは正常に作動しているし、衛生検査官が私たちに開始許可をくれた」と伝え、女性は❷「うちの店が来月開業したら、私たちのケーキや焼き菓子類は瞬く間に売れると確信している」と述べている。よって、話し手たちはパン屋を所有しており、その開業準備をしていると考えられる。own「～を所有する」。
(A) ウェブサイトや技術サポートに言及があるが、修理については述べられていない。repair「修理」。
(B) オンラインの新聞については述べられていない。
(D) medical supplies「医療用品」。

69 Look at the graphic. Which package will the speakers most likely choose?

(A) Package 1
(B) Package 2
(C) Package 3
(D) Package 4

図を見てください。話し手たちはどのパッケージを選ぶと考えられますか。

(A) パッケージ1
(B) パッケージ2
(C) パッケージ3
(D) パッケージ4

正解 C ウェブサイト制作のオンラインサービス業者が提供するパッケージの選択肢を示された女性は、❸「予算に関しては、月に30ドルより高くならないことが望ましい」と伝えている。また、❹で技術サポートは不要と述べる男性に賛同した後、女性は❺「私たちのパンがどのように作られるかを人々に見せるために、動画をアップロードできることが絶対に必要だ」と言っている。図を見ると、予算が月額30ドル以内で、技術サポートが含まれず、かつ動画対応可能なのはパッケージ3。よって、(C)が正解。

70 What does the man say he will do after lunch?

(A) Pick up a permit
(B) Make a call
(C) Watch a video
(D) Repair a device

男性は昼食後、何をするつもりだと言っていますか。

(A) 許可証を受け取る。
(B) 電話をする
(C) 動画を見る
(D) 機器を修理する

正解 B ウェブサイト制作のサービスパッケージの選択肢に関して女性と意見交換した後、男性は❻「ではその件は決まりだ。昼食後、彼らに電話する」と伝えている。よって、男性はBixterというウェブサイト制作業者に電話をすると分かる。
(A) 衛生検査官が許可をくれたとあるが、許可証の受け取りについては言及がない。pick up ～「～を受け取る」、permit「許可証」。
(C) 動画のアップロードが必要とあるが、男性は昼食後に動画を見るとは言っていない。
(D) device「機器」。

Words & Phrases

table 表　oven オーブン　health inspector 衛生検査官　go-ahead 開始許可、認可　pastry 焼き菓子
quickly すぐに　online オンラインの　create ～を創作する　option 選択肢　budget 予算
-wise 〈名詞・形容詞に付けて〉～に関して　tech support 技術サポート　★technical supportの略　Agreed 賛成、承知した
definitely 間違いなく　upload ～をアップロードする　video 動画　bread パン　settle ～に決着をつける
give ～ a call ～に電話する

表　builder 構築業者、建設業者　design tool デザインツール　unlimited 無制限の
storage capacity ストレージ容量、記憶容量　capable 利用可能な　package パッケージ、一括契約

Questions 71 through 73 refer to the following tour information.

🇨🇦 M

❶I'd like to start today's session by introducing our most unique exhibit: our rooftop sculpture garden! ❷Every now and then you'll be assigned this tour, so you'll need to become familiar with the sculptures on our roof. ❸Here—let me pass around a fact sheet with information on each sculpture. Now— ❹museum visitors need to buy a special pass to see this exhibit, so please remember to collect all passes before you start the tour.

問題71-73は次のツアー情報に関するものです。

本日のセッションは、私たちの非常に珍しい展示を紹介することから始めたいと思います。当館屋上の彫刻庭園です。時々、皆さんはこのツアーを割り当てられることになるので、当館屋上の彫刻作品に精通しておく必要があるでしょう。はい——各彫刻作品に関する情報が記載された概要説明書を順々に回します。さて——美術館の来館者はこの展示を見るために特別入場券を購入する必要があるので、ツアーを開始する前に忘れずに全ての入場券を回収してください。

---

71 Who most likely are the listeners?

(A) Ticket agents
(B) Art critics
(C) Janitorial staff
(D) Museum guides

聞き手は誰だと考えられますか。

(A) チケット販売員
(B) 芸術評論家
(C) 用務員
(D) 美術館の案内人

正解 D 話し手は❶で、当館屋上の彫刻庭園の紹介からセッションを始めると述べてから、❷「時々、皆さんはこのツアーを割り当てられることになる」と伝えている。さらに❹で、美術館の来館者への対応手順を説明していることからも、聞き手は美術館の案内人だと考えられる。
(A) ticket agent「チケット販売員」。
(B) 彫刻作品に精通する必要性が述べられているが、芸術評論に関する言及はない。critic「評論家」。
(C) janitorial「用務の、清掃の」。

---

72 What does the speaker hand out?

(A) New uniforms
(B) Instructor evaluations
(C) Fact sheets
(D) Security badges

話し手は何を配布していますか。

(A) 新しい制服
(B) 講師の評価表
(C) 概要説明書
(D) 警備員のバッジ

正解 C 話し手は❷で、聞き手が時々彫刻庭園のツアーの案内を担当することになると伝えた後、❸「はい——各彫刻作品に関する情報が記載された概要説明書を順々に回す」と概要説明書を配布している。hand out ～「～を配布する」。
(A) uniform「制服」。
(B) instructor「講師」、evaluation「評価表、評価」。
(D) security「警備」。

---

73 What are the listeners reminded to do?

(A) Submit application forms
(B) Print out brochures
(C) Prepare for an inspection
(D) Collect visitor passes

聞き手は何をするよう念を押されていますか。

(A) 申込用紙を提出する
(B) パンフレットを印刷する
(C) 点検に備える
(D) 来館者の入場券を回収する

正解 D 話し手は、彫刻庭園ツアーを担当する予定の聞き手に対し、❹「美術館の来館者はこの展示を見るために特別入場券を購入する必要があるので、ツアーを開始する前に忘れずに全ての入場券を回収してください」と注意を伝えている。remind ～ to do「～に…するよう念を押す」。
(A) submit「～を提出する」、application form「申込用紙」。
(B) print out ～「～を印刷する」、brochure「パンフレット」。
(C) prepare for ～「～に備える」、inspection「点検」。

Words & Phrases　information 情報　start ～ by doing ～を…することから始める　session セッション、会合　introduce ～を紹介する　unique 珍しい、他にはない　exhibit 展示　rooftop 屋上　sculpture 彫刻作品、彫刻　every now and then 時々　assign ～ … ～に…を割り当てる　familiar with ～ ～に精通している　roof 屋上　pass around ～ ～を順々に回す　fact sheet 概要説明書　★商品などの情報を簡潔にまとめたもの　pass 入場券　remember to do 忘れずに～する　collect ～を回収する

Questions 74 through 76 refer to the following excerpt from a meeting.

🇺🇸 W

Now that everyone has arrived, let's start our meeting. ❶I'm happy to announce that business has increased this month due to the new line of outdoor clothing we've added to our store. However, ❷since we moved things around to accommodate the additional jackets, gloves, and hats, people are having trouble finding what they're looking for. ❸Customers were really used to the old layout. So, ❹please keep this in mind and be extra helpful to our customers in the coming weeks.

問題74-76は次の会議の抜粋に関するものです。

全員が到着したので、会議を始めましょう。当店に加わったアウトドア用衣料品の新商品ラインのおかげで、今月取引が増えたことをお知らせできるのをうれしく思います。しかし、追加した上着、手袋、帽子を陳列するために私たちが物をあちこち動かしたので、皆さまご自分が探しているものを見つけるのに苦労されています。お客さまは以前のレイアウトにとても慣れていました。ですから、このことを念頭に置き、これからの数週間は特にお客さまのお役に立つようにしてください。

74 What kind of store does the speaker most likely manage?

(A) A stationery store
(B) An electronics store
(C) A grocery store
(D) A clothing store

話し手はどのような店を経営していると考えられますか。

(A) 文具店
(B) 電子機器店
(C) 食料雑貨店
(D) 衣料品店

正解 D 話し手は会議の開始を呼び掛けてから、❶「当店に加わったアウトドア用衣料品の新商品ラインのおかげで、今月取引が増えたことをお知らせできるのはうれしい」と述べている。よって、話し手の店は衣料品を扱っていると考えられる。manage「～を経営する」。
(A) stationery「文具」。
(B) electronics「電子機器」。
(C) grocery store「食料雑貨店」。

75 What are customers having difficulty with?

(A) Submitting orders
(B) Finding items
(C) Returning products
(D) Contacting staff

顧客は何に苦労していますか。

(A) 注文を送信すること
(B) 商品を見つけること
(C) 製品を返品すること
(D) スタッフに接すること

正解 B 話し手は❷「追加した上着、手袋、帽子を陳列するために私たちが物をあちこち動かしたので、皆さん自分が探しているものを見つけるのに苦労している」と商品配置の変更後、顧客が商品を見つけるのに苦労していることに言及している。have difficulty with ～「～に苦労する」。
(A) submit「～を提出する」。
(C) return「～を返品する」。
(D) contact「～に接する、～に連絡する」。

76 According to the speaker, what should the listeners do?

(A) Be helpful
(B) Arrive early
(C) Dress neatly
(D) Eat quickly

話し手によると、聞き手は何をすべきですか。

(A) 助けになるようにする
(B) 早めに到着する
(C) きちんとした服装をする
(D) 手早く食事する

正解 A 話し手は、❷で商品配置の変更後、顧客が商品を見つけるのに苦労していると述べている。さらに、❸「顧客は以前のレイアウトにとても慣れていた」と補足した上で、❹「このことを念頭に置き、これからの数週間は特に顧客の役に立つようにしてください」と聞き手に顧客の手助けを促している。
(C) dress「服を着る」、neatly「きちんと」。

Words & Phrases
now that ～ 今や～なので　arrive 到着する　be happy to do 喜んで～する　announce ～を知らせる　business 商取引、売買　increase 増える　due to ～ ～のために　line 商品ライン　clothing 衣料品　add ～ to … ～を…に追加する　move ～ around ～をあちこち動かす　accommodate ～を収める、～を収容する　additional 追加の　jacket 上着　glove 手袋　have trouble doing ～するのに苦労する　look for ～ ～を探す　customer 顧客　be used to ～ ～に慣れている　old 以前の、元の　layout レイアウト、配置　keep ～ in mind ～を覚えておく　extra 〈形容詞や副詞を修飾して〉特に　helpful to ～ ～に役立つ、～の助けになる　coming 次の、今度の

Questions 77 through 79 refer to the following telephone message.

🇦🇺 M

Hi, Amal. This is Jang-Ho Choi. ❶I'm calling to welcome you to the staff of the Sunrise Times Newspaper. ❷We're always glad to get skilled writers such as yourself on our team. Now, ❸I know that sometimes new employees have a lot of questions, because we often hire people fresh out of journalism school… but… <u>you have a lot of experience</u>. ❹We'll chat in person next week. ❺I'm leaving for vacation tomorrow for three days, and I'll see you when I return.

問題77-79は次の電話のメッセージに関するものです。

もしもし、Amal。Jang-Ho Choiです。あなたをSunrise Times新聞社のスタッフに喜んでお迎えするために電話しています。あなたのような熟練記者を私たちのチームの一員に迎えるのは、常にうれしいものです。さて、時として、新しい従業員は多くの質問があるということは理解しています、というのも私たちはジャーナリズム専門学校を出たばかりの人々を頻繁に雇用するので…ですが…あなたは多くの経験をお持ちです。来週、直接会って話しましょう。私は明日から3日間休暇で出掛けますので、戻った際にあなたにお会いします。

---

77 Where does the speaker work?

(A) At a newspaper
(B) At a travel agency
(C) At a hotel
(D) At a technology company

話し手はどこで働いていますか。

(A) 新聞社
(B) 旅行代理店
(C) ホテル
(D) テクノロジー企業

正解 A 話し手は聞き手に対し、❶「あなたをSunrise Times新聞社のスタッフに喜んで迎えるために電話している」と告げ、❷「あなたのような熟練記者を私たちのチームの一員に迎えるのは、常にうれしいものだ」と伝えている。よって、話し手は新聞社で働いていると分かる。
(B) agency「代理店」。
(D) technology「テクノロジー、科学技術」。

---

78 What does the speaker mean when he says, "<u>you have a lot of experience</u>"?

(A) The listener should take over a project.
(B) The listener will not need any assistance.
(C) The listener deserves a pay raise.
(D) The listener should teach an upcoming class.

話し手は "<u>you have a lot of experience</u>" という発言で、何を意味していますか。

(A) 聞き手はプロジェクトを引き継ぐべきだ。
(B) 聞き手は、何も手助けを必要としないだろう。
(C) 聞き手は昇給に値する。
(D) 聞き手は今度の講座を教えるべきだ。

正解 B 話し手は❸「時として、新しい従業員は多くの質問があるということは理解している、というのも私たちはジャーナリズム専門学校を出たばかりの人々を頻繁に雇用するからだ」と述べた後、「だが」と続け、下線部の発言をしている。よってこの発言で話し手は、聞き手が他の新しい従業員とは違って経験豊富なため、手助けを必要としないだろうと考えていると判断できる。assistance「手助け」。
(A) take over ～「～を引き継ぐ」。
(C) deserve「～に値する」、pay raise「昇給」。
(D) upcoming「今度の」。

---

79 What does the speaker say he is doing tomorrow?

(A) Attending a meeting
(B) Organizing a party
(C) Going on vacation
(D) Visiting a school

話し手は明日、何をすると言っていますか。

(A) 会議に出席する
(B) パーティーを企画する
(C) 休暇に出掛ける
(D) 学校を訪問する

正解 C 話し手は聞き手に対し、❹で来週直接会って話すことを提案し、❺「私は明日から3日間休暇で出掛ける」と予定を伝えている。leaving for vacationをgoing on vacationと言い換えている(C)が正解。go on vacation「休暇に出掛ける」。
(A) attend「～に出席する」。
(B) organize「～を企画する」。

Words & Phrases

welcome ～を喜んで迎える　newspaper 新聞社、新聞　skilled 熟練した
such as ～ ～のような　hire ～を雇用する　fresh out of ～ ～を出たばかりの　journalism ジャーナリズム、新聞学科
experience 経験　chat 雑談する　in person 直接会って　leave 出発する　vacation 休暇　return 戻る

Questions 80 through 82 refer to the following broadcast.

 W

❶Welcome to this broadcast of *Karla's Kitchen*! ❷Today I'd like to introduce a healthy breakfast food called overnight oatmeal. ❸It's a kind of cold cereal that can be prepared the night before you plan to eat it. All you have to do is combine oats and milk and soak them in the refrigerator overnight. Then, in the morning, you can add fruit, nuts, or spices. ❹I especially like that this recipe has very little sugar. The detailed recipe's on my Web site. ❺Now, I'd like to introduce today's guest, Carrie Nelson, author of the cookbook *Healthy Options*. ❻We'll talk to her about overnight oatmeal as well as her other favorite breakfast dishes.

今日の『Karla'sキッチン』の放送へようこそ。今日は、オーバーナイト・オートミールと呼ばれる健康的な朝食用の食べ物をご紹介します。それは、食べる予定の前の晩に準備できる冷たいシリアルの一種です。オート麦と牛乳を混ぜ合わせて、一晩冷蔵庫内で浸しておくだけです。それから朝に、果物、ナッツ類、スパイスなどを加えてもいいでしょう。このレシピは糖質が実に少ないという点が、私は特に気に入っています。詳しいレシピは私のウェブサイトにあります。それでは今日のゲストで、料理本『健康的な選択肢』の著者であるCarrie Nelsonをご紹介します。オーバーナイト・オートミールと、その他の彼女のお気に入りの朝食料理についても彼女とお話しします。

80 What is the topic of today's broadcast?

(A) Unusual desserts
(B) Breakfast foods
(C) Homemade energy drinks
(D) Cold vegetable soups

今日の放送のテーマは何ですか。

(A) 珍しいデザート
(B) 朝食用の食べ物
(C) 自家製栄養ドリンク
(D) 冷たい野菜スープ

正解 B 話し手は❶「今日の『Karla'sキッチン』の放送へようこそ」という番組冒頭の挨拶に続けて、❷「今日は、オーバーナイト・オートミールと呼ばれる健康的な朝食用の食べ物を紹介する」と今日の放送のテーマを伝えている。
(A) unusual「珍しい」。
(C) homemade「自家製の」、energy drink「栄養ドリンク、エネルギー飲料」。

81 What does the speaker say she likes about a recipe?

(A) It won an award.
(B) Its ingredients are inexpensive.
(C) It is low in sugar.
(D) It is easy to prepare.

話し手はレシピについて、何が気に入っていると言っていますか。

(A) それは賞を獲得した。
(B) その材料は安価である。
(C) それは糖質が少ない。
(D) それは準備するのが容易だ。

正解 C 話し手は❸で、オーバーナイト・オートミールという朝食の概要や作り方を説明した後、❹「このレシピは糖質が実に少ないという点が、私は特に気に入っている」と述べている。low「（数量が）少ない、低い」。
(A) win an award「賞を獲得する」。
(B) ingredient「材料」、inexpensive「安価な」。
(D) 話し手は準備の容易さに言及しているが、その点が気に入っているとは述べていない。

82 What will the speaker do next?

(A) Interview a guest
(B) Recommend an appliance
(C) Explain contest rules
(D) Provide a discount code

話し手は次に何をしますか。

(A) ゲストにインタビューする
(B) 電化製品を推奨する
(C) コンテストのルールを説明する
(D) 割引用コードを提供する

正解 A 話し手は、オーバーナイト・オートミールに関する説明の後、❺「それでは今日のゲストで、料理本『健康的な選択肢』の著者であるCarrie Nelsonを紹介する」と述べ、❻でそのゲストとこれから話す内容を続けて伝えている。よって、話し手は次にゲストにインタビューすると分かる。interview「～にインタビューする」。
(B) recommend「～を推奨する」、appliance「電化製品」。
(D) provide「～を提供する」。

Words & Phrases

broadcast 放送　introduce ～を紹介する　healthy 健康的な　overnight 〈形容詞で〉夜通しの、〈副詞で〉一晩中　oatmeal オートミール　cereal シリアル　prepare ～を準備する　combine ～を混ぜ合わせる　oats オート麦　soak ～を浸す　refrigerator 冷蔵庫　nut ナッツ　spice スパイス　especially 特に　recipe レシピ、調理法　sugar 糖質、砂糖　detailed 詳細な　author 著者　cookbook 料理の本　～ as well as … ～も…も

Questions 83 through 85 refer to the following telephone message.

問題83-85は次の電話のメッセージに関するものです。

 W

Hi, Diego. ❶This is Julie calling from E&F to let you know that your 3-D prototypes are ready for pickup. ❷We printed them using steel instead of plastic as you requested last week, but ❸now they are really heavy, well over 40 pounds total. ❹I'm letting you know so you can plan how you're going to carry them. Oh— ❺you mentioned you're interested in working for us? As it turns out, <u>our junior designer has just left</u>. Anyway, we're open until six, so feel free to come any time before then. Thanks!

もしもし、Diego。こちらはE&F社のJulieで、あなたの3Dの試作品が受け取れる状態だとお知らせするためにお電話しています。先週あなたにご依頼いただいた通り、当社はプラスチックではなくスチールを使用して印刷しましたが、現状でそれらは非常に重く、総重量は40ポンドを大幅に上回ります。あなたがそれらを運ぶ方法を計画できるよう、お知らせしています。ああ——あなたは当社で働きたいとおっしゃっていましたね。ふたを開けてみると、ちょうど当社の若手デザイナーが辞めたのです。いずれにしても、当社は6時まで営業しているので、それより前でしたらいつでも気軽においでください。よろしくお願いします。

---

83 Where does the speaker most likely work?

(A) At a printing business
(B) At a video game company
(C) At a plastics manufacturer
(D) At an employment agency

話し手はどこで働いていると考えられますか。

(A) 印刷業者
(B) ビデオゲーム会社
(C) プラスチック製造会社
(D) 人材紹介会社

正解 A 話し手は❶で、聞き手が依頼した3Dの試作品が引き渡せる状態になったことを知らせており、❷で、聞き手の依頼通りの素材で印刷したと述べている。よって、話し手は3D印刷を行う印刷業者で働いていると考えられる。printing「印刷業」。
(C) manufacturer「製造会社、メーカー」。
(D) employment agency「人材紹介会社」。

---

84 What is the speaker concerned about?

(A) A timeline may need to be revised.
(B) Some prototypes are very heavy.
(C) Some specifications are incorrect.
(D) A material is currently unavailable.

話し手は何について心配していますか。

(A) 日程を修正する必要があるかもしれない。
(B) 試作品が非常に重い。
(C) 仕様の一部が不正確だ。
(D) 素材が現在入手できない。

正解 B 話し手は準備した試作品について、❸「現状でそれらは非常に重く、総重量は40ポンドを大幅に上回る」と伝えている。さらに❹で、聞き手が試作品を運ぶ方法を計画できるよう知らせたと述べており、試作品が非常に重いと心配している。be concerned「心配している」。
(A) timeline「日程」、revise「〜を修正する」。
(C) specifications「仕様」、incorrect「不正確な」。
(D) material「素材」、currently「現在」、unavailable「入手できない」。

---

85 Why does the speaker say, "our junior designer has just left"?

(A) To explain why she is busy
(B) To complain about a delay
(C) To request that the listener return the next day
(D) To suggest that the listener apply for a job

話し手はなぜ "our junior designer has just left" と言っていますか。

(A) 自身がなぜ忙しいか説明するため
(B) 遅延について不満を言うため
(C) 聞き手に翌日また来るよう依頼するため
(D) 聞き手に職に応募するよう勧めるため

正解 D ❺で、以前に話し手の会社で働きたいと聞き手が言っていたことを述べてから、話し手は下線部の発言をしている。よって、話し手はデザイナーの職が空いたことを伝えて、聞き手にその職に応募するよう勧めていると判断できる。apply for 〜「〜に応募する」。
(B) complain about 〜「〜について不満を言う」、delay「遅延」。

Words & Phrases

3-D 3次元の ★three-dimensionalの略　prototype 試作品　ready for 〜 〜の準備ができた
pickup 受け取り　steel スチール　instead of 〜 〜ではなくて　plastic プラスチック
well over 〜 〜を大幅に上回って　pound ポンド ★重量単位で約454グラム　total 総量、総計　carry 〜を持ち運ぶ
mention 〜と言う　as it turns out 〜 ふたを開けてみると〜　junior 若手の、下級の　leave 辞職する、去る
anyway いずれにしても　feel free to do 気軽に〜する、遠慮なく〜する

Questions 86 through 88 refer to the following announcement.

問題86-88は次のお知らせに関するものです。

🇨🇦 M

❶I'm pleased to inform you today about a new employee benefit. The management team knows that many of you have had problems commuting to work by train, so **❷**our company president has agreed to provide a free shuttle service to and from the train station for all employees. **❸**All you need to do is show the driver your employee ID card each time you board. **❹**Interested employees should fill out the survey that was sent to you by e-mail no later than Friday. That way we'll know how many buses we'll need.

本日、従業員向けの新しい福利厚生について皆さんにお知らせでき、うれしく思います。経営陣は皆さんの多くが電車で通勤するのに苦労していることを理解しており、そのため社長は、全従業員のために鉄道駅からの往復の無料シャトルバス運行を提供することを、承諾しました。皆さんがする必要があるのは、乗車するたびに従業員IDカードを運転手に提示することだけです。関心のある従業員の方は金曜日までに、Eメールで皆さんに送付されたアンケート調査に必要事項を記入する必要があります。そうしますと、我々は、バスが何本必要になるか分かりますので。

86 What benefit is being discussed?

(A) A shuttle service
(B) A fitness center membership
(C) Additional vacation days
(D) Free financial advice

どんな福利厚生について述べられていますか。

(A) シャトルバスの運行
(B) フィットネスセンターの会員資格
(C) 追加の休暇日数
(D) 無料の金融アドバイス

正解 A 話し手は❶で、従業員向けの新しい福利厚生について知らせると述べ、❷「社長は、全従業員のために鉄道駅からの往復の無料シャトルバス運行を提供することを承諾した」と、新しい福利厚生の内容を説明している。
(B) membership「会員資格」。
(C) additional「追加の」。
(D) financial「金融の」。

87 What will employees have to show to receive the benefit?

(A) A letter from their supervisor
(B) A recent bank statement
(C) A driver's license
(D) A company identification card

従業員はこの福利厚生の恩恵を受けるために、何を提示する必要がありますか。

(A) 上司からの書状
(B) 最近の銀行取引明細書
(C) 運転免許証
(D) 社員証

正解 D 話し手は❷で、新しい福利厚生として全従業員のために無料シャトルバス運行を提供すると説明し、続けて❸「皆さんがする必要があるのは、乗車するたびに従業員IDカードを運転手に提示することだけだ」と述べている。your employee ID cardをa company identification cardと表している(D)が正解。
(A) letter「公式書状、手紙」、supervisor「上司」。
(B) recent「最近の」、bank statement「銀行取引明細書」。
(C) driver's license「運転免許証」。

88 What should some of the listeners do by Friday?

(A) Complete a survey
(B) Read an informational brochure
(C) Sign a contract
(D) Speak to a manager

一部の聞き手は金曜日までに何をすべきですか。

(A) アンケート調査の記入を完了する
(B) 情報提供用のパンフレットを読む
(C) 契約書に署名する
(D) 管理者に話す

正解 A 話し手は無料のシャトルバス運行という新しい福利厚生について説明し、❹「関心のある従業員は金曜日までに、Eメールで皆さんに送付されたアンケート調査に必要事項を記入する必要がある」と伝えている。fill out the surveyをcomplete「〜に全て記入する」を使って表している(A)が正解。
(B) informational「情報を提供する、情報の」、brochure「パンフレット」。
(C) sign「〜に署名する」、contract「契約書」。
(D) manager「管理者」。

Words & Phrases

be pleased to *do* 喜んで〜する　　inform 〜 about … 〜に…について知らせる
employee benefit 従業員福利厚生　　management team 経営陣　　have a problem 問題がある
commute to work 通勤する　　president 社長　　agree to *do* 〜することを承諾する　　provide 〜を提供する
shuttle service （バスなどの）シャトル運行、短距離定期往復便　　ID card IDカード、身元証明書　★identification cardの略
each time 〜 〜するたびに　　board （乗り物に）乗る　　interested 関心のある　　fill out 〜 〜に必要事項を記入する
survey アンケート調査　　no later than 〜 〜までに、〜より遅くなることなく

TEST 2 PART 4

131

Questions 89 through 91 refer to the following excerpt from a workshop.

問題89-91は次の講習会の抜粋に関するものです。

🇬🇧 W

Good morning. ❶Welcome to the City Water Department's new-employee workshop. ❷This morning, I'll be demonstrating the use of our specialized apparatus to test water for sodium and other mineral components. Although the workshop will take place here in our laboratory, ❸I'll also demonstrate how the equipment can test water at a project site. ❹It is surprisingly simple to use, which is a big advantage in the field. ❺At the end of the session, you'll receive a certificate of completion to show that you're qualified in the use of the equipment.

おはようございます。市の水道局の新規従業員向け講習会へようこそ。今日の午前中は、水にナトリウムや他の鉱物成分が含まれているかを検査するための専門器具一式の使用法を私が実演します。この講習会はこちらの研究室で行われますが、私はこの機器が作業現場でどのように水質を検査できるのかも実演します。それは驚くほど使いやすく、この点が実地での大きな利点です。この会の最後に皆さんは、機器の使用資格を持つことを示す修了証書を受け取ります。

---

89 What is the topic of the workshop?

(A) Testing water
(B) Preserving food
(C) Conserving energy
(D) Cleaning up a work site

講習会のテーマは何ですか。

(A) 水の検査
(B) 食物の保存
(C) エネルギーの節約
(D) 作業現場の清掃

正解 A 話し手は、❶の水道局の新規従業員向け講習会開始の挨拶に続けて、❷「今日の午前中は、水にナトリウムや他の鉱物成分が含まれているかを検査するための専門器具一式の使用法を私が実演する」と講習会のテーマを伝えている。
(B) preserve「～を保存する」。
(C) conserve「～を節約する」。
(D) 現場に言及はあるが、清掃については述べていない。clean up ～「～を清掃する」。

---

90 What advantage does the speaker mention about the equipment?

(A) It comes with accessories.
(B) It is inexpensive.
(C) It is lightweight.
(D) It is easy to use.

話し手はこの機器のどんな利点について述べていますか。

(A) それは付属品が付いている。
(B) それは安価である。
(C) それは軽量である。
(D) それは使いやすい。

正解 D 話し手は❸で、機器が現場でどのように水質を検査できるかも、この講習会で実演すると言ってから、❹「それは驚くほど使いやすく、この点が実地での大きな利点だ」と、述べている。simple to useをeasy to useと表している(D)が正解。
(A) come with ～「～が付いている」、accessories「付属品」。
(B) inexpensive「安価な」。
(C) lightweight「軽量な」。

---

91 What will happen at the end of the workshop?

(A) Photographs will be taken.
(B) Certificates will be awarded.
(C) Lunch will be served.
(D) Projects will be assigned.

講習会の最後には何が起こりますか。

(A) 写真が撮影される。
(B) 証明書が授与される。
(C) 昼食が出される。
(D) プロジェクトが割り当てられる。

正解 B 話し手は❷で、講習会で水質の検査器具の使用法について紹介すると伝え、❸でも講習の内容を説明している。さらに、❺「この会の最後に皆さんは、機器の使用資格を持つことを示す修了証書を受け取る」と伝えている。award「～を授与する」。
(A) photograph「写真」。
(C) serve「～（飲食物など）を出す」。
(D) assign「～を割り当てる」。

Words & Phrases

workshop 講習会　　department 局　　demonstrate ～を実演する　　specialized 専門の
apparatus 器具一式　　test ～ for … ～の…(の有無)を調べる　　sodium ナトリウム　　mineral 鉱物、ミネラル
component 成分　　take place 行われる　　laboratory 研究室　　equipment 機器　　site 現場、用地
surprisingly 驚くほど　　advantage 利点、優位　　in the field 実地で　　session セッション、集まり
receive ～を受け取る　　certificate 証明書　　completion 修了、完了　　qualified 資格のある、条件を満たした

Questions 92 through 94 refer to the following speech.

問題92-94は次のスピーチに関するものです。

M

❶I'm grateful and deeply honored to be inducted into the National Music Hall of Fame. It's great that a new generation of artists recognize their predecessors. ❷I remember when my first album was released. The success was beyond my wildest dreams. And the fans, wow! ❸I couldn't go out in public without people noticing me and trying to take my picture. ❹I've been retired for a long time though, and life has changed. I can go to a restaurant now. Retirement's not so bad. Anyway, there are a lot of people to thank, but ❺I should begin by thanking my manager, Manuel Garcia. Without him, my career could never have gotten started.

私は、全国音楽殿堂の一人として認められることに感謝し、心から光栄に思います。アーティストの新しい世代が自分たちの先任者たちを認めるのは、素晴らしいことです。私の初のアルバムが発売されたときを思い出します。その成功は夢にも思わなかったものでした。そしてファンの方々と言ったら、すごい! 人前に出れば必ず、人々は私に気付いて写真を撮ろうとしました。でも私は長い間引退しており、そして生活は変わりました。今では、私はレストランに行くことができます。引退もそれほど悪いものではありません。とにかく感謝すべき多くの人々がいますが、まず、私のマネジャーであるManuel Garciaに感謝すべきでしょう。彼なくして、私のキャリアは決して始まらなかったでしょうから。

92 Who most likely is the speaker?

(A) A musician
(B) A painter
(C) An athlete
(D) A photographer

話し手は誰だと考えられますか。

(A) 音楽家
(B) 画家
(C) スポーツ選手
(D) 写真家

正解 A 話し手は❶で、全国音楽殿堂の一人として認められたことに対する感謝の意を述べている。また❷「私の初のアルバムが発売されたときを思い出す」と回想しているので、殿堂入りを果たした音楽家だと考えられる。
(C) athlete「スポーツ選手」。

93 What does the speaker imply when he says, "I can go to a restaurant now"?

(A) He is not available for an interview.
(B) He is not recognized by fans.
(C) He is ready to start a project.
(D) He is receiving payments.

話し手は "I can go to a restaurant now" という発言で、何を示唆していますか。

(A) 彼はインタビューに応じることができない。
(B) 彼はファンに気付かれない。
(C) 彼はプロジェクトを開始する準備ができている。
(D) 彼は報酬を受け取っている。

正解 B 初アルバム発売時を回想した話し手は、ファンについて❸で、「人前に出れば必ず、人々は私に気付いて写真を撮ろうとした」と当時の状況を述べている。続けて❹「でも私は長い間引退しており、そして生活は変わった」と説明してから下線部で「今では、私はレストランに行くことができる」と言っている。よって、話し手は引退前の生活とは変わり、もはや自分が人前に出てもファンに気付かれない現状を伝えていると考えられる。
(C) be ready to do「~する準備ができている」。
(D) payment「報酬、支払い」。

94 Who does the speaker thank?

(A) His family
(B) His manager
(C) A reporter
(D) A competitor

話し手は誰に感謝していますか。

(A) 自分の家族
(B) 自分のマネジャー
(C) 記者
(D) 競争相手

正解 B 話し手は、感謝すべき多くの人がいると述べてから、❺「まず、私のマネジャーであるManuel Garciaに感謝すべきだ。彼なくして、私のキャリアは決して始まらなかっただろう」と自分のマネジャーに対する謝意を表している。
(C) reporter「記者」。
(D) competitor「競争相手」。

TEST 2 PART 4

Words & Phrases

be grateful to *do* ~であることをありがたく思う　be honored to *do* ~することを光栄に思う
deeply 深く　be inducted into ~ ~の一員として認められる　national 全国的な
Hall of Fame 栄誉の殿堂 ★功績者を表彰するための殿堂　generation 世代　recognize ~を認める、~に気付く
predecessor 先任者　release ~を発売する　success 成功　beyond *one's* wildest dreams 夢にも思わなかったような
in public 人前で、公然と　notice ~に気付く　retired 引退した　though でも、けれど　retirement 引退
begin by *doing* ~することから始める　career キャリア、職業

Questions 95 through 97 refer to the following telephone message and shirt options.

🏴 M

Hi, I'm Alexi Solokov. ❶I own a small business, and I'm interested in ordering some shirts from your company. See, ❷all of my employees are going to a trade show next month, and ❸I want them to wear shirts embroidered with our logo. ❹I looked at your design options, and I prefer the design with the logo on the sleeve of the shirt. But ❺before I place the order, I want to confirm that they'll be here in time for the trade show. ❻Please call me at 555-0134 and let me know when the shirts would be delivered. Thanks.

問題95-97は次の電話のメッセージとシャツの選択肢に関するものです。

もしもし、Alexi Solokovと申します。私は小さな店を所有しておりまして、御社にシャツを注文したいと思っています。あの、来月うちの従業員が全員、展示会に行くのですが、彼らには当店のロゴが刺しゅうされたシャツを着用してもらいたいと思っています。御社のデザインの選択肢を見てみたところ、私はシャツの袖にロゴが入ったデザインが気に入っています。でも、注文する前に、それらが展示会に間に合うようここに届くことを確認したいのです。555-0134まで私にお電話いただき、シャツがいつ配達されることになるか教えてください。よろしくお願いいたします。

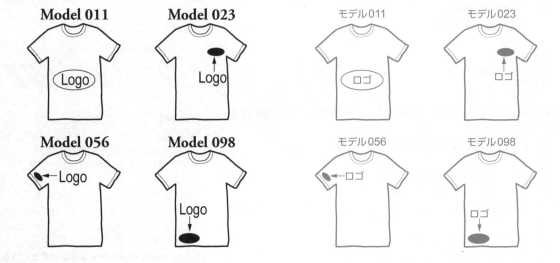

95 What will the speaker's employees do next month?

(A) Receive annual bonuses
(B) Act in a commercial
(C) Attend a trade show
(D) Celebrate an anniversary

話し手の従業員は来月、何をしますか。

(A) 年次賞与を受け取る
(B) コマーシャルに出演する
(C) 展示会に出席する
(D) 記念日を祝う

正解 C 話し手は❶で、自分が小さな店を所有しており、聞き手の会社にシャツを注文したいと伝え、❷「来月うちの従業員が全員、展示会に行く」と予定を述べている。このことをattend a trade showと表している(C)が正解。attend「〜に出席する」。

(A) annual「年次の」、bonus「賞与」。
(B) act in 〜「〜に出演する」、commercial「コマーシャル」。
(D) celebrate「〜を祝う」、anniversary「記念日」。

96 Look at the graphic. Which shirt design does the speaker prefer?

(A) Model 011
(B) Model 023
(C) Model 098
(D) Model 056

図を見てください。話し手はどのシャツのデザインを気に入りましたか。

(A) モデル011
(B) モデル023
(C) モデル098
(D) モデル056

正解 D ❶でシャツを注文したいと伝えた話し手は、❸で、来月の展示会で自分の従業員には自分の店のロゴが刺しゅうされたシャツを着用してほしいと、デザインの希望を述べている。さらに❹「御社のデザインの選択肢を見てみたところ、私はシャツの袖にロゴが入ったデザインが気に入っている」と言っている。図を見ると、袖にロゴが入っているデザインはモデル056なので、(D)が正解。

97 What does the speaker ask about?

(A) A delivery date
(B) A payment method
(C) Color options
(D) Shirt sizes

話し手は何について尋ねていますか。

(A) 配達日
(B) 支払方法
(C) 色の選択肢
(D) シャツのサイズ

正解 A ❹で、希望するシャツのデザインを伝えた話し手は、❺「注文する前に、それらが展示会に間に合うようここに届くことを確認したい」と述べ、続けて❻で、シャツがいつ配達されることになるか、自分に電話で知らせるよう頼んでいる。

(B) payment「支払い」。
(C)(D) 話し手はシャツについて話しているが、その色やサイズには言及していない。

TEST 2 PART 4

Words & Phrases

shirt シャツ　option 選択肢　own 〜を所有する　business 店、事業　order 〜を注文する　employee 従業員

trade show 展示会　embroider 〜 with … 〜に…を刺しゅうする　logo ロゴ　design デザイン

prefer 〜が気に入っている、〜の方を好む　sleeve 袖　place an order 注文する　confirm 〜を確認する

in time for 〜 〜に間に合って　deliver 〜を配達する

選択肢 model モデル、型

Questions 98 through 100 refer to the following excerpt from a meeting and schedule.

問題98-100は次の会議の抜粋と予定表に関するものです。

 W

OK, ❶next I want to discuss some of the current marketing campaigns we're working on. ❷It's great that we're handling the marketing for so many companies, but it does require careful planning. ❸Here's the schedule of the client meetings coming up in August. As you can see, one of them is with our newest client, the Bedham Corporation. ❹This is one of the largest accounts we've handled, so everyone should be here for that meeting. To familiarize you with this company, ❺I've prepared a packet of information about their history and major products. The packets are at the back of the room. Please be sure to pick up a packet on your way out.

さて次に、私たちが現在取り組んでいるマーケティングキャンペーンの何件かについて話し合いたいと思います。私たちが非常に多くの企業のマーケティングを受け持っているのは素晴らしいことです、しかしそれには綿密な計画がまさに必要です。こちらが、8月に入っている顧客との会合の予定表です。ご覧の通り、そのうちの1つは、私たちにとって一番新規の顧客であるBedham社とのものです。同社は私たちが受け持ってきた中で最も大口の顧客の1つなので、その会合のために全員がここに来る必要があります。皆さんにこの会社について詳しく知ってもらうために、同社の歴史や主要製品に関する情報資料の袋を用意しました。その袋は部屋の後方にあります。退出の際に、一袋必ず受け取ってください。

Upcoming Client Meetings	
August 3	Chung Associates
August 14	Bedham Corporation
August 18	Marsten Company
August 24	Satero Construction

今後の顧客との会合	
8月3日	Chung Associates社
8月14日	Bedham社
8月18日	Marsten社
8月24日	Satero建設会社

98 What type of business does the speaker work for?

    (A) A marketing firm
    (B) A Web-design company
    (C) A shipping service
    (D) A law firm

話し手はどのような業種で働いていますか。

    (A) マーケティング会社
    (B) ウェブデザイン会社
    (C) 運送サービス会社
    (D) 法律事務所

正解 A 話し手は❶「次に、現在私たちが取り組んでいるマーケティングキャンペーンの何件かについて話し合いたいと思う」と会議の議題を知らせ、続けて❷で自分たちは多くの企業のマーケティング案件を担当していると述べている。よって、話し手はマーケティング会社で働いていると分かる。firm「企業」。
(C) shipping「運送（業）、輸送（業）」。
(D) law firm「法律事務所」。

---

99 Look at the graphic. What day are the listeners asked to be available?

    (A) August 3
    (B) August 14
    (C) August 18
    (D) August 24

図を見てください。聞き手は何日に都合をつけるよう求められていますか。

    (A) 8月3日
    (B) 8月14日
    (C) 8月18日
    (D) 8月24日

正解 B 話し手は❸で、8月の顧客との会合の予定表を示し、そのうちの1つがBedham社との会合だと伝えている。さらにBedham社について、❹「同社は私たちが受け持ってきた中で最も大口の顧客の1つなので、その会合のために全員がここに来る必要がある」と聞き手に伝えている。図を見ると、Bedham社との会合が行われる日付は8月14日なので、(B)が正解。available「都合がつく、利用できる」。

---

100 What will the listeners find at the back of the room?

    (A) Name tags
    (B) Some product samples
    (C) Some refreshments
    (D) Information packets

聞き手は部屋の後方に何を見つけますか。

    (A) 名札
    (B) 製品サンプル
    (C) 軽食
    (D) 情報資料の袋

正解 D 話し手は、❹でBedham社という大口顧客との会合への全員の出席を求めてから、❺「同社の歴史や主要製品に関する情報資料の袋を用意した。その袋は部屋の後方にある」と言っている。
(A) name tag「名札」。
(C) refreshments「軽食」。

Words & Phrases

discuss ～について話し合う　　current 現在の、最新の　　marketing マーケティング　　campaign キャンペーン
work on ～ ～に取り組む　　handle ～を担当する　　require ～を必要とする　　careful 綿密な　　planning 計画
client 顧客　　come up 生じる、出てくる　　corporation 企業　　account 顧客、得意先
familiarize ～ with … ～を…に精通させる　　packet ひと包み、束　　major 主要な　　product 製品
be sure to *do* 必ず～する　　on *one's* way out 出る途中で

予定表 upcoming 今度の、近づいている　　construction 建設

PART 5

問題 特典 58-60

101 Summer interns at Fairview City Hall must ------- all city council meetings.

(A) attend
(B) attending
(C) to attend
(D) attends

フェアビュー市役所の夏期インターン生は、市議会の全ての会議に出席しなければなりません。

＊選択肢の訳は省略

正解 **A** 動詞attend「～に出席する」の適切な形を選ぶ。空所の前に助動詞mustがあり、後ろには名詞句all city council meetings「市議会の全ての会議」と続いているので、mustと共に文の述語動詞を作ることができる原形の(A) attendが適切。intern「インターン生、研修生」、city hall「市役所」、city council「市議会」。
(B) 現在分詞、または動名詞。(C) to不定詞。(D) 三人称単数現在形。

102 A ------- analysis of market trends can lead retailers to profitable results.

(A) careful
(B) care
(C) carefully
(D) cared

市場動向の綿密な分析は、小売業者を利益をもたらす結果に導くことができます。

(A) 綿密な
(B) 注意
(C) 注意深く
(D) 気にかけられた

正解 **A** 空所の前に冠詞aがあり、後ろに名詞analysis「分析」が続いているので、名詞を修飾する語が入る。形容詞の(A) careful「綿密な、注意深い」を入れると、「市場動向の綿密な分析は、小売業者を利益をもたらす結果に導くことができる」となり、文意が通る。market「市場」、trend「動向」、lead ～ to …「～を…(ある結果など)に導く」、retailer「小売業者」、profitable「利益をもたらす」。
(B) 名詞、または動詞「～を気にする」の原形。(C) 副詞。
(D) 動詞の過去分詞。名詞を修飾できるが、文意に合わない。

103 Please ------- a copy of each sales report on a separate piece of paper.

(A) pick
(B) tell
(C) reply
(D) print

それぞれの売上報告を1部ずつ、別々の紙に印刷してください。

(A) ～を選ぶ
(B) ～に伝える
(C) 返答する
(D) ～を印刷する

正解 **D** 選択肢は全て動詞の働きを持つ語。「それぞれの売上報告を1部ずつ、別々の紙に-------してください」と依頼する文。空所の後ろのa copy of each sales report「それぞれの売上報告を1部ずつ」を目的語として続けて文意に合うのは、(D) print「～を印刷する」。a copy of ～「1部の～」、sales report「売上報告」、a piece of ～「1つの～」、separate「別の」。

104 Ms. Wendt's -------, Daniel Novianto, will be answering her e-mails while she is on leave.

(A) assistant
(B) assistance
(C) assisting
(D) assists

Wendtさんの助手であるDaniel Noviantoが、Wendtさんの休暇の間、彼女宛てのEメールに返信します。

(A) 助手
(B) 支援
(C) 援助すること
(D) 援助

正解 **A** 文の述語動詞はwill be answeringで、前にあるMs. Wendt's ------ は、直後にカンマを挟んで続くDaniel Noviantoと同格の関係にあり、文の主語と考えられる。所有格のMs. Wendt'sに修飾される語として文意に合うのは、人物を表す名詞の(A) assistant「助手」。answer「～に返事をする」、on leave「休暇中で」。
(B) 名詞だが、人と同格にならない。
(C) 動詞「～を援助する」の動名詞。
(D) 名詞の複数形だとしても、人と同格にならない。

105 Do not keep perishable foods in the cooler beyond ------- expiration date.

(A) they
(B) their
(C) them
(D) themselves

腐りやすい食品は、その消費期限過ぎまで冷蔵庫内に保管しておかないでください。

(A) それらは
(B) それらの
(C) それらを
(D) それら自身

正解 **B** 選択肢は全て三人称複数の人称代名詞。空所の前に前置詞beyond「～を過ぎて」があり、後ろには名詞句expiration date「消費期限」が続いているので、空所には名詞句を修飾する語が入る。所有格の(B) theirが適切。their以降が「腐りやすい食品の消費期限」を表すので、文意にも合う。perishable「腐りやすい」、cooler「冷蔵庫」。
(A) 主格。(C) 目的格。(D) 再帰代名詞。

106 Erico Costa's new work of fiction is an ------- tale of mistaken identity.

(A) amuse
(B) amusement
(C) amusingly
(D) amusing

Erico Costaの小説の新作は、人違いに関する楽しい物語です。

(A) ～を楽しませる
(B) 楽しみ
(C) 楽しませるように
(D) 楽しい

正解 **D** 空所の前に冠詞anがあり、後ろには名詞tale「物語」が続いているので、名詞を修飾する語が入る。形容詞の(D) amusing「楽しい」が適切。work「作品」、fiction「小説、フィクション」、mistaken identity「人違い」。
(A) 動詞「～を楽しませる」の原形。
(B) 名詞。
(C) 副詞。

TEST 2 PART 5

107 Zantos Network is moving forward with the ------- to purchase a local radio station.

(A) property
(B) advancement
(C) proposal
(D) signature

Zantosネットワーク社は、地方ラジオ局を買収する計画を推進しています。

(A) 財産
(B) 前進
(C) 計画
(D) 署名

> **正解 C** 文意に合う名詞を選ぶ。文の述語動詞部分は is moving forward with 〜「〜を推進している」。空所に続くto purchase a local radio stationは「地方ラジオ局を買収するための」という意味なので、このto不定詞句によって修飾されて、文意に合うのは (C) proposal「(提案された)計画」。move forward with 〜「〜を推進する」、purchase「〜を買収する」、local「地方の」、radio station「ラジオ局」。

108 Over 95 percent of Kapp Hardware's clients have responded ------- in online reviews.

(A) favorable
(B) favorably
(C) favored
(D) to favor

Kappハードウエア社の顧客の95パーセント以上が、オンラインのレビューで好意的に反応しました。

(A) 好意的な
(B) 好意的に
(C) 好意を持たれている
(D) 〜に好意を示すために

> **正解 B** 空所は述語動詞have respondedの直後にあり、「顧客の95パーセント以上が、オンラインのレビューで反応した」という主旨の文が成立しているので、空所には述語動詞を修飾する副詞が入る。副詞の (B) favorably「好意的に」が適切。hardware「ハードウエア(電子機器装置)、金物類」、client「顧客」、respond「反応する」、online「オンラインの」、review「レビュー、評価」。
> (A) 形容詞。(C) 形容詞、または動詞「〜に好意を示す」の過去分詞。(D) to不定詞。

109 Ms. Kean mentioned the improved tool kit ------- at the meeting but did not discuss how we will promote it.

(A) closely
(B) repeatedly
(C) upwardly
(D) neatly

Keanさんは会議で、改良された工具一式に何度も言及しましたが、当社がそれをどのように売り込むかは述べませんでした。

(A) 綿密に
(B) 何度も
(C) 上方へ
(D) きちんと

> **正解 B** 選択肢は全て副詞。逆接を表す接続詞butの前までは、Ms. Keanを主語、mentionedを述語動詞とする文で、butの後ろは、同じ主語についてもう1つの述語動詞did not discussを並べて説明を加えている。(B) repeatedly「何度も」を入れると、会議で、改良された製品に何度も言及したものの、その売り込み方は述べなかった、となり、文意が通る。mention「〜に言及する」、improved「改良された」、tool kit「工具一式」、discuss「〜を論じる」、promote「〜を売り込む」。
> (A) (C) (D) mentionを修飾する副詞として不適切。

110 Once Mr. Braun had toured the conference -------, he paid the deposit fee.

　(A) location
　(B) locate
　(C) locating
　(D) locator

Braunさんは協議会の場所を見て回った後、すぐに手付金を支払いました。

　(A) 場所
　(B) ～を設置する
　(C) ～を設置している
　(D) 位置探査装置

正解 A 文頭からカンマまでは接続詞once「～するとすぐに」で始まる節。この節の述語動詞had touredの後ろは、the conference -------なので、conferenceと共に複合名詞となり、had touredの目的語となる名詞(A) location「場所」が適切。協議会を開催する場所を見て回った後、すぐに手付金を支払った、となり、文意も通る。tour「～を見て回る」、conference「協議会」、deposit fee「手付金」。
(B) 動詞「～を設置する」の原形。
(C) 現在分詞または動名詞。(D) 名詞だが、文意に合わない。

111 Management has asked Ms. Leung to meet ------- the new office supply vendor tomorrow.

　(A) at
　(B) with
　(C) for
　(D) of

経営陣は、事務用品の新規の供給業者と明日会うよう、Leungさんに頼みました。

　(A) ～で
　(B) ～と
　(C) ～のために
　(D) ～の

正解 B 選択肢は全て前置詞の働きを持つ語。空所の後ろは名詞句the new office supply vendor「事務用品の新規の供給業者」という「人物」なので、meet with ～で「(約束して)～と会う、～と会談する」という意味になる(B) withが適切。management「経営陣」、ask ～ to do「～に…するように頼む」、office supplies「事務用品」、vendor「供給業者」。

112 Mr. Farmingham will rearrange his schedule to have lunch at 2:00 P.M. ------- you are available then.

　(A) if
　(B) by
　(C) without
　(D) during

もしその時あなたの都合がつくならば、Farminghamさんは午後2時に昼食を取るように自分の予定を変更するでしょう。

　(A) もし～ならば
　(B) ～によって
　(C) ～なしに
　(D) ～の間中

正解 A 空所の前後に〈主語＋動詞〉の形があるので、空所には2つの文をつなぐことのできる接続詞が入る。適切なのは、条件や仮定を表す接続詞の(A) if「もし～ならば」。rearrange「～(約束の日時など)を変更する」、available「都合がつく」。
(B) (C) (D) 前置詞。2つの文をつなぐことができないので不適切。

141

113 Please include your employee number ------- filling out the room reservation form.

(A) although
(B) so
(C) when
(D) however

部屋の予約用紙に記入するときは、自分の従業員番号を入れてください。

(A) ～であるけれども
(B) それで
(C) ～するときに
(D) しかしながら

正解 C 文意に合う接続詞を選ぶ。空所の前のPlease include your employee number「自分の従業員番号を入れてください」と、空所の後ろのfilling out the room reservation form「部屋の予約用紙に記入する」をつなぐことができるのは、(C) when「～するときに」。予約用紙の記入時に従業員番号を含めるよう依頼する文になる。whenとfillingの間にはyou areが省略されていると考えられる。include「～を含める」、employee「従業員」、fill out ～「～に記入する」、reservation「予約」、form「用紙」。

114 Be sure to pack a water bottle for tomorrow's mountain hike, as it is ------- to stay hydrated.

(A) nutritious
(B) sensitive
(C) direct
(D) crucial

水分補給した状態でいることが非常に重要なので、明日の山歩きのために、必ず水筒を荷物に入れておいてください。

(A) 栄養のある
(B) 敏感な
(C) 直接の
(D) 非常に重要な

正解 D カンマの前までは、「明日の山歩きのために、必ず水筒を荷物に入れておいてください」という指示なので、接続詞asで始まる節では、水筒を荷物に入れておくべき理由を説明していると考えられる。(D) crucial「非常に重要な」を入れると、「水分補給した状態でいることが非常に重要なので」と、脱水症状を防ぐ助言をする文になる。be sure to do「必ず～する」、pack「～を荷物に入れる」、water bottle「水筒」、mountain hike「山歩き」、stay ～「～(ある状態)のままでいる」、hydrated「水分を保持した」。

115 Westmont Hospital announced that leading heart ------- Dr. Emily Chow will be joining the staff next month.

(A) special
(B) specialize
(C) specialist
(D) specialized

Westmont病院は、第一級の心臓専門医であるEmily Chow医師が来月、スタッフに加わることになっていると発表しました。

(A) 特別な
(B) 専門とする
(C) 専門医
(D) 専門化した

正解 C that節の述語動詞はwill be joiningなので、leading heart ------- Dr. Emily Chowまでが、その節内の主語に当たると考えられる。空所に名詞の(C) specialist「専門医」を入れると、leading heart specialistとDr. Emily Chowが同格の関係で結ばれ、「第一級の心臓専門医であるEmily Chow医師」となり、文が成立する。announce「～を発表する」、leading「一流の、卓越した」、join「～に加わる」。
(A) 形容詞。(B) 動詞「専門とする」の原形。(D) 形容詞。

116 The Midosuji branch of Tsurutani Bank is closed ------- because of a problem with the electrical system.

(A) slightly
(B) temporarily
(C) universally
(D) terminally

Tsurutani銀行のMidosuji支店は、電気系統の障害のため、一時的に休業しています。

(A) わずかに
(B) 一時的に
(C) 普遍的に
(D) 末期的に

正解 B 選択肢は全て副詞。空所までは「Tsurutani銀行のMidosuji支店は、-------休業している」という意味で、空所部分は述語動詞is closedを修飾している。空所の後ろでbecause of a problem with the electrical system「電気系統の障害のため」と、休業の理由が示されているので、文意が通るのは(B) temporarily「一時的に」。branch「支店」、because of ～「～のため、～ゆえに」、electrical system「電気系統」。

117 Funds raised by the community auction will be used to maintain the ------- Quill Street playground.

(A) aging
(B) glad
(C) utter
(D) brief

自治体のオークションで集められた資金は、老朽化したQuill通りの運動場の整備に使われます。

(A) 老朽化した
(B) うれしい
(C) まったくの
(D) 簡潔な

正解 A 選択肢は全て形容詞の働きを持つ語。文全体は「自治体のオークションで集められた資金は、------- Quill通りの運動場の整備に使われる」という意味。空所の後ろのQuill Street playgroundを修飾して動詞maintain「～を整備する」の目的語を作り、文意に合うのは(A) aging「老朽化した」。fund「資金」、raise「～（資金など）を集める」、community「自治体」、auction「オークション」、playground「運動場」。

118 United Carpet West received ------- higher customer satisfaction ratings than its competitors did.

(A) signify
(B) significance
(C) signifying
(D) significantly

United Carpet West社は、競合各社よりも著しく高い顧客満足度評価を受けました。

(A) ～を意味する
(B) 重要性
(C) ～を意味している
(D) 著しく

正解 D 文の主語はUnited Carpet West。空所直後に形容詞の比較級のhigherがあり、同社が受けた顧客満足度評価がthan以降の競合各社が受けた評価と比較して高かった、と述べている。空所には形容詞の比較級を修飾して程度を表す副詞の(D) significantly「著しく」が適切。customer satisfaction「顧客満足（度）」、rating「評価」、competitor「競合会社」。
(A) 動詞「～を意味する」の原形。(B) 名詞。(C) 現在分詞。

119 This month's tool catalog was edited to reflect that two items are not in -------.

(A) situation
(B) stock
(C) action
(D) asset

今月の用具カタログは、2つの商品の在庫がないことを反映して編集されました。

(A) 状況
(B) 在庫品
(C) 行動
(D) 資産

正解 B 選択肢は全て名詞の働きを持つ語。文頭からeditedまでは「今月の用具カタログは、編集された」という意味で、その後ろのto reflect that … 「…を反映するように」では、カタログの編集結果が述べられている。that節の主語はtwo itemsなので、in stockで「在庫して」という意味になる(B) stockを空所に入れると、「2つの商品の在庫がない」となり、文意が通る。tool「用具」、catalog「カタログ」、edit「〜を編集する」、reflect「〜を反映する」、item「品目」。
(C) in actionで「活動中の」という意味。文意に合わない。

120 On-site training programs are associated with ------- employee motivation.

(A) to increase
(B) increases
(C) increased
(D) increase

現地での研修プログラムは、従業員の意欲向上に結び付きます。

＊選択肢の訳は省略

正解 C 選択肢は動詞increase「〜を強める」の変化した形。空所の前に前置詞withがあり、後ろには名詞句employee motivation「従業員の意欲」が続いているので、名詞句を修飾する語が入る。形容詞の働きがある過去分詞の(C) increased「強められた」が適切。on-site「現地での」、be associated with 〜「〜と結び付く」、motivation「意欲」。
(A) to不定詞。(B) 動詞の三人称単数現在形、または名詞の複数形。
(D) 動詞の原形、または名詞の単数形。

121 The catering contract calls for flowers to be arranged ------- in a vase on each banquet table.

(A) honestly
(B) enormously
(C) hungrily
(D) attractively

そのケータリング契約は、宴会用の各テーブルの上にある花瓶に花が魅力的に飾られることを求めています。

(A) 正直に
(B) 莫大に
(C) むさぼるように
(D) 魅力的に

正解 D 選択肢は全て副詞。文の主語はThe catering contractで、述語動詞はcalls for。ケータリング契約で求められている内容を述べた文。to以降は、「宴会用の各テーブルの上にある花瓶に-------飾られる」という意味で、前の名詞flowersについて説明している。「花が飾られる」という行為を修飾する副詞として文意に合うのは(D) attractively「魅力的に」。catering「ケータリング」、contract「契約」、call for 〜 to do「〜が…するよう求める」、arrange「〜を配置する」、vase「花瓶」、banquet「宴会、夕食会」。

122 Fifty percent of the total landscaping cost is required now, and the ------- is due upon completion of the project.

(A) remains
(B) remain
(C) remained
(D) remainder

造園費用の総額のうち50パーセントは今求められており、残りはプロジェクトが完了次第支払われる必要があります。

(A) 残り物
(B) 残る
(C) 居残った
(D) 残り

正解 **D** 接続詞andで2つの文を並列している。カンマ以降の文の述語動詞はis. 空所を含むthe ------- がカンマ以降の文の主語に当たり、名詞の単数形で文意に合うものが入る。(D) remainder「残り」が適切。total「総計の」、landscaping「造園」、require「〜を必要とする」、due「支払われるべき」、completion「完了」。
(A) 複数扱いの名詞remains「残り物」。この名詞は通常複数形で使う。
(B) 動詞「残る」の原形。
(C) 動詞の過去形または過去分詞。

123 The date of the building's grand opening was moved ------- President Daniels could be there to officiate.

(A) so that
(B) such as
(C) due to
(D) except for

Daniels社長が式を執り行うためにその場にいられるよう、その建物のグランドオープンの日にちは変更されました。

(A) 〜するために
(B) 〜のような
(C) 〜のせいで
(D) 〜を除いて

正解 **A** 空所の前後に〈主語＋動詞〉の形があるので、空所には2つの文をつなぐ接続詞の働きをするものが入る。文を接続できるのは、目的を表す(A) so that「〜するために」のみ。grand opening「グランドオープン、開店記念」、move「〜（日時など）を変更する、〜を移動する」、officiate「式を執り行う」。
(B) (C) (D) いずれも前置詞句で、2文をつなぐことはできない。

124 New patients ------- miss their initial visit at Pratha Medical Clinic without advance notice will not be rescheduled.

(A) what
(B) where
(C) who
(D) why

Pratha診療所の新規患者で事前連絡なく初回の来院をしなかった方には、予定の組み直しは行われません。

(A) 〜するもの
(B) 〜する（場所）
(C) 〜する（人）
(D) 〜する（理由）

正解 **C** 文頭からnoticeまでがこの文の主語に当たり、will not be rescheduledが述語動詞。空所直前の名詞句 New patientsは「人物」なので、これを先行詞として受け、後ろに動詞を続けることのできる主格の関係代名詞の(C) whoが適切。patient「患者」、miss「〜しそこなう」、initial「最初の」、medical clinic「診療所」、advance「事前の」、notice「通知」、reschedule「〜の予定を組み直す」。
(A) 関係代名詞。先行詞なしで用いるので不適切。
(B) (D) 関係副詞。「人物」を先行詞としないので不適切。

125 Mr. Lewis deserves ------- for the thoughtful service he always provides to customers.

   (A) content
   (B) experience
   (C) community
   (D) recognition

Lewisさんは、いつも顧客に提供している心のこもったサービスに対して評価を受けるに値します。

   (A) 満足
   (B) 経験
   (C) 地域社会
   (D) 評価

正解 **D** 選択肢は全て名詞の働きを持つ語。文の主語はMr. Lewis、述語動詞はdeservesで、空所直後には前置詞for がある。recognition for ～ で「～に対する評価」を表す(D) recognitionを入れると文意が通る。deserve「～を受けるに値する」、thoughtful「心のこもった」、provide「～を提供する」、customer「顧客」。

126 ------- the growing demand for steel, there is still a large supply available.

   (A) Likewise
   (B) Despite
   (C) Though
   (D) While

鋼鉄に対して増大する需要にもかかわらず、まだ十分な供給が得られています。

   (A) 同様に
   (B) ～にもかかわらず
   (C) ～だけれども
   (D) ～している間に

正解 **B** カンマまでは、空所と名詞句the growing demand for steel だけなので、空所に前置詞を入れて前置詞句にすると、カンマの後ろとつながる。カンマまでは「鋼鉄に対して増大する需要-------」で、カンマの後ろでは「まだ十分な供給が得られている」と相反する内容が述べられている。よって、逆接を表す前置詞の(B) Despite「～にもかかわらず」が適切。growing「増大する」、demand「需要」、steel「鋼鉄」、supply「供給」、available「利用可能な」。
(A) 副詞。(C) (D) 接続詞。

127 Maria Pennfield's Star Signs Company ------- two decades ago.

   (A) has established
   (B) establishes
   (C) was established
   (D) establishing

Maria Pennfield の Star Signs社は、20年前に設立されました。

＊選択肢の訳は省略

正解 **C** 動詞establish「～を設立する」の適切な形を選ぶ。主語であるStar Signs Companyは設立される対象なので、受動態の文。two decades ago「20年前に」と過去の特定の時点を示す句があるので、時制は過去。受動態で過去形の(C) was establishedが三人称単数の Star Signs Companyにも合い、適切。decade「10年間」。
(A) 現在完了形。能動態なので不適切。(B) 三人称単数現在形。
(D) 現在分詞。この文には述語動詞がないので、空所に述語動詞が必要。

128 The paintings ------- the outside wall of the Klampton Hotel feature the art of Ah Lam Zhang.

(A) unto
(B) instead of
(C) in case of
(D) along

Klampton ホテルの外壁沿いの絵画は、Ah Lam Zhang の作品を目玉にしています。

(A) ～に
(B) ～の代わりに
(C) ～の場合
(D) ～沿いの

正解 D 選択肢は全て前置詞の働きを持つ語句。文の主語は The paintings で、述語動詞は feature なので、空所と the outside wall of the Klampton Hotel が、The paintings を修飾して、どのようなものかを説明していると考えられる。(D) along「～沿いの」を入れると、「ホテルの外壁沿いの絵画」となり、文意が通る。painting「絵画」、outside wall「外壁」、feature「～を目玉にする、～を特色にする」、art「芸術作品」。

129 Please ------- the handrail when going down the Palmer Theater's marble staircase.

(A) catch up
(B) run out of
(C) find out
(D) hold on to

Palmer 劇場の大理石の階段を下りる際には、手すりにしっかりつかまってください。

(A) ～をさっとつかみ上げる
(B) ～がなくなる
(C) ～を見つけ出す
(D) ～にしっかりつかまる

正解 D 選択肢は全て句動詞。空所の後ろにある the handrail「手すり」を目的語に取って文意に合うものを選ぶ。階段を下りる際の、手すりに対する行為として適切なのは (D) hold on to「～にしっかりつかまる」。when の直後に you are が省略されていると考えられる。marble「大理石」、staircase「(手すりなどを含めた一続きの)階段」。

130 Until the office heating system ------- , employees are permitted to work from home.

(A) will be fixed
(B) is being fixed
(C) has been fixed
(D) had been fixed

オフィスの暖房装置の修理が完了するまで、従業員は在宅勤務が認められます。

＊選択肢の訳は省略

正解 C 動詞 fix「～を修理する」の受動態の適切な時制を選ぶ。カンマの後ろは「従業員は在宅勤務が認められる」、カンマまでは時の継続を表す接続詞 Until で始まる節で、the office heating system までが主語と考えられる。カンマまでを「オフィスの暖房装置の修理が完了するまで」として在宅勤務の期限を述べる節にすると文意が通る。現在完了形の (C) が適切。heating system「暖房装置」、permit ～ to do「～に…することを許可する」、work from home「在宅勤務をする」。
(A) 未来形の受動態。(B) 現在進行形の受動態。(D) 過去完了形の受動態。

PART 6

Questions 131-134 refer to the following article.

---

❶ CALGROVE (November 4)—The Calgrove Transportation Bureau announced today that it recently contracted with Tazuco Corporation to provide the city with new traffic-signal control cabinets. These cabinets contain the computers that manage the timing of automated -------. **131.** According to a Tazuco spokesperson, the cabinets are designed with roll-up doors for easy access, so that sidewalks are not blocked when maintenance teams service them. -------. The **132.** cabinets are also equipped with a backup battery designed to keep the signals running ------- **133.** an electrical outage, so that vehicular traffic can move smoothly.

❷ Calgrove plans ------- several Tazuco cabinets in the West Bay neighborhood during an initial trial **134.** period. After collecting data from those, transportation officials will decide whether further units should be placed throughout the city.

問題 131-134 は次の記事に関するものです。

Calgrove (11 月 4 日)——本日、Calgrove 市交通局は、Tazuco 社が同市に新しい交通信号制御キャビネットを供給する契約を最近結んだと発表した。これらのキャビネットには、自動式交通信号のタイミングを管理するコンピューターが入っている。Tazuco 社の広報担当者によると、キャビネットは内部にアクセスしやすい巻き上げ式扉の設計になっており、従って保守チームがそれらの修理点検を行う際に歩道がふさがれることがない。*この特徴が地元の歩行者に歓迎されるのは確実だ。またキャビネットには、停電の場合に信号が作動し続けるように設計された予備電池が備え付けてあり、車両通行がスムーズに流れるようになっている。

Calgrove 市は最初の試用期間中に、ウエストベイ地区に Tazuco 社のキャビネットを数台取り付ける計画である。それらからデータを収集後、交通当局は、さらに追加の装置を市の全域に設置すべきかどうかを決定することになる。

*問題 132 の挿入文の訳

Words & Phrases

❶ transportation 交通　bureau （官庁の）局　announce ～を発表する　recently 最近　contract with ～ to do …する契約を～と結ぶ　provide ～ with … …に…を供給する　traffic-signal 交通信号の　control 制御　cabinet キャビネット、保管庫　contain ～が入っている、～を含む　manage ～を管理する　timing タイミング、時間調整　automated 自動の　spokesperson 広報担当者　design ～を設計する　roll-up 巻き上げ式の　access アクセス、接近　sidewalk 歩道　block ～をふさぐ　maintenance 保守、整備　service ～の修理点検をする　backup 予備(の)　run 作動する　electrical outage 停電　vehicular 車両の　traffic 通行、交通　smoothly スムーズに　❷ neighborhood 地区　initial 最初の　trial period 試用期間　collect ～を収集する　data データ　official 当局者、役人　further さらに付け加えられた　unit 装置一式　place ～を設置する　throughout ～の全体にわたって、～の至る所に

Expressions

be equipped with ～ 「～が備え付けてある」（❶ 6行目）

All the conference rooms are equipped with large projector screens.
全ての会議室には、大型のプロジェクタースクリーンが備え付けてあります。

131
(A) stoplights
(B) sprinklers
(C) tellers
(D) messages

(A) 交通信号
(B) スプリンクラー
(C) 窓口係
(D) メッセージ

> **正解 A** ❶1～3行目より、この記事はCalgrove市交通局とTazuco社の間で、新しい交通信号制御キャビネットを市に供給する契約が結ばれたことを知らせるものだと分かる。空所を含む文は、「これらのキャビネットには、自動式------のタイミングを管理するコンピューターが入っている」という意味で、直前の文のnew traffic-signal control cabinets「新しい交通信号制御キャビネット」をThese cabinetsと表して、その説明をしている。よって、空所に(A) stoplights「交通信号」を入れると、キャビネットの内部には交通信号を制御するコンピューターが入っているという内容になり、文意が通る。

132
(A) This will provide added space for kitchen utensils.
(B) Local sports fans are already lining up for tickets.
(C) Drivers will appreciate the additional drive-up convenience.
(D) This feature is sure to be welcomed by local pedestrians.

(A) これは、台所用品のための追加のスペースを与えるものだ。
(B) 地元のスポーツファンは、すでにチケットを求めて列に並んでいる。
(C) 運転者は、追加されるドライブスルーの利便性をありがたく思うだろう。
(D) この特徴が地元の歩行者に歓迎されるのは確実だ。

> **正解 D** 空所直前の文では、交通信号制御キャビネットが巻き上げ式扉の設計のため、歩道をふさがずに修理点検が可能だと述べられている。空所に(D)を入れるとThis featureが巻き上げ式扉で歩道をふさがずに修理点検が可能というキャビネットの特徴を指し、それが歩行者に歓迎されることは確実だという意味になるので、流れとして自然。be sure to do「～するのは確実だ」、welcome「～を歓迎する」、pedestrian「歩行者」。
> (A) provide「～を提供する」、added「追加の、余分な」、kitchen utensils「台所用品」。
> (B) line up「列に並ぶ」。
> (C) appreciate「～をありがたく思う、～を高く評価する」、additional「追加の」、drive-up「ドライブスルーの、車に乗ったままサービスを受けられる」、convenience「利便性」。

133
(A) by means of
(B) on top of
(C) in the event of
(D) on behalf of

(A) ～によって
(B) ～に加えて
(C) ～の場合には
(D) ～に代わって

> **正解 C** 空所を含む文は、「またキャビネットには、停電------信号が作動し続けるように設計された予備電池が備え付けてあり、車両通行がスムーズに流れるようになっている」という意味。予備電池は停電時にも信号を作動させ続けるためのものだと考えられるので、(C) in the event of「～の場合には」を入れると文意が通る。
> (A) (B) (D) いずれも文意が通らない。

134
(A) install
(B) to install
(C) have installed
(D) will install

＊選択肢の訳は省略

> **正解 B** 選択肢は動詞install「～を取り付ける」とその変化した形。空所を含む文の主語はCalgroveで、述語動詞であるplansの後ろに続けるのに適切な形を選ぶ。❶で、市が交通信号制御キャビネットの供給契約を結んだことが報じられ、キャビネットの特徴が説明されている。❷の空所を含む文では、during an initial trial period「最初の試用期間中に」とあり、直後の文で「それらからデータを収集後、交通当局は、さらに追加の装置を市の全域に設置すべきかどうかを決定することになる」とキャビネットの設置に関する今後の計画が述べられている。plan to doは「～することを計画する」を表すので、(B) to installを入れると、キャビネット設置のための今後の計画を段階的に説明する流れとなり、適切。
> (A) 原形。
> (C) 現在完了形。
> (D) 未来形。

Questions 135-138 refer to the following brochure.

❶ Most car buyers take out the expensive loans that are offered by auto dealership salespeople. This likely means the buyer will pay loan interest both to the lender and to the dealership. Do not make this ------- . We at Athena Bank invite you to consider an ------- . Why not secure
135.　　　　　　　　　　　　　　　　　　136.
a loan directly through Athena first, before ever entering a dealership? You could save hundreds. We are even willing to guarantee our lowest loan rate. ------- . Our representatives
137.
will be ------- to answer any questions that you may have.
138.

問題135-138は次のパンフレットに関するものです。

　自動車購入者の大多数は、自動車販売店の販売員に提示される高いローンを組みます。これによりおそらく、購入者は貸主と販売店の両方に対して、ローンの金利を支払うことになります。この失敗を犯さないでください。私どもAthena銀行はお客さまに、別の選択肢を検討なさることをお勧めします。そもそも販売店に入る前に、まず直接Athena銀行を通してローンを組んではいかがでしょうか。何百ドルものお金を節約できるかもしれません。私どもは、当行のローンの最低金利でさえも保証する用意があります。*当行は低金利の自動車ローンを専門としているため、これができるのです。当行の担当者は、お客さまがお持ちになるかもしれないどのような疑問にも喜んでお答えいたします。

*問題137の挿入文の訳

135
(A) impression
(B) comment
(C) mistake
(D) revision

(A) 印象
(B) コメント
(C) 失敗
(D) 修正

正解 C ❶1～2行目で、自動車購入者の大多数は販売店が提示する高金利のローンを組んだ結果、貸主と販売店の両方に対して金利を支払うことになる、と述べられている。空所に(C) mistakeを入れると、this mistakeが前の2つの文で説明されている「(高金利のローンを組んで)二重に金利を払うこと」を指し、そのような失敗はしないでください、と注意を促す流れになるので適切。
(A)(B)(D)いずれも文意に合わない。

136
(A) alternatively
(B) alternative
(C) alternatives
(D) alternating

(A) 代わりに
(B) 別の選択肢
(C) 別の選択肢
(D) 交互に起こること

正解 B 空所の前に動詞consider「～を検討する」と冠詞anがあるので、空所にはconsiderの目的語となる名詞の単数形が入る。(B) alternative「別の選択肢」が適切。自動車販売店が提示する高金利のローンを組む代わりに直接Athena銀行を通してローンを組むことを、別の選択肢として勧める文となる。
(A) 副詞。
(C) 名詞の複数形。直前は冠詞anなので、続けられない。
(D) 動詞alternate「交互に起こる」の動名詞、または形容詞で「交互の」。

137
(A) This was a great choice for a home loan.
(B) Feel free to take a test drive at any time.
(C) However, you will still need to purchase an auto insurance policy.
(D) We can do this because we specialize in low-interest auto loans.

(A) これは、住宅ローンのための素晴らしい選択でした。
(B) いつでもお気軽に試乗してください。
(C) しかしながら、お客さまは依然として自動車保険契約を結ぶ必要があるでしょう。
(D) 当行は低金利の自動車ローンを専門としているため、これができるのです。

正解 D 空所の直前の文に、「私たちは、当行のローンの最低金利でさえも保証する用意がある」とある。空所に(D)を入れると、thisが最低金利を保証することを指して、それができる理由を説明する文が続くこととなり、流れとして自然。specialize in ～「～を専門にする」。
(A) choice「選んだもの、選択」、home loan「住宅ローン」。
(B) feel free to do「気軽に～する、遠慮なく～する」、test drive「試乗」。
(C) purchase「～を購入する」、insurance policy「保険証券、保険証書」。

138
(A) proper
(B) happy
(C) successful
(D) pleasant

(A) 適切な
(B) 喜んで
(C) 成功した
(D) 好ましい

正解 B 選択肢は全て形容詞。このパンフレットは❶3～4行目で、直接Athena銀行でローンを組むことを読み手に勧めており、続けてその利点を強調している。空所を含む文の主語はOur representatives「当行の担当者」。be happy to doは「喜んで～する」を表すので、空所に(B) happyを入れると、空所を含む文が「当行の担当者は、あなたが抱くどんな疑問にも喜んで答える」という意味になり、文意が通る。
(D) It is pleasant to do「～するのが好ましい」という形式主語を用いた形で使うので、ここでは不適切。

Questions 139-142 refer to the following e-mail.

To: Leni Bischof <lbischof@curiousgardengoods.de>
From: Brian Adler <badler@curiousgardengoods.co.uk>
Subject: Information
Date: 31 March
Attachment: Adler_1

Dear Ms. Bischof:

① After our meeting in London last week, I did some research into the feasibility of using robots in the Hamburg warehouse. -------. Despite the initial expenditure we would have to make, I think
139.
we would end up saving money in the long run. -------, robots can be programmed to
140.
accomplish simple, automated tasks. Robots can also perform the same task over and over again. This allows employees to concentrate on jobs that require more ------- skills. I have
141.
attached a brief report on the costs and benefits of ------- robotic technology. Please let me
142.
know what you think.

Sincerely,

Brian Adler

問題139-142は次のEメールに関するものです。

受信者：Leni Bischof <lbischof@curiousgardengoods.de>
送信者：Brian Adler <badler@curiousgardengoods.co.uk>
件名：情報
日付：3月31日
添付ファイル：Adler_1

Bischof様

先週のロンドンでの私たちの打ち合わせの後、ハンブルクの倉庫でロボットを使用することの実現可能性について、私は少し調査をしました。*それは検討に値するアイデアであると私は思います。初期費用はかかるものの、長期的に見れば最終的には費用の節約になるだろうと考えます。1つには、ロボットは単純で自動化された作業をやり遂げるようにプログラムすることができます。また、ロボットは同じ作業を何度も繰り返し行うことができます。これは従業員がより分析的な技能を要する仕事に集中することを可能にします。ロボット技術を使用することの費用と効果に関する簡潔な報告書を添付しました。あなたのお考えをお知らせください。

敬具

Brian Adler

*問題139の挿入文の訳

139
(A) I think it is an idea worth considering.
(B) It is the oldest building on the campus.
(C) I saw a photo of robots in a magazine.
(D) Technology changes rapidly these days.

(A) それは検討に値するアイデアであると私は思います。
(B) それは構内で最も古い建物です。
(C) 私は雑誌でロボットの写真を見ました。
(D) 科学技術は近ごろ急速に変化しています。

正解 A 空所直前の文には、倉庫におけるロボットの使用の実現可能性について調査したとあり、空所直後の文では、Despite the initial expenditure we would have to make, I think we would end up saving money in the long run. 「初期費用はかかるものの、長期的に見れば最終的には費用の節約になるだろうと考える」という見込みが述べられている。空所に (A) を入れると、ロボットを使用するアイデアについて、「それは検討に値する」と調査に基づく肯定的見解を述べた後、長期的な費用の節約の見込みというロボット使用の利点を根拠として挙げる流れとなり、適切。worth *doing*「〜する価値がある」、consider「〜を検討する」。
(B) campus「(大学・会社などの)構内」。(D) rapidly「急速に」、these days「最近」。

140
(A) Otherwise
(B) Even so
(C) Nevertheless
(D) For one thing

(A) さもなければ
(B) たとえそうでも
(C) それにもかかわらず
(D) 1つには

正解 D 選択肢は全て接続詞的な働きをするもの。空所を含む文は、「------、ロボットは単純で自動化された作業をやり遂げるようにプログラムすることができる」という意味。直前の文で、長期的に見れば費用の節約になるという見込みが述べられ、空所を含む文とその後ろの文では、ロボット使用の具体的利点がそれぞれ挙げられている。従って、空所を含む文では利点の1つ目が説明されていると考えられる。理由を列挙する際に用いる (D) For one thing「1つには」が適切。
(A) 副詞。(C) 副詞。
(A) (B) (C) 前後の話の内容が論理的につながらない。

141
(A) analyze
(B) have analyzed
(C) analytical
(D) to analyze

＊選択肢の訳は省略

正解 C 空所の前は more、後ろは名詞 skills で、この3語が動詞 require の目的語になっている。ここでは more に続けられ、名詞を修飾できる形容詞の (C) analytical「分析的な」が適切。前文では、同じことの繰り返し作業はロボットに任せられることが述べられており、空所を含む文では、そうすることによって人間がより分析的な技能を要する仕事に集中できることが示されている。
(A) analyze「〜を分析する」の原形。(B) 現在完了形。(D) to 不定詞。

142
(A) used
(B) using
(C) to use
(D) being used

＊選択肢の訳は省略

正解 B 動詞 use「〜を使う」の適切な形を選ぶ。空所を含む文は、「ロボット技術を-------の費用と効果に関する簡潔な報告書を添付した」という意味。空所の前の前置詞 of に続くことができて、後ろに名詞句 robotic technology を置けるのは、これを目的語として取ることができる動名詞の (B) using。「ロボット技術を使うこと」という意味になり、文意も通る。
(A) 過去分詞。「使い古した」では文意に合わない。
(C) to 不定詞。
(D) use の受動態で目的語が後ろに残っているのは文法的に不適切。

Words & Phrases

attachment 添付ファイル ❶ research 調査 feasibility 実現可能性 robot ロボット warehouse 倉庫 despite 〜にもかかわらず initial 初期の expenditure 費用、経費 end up *doing* 最終的には〜することになる save 〜を節約する in the long run 長期的に見れば program 〜 to *do* 〜を…するようにプログラムする accomplish 〜をやり遂げる simple 単純な automated 自動化された task 作業 perform 〜を行う over and over again 何度も繰り返して employee 従業員 concentrate on 〜 〜に集中する require 〜を必要とする skill 技能 attach 〜を添付する brief 簡潔な、簡単な report 報告書 cost 費用 benefit 利益 robotic ロボットの technology 科学技術

Expressions

allow 〜 to *do* 「〜が…することを可能にする」(❶ 5行目)
The money allowed me to start a new online business.
そのお金で、私は新しいオンラインビジネスを始めることができました。

Questions 143-146 refer to the following letter.

Anabel Faren
183 Maple Road
Irvine, CA 92621

September 12

Arun Khatri
Product Development
Better Barley Company
2800 Clearview Drive
Los Angeles, CA 90040

Dear Mr. Khatri,

❶ Thank you for your interest in my food blog, *Cooking with Anabel 365*. I am a trained chef who has been creating original recipes for the home cook for the past eleven years. I currently have more than 50,000 followers who respond ------- to my posts. From their many comments, one **143.** fact stands out—they are eager to purchase the products I -------. **144.**

❷ -------. I can create recipes using your products and feature your products on my site. I use the **145.** services of a professional photographer ------- the products I use to their best advantage. **146.** Please let me know if you would like to talk further about the brands I work with or about using your products on my blog.

Very truly yours,

Anabel Faren

問題 143-146 は次の手紙に関するものです。

Anabel Faren
メープル通り 183 番地
アーバイン、CA 92621

9月12日

Arun Khatri 様
商品開発部
Better Barley 社
クリアビュー通り 2800 番地
ロサンゼルス、CA 90040

Khatri 様

私の料理ブログ『Anabel と一緒にクッキング 365 日』に関心を寄せていただき、ありがとうございます。私は熟練のシェフで、この 11 年間、家庭で料理を作る人向けに独自のレシピを創作し続けております。現在私には、投稿に頻繁に反応してくれるフォロワーが 5 万人以上います。彼らの多数のコメントからは、1 つの事実が浮き彫りになっています——彼らは、私が推薦する製品を非常に買いたがっているのです。

*私は御社と一緒にお仕事ができればうれしく思います。私は御社の製品を使用するレシピを創作し、私のサイトで御社の製品を大きく取り上げることができます。自分が使う製品の良さを最大限に引き立てて見せるために、私はプロのカメラマンのサービスを利用しています。私が一緒に仕事をしているブランドや私のブログで御社の製品を使用することについて、さらにお話しすることをご希望でしたら、どうぞお知らせください。

敬具

Anabel Faren

*問題 145 の挿入文の訳

143
(A) quietly
(B) frequently
(C) negatively
(D) aggressively

(A) 静かに
(B) 頻繁に
(C) 否定的に
(D) 攻撃的に

正解 B　選択肢は全て副詞。空所を含む文は、「現在私には、投稿に------反応してくれるフォロワーが5万人以上いる」という意味。空所直後の文より、それらの人々から多数のコメントが寄せられることが分かるので、文意に合うのは(B) frequently「頻繁に」。

144
(A) design
(B) restore
(C) recommend
(D) manufacture

(A) ～を企画する
(B) ～を修復する
(C) ～を推薦する
(D) ～を製造する

正解 C　選択肢は全て動詞の働きを持つ語。空所を含む文は、「彼らのコメントからは、1つの事実が浮き彫りになる——彼らは、私が------製品を非常に買いたがっている」という意味。この後ろの❷1行目でI can create recipes using your products and feature your products on my site.「私は、御社の製品を使用するレシピを創作し、私のサイトで御社の製品を大きく取り上げることができる」と、ブログ上で製品を販売促進するアイデアが述べられているので、空所に(C) recommend「～を推薦する」を入れると、Farenさんが製品を薦めると購買促進につながることを表し、文意が通る。
(A) (B) ❷で述べている、Farenさんのブログで製品を取り上げるという文意に合わない。
(D) 製品を製造するのはFarenさんではなく、手紙の受取人が勤務するBetter Barley社なので不適切。

145
(A) Original recipes are often preferred.
(B) I would be happy to work with you.
(C) Many have eaten in the best restaurants.
(D) I will soon rearrange my kitchen.

(A) 独自のレシピの方が、多くの場合好まれます。
(B) 私は御社と一緒にお仕事ができればうれしく思います。
(C) 多くの人は一流レストランで食事をしたことがあります。
(D) 私は間もなくキッチンの模様替えをします。

正解 B　❶1行目から、この手紙の受取人であるBetter Barley社のKhatriさんは、差出人のFarenさんのブログに興味を示していたことが分かる。また、空所直後で、「私は御社の製品を使用するレシピを創作し、私のサイトで御社の製品を大きく取り上げることができる」と自分の強みを述べているので、FarenさんもBetter Barley社と仕事をすることに前向きだと考えられる。よって、喜んで一緒に仕事をしたいという意思を伝えている(B)が適切。
(A) prefer「～の方を好む」。
(D) rearrange「～の模様替えをする」。

146
(A) to display
(B) it displays
(C) a display of
(D) has displayed

(A) ～を見せるために
(B) それは～を見せる
(C) ～の展示
(D) ～を見せた

正解 A　空所の直前にI use the services of a professional photographer「私はプロのカメラマンのサービスを利用している」とあり、この部分のみでも文が成立している。よって、to不定詞の(A) to displayを入れると、目的を表す副詞的用法となり、後ろの部分とつながる。「自分が使う製品の良さを最大限に引き立てて見せるために」と、プロのカメラマンのサービスを利用する目的を表す内容となり、適切。
(B) (D) 文が成立しない。
(C) この文の述語動詞のuseは目的語を2つ取らないので不適切。

Words & Phrases

product development　商品開発　❶ interest　関心　blog　ブログ　trained　熟練の、訓練を受けた
chef　シェフ、料理長　create　～を創作する　original　独自の　recipe　レシピ、料理法　cook　料理を作る人
past　過去の　currently　現在　follower　（SNSなどの）フォロワー、ファン　respond to ～　～に反応する　post　投稿
comment　コメント　fact　事実　stand out　際立つ　purchase　～を購入する
❷ feature　～を大々的に扱う、～を目玉にする　service　サービス　professional　プロの、専門家の
photographer　カメラマン、写真家　to one's advantage　～の長所を引き立たせて　brand　ブランド、銘柄

Expressions

be eager to do　「しきりに～したがる」（❶ 4行目）
Our hotel staff members are eager to serve the guests.
当ホテルのスタッフは、お客さまのために尽くすことに意欲的です。

Questions 147-148 refer to the following announcement.

① **The Chelham Chamber of Commerce**
Presents
Building a Professional Wardrobe
Speaker: Alice Ferry

② Ms. Ferry, owner of Ferry Goods, will focus her presentation on the type of attire and accessories appropriate for the business environment. Whether the dress code in your office is formal, casual, or something in between, Ms. Ferry's expertise can help you create a proper look. All are welcome, but the workshop will be especially helpful for community members seeking employment. Following the presentation, light refreshments will be served free of charge.

③ Thursday, April 6, 6:00–8:00 P.M.
Coventry Hotel
1770 Bloomington Street, Chelham

問題147-148は次のお知らせに関するものです。

チェルハム商工会議所
提供
『プロフェッショナルな服装を組み立てるには』
講演者：Alice Ferry

Ferry Goods社のオーナーであるFerryさんはご自身のプレゼンテーションで、ビジネスの環境にふさわしい種類の服装とアクセサリーに焦点を当てます。あなたの職場の服装規定がフォーマル、カジュアル、あるいはその中間的なもののいずれであれ、Ferryさんの専門知識は、あなたがきちんと見えるようにするのを手助けしてくれます。どなたでも歓迎いたしますが、この講習会は職を求めている地域の方々にとって特に有益でしょう。プレゼンテーションの後には、ささやかな軽食を無料でお出しします。

4月6日木曜日、午後6時～8時
Coventryホテル
ブルーミントン通り1770番地、チェルハム

147 What will Ms. Ferry speak about?

   (A) How to start a business
   (B) How to write a résumé
   (C) Where to look for jobs
   (D) What to wear to work

Ferryさんは何について話しますか。

   (A) 事業の始め方
   (B) 履歴書の書き方
   (C) 職を探す場所
   (D) 職場に着ていくべきもの

正解 D

❶ 3～4行目より、Ferryさんとは『プロフェッショナルな服装を組み立てるには』というテーマで話をする講演者だと分かる。❷ 1～2行目で、Ferryさんのプレゼンテーションの焦点は、ビジネスの環境にふさわしい服装とアクセサリーだと述べられ、続く同2～4行目では、「職場の服装規定がどのようなものであっても、Ferryさんの専門知識は、あなたがきちんと見えるようにするのを手助けしてくれる」と説明されている。よって、Ferryさんは職場に着ていくべき服装について話をすると分かる。
(A) business「事業、店」。
(B) résumé「履歴書」。
(C) ❷ 4～5行目で職を求めている人に言及はあるが、探す場所について述べてはいない。look for ～「～を探す」。

---

148 What is indicated about the event?

   (A) It is held every year.
   (B) It is open to the public.
   (C) A full dinner will be provided.
   (D) There is a fee for admission.

イベントについて何が示されていますか。

   (A) それは毎年開催される。
   (B) それは一般に公開されている。
   (C) フルコースの夕食が提供される。
   (D) 入場には料金がかかる。

正解 B

❷ 4～5行目に、All are welcome, but the workshop will be especially helpful for community members seeking employment.「どなたでも歓迎するが、この講習会は職を求めている地域の人々にとって特に有益だろう」とある。よって、Ferryさんが講演する講習会は、一般に公開されたイベントだと分かる。open「公開の」、the public「一般の人々」。
(A) 開催頻度に関する記載はない。hold「～を開催する」。
(C) ❷ 5～6行目より、提供されるのは軽食。full dinner「フルコースの夕食」、provide「～を提供する」。
(D) 入場料については述べられていない。fee「料金」、admission「入場」。

Expressions

whether A, B, or C　「A、B、Cのいずれであれ」（❷2～3行目）
Whether you visit the museum by car, bus, or taxi, you should arrive early in the morning.
博物館を車、バス、タクシーのいずれで訪れるのであれ、午前中早めに着くのが良いでしょう。

Questions 149-150 refer to the following online customer-service exchange.

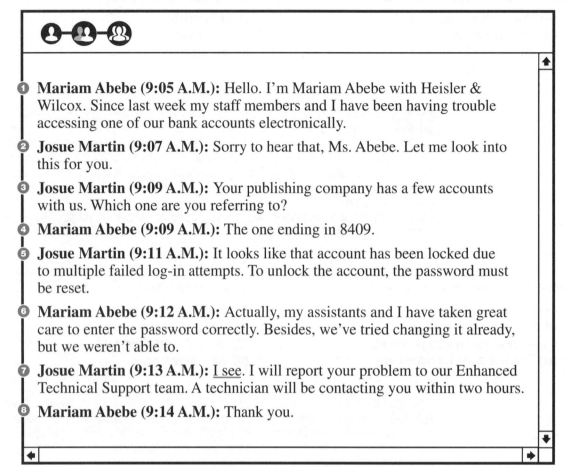

① Mariam Abebe (9:05 A.M.): Hello. I'm Mariam Abebe with Heisler & Wilcox. Since last week my staff members and I have been having trouble accessing one of our bank accounts electronically.

② Josue Martin (9:07 A.M.): Sorry to hear that, Ms. Abebe. Let me look into this for you.

③ Josue Martin (9:09 A.M.): Your publishing company has a few accounts with us. Which one are you referring to?

④ Mariam Abebe (9:09 A.M.): The one ending in 8409.

⑤ Josue Martin (9:11 A.M.): It looks like that account has been locked due to multiple failed log-in attempts. To unlock the account, the password must be reset.

⑥ Mariam Abebe (9:12 A.M.): Actually, my assistants and I have taken great care to enter the password correctly. Besides, we've tried changing it already, but we weren't able to.

⑦ Josue Martin (9:13 A.M.): <u>I see</u>. I will report your problem to our Enhanced Technical Support team. A technician will be contacting you within two hours.

⑧ Mariam Abebe (9:14 A.M.): Thank you.

問題149-150は次のオンライン顧客サービスのやりとりに関するものです。

Mariam Abebe (午前9時5分)：こんにちは。Heisler & Wilcox社のMariam Abebeです。先週からスタッフと私は、当社の銀行口座の1つにオンラインでアクセスできなくて困っています。

Josue Martin (午前9時7分)：それはお気の毒に思います、Abebe様。お客さまのために、この件を調べさせてください。

Josue Martin (午前9時9分)：お客さまの出版社は、当行に幾つかの口座をお持ちですね。どの口座のことをおっしゃっていますか。

Mariam Abebe (午前9時9分)：末尾が8409のものです。

Josue Martin (午前9時11分)：その口座は、ログインの試みに複数回失敗したためにロックされているようです。この口座のロックを解除するには、パスワードがリセットされる必要があります。

Mariam Abebe (午前9時12分)：実のところ、アシスタントたちと私はパスワードを正確に入力するよう、相当気を付けていました。それに、私たちはすでにそれを変更しようと試みたのですが、できなかったのです。

Josue Martin (午前9時13分)：分かりました。私が、当行の高度技術サポートチームにお客さまの問題を報告します。2時間以内に技術者がお客さまにご連絡いたします。

Mariam Abebe (午前9時14分)：ありがとうございます。

149 What most likely is true about Ms. Abebe?

    (A) She has been locked out of her office before.

    (B) She oversees staff at a publishing company.

    (C) She will be submitting a report in two hours.

    (D) She had contacted Mr. Martin last week.

Abebeさんについて正しいと考えられることは何ですか。

    (A) 彼女は以前、自分の執務室の中に入れなくなってしまったことがある。

    (B) 彼女は出版社でスタッフを監督している。

    (C) 彼女は2時間後に報告書を提出することになっている。

    (D) 彼女は先週、Martinさんに連絡していた。

正解 B Abebeさんは❶で、自分とスタッフは、自社の銀行口座の1つにオンラインでアクセスできなくて困っている、と問題を伝えている。❸より、Abebeさんの勤務先は出版社と分かる。また、Abebeさんは❻でmy assistants and I「私のアシスタントたちと私」と書いていることから、彼女は出版社で部下を持つ立場にあると考えられる。よって、(B)が正解。oversee「～を監督する」。

(A) lock ～ out of …「～を…から閉め出す」。

(C) submit「～を提出する」、report「報告書」。

150 At 9:13 A.M., what does Mr. Martin most likely mean when he writes, "I see"?

    (A) He knows that Ms. Abebe tried to access the account repeatedly.

    (B) He noticed that Ms. Abebe had changed her password.

    (C) He understands why Ms. Abebe rejects his suggestion.

    (D) He realizes why Ms. Abebe needs on-site assistance.

午前9時13分に、Martinさんは "I see" という発言で、何を意味していると考えられますか。

    (A) 彼は、Abebeさんが繰り返し口座にアクセスしようとしたことを知っている。

    (B) 彼は、Abebeさんがパスワードを変更していたことに気付いた。

    (C) 彼は、なぜAbebeさんが彼の提案を却下するのかを理解している。

    (D) 彼は、なぜAbebeさんが現場での手助けを必要とするのか分かっている。

正解 C ❶の、銀行口座にオンラインでアクセスできないというAbebeさんからの問い合わせに、Martinさんは❺で、口座のロックを解除するにはパスワードのリセットが必要だと伝えている。それに対しAbebeさんは❻で、パスワードを入力する際には注意を払ってきたと述べた後、「私たちはすでにそれを変更しようと試みたが、できなかった」と、Martinさんの提案を退けている。それに返答してMartinさんは下線部の発言をし、続けて問題を高度技術サポートチームに報告すると申し出ている。よって、Martinさんは、Abebeさんが自分の提案に同意しなかった理由を理解したため、下線部の発言をしたと考えられる。reject「～を却下する」、suggestion「提案」。

(A) repeatedly「繰り返し」。

(B) ❻でAbebeさん自身が、パスワード変更を試みたができなかったと述べている。notice「～に気付く」。

(D) realize「～がよく分かる、～を認識する」、on-site「現場での」、assistance「手助け」。

Words & Phrases

customer-service 顧客サービスの　　exchange やりとり　❶ with ～に勤めて　　access ～にアクセスする
bank account 銀行口座　　electronically 電子的に、オンラインで　❷ look into ～ ～を調べる
❸ publishing company 出版社　　refer to ～ ～に言及する　❹ end in ～ 末尾が～である、～で終わる
❺ It looks like ～ ～のようである　　lock ～をロックする　　due to ～ ～のために　　multiple 複数の　　failed 失敗した
attempt 試み　　unlock ～のロックを解除する　❻ actually 実のところ、実際に　　assistant アシスタント、助手
take care to *do* ～するように気を付ける　　enter ～を入力する　　correctly 正確に　　besides その上
be able to *do* ～することができる　❼ enhanced 高めた、強化した　　technical 技術的な　　technician 技術者

Expressions

have trouble *doing* 「～するのに苦労する」(❶)
Mr. Cole is having trouble rescheduling the luncheon with his client.
Coleさんは、顧客との昼食会の予定を変更するのに苦労しています。

Questions 151-152 refer to the following e-mail.

From:	Thiago Ayala
To:	All staff members
Subject:	Elevator inspections
Date:	November 15, 8:00 A.M.

❶ The annual state-mandated inspection of our elevators is scheduled to take place starting at 11:00 A.M. today. If all goes well, the inspection will be finished by 2:00 P.M. During this time, the fire doors will be closed as a normal part of the process. You are not likely to hear any alarms, but there is always a possibility one will go off. Each of the elevators will be out of service at some point during the inspections, but at least one elevator will be available at all times.

❷ Should you have any questions or concerns, I will be in my office until 10:45 this morning. Past that point, it would be best to text me on my cell phone at 555-0011.

Thiago Ayala, Facilities Supervisor
Brogolio, Inc.

問題151-152は次のEメールに関するものです。

送信者：Thiago Ayala
受信者：全スタッフ
件名：エレベーター点検
日付：11月15日、午前8時

州により義務付けられたエレベーターの年次点検が、本日午前11時から行われる予定です。全てが順調に進めば、点検は午後2時までに終了します。この時間中、通常の手順の一環として、防火扉は閉じられます。皆さんは警報音を聞くことはないと思われますが、それが鳴る可能性は常にあります。エレベーターの各基は点検中どこかの時点で運転休止になりますが、少なくとも1基のエレベーターは常に利用可能です。

もし質問や懸念がありましたら、私は本日午前10時45分まで自分の執務室におります。それ以降は、私の携帯電話の555-0011までテキストメッセージを送っていただくのが一番良いと思います。

Thiago Ayala、施設部責任者
Brogolio社

Words & Phrases

elevator エレベーター　inspection 点検　❶ annual 年に1度の　state-mandated 州によって義務付けられた
be scheduled to do ～する予定である　take place 行われる　fire door 防火扉　a part of ～ ～の一環
normal 通常の　process 手順、処置　be likely to do ～しそうである　alarm 警報音　possibility 可能性
go off （警報などが）鳴る　out of service 運転中止になって　point 時点　at least 少なくとも
available 利用可能な　❷ concern 懸念　past ～を過ぎて　text ～にテキストメッセージを送る
cell phone 携帯電話　facility 施設、設備　supervisor 管理者

151 What is indicated about the inspection?

(A) It takes place every two years.
(B) It involves checks over a two-day period.
(C) It includes testing the alarm system.
(D) It is required by a government agency.

点検について何が示されていますか。

(A) それは2年ごとに行われる。
(B) それは2日間にわたる検査を必要とする。
(C) それは警報設備のテストを含む。
(D) それは政府機関によって義務付けられている。

正解 D 宛先と件名より、このEメールは全スタッフ宛てにエレベーター点検について通知するもの。❶1～2行目に、The annual state-mandated inspection of our elevators is scheduled to take place starting at 11:00 A.M. today.「州により義務付けられたエレベーターの年次点検が、本日午前11時から行われる予定だ」とあることから、点検は州政府命令に従って行われると分かる。よって、(D)が正解。require「～を義務付ける」、government agency「政府機関」。
(A) ❶1行目より、エレベーターの点検は1年に1度。every ～「～ごとに」。
(B) ❶1～2行目より、エレベーターの点検は午前11時に始まり、同日午後2時までに終わる予定。involve「～を必要とする」、check「検査」、period「期間」。
(C) ❶3～4行目で、警報音が鳴る可能性があると述べられているだけで、警報設備のテストについての言及はない。include「～を含む」。

---

152 When are both elevators anticipated to be operational again?

(A) At 8:00 A.M.
(B) At 10:45 A.M.
(C) At 11:00 A.M.
(D) At 2:00 P.M.

両方のエレベーターが再び利用できる状態になるのは、いつだと予想されていますか。

(A) 午前8時
(B) 午前10時45分
(C) 午前11時
(D) 午後2時

正解 D ❶2行目で、If all goes well, the inspection will be finished by 2:00 P.M.「全てが順調に進めば、点検は午後2時までに終了する」と、エレベーター点検の終了予定時刻が述べられている。anticipate「～を予想する」、operational「使用できる（状態の）」。
(A) このメールの送信時刻。
(B) ❷1～2行目より、Eメールの送信者のAyalaさんが、それまで自分の執務室にいると述べている時刻。
(C) ❶1～2行目より、エレベーター点検の開始時刻。

Expressions

Should you do 「もしあなたが～するなら」（❷1行目）
★丁寧な言い回し。If you should do のIfが省略され、shouldが文頭に置かれた倒置の文。
Should you need any help, don't hesitate to contact me.
もし少しでも助けが必要でしたら、ご遠慮なく私に連絡してください。

Questions 153-154 refer to the following advertisement.

Pro Clean Dry Cleaners

❶ Count the ways we work to serve you!
1. Customer drop-off 24 hours a day through our drop box
2. Expert stain removal using the most up-to-date cleaning equipment and solutions
3. Tailoring services, including button and zipper replacement
4. Long-term on-site garment storage

❷ Monthly special: During the month of March, first-time customers get 30 percent off their dry-cleaning service, plus a free garment bag! Watch our mailings for future discounts.

問題153-154は次の広告に関するものです。

Pro Clean ドライクリーニング店

お客さまのお役に立つために当店が行うサービスを数えてみてください！
1. お客さまは当店の投入ボックスを通じて、24時間お預けが可能
2. 最先端の洗浄装置と洗浄液を使用した、プロの技による染み抜き
3. ボタンやファスナーの付け替えを含む、仕立てサービス
4. 店舗での衣服の長期保管

月例の特別提供：3月中は、初回のお客さまはドライクリーニング・サービスが30パーセント引きになり、さらに無料の衣装袋を1つもらえます！今後の割引については、当店からの郵便物をご覧ください。

153 What service does Pro Clean Dry Cleaners offer?

(A) Delivery of orders to customers' homes
(B) Removal of stains using current processes
(C) Free replacement of buttons and zippers
(D) Advice on proper long-term garment storage

Pro Clean ドライクリーニング店はどんなサービスを提供していますか。

(A) 顧客の自宅への注文品の配達
(B) 最新の方法を用いた染み抜き
(C) ボタンとファスナーの無料付け替え
(D) 衣服の適切な長期保管に関する助言

正解 B Pro Clean ドライクリーニング店が提供しているサービス内容は❶に列挙されている。その2項目目に、Expert stain removal using the most up-to-date cleaning equipment and solutions「最先端の洗浄装置と洗浄液を使用した、プロの技による染み抜き」とあるので、(B)が正解。current「最新の」、process「方法」。
(A) 配達に関する言及はない。delivery「配達」、order「注文品」。
(C) ❶3項目目にボタンとファスナーの付け替えに言及があるが、無料とは書かれていない。
(D) ❶4項目目に衣服の長期保管サービスについて述べられているが、助言に関する言及はない。

---

154 How can some customers receive a discount?

(A) By placing their first order in March
(B) By spending more than $30
(C) By responding to a customer survey
(D) By purchasing a garment bag

一部の顧客はどうすれば割引を受けられますか。

(A) 3月に初めて注文をすることによって
(B) 30ドルより多くお金を支払うことによって
(C) 顧客アンケート調査に回答することによって
(D) 衣装袋を購入することによって

正解 A ❷1～2行目に、During the month of March, first-time customers get 30 percent off their dry-cleaning service「3月中は、初回のお客さまはドライクリーニング・サービスが30パーセント引きになる」とある。よって、3月中に初めて同店のサービスを利用すると割引が受けられるので、(A)が正解。place an order「注文をする」。
(C) respond to ～「～に答える」、survey「アンケート調査」。
(D) ❷1～2行目より、衣装袋は新規顧客に対し店が無料で提供するもの。purchase「～を購入する」。

Expressions

24 hours a day 「24時間いつでも」(❶2行目)
  MMT Store is open 24 hours a day, seven days a week.
  MMT店は、24時間営業で年中無休です。

Questions 155-157 refer to the following article.

Burger City Bistro to Become BC Bistro

By Lola Jimenez

❶ Burger City Bistro has announced that it will soon be known as BC Bistro. All advertisements, packaging, signage, and social media accounts are being updated in line with the new name. — [1] —.

❷ "Over the years, our organization has expanded its menu to feature healthful items such as salads, sandwich wraps, and grilled chicken, in addition to burgers," company president Howard Shuman said. "We want our guests to think of us as a place where everyone can find tasty options." — [2] —.

❸ Burger City Bistro has traditionally appealed to young adults and teenagers. But women aged 25–49 currently make up only 23 percent of the company's annual sales. — [3] —. The company recently announced that it had hired celebrity Isobel Wu as a spokesperson to help appeal to that market segment. Ms. Wu, who performs on the television program *Star Dancers*, will appear in television and print advertisements featuring BC Bistro as part of a healthy lifestyle.

❹ "Ms. Wu will bring a new voice to our company that will reach potential customers who don't yet know that our menu has shifted away from what it was years ago," Mr. Shuman noted. — [4] —.

問題155-157は次の記事に関するものです。

Burger CityビストロがBCビストロに

Lola Jimenez記

Burger Cityビストロは、間もなく同社がBCビストロという名で知られるようになると発表した。広告、包装、看板、そしてソーシャルメディアのアカウントの全てが新しい名称に合わせて更新されているところだ。

「当組織は長年にわたり、ハンバーガーに加えて、サラダ、ラップサンドイッチ、グリルチキンのような健康に良いものを目玉としてメニューを拡大してきました」とHoward Shuman社長は述べた。「われわれは、お客さまがうちの店を誰もがおいしい選択肢を見つけられる場所だと思ってくださることを望んでいます」。

Burger Cityビストロは従来、若い成人や10代の若者に受けてきた。しかし、25歳～49歳の女性は現在、同社の年間売り上げの23パーセントしか占めていない。同社は最近、その市場区分にアピールする一助となるよう、著名人のIsobel Wuを広報役に採用したと発表した。Wuさんは、テレビ番組『スター・ダンサーズ』に出演中で、BCビストロを健康的なライフスタイルの一環として紹介するテレビ広告と印刷広告に登場することになる。

「当社のメニューが、何年も前のものから方向転換したことをまだ知らない潜在顧客に届く新たな発言力を、Wuさんは当社にもたらすでしょう」とShuman氏は述べた。＊Wuさんを起用する広告は、社名が切り替わるとすぐ始められるように用意ができている。

＊問題157の挿入文の訳

Words & Phrases

burger ハンバーガー　bistro ビストロ、小さなレストラン　❶ announce ～を発表する
be known as ～ ～の名で知られる　advertisement 広告　packaging 包装　signage 看板
social media ソーシャルメディア　account （コンピューターの）アカウント　in line with ～ ～と一致して
❷ organization 組織　expand ～を拡大する　feature ～を目玉とする、～を紹介する　healthful 健康に良い
item 品目　such as ～ ～のような　sandwich wrap ラップサンドイッチ　grilled chicken グリルチキン
in addition to ～ ～に加えて　company president 社長　think of ～ as … ～を…だと思う　tasty おいしい
option 選択肢　❸ traditionally 従来、伝統的に　appeal to ～ ～に受ける、～にアピールする　young adult 若い成人
teenager 10代の若者　aged ～ ～歳の　currently 現在　annual 年間の　sales 売上(高)　recently 最近
hire ～を採用する　celebrity 著名人　spokesperson 広報役　market segment 市場区分　perform 演じる
appear in ～ ～に出演する、～に掲載される　print 印刷物　healthy 健康的な　lifestyle ライフスタイル
❹ voice 発言力、ものを言いうる力　reach ～に届く、～に影響を与える　potential customer 潜在的顧客
yet 〈否定文で〉まだ　shift from ～ ～から方向を変える　away 別の方向へ　note ～と述べる

Expressions

make up ～「～を占める」(❸ 3～4行目)
Women make up about 70 percent of our Accounting Department.
当社の経理部の約70パーセントを女性が占めています。

155 According to the article, why is the company changing its name?

(A) To make the name easier to remember
(B) To better reflect the company's current image
(C) Because it has been sold to another company
(D) Because it is no longer selling burgers

記事によると、会社はなぜその名称を変更するのですか。

(A) 名称をより覚えやすくするため
(B) 会社の現在のイメージをより適切に表すため
(C) 同社は別会社に売却されたから
(D) 同社は、もはやハンバーガーを販売していないから

正解 B ❶より、Burger Cityビストロという会社が名称変更をすると分かる。❷1〜4行目に、「当組織は長年にわたり、ハンバーガーに加えて、健康に良いものを目玉としてメニューを拡大してきた」という同社社長の発言がある。さらに同5〜7行目に、We want our guests to think of us as a place where everyone can find tasty options.「われわれは、お客さまが当店を誰もがおいしい選択肢を見つけられる場所だと思ってくれることを望む」と同社社長の話が続いている。よって社名の変更は、ハンバーガーだけでなく健康的なメニューを取りそろえるようになった同社の現在のイメージを、より適切に表すためと分かる。reflect「〜を表す、〜を反映する」、current「現在の」、image「イメージ、印象」。
(D) no longer「もはや〜ない」。

156 According to the article, what does the company hope to accomplish by hiring Ms. Wu?

(A) More women will visit BC Bistro locations.
(B) More teenagers will become interested in BC Bistro.
(C) There will be a larger audience for *Star Dancers*.
(D) Free dance classes will be held at all locations.

記事によると、会社はWuさんを採用することによって何を成し遂げたいと思っていますか。

(A) より多くの女性がBCビストロの店舗を訪れる。
(B) より多くの10代の若者がBCビストロに興味を持つようになる。
(C) 『スター・ダンサーズ』の視聴者がより多くなる。
(D) 無料のダンス講座が全店舗で開催される。

正解 A ❸5〜8行目に、The company recently announced that it had hired celebrity Isobel Wu as a spokesperson to help appeal to that market segment.「同社は最近、その市場区分にアピールする一助となるよう、著名人のIsobel Wuを広報役に採用したと発表した」とある。ここでのthat market segment「その市場区分」とは、直前の文にある、同社の年間売り上げの23パーセントしか占めていない「25歳〜49歳の女性」を指している。つまり、会社はWuさんを起用することによって、現在の主要顧客層ではない年代の女性にアピールし、より多くの女性顧客を取り込む狙いがあると分かる。よって(A)が正解。accomplish「〜を成し遂げる」。location「店舗」。
(C) audience「視聴者、観客」。

157 In which of the positions marked [1], [2], [3], and [4] does the following sentence best belong?

"Advertisements featuring Ms. Wu are set to begin when the name changes."

(A) [1]
(B) [2]
(C) [3]
(D) [4]

正解 D 挿入文は、Wuさんを起用した広告について述べているもの。Wuさんについて初めて言及しているのは❸6行目なので、挿入文はこれ以降に入ると考えられる。❹1〜4行目で、Wuさんを起用する広告について、「当社のメニューが、何年も前のものから方向転換したことをまだ知らない潜在顧客に届く新たな発言力を、Wuさんは当社にもたらすだろう」とその期待が述べられている。この直後の(D) [4]に、Wuさんを起用した広告が始まるタイミングを知らせる挿入文を入れると、Wuさん起用の広告に関する一連の流れとなり適切。be set to *do*「〜する用意ができている」。

[1]、[2]、[3]、[4]と記載された箇所のうち、次の文が入るのに最もふさわしいのはどれですか。

「Wuさんを起用する広告は、社名が切り替わるとすぐ始められるように用意ができている」

Questions 158-160 refer to the following invoice.

All Sounds Music

Equipment, repairs, and rentals
Established 1954

All Sounds Music
4 Oak Street
Foustown, Pennsylvania 17404

❶

Store Hours
10:00 A.M. – 6:00 P.M., seven days a week

Date: *March 14*

Phone: *717-555-0102*

Salesperson: *Winston Sajek*

Customer: *Karen Ahn*

❷

QUANTITY	DESCRIPTION	PRICE
2	GR-48 Speakers	$160.00
	Subtotal	$160.00
	Sales tax	$9.60
	Total refund	–$169.60
	In-store credit	$169.60

❸ **Return policy:**

No returns on discounted sale items.
All other items may be returned as long as they are in the same condition as purchased
and an original receipt is submitted.
Customers returning items up to 14 days after purchase will receive a full refund.
Customers returning items between 15 and 30 days after purchase are eligible for in-store
credit only. Store credit is good for 90 days from the date it was issued.
Repaired items not picked up within 60 days become the property of All Sounds Music.

問題158-160は次の請求明細書に関するものです。

All Sounds Music社
機材・修理・レンタル
1954年設立

All Sounds Music社
オーク通り4番地
ファウスタウン、ペンシルベニア 17404

店舗営業時間
午前10時〜午後6時、年中無休

日付：3月14日
電話：717-555-0102

販売担当者：Winston Sajek
お客さま： Karen Ahn様

数量	品目	価格
2	GR-48スピーカー	160.00ドル
	小計	160.00ドル
	売上税	9.60ドル
	払戻額合計	−169.60ドル
	店内クレジット	169.60ドル

返品方針：

割引されたセール品の返品はできません。
その他全ての品物は、購入時と同じ状態で、かつ領収書の原本が提出される限りにおいて、返品可能です。
購入後14日までに返品したお客さまは、全額払い戻しを受けられます。
購入後15日から30日の間に返品したお客さまは、店内クレジットによる払い戻しのみの対象となります。店のクレジットは、発行された日付から90日間有効です。
60日以内に引き取りがない修理品は、All Sounds Music社の所有物となります。

158 What is indicated about All Sounds Music?

(A) Its store in Foustown is new.
(B) Its owner is Mr. Sajek.
(C) It has multiple locations.
(D) It is open every day.

All Sounds Music社について何が示されていますか。

(A) ファウスタウンにある同社の店舗はできたばかりだ。
(B) 同社のオーナーはSajekさんである。
(C) 同社は複数の店舗を持つ。
(D) 同社は毎日営業している。

> **正解 D** All Sounds Music社の請求明細書の❶のStore Hours「店舗営業時間」の欄に、seven days a week「年中無休」と書かれているので、All Sounds Music社は毎日営業していると分かる。(D)が正解。
> (B) ❶右欄の「販売担当者」の行にSajekさんの名前があるが、オーナーだという記載はない。
> (C) multiple「複数の」、location「店舗、所在地」。

159 What is suggested about the GR-48 speakers?

(A) They were purchased at a discount.
(B) They were returned in damaged condition.
(C) They were returned with a purchase receipt.
(D) They were rented from All Sounds Music.

このGR-48スピーカーについて何が分かりますか。

(A) それらは割引価格で購入された。
(B) それらは破損した状態で返品された。
(C) それらは購入時の領収書と共に返品された。
(D) それらはAll Sounds Music社から貸し出された。

> **正解 C** ❷のDESCRIPTION「品目」の欄に「GR-48スピーカー」とあり、同表最下行のIn-store credit「店内クレジット」の欄に「169.60ドル」とあるので、GR-48スピーカーの購入時の代金は店内クレジットによる払い戻しとなったことが分かる。返品方針を示した❸ 3～4行目に、All other items may be returned as long as they are in the same condition as purchased and an original receipt is submitted.「その他全ての品物は、購入時と同じ状態で、かつ領収書の原本が提出される限りにおいて、返品可能だ」とある。よって、店内クレジットによる払い戻しとなった、このGR-48スピーカーは、購入時の領収書と共に返品されたと考えられる。(C)が正解。
> (A) (B) ❸2行目より、割引商品は返品を受け付けておらず、また同3～4行目より、破損品の返品は受け付けていない。❷より、この請求書のGR-48スピーカーは払い戻しが認められているので、割引品でも破損品でもないと分かる。(A) at a discount「割引価格で」。(B) damaged「破損した」。

160 For how long is Ms. Ahn's store credit valid?

(A) 14 days
(B) 30 days
(C) 60 days
(D) 90 days

Ahnさんの店内クレジットはどのくらいの期間有効ですか。

(A) 14日間
(B) 30日間
(C) 60日間
(D) 90日間

> **正解 D** ❶右欄のCustomer「お客さま」の行より、AhnさんとはAll Sounds Music社から商品のGR-48スピーカーを購入した客。❷の最下行のIn-store credit「店内クレジット」の価格欄に「169.60ドル」とあり、店内クレジットが提供されている。❸7行目に、Store credit is good for 90 days from the date it was issued.「店のクレジットは、発行された日付から90日間有効だ」と記載があるので、(D)が正解。valid「有効な」。
> (A) ❸5行目より、14日間は全額払い戻しを受けられる返品期限。
> (B) ❸6～7行目より、30日間は店内クレジットのみによる払い戻しを受けられる返品期限。
> (C) ❸8行目より、60日間は引き取りのない修理品がAll Sounds Music社の所有物となる期限。

Words & Phrases

invoice 請求明細書、送り状　equipment 機材　repair 修理　rental レンタル　establish ～を設立する
❶ hours 営業時間　seven days a week 年中無休　salesperson 販売員　customer 顧客　❷ quantity 数量
description 品目　speaker スピーカー　subtotal 小計　sales tax 売上税　total 合計の
refund 払い戻し、返金(額)　in-store credit 店内クレジット　★その店舗のみで今後の商品購入などに利用できる金額に相当
❸ return 返品　policy 方針　discounted 割引された　sale item セール品　as long as ～ ～する限り
condition 状態　purchase 〈動詞で〉～を購入する、〈名詞で〉購入　original 元の　receipt 領収書、レシート
submit ～を提出する　up to ～ 最大で～まで　full 完全な　be eligible for ～ ～の資格がある
good for ～ ～の間有効な　issue ～を発行する　pick up ～ ～を受け取る　property 所有物

Questions 161-163 refer to the following memo.

MEMO

① To: All Lawson's Repair Technicians
From: Joel Gaos
Subject: New Process
Date: 3 April

② Beginning on 5 April, our cost estimates for repairs will be processed electronically and sent to customers via e-mail. Whenever you visit customers to assess damage to their items, be sure to have your mobile phone or a tablet with you so that you can take pictures of the damage. You will fill out the estimate form on our Web site, attach the photos, and e-mail the estimate to the customer. Estimates should be filled out within 24 hours of your visit to a customer's home or business. We will likely have a few customers who will want handwritten estimates. If this is the case, you will still need to fill out the electronic form for our records and upload a copy of the handwritten estimate.

③ As always, carefully check warranties to find out which repairs are <u>covered</u> and which repairs the customer is responsible for. The computer desks now have only a three-month warranty, and the sofas, chairs, and dining sets have a much more limited warranty than before.

問題 161-163 は次のメモに関するものです。

メモ

宛先：Lawson's 社の修理技術者各位
差出人：Joel Gaos
件名：新しい手順
日付：4月3日

4月5日より、当社の修理費用見積書は電子媒体で処理され、Eメールで顧客に送信されるようになります。顧客を訪問して商品の損傷を査定する際は常に、損傷の写真を撮ることができるよう携帯電話またはタブレット端末を必ず持参してください。あなた方は、当社のウェブサイトで見積もりフォームに入力し、その写真を添付の上、見積書を顧客にEメールで送ることになります。見積書は、顧客の自宅または事業所を訪問した後24時間以内に入力する必要があります。おそらく、手書きの見積書を希望する顧客が多少いるでしょう。この場合にも、あなた方は社内記録用に、やはり電子フォームに入力し、手書きの見積の写しをアップロードする必要があります。

従来通り、どの修理が保証対象に入り、どの修理が顧客の責任となるかを見分けるために、保証書を入念に確認してください。コンピューター用デスクは現在わずか3カ月間の保証しかなく、ソファ、椅子、ダイニングセットは以前よりもはるかに限られた保証になっています。

Words & Phrases

❶ repair 修理　technician 技術者　process 〈名詞で〉手順、〈動詞で〉～を処理する　**❷** estimate 見積書、見積もり　electronically 電子的に、コンピューターを使って　via ～によって　assess ～を査定する　damage 損傷　be sure to do 必ず～する　mobile phone 携帯電話　tablet タブレット端末　fill out ～ ～に記入する　attach ～を添付する　business 事業所、会社　likely おそらく　a few 多少の　handwritten 手書きの　electronic 電子的な　record 記録　upload ～をアップロードする　**❸** as always 例のごとく、いつものように　warranty 保証、保証書　cover ～を保証対象とする　be responsible for ～ ～に責任がある　limited 限られた

Expressions

If this is the case, ～　「この場合には、～」（**❷** 8～9行目）
You might want to try some other options. If this is the case, please give us a call.
お客さまは、他の選択肢を試したいとお思いになるかもしれません。このような場合には、ぜひ当社にお電話ください。

161 What is indicated about Lawson's customers?

(A) They must provide photographs of damaged items.

(B) They must send an e-mail request for repair service.

(C) They may request that technicians write out an estimate.

(D) They may record complaints about the warranties electronically.

Lawson's社の顧客について何が示されていますか。

(A) 彼らは、損傷品の写真を提供しなければならない。

(B) 彼らは、修理サービスを依頼するEメールを送信しなければならない。

(C) 彼らは、技術者が見積書を手書きすることを求めるかもしれない。

(D) 彼らは、保証に関する苦情をコンピューター上の記録に残すかもしれない。

正解 C ❶の宛先の「Lawson's社の修理技術者各位」より、同社は修理業務を行うと分かる。❷ 1〜2行目に、修理費用見積書を電子媒体で処理することになったとあり、同5〜6行目で、自社のウェブサイト上での見積書の作成手順が説明されている。その一方、同7〜8行目ではWe will likely have a few customers who will want handwritten estimates.「おそらく、手書きの見積書を希望する顧客が多少いるだろう」とあり、続く同8〜10行目に、この場合の対応の説明がある。よって、Lawson's社では、見積書の電子媒体処理移行後も、顧客の一部が見積書を手書きするよう求める可能性があると考えていることが分かる。write out〜「〜を手書きする」。
(A) ❷4行目より、写真を撮影するのは顧客ではなく、Lawson's社の技術者。provide「〜を提供する」。
(B) ❷5〜6行目より、Eメールを送るのは顧客ではなく、見積書を送るLawson's社の技術者。
(D) complaint「苦情」。

---

162 The word "covered" in paragraph 2, line 1, is closest in meaning to

(A) replaced

(B) included

(C) retrieved

(D) concealed

第2段落・1行目にある "covered" に最も意味が近いのは

(A) 交換されて

(B) 含まれて

(C) 回収されて

(D) 隠されて

正解 B ❷より、Lawson's社の技術者は修理のために顧客訪問を行うと分かる。該当する語を含む❸1〜2行目の文は、顧客訪問時に従来通り保証書を入念に確認するよう技術者に促しており、その目的を修理が保証対象かどうか見分けるため、と2つのwhichを用いて説明している。2つ目のwhich repairs the customer is responsible forは「どの修理が顧客の責任となるか」を表している。よって、該当する語を含む1つ目のwhich repairs are coveredは「どの修理が商品の保証対象に入るか」を意味すると考えられるので、include「〜を含む」の過去分詞である(B) includedが適切。
(A) replace「〜を交換する」の過去分詞。(C) retrieve「〜を回収する」の過去分詞。
(D) conceal「〜を隠す」の過去分詞。

---

163 What do Lawson's technicians repair?

(A) Cameras

(B) Mobile phones

(C) Homes

(D) Furniture

Lawson's社の技術者は何を修理しますか。

(A) カメラ

(B) 携帯電話

(C) 住宅

(D) 家具

正解 D ❸1〜2行目で、Lawson's社の技術者に対し、修理時の保証書の確認指示が出されている。続いて同2〜4行目で、The computer desks now have only a three-month warranty, and the sofas, chairs, and dining sets have a much more limited warranty than before.「コンピューター用デスクは現在わずか3カ月間の保証しかなく、ソファ、椅子、ダイニングセットは以前よりもはるかに限られた保証になっている」と家具類の保証期間について注意が述べられているので、Lawson's社の技術者が修理するのは、これら家具類と判断できる。

Questions 164-167 refer to the following text-message chain.

---

① Linda Farr (8:48 A.M.) Megumi and Ricardo, I suggest going to Sofia's Place for our weekly meeting instead of gathering here in our usual conference room. The three of us could easily report on progress made on the Humbert project over lunch. Thoughts?

② Megumi Sugiyama (8:50 A.M.) I could use a break from the office.

③ Ricardo Thompson (8:51 A.M.) Alright by me. But what about staying close by and going to Crab Bay Café?

④ Linda Farr (8:52 A.M.) It's closer, but there's usually a wait because seating is limited. I don't want to go over an hour. Plus, I love the salads at Sofia's.

⑤ Ricardo Thompson (8:53 A.M.) True. They're great.

⑥ Megumi Sugiyama (8:55 A.M.) Sofia's it is then! But could we change the time? I find our usual meeting time a bit early for lunch.

⑦ Linda Farr (8:56 A.M.) Yes, 11:00 is a bit early for lunch, isn't it? OK, what time works best? 11:30? 12:00?

⑧ Ricardo Thompson (8:57 A.M.) Hmmm. How about 12:30?

⑨ Megumi Sugiyama (8:58 A.M.) Perfect!

⑩ Linda Farr (8:59 A.M.) Sounds good. See you then!

問題 164-167 は次のテキストメッセージのやりとりに関するものです。

Linda Farr（午前8時48分）　Megumi、そして Ricardo、毎週の定例ミーティングで、ここのいつもの会議室に集まるのではなく Sofia's Place に行くのはどうかしら。私たち3人で、昼食を取りながら Humbert プロジェクトの進捗について気楽に伝えられるし。どう思う？

Megumi Sugiyama（午前8時50分）　私はオフィスから離れて一息つけるとありがたいわ。

Ricardo Thompson（午前8時51分）　僕は構わないよ。でも、近場にとどまって、Crab Bay カフェに行くのはどうかな？

Linda Farr（午前8時52分）　そこはもっと近いけれど、席数が限られているから、たいてい待ち時間があるのよ。私は1時間以上かけたくないわ。それに、私は Sofia's のサラダが大好きなの。

Ricardo Thompson（午前8時53分）　確かに。あれはすごくおいしいよね。

Megumi Sugiyama（午前8時55分）　では、Sofia's に決まりね! ただ、時間を変更できるかしら？ いつものミーティングの時間は昼食には少し早いと思うの。

Linda Farr（午前8時56分）　そうね、11時は昼食には少し早いわね。それなら、何時が一番都合がいいかしら？ 11時30分？ 12時？

Ricardo Thompson（午前8時57分）　うーん。12時30分はどう？

Megumi Sugiyama（午前8時58分）　完璧!

Linda Farr（午前8時59分）　いいわね。そのときに会いましょう!

Words & Phrases

① suggest *doing* 　～することを提案する　　place 店　　weekly 毎週の
instead of *doing* 　～するのではなく、～する代わりに　　gather 集まる　　conference room 会議室　　easily 気軽に
progress 進捗、進展　　over ～をしながら　　thought 考え　② could use ～ 　～を得られたらありがたい、～が欲しい
break 休憩　③ close by すぐそばに　④ wait 待ち時間　　seating 座席数、座席　　limited 限られた
go over ～ 　～を超える　　plus 加えて、それに　⑥ a bit 少し　⑦ work 都合が良い、うまくいく

164 What is indicated about the upcoming meeting?

(A) Staff will give updates on a project.
(B) Staff will be joined by several clients.
(C) Staff will celebrate a recent success.
(D) Staff will make some important decisions.

今度のミーティングについて何が示されていますか。

(A) スタッフがプロジェクトの最新情報を報告する。
(B) スタッフと一緒に数名の顧客が参加する。
(C) スタッフが最近の成功を祝う。
(D) スタッフが幾つか重要な決断を下す。

正解 A Farrさんは❶で、今度のミーティングを行う場所について提案を行い、The three of us could easily report on progress made on the Humbert project over lunch.「私たち3人で、昼食を取りながらHumbertプロジェクト の進捗について気楽に伝えられる」と述べているので、(A)が正解。upcoming「今度の」。update「最新情報」。
(C) celebrate「〜を祝う」、recent「最近の」。
(D) make a decision「決断を下す」。

165 At 8:50 A.M., what does Ms. Sugiyama mean when she writes, "I could use a break from the office"?

(A) She approves of meeting elsewhere.
(B) She wants to ask for time off from work.
(C) She is looking forward to her vacation.
(D) She is happy to run an errand for Ms. Farr.

午前8時50分に、Sugiyamaさんは "I could use a break from the office" という発言で、何を意味していますか。

(A) 彼女は他の場所で会合することに賛成している。
(B) 彼女は仕事を休むことを願い出たいと思っている。
(C) 彼女は自分の休暇を楽しみにしている。
(D) 彼女は喜んでFarrさんのために用事をする。

正解 A Farrさんは❶で、今度のミーティングをいつも利用している社内の会議室ではなくSofia's Placeという飲食店で行うことを提案し、他の2人にどう思うかと意見を求めている。それに対し、Sugiyamaさんは下線部で「私はオフィスから離れて一息つけるとありがたい」と答えているので、他の場所でミーティングを行うことに賛成していると考えられる。よ って、(A)が正解。approve of 〜「〜に賛成する」、meet「会合する」、elsewhere「他の場所で」。
(B) ask for 〜「〜を求める」、time off from 〜「〜を休むこと」。
(D) be happy to do「喜んで〜する」、run an errand for 〜「〜の使い走りをする」。

166 What concern does Ms. Farr express about Crab Bay Café?

(A) It is too expensive.
(B) It is somewhat noisy.
(C) It does not offer Internet service.
(D) It cannot accommodate many people.

Farrさんは、Crab Bayカフェについてどんな懸念を述べていますか。

(A) 同店は値段が高過ぎる。
(B) 同店は少し騒々しい。
(C) 同店はインターネットサービスを提供していない。
(D) 同店は大勢の人を収容できない。

正解 D Crab Bayカフェについて、Farrさんは❹で、It's closer, but there's usually a wait because seating is limited.「そこはもっと近いが、席数が限られているから、たいてい待ち時間がある」と述べているので、(D)が正解。concern「懸念」、express「〜を述べる、〜を表す」。accommodate 「〜を収容する」。
(A) expensive「値段が高い」。
(B) somewhat「少し、幾分」、noisy「騒々しい」。

167 What time does the group normally meet?

(A) At 11:00 A.M.
(B) At 11:30 A.M.
(C) At 12:00 noon
(D) At 12:30 P.M.

このグループは通常、何時に会合しますか。

(A) 午前11時
(B) 午前11時30分
(C) 正午12時
(D) 午後12時30分

正解 A ❻でSugiyamaさんが、I find our usual meeting time a bit early for lunch.「いつものミーティングの時間は昼食には少し早いと思う」と述べたのに対し、❼でFarr さんが、Yes, 11:00 is a bit early for lunch「そうね、11時は昼食には少し早い」と同意しているので、通常このグループは毎週午前11時に会合していると分かる。normally「通常は」。

Questions 168-171 refer to the following information.

Crofton Power

❶ Crofton Power is consistently given high ratings for its commitment to customers. Service representatives are available at all times to promptly address power concerns. Customer satisfaction is backed with several key guarantees. — [1] —. Our assurances to customers are outlined below.

❷ **Billing:** Customer inquiries should be directed to the billing department at 604-555-0101 or made online through the Crofton Power customer portal. — [2] —. If your question requires further investigation, please allow up to three business days for a response. Should the response be delayed by more than three days, the customer's account will be credited $25.

❸ **Appointments:** Crofton Power aims to keep all appointments with customers. Crofton service technicians are scheduled to arrive within a two-hour time frame. On any occasion that this time frame is not honored, the customer's account will be credited $40.

❹ **Planned Outages:** If Crofton Power needs to turn off power temporarily for construction or maintenance work, customers who may be affected will be notified at least 48 hours in advance. — [3] —. In the rare case that a service interruption notice has not been provided and a power outage occurs, the customer's account will be credited $80.

❺ The aim of Crofton Power is to provide service that is fair and transparent. — [4] —. Thank you for trusting Crofton Power with your energy needs.

Words & Phrases

power 電力　❶ consistently 一貫して　rating 評価　commitment 献身、責任　representative 担当者
available 応対可能な　at all times いつでも　promptly 迅速に　address ～に対処する　concern 用事、事柄
customer satisfaction 顧客満足(度)　be backed with ～ ～で裏打ちされる　key 要の、主要な　guarantee 保証
assurance 保証、請け合い　outline ～の概略を述べる　below 以下に　❷ billing 請求書の作成・送付
inquiry 問い合わせ　department 部門　portal ポータルサイト　require ～を必要とする　further さらなる
investigation 調査　allow ～ for … …に～の余裕を見ておく　up to ～ 最大で～　business day 営業日
response 回答　delay ～を遅らせる　account 顧客アカウント　credit ～ … ～(人)の貸方に…(金額)を記入する
❸ aim to do ～することを目指す　keep an appointment 約束の時間を守る　service technician 点検修理技術者
be scheduled to do ～する予定である　within ～以内に　time frame 時間枠　occasion 場合、機会
honor ～(約束など)を順守する　❹ planned 計画的な　outage 停電　turn off ～ ～を止める
temporarily 一時的に　construction 建設工事　maintenance 保守、維持管理　affect ～に影響を与える
notify ～に通知する　at least 少なくとも　in advance 前もって　rare まれな、珍しい
service interruption 供給中断　notice 通知　provide ～を提供する　occur 発生する　❺ aim 目標
fair 公正な　transparent 透明性のある　trust ～ with … ～に…を信頼して任せる　energy エネルギー
needs 需要、ニーズ

問題168-171は次の案内に関するものです。

Crofton 電力社

Crofton 電力社は、お客さまへの献身に対して一貫して高い評価を頂いております。サービス担当者は、電力に関するご用件に迅速に対処すべく常時応対可能です。お客様満足度は、幾つかの要となる保証によって裏打ちされています。お客さまへのお約束については、以下に概要を記しております。

請求書の作成・送付：お客さまからのお問い合わせは、請求書担当部門宛てに 604-555-0101 までお寄せいただくか、Crofton 電力社お客さま用ポータルサイトを通じてオンラインで行ってください。*お客さまは通常、オンラインでのご依頼を送信後、2 時間以内に回答を受け取ります。お客さまのご質問にさらなる調査が必要な場合は、回答に最長 3 営業日の余裕を見てください。万一、回答が 3 日よりも遅れた場合は、お客さまのアカウントに当社に対して 25 ドルの貸しがあることが記録されます。

予約：Crofton 電力社はお客さまとのお約束の時間を全て守ることを目指しています。Crofton 社の点検修理技術者は 2 時間の時間枠内に到着するように予定しています。この時間枠が順守されなかった際にはどのような場合も、お客さまのアカウントに当社に対して 40 ドルの貸しがあることが記録されます。

計画停電：建設工事や保守作業のために Crofton 電力社が一時的に電力供給を停止する必要がある場合、影響を受ける可能性のあるお客さまは、遅くとも 48 時間前には通知されます。供給中断の通知が提供されないまま、停電が発生するというめったにないケースでは、お客さまのアカウントに当社に対して 80 ドルの貸しがあることが記録されます。

Crofton 電力社が目指すのは、公正で透明性のあるサービスを提供することです。お客さまのエネルギー需要を Crofton 電力社にお任せくださいまして、ありがとうございます。

*問題171の挿入文の訳

---

168 What is suggested in the information?

 (A) Equipment has been recently upgraded.

 (B) Delayed bill payments may result in a late fee.

 (C) Quality service is a priority.

 (D) A service area has expanded.

案内では何が分かりますか。

 (A) 設備の性能が最近高められた。

 (B) 料金支払いが遅れると、延滞料が発生することがある。

 (C) 質の高いサービスが優先事項である。

 (D) サービス提供エリアが拡大した。

正解 C Crofton電力社の案内の❶1行目で、同社は顧客への献身的なサービスに対し一貫して高評価を受けていると述べられており、続く同1〜2行目にService representatives are available at all times to promptly address power concerns.「サービス担当者は、電力に関する用件に迅速に対処すべく常時応対可能だ」とある。さらに、❷〜❹ではサービスに関する顧客への約束の概要が記載され、❺1行目で「Crofton電力社が目指すのは、公正で透明性のあるサービスを提供することだ」と述べられている。これらのことから、同社は顧客サービスに力を入れていると判断できるので、(C)が正解。quality「質の高い」、priority「優先事項」。

(A) equipment「設備、機材」、upgrade「〜の性能を高める」。

(B) result in 〜「〜という結果になる」、late fee「延滞料」。

(D) expand「拡大する」。

---

169 In what case will a customer receive a $40 credit from Crofton Power?

 (A) When a power outage lasts more than three days

 (B) When an inquiry is not addressed quickly

 (C) When equipment requires emergency maintenance

 (D) When a service technician's arrival is delayed

どんな場合に、顧客はCrofton電力社から40ドルの貸しを得ますか。

 (A) 停電が3日よりも長く続く場合

 (B) 問い合わせが早急に対処されない場合

 (C) 設備が緊急保守を要する場合

 (D) 点検修理技術者の到着が遅れた場合

正解 D ❸1〜2行目に、Crofton service technicians are scheduled to arrive within a two-hour time frame.「Crofton社の点検修理技術者は2時間の時間枠内に到着するように予定している」とあり、続く同2〜3行目でOn any occasion that this time frame is not honored, the customer's account will be credited $40.「この時間枠が順守されなかった際にはどのような場合も、お客さまのアカウントに当社に対して40ドルの貸しがあることが記録される」と述べられている。よって、(D)が正解。credit「貸し勘定」。arrival「到着」。

(A) (C) ❹に、保守作業などによる計画停電の際、事前通知なしに停電が発生した場合に顧客が得る額は80ドルとある。(A) last「続く」。(C) emergency「緊急(の)」。

(B) ❷3〜4行目に、問い合わせへの回答が3日よりも遅れた場合に顧客が得る額は25ドルとある。

170 What will Crofton Power do when a power outage is planned?

(A) Renew a service contract
(B) Update a billing cycle
(C) Give advance notice
(D) Hire additional technicians

停電が計画された場合、Crofton電力社は何をすることになっていますか。

(A) 供給契約を更新する
(B) 請求書作成周期を改定する
(C) 事前の通知をする
(D) 追加の技術者を雇う

正解 **C** Planned Outages「計画停電」について記載されている❹1〜3行目で、建設工事や保守作業のためにCrofton電力社が一時的に電力供給を停止する必要がある場合、影響を受ける可能性のある顧客には、遅くとも48時間前には通知することが述べられているので、(C)が正解。advance「事前の」。
(A) renew「〜を更新する、〜を延長する」。
(B) update「〜を改定する、〜を更新する」、cycle「周期」。
(D) ❸で技術者に言及があるが、顧客訪問時の約束に関するもので、技術者を追加雇用するとは述べられていない。additional「追加の」。

171 In which of the positions marked [1], [2], [3], and [4] does the following sentence best belong?

"Customers typically receive a response within two hours after an online request is made."

(A) [1]
(B) [2]
(C) [3]
(D) [4]

[1]、[2]、[3]、[4]と記載された箇所のうち、次の文が入るのに最もふさわしいのはどれですか。

「お客さまは通常、オンラインでのご依頼を送信後、2時間以内に回答を受け取ります」

正解 **B** 挿入文は顧客に対し、オンラインで問い合わせた場合について案内するもの。❷1〜2行目で、「お客さまからの問い合わせは、請求書担当部門宛てに604-555-0101まで寄せていただくか、Crofton電力社お客さま用ポータルサイトを通じてオンラインで行ってください」と、顧客が問い合わせる際の方法を案内している。この後ろの(B) [2]に挿入文を入れると、顧客がオンラインで問い合わせを行った後に回答を受け取るまでの所要時間を示すことになり、流れとして適切。typically「通例、一般的には」。

Questions 172-175 refer to the following customer reviews.

Home	Products	**Reviews**	Contact Us

① Adrianna Rossi ★ ★ ★ ★ ★

Mr. Prescott runs a top-notch online business. I have never worked with a designer this talented before. I was able to give a very specific description of what I wanted and my expectations were exceeded. I could have never imagined my wedding invitations turning out so beautiful! A friend needs new brochures for her business, and I will definitely refer her to this shop. Thanks!

② Prisha Deol ★ ★ ☆ ☆ ☆

I am not pleased with my recent order. I had bought birthday party invitations previously from this store and was satisfied. This time, I ordered customized programs for my piano recital. I loved the proof that I was sent, but these do not look like the proof at all. The printing looks grainy and cheap. Also, the programs have a white mark at the top on the front and the back. It just does not look very professional.

③ Isak Larsson ★ ★ ★ ★ ★

The owner was fast to respond to my questions before I had even purchased anything. My business cards were designed in days and arrived quickly, even with international shipping to Sweden. They were exactly how I wanted them, even though I gave the designer only a few details and asked whether they could be completed in a hurry. This was a great experience.

問題172-175は次の顧客レビューに関するものです。

ホーム	製品	レビュー	お問い合わせ

Adrianna Rossi ★★★★★

Prescottさんは最高のオンラインの事業を運営しています。私は、これほど才能のあるデザイナーの方にお仕事していただいたことは、これまで一度もありません。私は希望していたことを非常に具体的に説明させてもらうことができました、そして、私の期待を上回るものになりました。私は自分の結婚式の招待状がこんなに美しいものになるとは全く想像していませんでした! 友人が自分の事業のために新しいパンフレットを必要としているので、私は断然、彼女にこの店を紹介します。ありがとうございました!

Prisha Deol ★★☆☆

私は最近の注文品には満足していません。私は以前この店で誕生日パーティーの招待状を購入したことがあり、満足でした。今回、自分のピアノリサイタル用に特注プログラムを注文しました。私は送られてきた校正刷りをとても気に入ったのですが、今回のものは、校正刷りと同じようには全く見えません。印刷は粗くて安っぽく見えます。また、プログラムの表と裏の上部に白い染みがあります。プロの仕上がりにはとても見えません。

Isak Larsson ★★★★★

まだ何かを購入する前でさえ、私の質問への店主の返答は迅速でした。私の名刺は数日でデザインされ、スウェーデンへの国際配送にもかかわらず早々に到着しました。私はデザイナーの方にほんのわずかな詳細しかお伝えせず、急いで仕上げられるかどうか尋ねたのですが、それらはまさに私が希望した通りの出来でした。これは素晴らしい経験でした。

Words & Phrases

customer review 顧客レビュー　❶ run ～を運営する　top-notch 最高の、一流の　talented 才能のある
specific 詳細な　description 説明　expectation 期待されるもの　exceed ～を上回る　invitation 招待、招待状
turn out ～ ～の結果になる　brochure パンフレット　definitely 断然　refer ～ to … ～を…に紹介する
❷ be pleased with ～ ～に満足している　recent 最近の　previously 以前に　satisfied 満足して
customized 特別注文による　recital リサイタル、独奏会　proof 校正刷り　printing 印刷
grainy 粒子の粗い、粒状の　cheap 安っぽい　mark 染み　professional プロの　❸ owner 所有者
respond to ～ ～に返答する　even ～さえ　purchase ～を購入する　business card 名刺　arrive 届く
international 国際的な　shipping 配送　exactly まさに　details 詳細　complete ～を完成させる
in a hurry 急いで　experience 経験

Expressions

even though ～ 「～けれども、～にもかかわらず」(❸ 4～5行目)
　The farmers' market was held on Sunday as scheduled, even though it rained.
　雨が降りましたが、農産物市は予定通り日曜日に開催されました。

172 What type of service does the business most likely provide?

(A) Home decorating
(B) Event planning
(C) Custom printing
(D) Fashion accessorizing

この店はどんな種類のサービスを提供していると考えられますか。

(A) 住居の装飾
(B) イベントの企画
(C) 特注の印刷
(D) ファッション小物使い

正解 C ❶で、Rossiさんがこの店で結婚式の招待状を作成したこと、そして個人事業用のパンフレットを必要とする友人に同店を紹介することが述べられている。❷では、Deolさんが過去に同店で誕生日パーティーの招待状を購入したこと、今回は自分のピアノリサイタル用の特注プログラムを注文

したことが述べられており、❸では、Larssonさんが名刺を注文したことが分かる。よって、この店が提供しているサービスは特注の印刷と考えられる。
(D) accessorize「〜にアクセサリーを付ける」。

---

173 What does Ms. Rossi indicate about her items?

(A) They were made according to her instructions.
(B) They were shipped to another country.
(C) They were constructed with inexpensive materials.
(D) They were not the correct color.

Rossiさんは自分の品物について何を示していますか。

(A) それらは彼女の指示に従って作られた。
(B) それらは別の国へ配送された。
(C) それらは安価な材料で組み立てられた。
(D) それらは正しい色ではなかった。

正解 A ❶3〜4行目で、Rossiさんは注文した結婚式の招待状について、I was able to give a very specific description of what I wanted and my expectations were exceeded.「私は希望していたことを非常に具体的に説明させてもらうことができた、そして、私の期待を上回るものになった」と述べているので(A)が正解。according to 〜「〜に従って」、

instructions「指示」。
(B) ❸より、外国への配送について言及しているのはRossiさんではなくLarssonさん。
(C) (D) 材料や色についての言及はない。(C) construct「〜を組み立てる」、inexpensive「安価な」。

---

174 What made a customer unhappy?

(A) A product option
(B) Business hours
(C) A party venue
(D) Recital programs

何が、ある顧客に不満を抱かせましたか。

(A) 製品の選択肢
(B) 営業時間
(C) パーティー会場
(D) リサイタルのプログラム

正解 D レビューの星の数で低評価をつけているのは❷のDeolさん。Deolさんは同2行目で、I am not pleased with my recent order.「私は最近の注文品には満足していない」と述べ、同3〜6行目で、ピアノリサイタルの特注プログラムを注文したものの、印刷が粗くて安っぽく見え、また白い

染みがあり、プロの仕上がりには見えない、とプログラムの出来に対する不満を書いている。よって、(D)が正解。unhappy「不満な」。
(C) venue「開催地」。

---

175 What does Mr. Larsson discuss in his review?

(A) The instructions for placing an order
(B) The variety of product choices
(C) The efficiency of the business
(D) The weight of the merchandise

Larssonさんはレビューで何について述べていますか。

(A) 注文するための説明
(B) 製品の選択肢の多様性
(C) その店の手際の良さ
(D) 商品の重量

正解 C Larssonさんは❸で、名刺を注文した際の店の対応について評価を述べている。同2行目で、商品の購入前でも店主が迅速に質問に回答してくれたこと、続く同2〜4行目で、国際配送という状況でも商品到着が早かったこと、同4〜5行目で、詳細のわずかな説明と至急の納品であっても、希望通りの出来だったことを述べている。よって、Larssonさんはレ

ビューで、店の手際が良かったことを説明していると言えるので、(C)が正解。discuss「〜について論じる」。efficiency「(仕事上の)手際の良さ、効率の良さ」。
(A) instructions「説明」、place an order「注文する」。
(B) variety「多様性」。
(D) weight「重量」、merchandise「商品」。

Questions 176-180 refer to the following tracking information and e-mail.

National Package Service (NPS) Package Tracking
Shipment number: DM5671

Location	Date	Local time	Action
Baltimore, MD	May 2	7:15 A.M.	Origin scan
Baltimore, MD	May 2	8:22 A.M.	Departure scan
Hartford, CT	May 3	4:48 P.M.	Arrival scan
Hartford, CT	May 4	6:30 A.M.	Departure scan
Lowell, MA	May 4	3:43 P.M.	Arrival scan
Lowell, MA	May 5	9:47 A.M.	Departure scan
Windham, NH	May 5	1:26 P.M.	Arrival scan
Windham, NH	May 5	5:17 P.M.	Loaded for delivery
Windham, NH	May 6	7:34 A.M.	Delivered

Shipped by: Deymantis, Inc.　　**Weight:** 23.5 kilograms
Shipment category: Package　　**Service:** Ground shipment
Billed on: May 1　　**Message on package:**
Shipment of part number 264

To:	Mervin Hartley
From:	Caroline Launey
Date:	May 11
Subject:	Re: Deymantis package

Dear Mr. Hartley,

We received the package ahead of schedule and were able to install the Deymantis blade (part 264) on the day it arrived and test it the next day. We closed the mill to test the blade on various lengths and types of damaged lumber. The tests with the new cutting blade were successful, and so Monday was our first day at full operational status. I will send you an initial report on our revised processing times by the end of this week.

Sincerely,

Caroline Launey
Milford Lumber Mill

問題176-180は次の追跡情報とEメールに関するものです。

全国小包配送便（NPS）小包追跡

配送番号：DM5671

場所	日付	現地時間	実施（事項）
ボルティモア、MD	5月2日	午前7時15分	発送元読み取り
ボルティモア、MD	5月2日	午前8時22分	出発読み取り
ハートフォード、CT	5月3日	午後4時48分	到着読み取り
ハートフォード、CT	5月4日	午後6時30分	出発読み取り
ローウェル、MA	5月4日	午後3時43分	到着読み取り
ローウェル、MA	5月5日	午前9時47分	出発読み取り
ウィンダム、NH	5月5日	午後1時26分	到着読み取り
ウィンダム、NH	5月5日	午後5時17分	配達のため積載完了
ウィンダム、NH	5月6日	午前7時34分	配達完了

発送者：Deymantis社　　　　　　　重量：23.5キログラム

配送区分：小包　　　　　　　　　　運送：陸送

請求日：5月1日　　　　　　　　　　小包の伝達事項：番号264の部品の配送

受信者：Mervin Hartley

送信者：Caroline Launey

日付：5月11日

件名：Re：Deymantis社の小包

Hartley様

私たちは予定よりも早く小包を受け取り、到着したその日にDeymantis社製の刃（部品264）を取り付け、翌日にはそれをテストすることができました。私たちは製材所を休業して、さまざまな長さや種類の傷んだ木材でその刃をテストしました。この新しい切断用の刃を使ったテストは成功し、従って月曜日は当製材所のフル稼働初日となりました。今週末までに、あなたに修正された処理時間に関する初回報告書をお送りします。

敬具

Caroline Launey

Milford製材所

176 According to the tracking information, where was the package on the evening of May 4?

(A) In Baltimore
(B) In Hartford
(C) In Lowell
(D) In Windham

追跡情報によると、小包は5月4日の晩にはどこにありましたか。

(A) ボルティモア
(B) ハートフォード
(C) ローウェル
(D) ウィンダム

正解 C **1**の小包の追跡情報を見ると、**❶**6行目に「ローウェル、MA 5月4日 午後3時43分 到着読み取り」とあり、同7行目に「ローウェル、MA 5月5日 午前9時47分 出発読み取り」とあるので、小包は5月4日午後にローウェルに到着して、翌日の5日午前にローウェルを出発したと分かる。よって、5月4日の晩に小包はローウェルにあったと判断できるので、(C)が正解。

177 According to the tracking information, how was the package most likely transported?

(A) By NPS airplane
(B) By NPS truck
(C) By Deymantis airplane
(D) By Deymantis truck

追跡情報によると、小包はどのように輸送されたと考えられますか。

(A) NPSの飛行機で
(B) NPSのトラックで
(C) Deymantis社の飛行機で
(D) Deymantis社のトラックで

正解 B **1**の見出しより、この配送はNational Package Service（NPS）と呼ばれる小包配送サービスを利用していると分かる。同**❷**右欄の2行目に、Service: Ground shipment「運送：陸送」と記載があるので、NPSのトラックで陸上輸送されたと考えられる。transport「～を輸送する」。
(C) (D) **2**の**❶**1行目より、Deymantis社は刃を取り扱うメーカーと分かる。また、**1**の**❷**「発送者：Deymantis社」から、小包の送り主が同社だと判断できる。

178 Why did Ms. Launey write the e-mail?

(A) To provide an update
(B) To explain a delay
(C) To order a new part
(D) To request a report

LauneyさんはなぜEメールを書いたのですか。

(A) 最新情報を提供するため
(B) 遅延について説明するため
(C) 新しい部品を注文するため
(D) 報告を求めるため

正解 A Launeyさんは**2**のEメールの**❶**1～2行目で「私たちは予定よりも早く小包を受け取り、到着したその日にDeymantis社製の刃（部品264）を取り付け、翌日にはそれをテストすることができた」と知らせている。さらに同3～4行目で、The tests with the new cutting blade were successful, and so Monday was our first day at full operational status.「この新しい切断用の刃を使ったテストは成功し、従って月曜日は当製材所のフル稼働初日となった」と、届いた部品を試した結果と製材所の稼働状況を報告している。よって、Launeyさんは最新の状況を伝えるためにHartleyさん宛てにEメールを書いたと分かる。provide「～を提供する」、update「最新情報」。
(B) explain「～を説明する」、delay「遅延」。
(D) **2**の**❶**4～5行目で、Launeyさんは報告書を送ると述べており、求めてはいない。request「～を求める」。

179 When was part number 264 tested?

(A) On May 2
(B) On May 6
(C) On May 7
(D) On May 11

番号264の部品はいつテストされましたか。

(A) 5月2日
(B) 5月6日
(C) 5月7日
(D) 5月11日

正解 C	❷の❶ 1～2行目に、We ...... were able to install the Deymantis blade (part 264) on the day it arrived and test it the next day.「私たちは到着したその日にDeymantis社製の刃（部品264）を取り付け、翌日にはそれをテストすることができた」とある。❶の❶右端欄の「実施（事項）」の10行目のDelivered「配達完了」より、番号264の部品の小包配達が完了したのは5月6日なので、テストが行われたのはその翌日の5月7日と分かる。

180 According to the e-mail, what will part number 264 most likely be used for?

(A) Breaking concrete
(B) Polishing metal
(C) Shaping glass
(D) Cutting wood

Eメールによると、番号264の部品は何のために使用されると考えられますか。

(A) コンクリートを破砕するため
(B) 金属を研磨するため
(C) ガラスを成形するため
(D) 木材を切断するため

正解 D	❷の最後にある送信者の所属先にMilford Lumber Mill「Milford製材所」とある。また、同❶ 1～2行目に、the Deymantis blade (part 264)「Deymantis社製の刃（部品264）」とあることから、番号264の部品とは刃であると分かる。続けて、同2～3行目でその刃について、We closed the mill to test the blade on various lengths and types of damaged lumber.「私たちは製材所を休業して、さまざまな長さや種類の傷んだ木材でその刃をテストした」と述べ、さらに同3～4行目でThe tests with the new cutting blade were successful「この新しい切断用の刃を使ったテストは成功した」と伝えている。よって、番号264の部品は木材を切るために使用されると考えられる。 (A) concrete「コンクリート」。 (B) polish「～を磨く」、metal「金属」。 (C) shape「～を成形する」。

Words & Phrases

❶ 追跡情報 tracking information　追跡情報
package　小包、荷物　　shipment　配送　　❶ location　場所　　local　現地の、地元の　　origin　出所、起源
scan　読み取り、スキャン　　departure　出発　　arrival　到着　　load　～を積む　　delivery　配達
❷ ship　～を発送する　　category　区分、種類　　bill　～に請求する　　weight　重量　　ground　地上（の）
message　伝達事項　　part　部品

❷ Eメール ❶ be able to do　～することができる　　install　～を取り付ける　　blade　刃
test　〈動詞で〉～をテストする、〈名詞で〉テスト　　mill　製造所、工場　　various　さまざまな　　length　長さ
type　種類　　damaged　損傷した　　lumber　木材　　cutting blade　切断用の刃　　successful　成功した
at full operational status　フル稼働状況で　　initial　最初の　　revise　～を修正する、～を更新する
processing time　処理時間

Expressions

ahead of ～　「～より前に」（❷の❶ 1行目）
The bus to downtown arrived five minutes ahead of time.
市街地行きのバスは定刻より5分早く到着しました。

Questions 181-185 refer to the following e-mail and certificate.

1 E メール

From:	Month of Giving Committee
To:	All Vernment Employees
Date:	April 26
Subject:	Only a few days left

① As our company's Month of Giving comes to a close, I would like to <u>draw</u> your attention to one more charity to consider. We have been profiling some of the lesser-known, but well-respected, organizations that are important to our colleagues. If you have not already made your voluntary contribution, take a moment to learn about this worthy cause. Remember that as your employer, Vernment, Inc., will match up to $100 of your contributions to eligible charities during this month.

② Arborlee International works with communities in North America, South America, and Asia to establish young trees in areas that need to be reforested. Experts assist their partners in choosing the most appropriate native trees to plant. Local citizens are hired and taught the skills required to plant the trees and to care for them. Arborlee wants the trees to grow strong and provide shade, oxygen, and soil stabilization for previously barren areas. Every dollar donated goes toward the planting of trees; a gift of $1,000, for example, funds the planting of 1,000 trees. Go to www.arborlee.org to learn more.

2 証明書

ARBORLEE INTERNATIONAL

CERTIFICATE OF APPRECIATION

FOR

Vernment, Inc.

① Many thanks for the generous gift of $7,260 generated by your company and for spreading the word about Arborlee International and its mission. In recognition of your contribution, your company's name will be displayed on a plaque at the entrance gate of the Rio Alto Forest Reserve in Bolivia, a project completed with the help of your funds.

Jennifer Price

Jennifer Price, President, Arborlee International

問題181-185は次のEメールと証明書に関するものです。

送信者：寄付月間委員会
受信者：Vernment社全従業員
日付：4月26日
件名：残りわずか数日

当社の寄付月間が終わりに近づいてきましたので、検討すべきもう一つの慈善団体に皆さんの注目を集めたいと思います。当委員会ではこれまで、あまり知られていないながらも非常に高く評価され、同僚の皆さんにとって注目すべき団体を幾つか紹介してきました。あなたがまだ自発的な寄付をしていないのであれば、少し時間を取ってこの価値ある理念について知ってください。皆さんの雇用主としてVernment社は今月中、対象となる慈善団体へのあなたの寄付額のうち最大100ドルまで同額を拠出するということを覚えておいてください。

Arborlee Internationalは、森林再生が必要な地域で若木を根付かせるために、北米、南米、そしてアジアの地域社会と共に力を尽くしています。最も植栽に適したその土地固有の木を選ぶにあたって、専門家がその共同事業者たちに手を貸しています。地元住民が雇用され、木を植えてそれらを手入れするのに必要な技術を教わっています。Arborleeは木が丈夫に成長し、それらが以前は不毛だった地帯に木陰、酸素、土壌の安定化をもたらすことを望んでいます。寄付金は全て、植林に使われます。例えば1,000ドルの寄贈なら、1,000本の植林の資金となります。さらに知るにはwww.arborlee.orgにアクセスしてください。

ARBORLEE INTERNATIONAL
感謝状
Vernment社

貴社が集められた7,260ドルという多額のご献金、そしてArborlee Internationalとその使命に関する情報を広めてくださったことに対し、深く感謝いたします。貴社の貢献をたたえまして、貴社の資金協力によって完成したプロジェクトである、ボリビアのRio Alto保護林の入り口の門にある記念プレートに貴社名を掲示いたします。

Jennifer Price（署名）
Jennifer Price、Arborlee International代表

181 What is the purpose of the e-mail?

(A) To announce a business acquisition
(B) To inform employees of a charitable giving option
(C) To recognize an employee's community service
(D) To encourage organizations to conserve resources

Eメールの目的は何ですか。

(A) 事業の買収を発表すること
(B) 従業員に慈善事業への寄付の一つの選択肢を知らせること
(C) 従業員の地域社会への奉仕活動を評価すること
(D) 団体に資源を保護するよう奨励すること

正解 B　**1**のEメールは、Vernment社の寄付月間委員会が全従業員宛てに送信したもの。同**❶** 1～2行目で、I would like to draw your attention to one more charity to consider.「検討すべきもう一つの慈善団体に皆さんの注目を集めたいと思う」と述べ、同**❷**では、森林再生活動に尽力しているArborlee Internationalという団体について詳しく紹介している。よって、寄付先の選択肢として同団体をVernment社の従業員に知らせることがEメールの目的だと考えられるので、(B)が正解。inform ～ of … 「～に…を知らせる」、charitable giving「慈善事業への寄付」、option「選択肢」。
(A) announce「～を発表する」、acquisition「買収、取得」。
(C) recognize「～を評価する、～を認める」、community service「地域社会への奉仕活動」。
(D) encourage ～ to *do*「～に…するよう奨励する」、conserve「～を保護する」、resource「資源」。

182 In the e-mail, the word "draw" in paragraph 1, line 1, is closest in meaning to

(A) provide
(B) picture
(C) create
(D) attract

Eメールの第1段落・1行目にある "draw" に最も意味が近いのは

(A) ～を提供する
(B) ～を描写する
(C) ～を作り出す
(D) ～を引き付ける

正解 D　該当の語を含む文に続いて、We have been profiling some of the lesser-known, but well-respected, organizations「私たちはこれまで、あまり知られていないながらも非常に高く評価されている団体を幾つか紹介してきた」とあり、寄付月間委員会が慈善団体を紹介してきたことが分かる。よって、該当する語を含む文は、「検討すべきもう一つの慈善団体に皆さんの注目-------たいと思う」と、新たな慈善団体に従業員の関心を引きたい旨を述べた文だと判断できる。(D)が適切。

183 According to the e-mail, who will plant trees?

(A) People living in deforested areas
(B) Representatives from government agencies
(C) The Month of Giving committee
(D) Volunteers from Vernment, Inc.

Eメールによると、誰が木を植えますか。

(A) 森林伐採地域に暮らす人々
(B) 政府機関の代表者
(C) 寄付月間委員会
(D) Vernment社のボランティア

正解 A　**1**の**❷** 1～2行目に、Arborlee Internationalという団体が森林再生が必要な場所で若木を根付かせるために世界各地の地域社会と共に尽力していることに言及があり、同3～4行目に、Local citizens are hired and taught the skills required to plant the trees and to care for them.「地元住民が雇用され、木を植えてそれらを手入れするのに必要な技術を教わっている」とある。よって、木を植えるのは、森林再生が必要な地域に暮らす地元住民と分かるので、(A)が正解。deforest「～の森林を伐採する」。
(B) representative「代表者」、government「政府」、agency「機関」。

184 What is the purpose of planting the trees?

 (A) To provide inexpensive building materials
 (B) To increase incomes in an area
 (C) To improve the environment
 (D) To beautify a city

木を植える目的は何ですか。

 (A) 安価な建築資材を提供すること
 (B) 地域の収入を増やすこと
 (C) 環境を改善すること
 (D) 都市を美化すること

> **正解 C**　**1**の**2** 1～2 行目に、Arborlee Internationalは森林再生が必要な場所で植林のために各地の地域社会と連携しているとあり、同 4～6 行目には Arborlee wants the trees to grow strong and provide shade, oxygen, and soil stabilization for previously barren areas.「Arborlee は木が丈夫に成長し、それらが以前は不毛だった地帯に木陰、酸素、土壌の安定化をもたらすことを望んでいる」とある。よって、植林の目的は森林伐採地域の環境を改善することと分かる。
> (A) inexpensive「安価な」、material「材料」。(B) income「収入」。(D) beautify「～を美化する」。

185 For what was the contribution from Vernment, Inc., most likely used?

 (A) Planting thousands of new trees
 (B) Making improvements to the landscaping on a corporate campus
 (C) Saving native trees from being harvested
 (D) Printing materials that outline the mission of Arborlee International

Vernment社からの寄付金は、何のために使われたと考えられますか。

 (A) 何千本もの新しい木を植えること
 (B) 会社の敷地内の景観を改善すること
 (C) 自生樹木が伐採されるのを防ぐこと
 (D) Arborlee internationalの使命を概説する資料を印刷すること

> **正解 A**　**1**の**2** 6 行目より、Arborlee Internationalへの寄付金は全て植林に使われると分かり、同 6～7 行目に「例えば 1,000 ドルの寄贈なら、1,000 本の植林の資金となる」とある。同団体からVernment社へ贈られた**2**の感謝状を見ると、**1** 1 行目より同社の寄付額は 7,260 ドルと分かる。さらに同 4～5 行目には、the Rio Alto Forest Reserve in Bolivia, a project completed with the help of your funds「貴社の資金協力によって完成したプロジェクトである、ボリビアのRio Alto 保護林」とあることから、Vernment社からの寄付金は保護林に 7,260 本の木を植えることに充てられたと考えられる。
> (B) improvement「改良」、landscaping「景観設計」、corporate「会社の」、campus「敷地」。
> (C) save ～ from *doing*「～が…しないで済むようにする」、harvest「～を伐採する、～を収穫する」。
> (D) outline「～を概説する」。

Words & Phrases

 certificate　証明書

1 E メール　committee　委員会　**1** come to a close　終わりに近づく　attention　注目　charity　慈善団体
consider　～を検討する　profile　～を紹介する　lesser-known　あまり知られていない
well-respected　非常に評価の高い　organization　団体　colleague　同僚　voluntary　自発的な
contribution　寄付、寄付金、貢献　take a moment to *do*　少し時間を取って～する　worthy　価値のある
cause　大義　match　～に匹敵する資金を供給する　up to ～　最大～まで　eligible　適格な、選ばれる資格のある
2 community　地域社会　establish　～を新しい土地に定着させる　reforest　～に森林を再生させる
assist ～ in *doing*　～が…するのを援助する　partner　共同事業者　appropriate　ふさわしい
native　その土地固有の　plant　～を植える　citizen　住民　hire　～を雇用する　skill　技術
require　～を必要とする　care for ～　～を手入れする、～を世話する　provide ～ for …　…に～を与える
shade　日陰　oxygen　酸素　soil　土壌　stabilization　安定化　previously　以前は　barren　不毛な
donate　～を寄付する　go toward ～　～に使われる　fund　〈動詞で〉～に資金を提供する、〈名詞で〉資金

2 証明書　appreciation　感謝　**1** generous　たくさんの、寛大な　generate　～を生み出す
spread the word about ～　～に関する情報を広める　mission　使命　in recognition of ～　～をたたえて
display　～を掲示する、～を表示する　plaque　記念銘板、装飾用プレート　forest reserve　保護林

Expressions

Many thanks for ～　「～に大変感謝しています」（**2**の**1** 1～2行目）
 Many thanks for your help in arranging the meeting.
 会議の手配を手伝っていただいたことに大変感謝しています。

Questions 186-190 refer to the following advertisement, invoice, and e-mail.

1 広告

GREEN LYRE OFFICE FURNITURE DECEMBER SALE

❶ We are making room for new models and products. Save 40 percent off all in-stock Green Lyre brand furniture, and save 30 percent off all other furniture brands in stock. All sales are final.

❷ Delivery service is available and free to locations within Somerfield city limits. Pick-up and disposal of old furniture is also offered.

❸ Start shopping now! Go to www.greenlyreofficefurniture.com or visit our showroom at 174 E. Landover Street.

2 請求書

Green Lyre Office Furniture Invoice

❶ **Purchased by:**
Jasmine Kai, Office Manager
Hainey Medical Clinic

Phone: (210) 555-0108

Order number: G90123

❷

Description	Item Number	Color	Quantity	Total Price
Reception Chair	MT-5047	Gray	2	$376.00
Lounge Chair	MT-2956	Gray	2	$1,100.00
Accent Chair	MT-0632	Black	1	$330.00
Leather Sofa	MT-4278	Gray	1	$1,325.00

Subtotal:	$3,131.00
Discount (40%):	- $1,252.40
Delivery:	+ $100.00
Total Charges:	**$1,978.60**

3 Eメール

To:	Jasmine Kai <jkai@haineymed.com>
From:	Colin Byrne <cbyrne@greenlyreofficefurniture.com>
Date:	December 10
Subject:	Your recent voicemail

Dear Ms. Kai:

❶ I received your voicemail regarding your order number G90123, but your office was closed when I tried to return your call. You mentioned that you realized the sofa you ordered is unlikely to fit in the intended space in your clinic's waiting area. Then you asked whether you could receive a refund. Unfortunately, your purchase is not refundable, but I would like to accommodate you by offering an exchange. I can provide you with a Green Lyre Leather Love Seat in place of the sofa. And if you accept the love seat, I would also let you have an additional Green Lyre Reception Chair, all for the same total price as on the original invoice. Let me know if this will work.

❷ Thank you for shopping at Green Lyre Office Furniture.

Sincerely yours,

Colin Byrne, Sales Manager

問題186-190は次の広告、請求書、Eメールに関するものです。

Green Lyre オフィス家具店
12月のセール

当店は現在、新モデルや新製品のためのスペースを準備中です。Green Lyre ブランドの家具の全在庫品が40パーセント引き、その他の家具ブランドの全在庫品は30パーセント引きでお買得です。特売は全て最終です。

配送サービスがご利用可能で、サマーフィールド市内の場所であれば無料です。古い家具の集荷と処分も行っております。

今すぐ買い物を始めましょう！ www.greenlyreofficefurniture.com にアクセスしていただくか、もしくは東ランドオーバー通り174番地の当店ショールームへお越しください。

Green Lyre オフィス家具店請求書

購入者：
Jasmine Kai、事務長
Hainey 診療所

電話：(210)555-0108

注文番号：G90123

品目	商品番号	色	数量	合計価格
レセプションチェア	MT-5047	グレー	2	376.00ドル
ラウンジチェア	MT-2956	グレー	2	1,100.00ドル
アクセントチェア	MT-0632	黒	1	330.00ドル
レザーソファ	MT-4278	グレー	1	1,325.00ドル

小計： 3,131.00ドル
割引（40パーセント）：－1,252.40ドル
配送料：＋ 100.00ドル
合計請求金額： **1,978.60ドル**

受信者：Jasmine Kai <jkai@haineymed.com>
送信者：Colin Byrne <cbyrne@greenlyreofficefurniture.com>
日付：12月10日
件名：お客さまの先の留守番電話

Kai 様

ご注文番号G90123に関するあなたの留守番電話を受信いたしましたが、私が折り返しお電話を差し上げようとしたところ、貴診療所は業務を終了しておりました。あなたは、ご注文なさったソファが診療所の待合室内の計画していたスペースに収まりそうにないことが分かったとおっしゃいました。それからあなたは、払い戻しを受けられるかどうかお尋ねでした。あいにく、今回のご購入は払い戻しが利きませんが、交換をご提供することによってご要望に応じたいと存じます。そのソファの代わりに、Green Lyre の二人掛けレザーソファを提供することが可能です。もしこの二人掛けソファをご了承いただけるようでしたら、全て合わせて元の請求書にあるのと同じ合計金額で追加のGreen Lyre レセプションチェアも1脚お付けしたいと思います。こちらでよろしいかどうかご連絡ください。

Green Lyre オフィス家具店でご購入いただき、ありがとうございます。

敬具

Colin Byrne、販売部長

186 What is indicated about Green Lyre Office Furniture?

    (A) It will soon close one of its stores.

    (B) It accepts online orders only.

    (C) It is offering a 40 percent discount on all merchandise.

    (D) It offers to remove used furniture.

Green Lyreオフィス家具店について何が示されていますか。

    (A) 同店は間もなく店舗の1つを閉鎖する。

    (B) 同店はオンライン注文のみを受け付ける。

    (C) 同店は全商品の40パーセント引きを行っている。

    (D) 同店は中古の家具の撤去作業を提供している。

> **正解 D**　**１**のGreen Lyreオフィス家具店の広告の**❷**2行目に、Pick-up and disposal of old furniture is also offered. 「古い家具の集荷と処分も行っている」とあるので、(D)が正解。offer to *do*「～しようと申し出る」、remove「～を持ち去る、～を取り除く」、used「中古の」。
> (B) online「オンラインの」。
> (C) **１**の**❶**2～4行目より、40パーセント引きになるのはGreen Lyreブランドの家具のみ。merchandise「商品」。

---

187 What is suggested about Hainey Medical Clinic?

    (A) It is not located in Somerfield.

    (B) Its waiting room includes a children's play area.

    (C) It has just enlarged its waiting room.

    (D) It has recently moved to a new location.

Hainey診療所について何が分かりますか。

    (A) 同診療所はサマーフィールド市内に位置していない。

    (B) 同診療所の待合室には子どもの遊び場がある。

    (C) 同診療所は待合室を拡張したばかりである。

    (D) 同診療所は最近、新しい場所に移った。

> **正解 A**　**１**の家具店の広告の**❷**1行目に、Delivery service is available and free to locations within Somerfield city limits. 「配送サービスが利用可能で、サマーフィールド市内の場所なら無料だ」とある。**２**の請求書は**❶**3行目より、同店からHainey診療所に宛てたもの。同**❷**右下のDelivery「配送料」の欄に100.00ドルと記載があるので、注文には配送料がかかっている。よって、Hainey診療所はサマーフィールド市内には位置していないと分かる。be located in ～「～に位置している、～にある」。
> (B) waiting room「待合室」、include「～を含む」、play area「遊び場」。
> (C) enlarge「～を拡張する」。

---

188 Why did Mr. Byrne send the e-mail?

    (A) To make a purchase

    (B) To answer a question

    (C) To schedule an appointment

    (D) To describe some product features

ByrneさんはなぜEメールを送ったのですか。

    (A) 購入をするため

    (B) 質問に答えるため

    (C) 約束の日程を取り決めるため

    (D) 製品の特徴を説明するため

> **正解 B**　**３**のEメールは、Green Lyreオフィス家具店のByrneさんが、Hainey診療所のKaiさん宛てに送信したもの。Byrneさんは、同**❶**1～2行目で、Kaiさんからの留守番電話を受け、折り返し電話したが、診療所は業務を終了していたと述べている。同3～4行目で、Then you asked whether you could receive a refund. 「それからあなたは、払い戻しを受けられるかどうか尋ねた」と述べてから、続く4～5行目で、Unfortunately, your purchase is not refundable, but I would like to accommodate you by offering an exchange. 「あいにく、今回の購入は払い戻しが利かないが、交換を提供することによって要望に応じたいと思う」と、Kaiさんの質問に回答しているので、(B)が正解。
> (A) make a purchase「購入する」。
> (D) **３**の**❶**5～8行目で、Byrneさんは交換する製品に言及しているが、その特徴を説明してはいない。describe「～を説明する」、feature「特徴」。

189 What did Ms. Kai indicate about the leather sofa?

(A) It was not the correct item.
(B) It was the wrong color.
(C) It was somewhat damaged.
(D) It was not suitable for the space.

Kaiさんはレザーソファについて何を示しましたか。

(A) それは正しい商品ではなかった。
(B) それは間違った色だった。
(C) それはやや損傷していた。
(D) それはスペースに合わなかった。

正解 D　Byrneさんが Kai さんに宛てた E メールである **3** の **❶** 2~3行目に、You mentioned that you realized the sofa you ordered is unlikely to fit in the intended space in your clinic's waiting area.「あなたは、注文したソファが診療所の待合室内の計画していたスペースに収まりそうにないことが分かった、と言った」とある。**2** の請求書は **❶** の購入者名より、Kai さんの注文分と分かるので、この Kai さんが言うソファとは、同 **2** の表最下行に記載されたレザーソファだと判断できる。よって、(D)が正解。be suitable for ~「~に適している」。
(A) correct「正しい」。
(C) somewhat「多少」、damage「~を損傷する」。

190 What extra item does the store offer to add to the order?

(A) MT-5047
(B) MT-2956
(C) MT-0632
(D) MT-4278

店は、注文分にどの追加商品を加えると申し出ていますか。

(A) MT-5047
(B) MT-2956
(C) MT-0632
(D) MT-4278

正解 A　**3** の **❶** 5~6行目で、Green Lyre オフィス家具店の Byrne さんは、Kai さんが注文したソファの代わりに Green Lyre の二人掛けレザーソファを提供することを申し出てから、続く同 6~8行目で if you accept the love seat, I would also let you have an additional Green Lyre Reception Chair, all for the same total price as on the original invoice「もしこの二人掛けソファを了承してくれるなら、全て合わせて元の請求書にあるのと同じ合計金額で追加の Green Lyre レセプションチェアも1脚付けたい」と述べている。**2** の請求書の **❷** で、Reception Chair「レセプションチェア」の Item Number「商品番号」は MT-5047 と記されているので、(A)が正解。extra「追加の、余分の」、add ~ to …「~を…に追加する」。

Words & Phrases

invoice　請求明細書、送り状

1 広告　furniture　家具　　sale　特売、セール　　**❶** make room for ~　~のためのスペースを作る　　model　モデル、型　save　~を節約する　　off　~から割り引いて　　in-stock　在庫のある　　brand　ブランド　　in stock　在庫の　final　最終の　　**❷** available　利用できる　　location　場所、居住地　　within ~ limits　~の区域内で　pick-up　集荷　　disposal　処分　　offer　~を提供する　　**❸** showroom　ショールーム、展示室

2 請求書　**❶** purchase　~を購入する　　office manager　事務長　　medical clinic　診療所　　**❷** description　品目　item　商品　　quantity　数量　　total price　合計価格　　reception chair　レセプションチェア　★受付用の椅子　lounge chair　ラウンジチェア　★ゆったりとした椅子　accent chair　アクセントチェア　★インテリアのアクセントとなる椅子　　leather　レザーの、革製の　　subtotal　小計　discount　割引　　charge　請求金額、料金

3 Eメール　recent　最近の　　voicemail　留守番電話、ボイスメール　　**❶** regarding　~に関して　　mention　~と言う　realize　~とよく分かる　　be unlikely to *do*　~しそうにない　　fit in ~　~にぴったりはまる　intended　意図された　　waiting area　待合室　　refund　払い戻し　　unfortunately　あいにく　purchase　購入　　refundable　払い戻しの可能な　　accommodate　~の便宜を図る　　exchange　交換品、交換　provide ~ with …　~に…を提供する　　love seat　二人掛けのソファ、ラブシート　　accept　~を受け入れる　additional　追加の　　original　元の

Expressions

in place of ~　「~の代わりに」（**3** の **❶** 6行目）
I attended the regional event in place of Mr. Wilson.
私は Wilson さんの代わりに、その地域イベントに出席しました。

Questions 191-195 refer to the following e-mail, article, and Web site post.

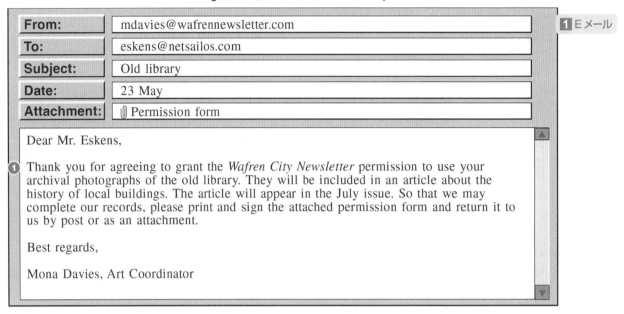

From:	mdavies@wafrennewsletter.com
To:	eskens@netsailos.com
Subject:	Old library
Date:	23 May
Attachment:	📎 Permission form

1 E メール

Dear Mr. Eskens,

Thank you for agreeing to grant the *Wafren City Newsletter* permission to use your archival photographs of the old library. They will be included in an article about the history of local buildings. The article will appear in the July issue. So that we may complete our records, please print and sign the attached permission form and return it to us by post or as an attachment.

Best regards,

Mona Davies, Art Coordinator

---

2 記事

From the Editorial Board

Welcome to the July issue of the *Wafren City Newsletter*. Featured on the front page is a photo of the renovated City Park. Read about how it has been transformed to better serve our community. This year, for the first time, it will host the popular Vegetable and Fruit Market, featuring produce from local farmers. Also covered in this issue are music performances and a drama festival.

Learn more about how City Hall works closely with local businesses. For example, you can read about a recent job-training initiative, fully financed by City Hall, which resulted in a number of Wafren residents being hired as drivers by transport companies in the area.

We welcome contributions from our readers, which can be found on pages 2–3. Letters to the editor, notices, and other submissions must be received by the tenth of the month to be considered for the next issue.

Also in this issue:
Street Improvements Pending–Page 4
Then and Now: Wafren Historical Landmarks–Page 6
Food Trucks: Locations and Schedules–Page 9
City Calendar and Phone Directory–Page 14

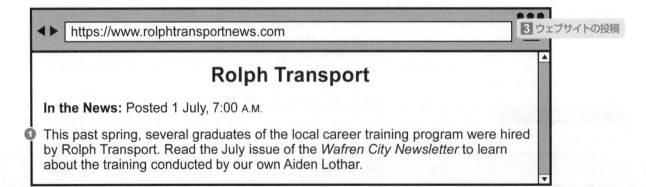

https://www.rolphtransportnews.com

3 ウェブサイトの投稿

Rolph Transport

In the News: Posted 1 July, 7:00 A.M.

This past spring, several graduates of the local career training program were hired by Rolph Transport. Read the July issue of the *Wafren City Newsletter* to learn about the training conducted by our own Aiden Lothar.

問題191-195は次のEメール、記事、ウェブサイトの投稿に関するものです。

送信者：mdavies@wafrennewsletter.com
受信者：eskens@netsailos.com
件名：旧図書館
日付：5月23日
添付：承諾書

Eskens様

『Wafren市公報』に、旧図書館のあなたの記録写真の使用許可を与えることに同意してくださり、ありがとうございます。これらのものは、地元の建造物の歴史に関する記事に盛り込まれる予定です。この記事は7月号に掲載されることになっています。双方合意の記録を当方に残すため、添付の承諾書を印刷してご署名いただき、郵便でもしくは添付ファイルにて私どもにご返送ください。

敬具

Mona Davies、アートコーディネーター

編集委員会より

『Wafren市公報』の7月号へようこそ。第1面で取り上げられているのは、改修された市立公園の写真です。同公園が私たちの地域社会により役立つよう、どう変貌したかについてお読みください。今年同公園では初めて、地元農家からの農産物を目玉とする人気の青果市が開催されます。本号では、音楽公演と演劇祭も扱っています。

市役所がいかに地元の企業と密接に連携しているかについて、もっと知ってください。例えば、市役所によって全面的に資金提供された最近の職業訓練の施策についてお読みいただけます。これによって、多くのWafren市民が運転手として地域の運送会社に雇用される結果となりました。

当誌では読者の方々からの寄稿を歓迎しており、それらは2～3ページでご覧いただけます。投書、お知らせ、その他の投稿は、次号掲載の検討対象となるよう、当月の10日までに受け付けられる必要があります。

他の本号掲載内容：
審議中の道路改良工事 ―― 4ページ
当時と現在：Wafren市の歴史的建造物 ―― 6ページ
移動式屋台：場所と日程表 ―― 9ページ
市の行事表と電話番号案内 ―― 14ページ

---

https://www.rolphtransportnews.com

Rolph運送会社

新しいお知らせ：7月1日午前7時に投稿

この春、地元の職業訓練プログラムの卒業生が数名、Rolph運送会社に雇用されました。当社のAiden Lotharによって指導された、その訓練について知るには、『Wafren市公報』の7月号をお読みください。

191 In the e-mail, what is Mr. Eskens asked to do?

(A) Subscribe to a newsletter
(B) Update his photograph
(C) Sign a document
(D) Visit the library

Eメールで、Eskensさんは何をするよう求められていますか。

(A) 公報を定期購読する
(B) 彼の写真を最新のものにする
(C) 書類に署名する
(D) 図書館を訪問する

> **正解 C** ❶のEメールは、冒頭の宛名と最後の差出人名より、Eskensさん宛てにDaviesさんが送信したもの。同❶の1～2行目で、Eskensさんが写真の使用を許可したことへのお礼が述べられ、続けて同3～5行目で、So that we may complete our records, please print and sign the attached permission form and return it to us by post or as an attachment. 「双方合意の記録を当方に残すため、添付の承諾書を印刷して署名いただき、郵便でもしくは添付ファイルにて私どもに返送してください」とEskensさんは書類に署名するよう求められているので、(C)が正解。
> (A) subscribe to ～「～を定期購読する」。
> (B) ❶の❶1～2行目でEskensさんの図書館写真の使用に言及はあるが、最新版への差し替えは求められていない。update「～を最新のものにする」。

192 According to the article, what will take place at a new location?

(A) A food market
(B) A training program
(C) A drama festival
(D) A music concert

記事によると、新しい場所で何が行われますか。

(A) 食べ物市
(B) 訓練プログラム
(C) 演劇祭
(D) 音楽コンサート

> **正解 A** a new location「新しい場所」とは、❷の記事の❶2行目のthe renovated City Park「改修された市立公園」のことだと考えられる。同3～4行目に、This year, for the first time, it will host the popular Vegetable and Fruit Market, featuring produce from local farmers. 「今年同公園では初めて、地元農家からの農産物を目玉とする人気の青果市が開催される」と青果市の開催が伝えられている。この文のitは、前にあるthe renovated City Park「改修された市立公園」を指すので、(A)が正解。location「場所」。
> (C) (D) ❷の❶4～5行目で音楽公演と演劇祭に言及があるが、新しい開催場所とは書かれていない。

193 What page in the newsletter most likely features materials provided by Mr. Eskens?

(A) Page 4
(B) Page 6
(C) Page 9
(D) Page 14

Eskensさんから提供された資料が取り上げられるのは、公報の何ページだと考えられますか。

(A) 4ページ
(B) 6ページ
(C) 9ページ
(D) 14ページ

> **正解 B** Eskensさんから公報に提供された資料とは、❶のEメールの❶1～2行目にあるyour archival photographs of the old library「旧図書館のあなたの記録写真」を指すと考えられる。同2～3行目に、They will be included in an article about the history of local buildings. 「これらのものは、地元の建造物の歴史に関する記事に盛り込まれる予定だ」とあり、続けて「この記事は7月号に掲載される」と書かれている。❷の❶と❹から、❹では公報の7月号の掲載内容を紹介していることが分かり、同3行目に、Then and Now: Wafren Historical Landmarks — Page 6「当時と現在：Wafren市の歴史的建造物──6ページ」と記載がある。よって、Eskensさんの提供資料が取り上げられるのはこの6ページと考えられる。material「資料」、provide「～を提供する」。

Expressions

result in ～ 「～という結果になる」（❷の❷2～3行目）
　Thomas' efforts resulted in sales success.
　Thomasの努力は販売の成功という結果をもたらしました。

194 Who must follow the deadline mentioned in the article?

    (A) Workers applying for jobs
    (B) Artists requesting funds
    (C) Readers canceling subscriptions
    (D) Writers submitting articles

誰が、記事の中で述べられている期限を守る必要がありますか。

    (A) 職に応募する労働者
    (B) 資金を求める芸術家
    (C) 定期購読を中止する読者
    (D) 記事を投稿する書き手

> **正解 D** ❷の❸1行目で、読者に対し寄稿を歓迎する旨が述べられている。同1〜3行目に、Letters to the editor, notices, and other submissions must be received by the tenth of the month to be considered for the next issue.「投書、お知らせ、その他の投稿は、次号掲載の検討対象となるよう、当月の10日までに受け付けられる必要がある」と期限が伝えられているので、(D)が正解。follow「〜を守る」、deadline「期限、締め切り」。submit「〜を投稿する」。
> (A) apply for 〜「〜に応募する」。
> (B) request「〜を求める」、fund「資金」。
> (C) cancel「〜を中止する」、subscription「定期購読」。

195 What is indicated about the training given by Mr. Lothar?

    (A) Residents requested it.
    (B) Local authorities paid for it.
    (C) It can be attended online.
    (D) It will be postponed.

Lotharさんによって行われる訓練について、何が示されていますか。

    (A) 住民がそれを要求した。
    (B) 地方自治体がその代金を支払った。
    (C) それはオンラインで出席ができる。
    (D) それは延期されることになっている。

> **正解 B** ❸のRolph運送会社のウェブサイトの投稿の❶1〜2行目で、「この春、地元の職業訓練プログラムの卒業生が数名、Rolph運送会社に雇用された」と述べられ、続く同2〜3行目にRead the July issue of the *Wafren City Newsletter* to learn about the training conducted by our own Aiden Lothar.「当社のAiden Lotharによって指導された、その訓練について知るには、『Wafren市公報』の7月号を読んでください」とある。❷の記事の❷1〜2行目に、you can read about a recent job-training initiative, fully financed by City Hall「市役所によって全面的に資金提供された最近の職業訓練の施策について読むことができる」とあり、続けて、その結果多くのWafren市民が運転手として地域の運送会社に雇用されたと書かれている。Lotharさんによる訓練とは、この職業訓練の施策によるものだと判断できるので、(B)が正解。local authority「地方自治体」、pay for 〜「〜の代金を支払う」。
> (D) postpone「〜を延期する」。

Words & Phrases

post 投稿、掲示

1 Eメール
attachment 添付　　permission 許可　　form 用紙　　❶ agree to *do* 〜することに同意する　grant 〜 … 〜に…を与える　　newsletter 公報　　archival 記録文書の　　photograph 写真　include 〜を含める　　local 地元の　　appear （記事などが）掲載される　　issue （雑誌などの)号　so that 〜 may … 〜が…できるように　　complete 〜を完全なものにする　　sign 〜に署名する　attached 添付の　　by post 郵便で　　coordinator コーディネーター

2 記事
editorial board 編集委員会　　❶ feature 〜を大々的に扱う、〜を目玉とする　　front page 第1面　renovate 〜を改修する　　transform 〜を変貌させる　　serve 〜に役立つ　　community 地域社会　for the first time 初めて　　host 〜を主催する　　produce 農産物　　cover 〜(話題など)を扱う　performance 公演　　drama 演劇　　❷ City Hall 市役所　　closely 密接に　　recent 最近の　job-training 職業訓練の　　initiative 新しい試み、新規行動計画　　fully 完全に　　finance 〜に資金提供する　a number of 〜 多くの〜　　resident 住民　　hire 〜を雇用する　　transport 運送　❸ welcome 〜を歓迎する　　contribution 寄稿　　letter to the editor 投書　　notice お知らせ　submission 投稿、提出　　❹ improvement 改良工事　　pending 未決定の、係争中の　historical 歴史的な　　landmark 歴史的建造物　　food truck 移動式屋台　　phone directory 電話帳

3 ウェブサイトの投稿
in the news 話題になっている　　❶ several 幾つかの　　graduate 卒業生　　career 職業、キャリア　conduct 〜を指導する　　*one's* own 〜自身の

Questions 196-200 refer to the following advertisement and e-mails.

ADELETTO AND SONS

Our family business has been processing and dyeing fine leather since 1849. Whatever your factory product line, our experts will help you to wrap and finish your items beautifully by providing you with the highest-quality leather tailored to your specifications. Speedy worldwide shipping is guaranteed. Choose from the following collections, all of which are available in a variety of finishes and in over 100 designer colors.

- ROMA COLLECTION, for automotive, aviation, and seagoing use

- GENOA COLLECTION, for fine furniture

- VICENZA COLLECTION, for both dress shoes and casual footwear

- MILANO COLLECTION, for handbags and personal accessories

To:	Domenico Grande <d.grande@adeletto.it>
From:	Youngjoon Cho <yjcho@jaehakmarine.co.kr>
Date:	15 February
Subject:	Touring Line seating

Dear Mr. Grande:

We received the sample shipment of leather for the seats in our line of touring boats. While the color and texture are very pleasing, this leather is much too fine and thin for our purposes. It seems to be more like a glove leather, appropriate for small personal items. We are concerned that it will easily tear and become worn out, even with normal use.

Jaehak Marine builds boats for touring companies to use for weddings, corporate parties, and gala events. Naturally, the seating must be comfortable, but the surface should be sturdy and durable enough to withstand weight and friction as well as continual exposure to moisture. Most importantly, we must choose a leather that will stand up to the frequent spills that occur when food and beverages are served. Damage from spills is an issue we have had with our seats in the past, so we want to be certain to make the right choice this time. Please help us identify the best Adeletto and Sons material to meet these needs.

We look forward to your recommendation.

Sincerely,

Youngjoon Cho
Product Development, Jaehak Marine

To:	Youngjoon Cho <yjcho@jaehakmarine.co.kr>
From:	Domenico Grande <d.grande@adeletto.it>
Date:	16 February
Subject:	RE: Touring Line seating

Dear Mr. Cho:

We are so sorry for the error. Your sample should never have been prepared with our softest and most delicate leather product. We will send you new samples.

Given what you have said about the usage your seating must withstand, we think you may also be interested in our special stain-resistant leather treatment. This type of finishing treatment is very popular with clients whose products are subject to heavy, repeated use. Please let us know if you would like to add this option to your sample order. Also, let us know if you would like your new samples in the same neutral color that you originally requested.

Adeletto and Sons can have your samples delivered to you in Jeju City within three days, and we will offer a 10 percent discount when you are ready to place a full order.

Thank you,

Domenico Grande
Director of Client Relations, Adeletto and Sons

問題196-200は次の広告と2通のEメールに関するものです。

ADELETTO AND SONS社

家族経営会社である私どもは1849年以来、上質な革を加工し染め続けてきました。貴社の工場製品ラインがどのようなものであれ、当社の熟練工が貴社の仕様に合わせた最高品質の革をご提供することによって、貴社製品の表面を美しく装い仕上げるお手伝いをします。世界中に迅速な配送を保証いたします。下記のコレクションからお選びください。これらは全て、さまざまな仕上げと100を超えるデザイナーカラーにてご用意できます。

・ローマコレクション　自動車、航空機、船舶使用に
・ジェノバコレクション　上質な家具に
・ビチェンツァコレクション　正装用の靴とカジュアルな履物のどちらにも
・ミラノコレクション　ハンドバッグや身の回りの装身具に

受信者：Domenico Grande <d.grande@adeletto.it>
送信者：Youngjoon Cho <yjcho@jaehakmarine.co.kr>
日付：2月15日
件名：周遊船製品ラインの座席

Grande様

当社が製造する周遊船の座席に使う革の見本の荷物を受け取りました。色や手触りは大変魅力的なのですが、この革は私たちの用途にはあまりにも繊細で薄過ぎます。むしろ手袋の革のような、小さな身の回り品に適しているようです。たとえ通常の使い方でも、簡単に裂けて擦り切れてしまうことを私たちは懸念しています。

当Jaehak Marine社はツアー会社向けに、結婚式、企業のパーティー、また祝賀会に利用する船を造っています。当然ながら、座席は快適でなければなりませんが、その表面は重量や摩擦だけでなく、湿気に継続的にさらされることにも耐えられるだけ十分に丈夫で耐久性があることが望まれます。そして最も重要なことですが、私たちは、飲食物提供時に頻繁にこぼれても耐え得る革を選ばなければなりません。こぼれた飲食物による損傷は、これまで私たちが当社の座席に関して抱えてきた課題ですので、今回は必ず正しい選択をしたいと思っています。これらのニーズを満たす、Adeletto and Sons社の最適な素材を見極める手助けをお願いいたします。

貴社のご提案をお待ちしております。

敬具

Youngjoon Cho
製品開発部、Jaehak Marine社

受信者：Youngjoon Cho <yjcho@jaehakmarine.co.kr>
送信者：Domenico Grande <d.grande@adeletto.it>
日付：2月16日
件名：RE：周遊船製品ラインの座席

Cho様

このたびの間違いにつきまして大変申し訳なく存じます。貴社のための見本は、当社の最も柔らかく繊細な革でご用意すべきではございませんでした。新しい見本をお送りいたします。

あなたがご説明くださった、座席が耐久性を必要とする使い方を考慮しますと、貴社は当社の革の特殊防汚加工処理にもご興味をお持ちになる可能性があると存じます。このタイプの仕上げ処理は、繰り返し苛酷に使用される製品を取り扱うお客様方に大変好評です。見本のご注文にこのオプションを追加なさりたいかどうかお知らせください。また、新しい見本を最初に貴社がご要望になったのと同じ中間色でご希望かどうかもお知らせください。

Adeletto and Sons社は見本をチェジュ市の貴社の元に3日以内にお届けすることができます。また正式にご注文していただけるのであれば10パーセント引きをご提供いたします。

よろしくお願いいたします。

Domenico Grande
顧客相談窓口担当部長、Adeletto and Sons社

196 What is suggested about Adeletto and Sons?

(A) It creates products made of artificial leather.
(B) It produces shoes and handbags.
(C) It plans to open a new international office soon.
(D) It sells leather to manufacturing companies.

Adeletto and Sons 社について何が分かりますか。

(A) 同社は合成皮革製の製品を作る。
(B) 同社は靴やハンドバッグを製造する。
(C) 同社は間もなく新たな海外事務所を開く予定である。
(D) 同社は製造業の企業に革を販売する。

> **正解 D** 1のAdeletto and Sons 社の広告の❶1行目で、同社は1849年以来、革の加工と染色を行ってきたと述べられ、続く同2～4行目に、「貴社の工場製品ラインがどのようなものでも、当社の熟練工が貴社の仕様に合わせた最高品質の革を提供することによって、貴社製品の表面を美しく装い仕上げる手伝いをする」とあるので、同社は製造業の企業に革を販売すると分かる。manufacturing「製造業の」。
> (A) made of ～「～でできた」、artificial leather「合成皮革」。
> (B) 1の❷3～4行目で靴やハンドバッグ向けの革のコレクションが列挙されているが、靴やハンドバッグそのものを製造していると述べられてはいない。produce「～を製造する」。
> (C) international「海外の、国際的な」。

197 What is one purpose of the first e-mail?

(A) To promote boat rentals for events
(B) To complain about a late shipment
(C) To ask for advice about seat coverings
(D) To request instructions for preserving a delicate material

1通目のEメールの1つの目的は何ですか。

(A) 行事向けの船のレンタルを促進すること
(B) 発送の遅延に不満を述べること
(C) 座席張りに関する助言を求めること
(D) 繊細な素材を保護するための説明を要望すること

> **正解 C** 1通目のEメールである2は、造船業のJaehak Marine 社のChoさんが革加工会社であるAdeletto and Sons 社のGrandeさん宛てに送信したもので、件名には「周遊船製品ラインの座席」とある。Choさんは同❶1～3行目で、受け取った見本は座席に使う革としては繊細で薄過ぎると述べ、同❷2～4行目で、丈夫で耐久性のある革が必要だと書いている。同❷5～7行目では、「こぼれた飲食物による損傷は、これまで私たちが当社の座席に関して抱えてきた課題なので、今回は必ず正しい選択をしたい。これらのニーズを満たす、Adeletto and Sons 社の最適な素材を見極める手助けをお願いしたい」とニーズを伝えた上で座席張りについての助言を求めているので、(C)が正解。seat covering「座席張り」。
> (A) promote「～を促進する」、rental「レンタル、賃借」。
> (B) complain about ～「～に不満を述べる」。
> (D) instructions「指示」、preserve「～を保護する」、delicate「繊細な」。

198 What collection best suits Mr. Cho's needs?

(A) Roma
(B) Genoa
(C) Vicenza
(D) Milano

どのコレクションがChoさんのニーズに最も合いますか。

(A) ローマ
(B) ジェノバ
(C) ビチェンツァ
(D) ミラノ

> **正解 A** Choさんが求めているものは、1通目のEメールの2の❶1行目のleather for the seats in our line of touring boats「当社が製造する周遊船の座席に使う革」である。さらにChoさんは同❷で、耐久性が重要な座席の革の条件について述べている。従って、1の❷1行目に、「ローマコレクション 自動車、航空機、船舶使用に」とある、船舶向けのローマコレクションがChoさんのニーズに最も合うと判断できる。suit「～に合う」。

Expressions

A as well as *B* 「*B*だけでなく*A*も」（2の❷3～4行目）
Rosemary has experience as well as knowledge in international trade.
Rosemaryには、国際貿易についての知識だけでなく経験もあります。

199 What is the reason for Mr. Grande's apology in the second e-mail?

(A) A sample arrived with significant water damage.
(B) The wrong material was used in preparing a sample.
(C) An order confirmation was not sent.
(D) A discount was not applied to an order.

2通目のEメールにおけるGrandeさんの謝罪の理由は何ですか。

(A) 見本が水による著しい損傷を伴って届いた。
(B) 見本の用意に間違った素材が使われた。
(C) 注文確認書が送付されなかった。
(D) 割引が注文に適用されなかった。

正解 **B**　2通目のEメールの❸は、革加工会社であるAdeletto and Sons社のGrandeさんが、顧客であるJaehak Marine社のChoさんに返信したもの。Grandeさんは同❶ 1行目で、「このたびの間違いについて大変申し訳なく思う」と謝罪し、続けてYour sample should never have been prepared with our softest and most delicate leather product.「貴社のための見本は、当社の最も柔らかく繊細な革で用意すべきではなかった」と、送付見本が適切でなかったと述べている。apology「謝罪」。
(A) significant「著しい」。(C) order comfirmation「注文確認書」。
(D) apply ~ to …「~を…に適用する」。

200 What will probably be most important to Mr. Cho when he places a full order?

(A) The shipping time
(B) The amount of the discount
(C) The color selection
(D) The finishing treatment

正式注文をする際に、Choさんにとっておそらく何が最も重要ですか。

(A) 運送時間
(B) 割引額
(C) 色の選択
(D) 仕上げ処理

正解 **D**　❸の❷ 1~2行目で、GrandeさんはChoさんの説明から判断すると、Choさんの会社が革の防汚加工処理に興味を持つ可能性に言及し、同2~4行目で、苛酷に使用される製品を取り扱う顧客に評判の仕上げ処理を紹介した後、Choさんに見本注文にそのオプションの追加を希望するかどうか尋ねている。❷の❷ 4~7行目でChoさんは、Most importantly「最も重要なことだが」と言って、座席への飲食物のこぼれに対する革の損傷を以前からの課題として挙げ、素材の見極めの手助けを頼んでいる。よって、Choさんにとって汚れに対して耐性を持たせる仕上げ処理が最重要だと判断できる。
(C) selection「選択」。

Words & Phrases

1 広告　❶ family business 家族経営会社　process ~を加工する　dye ~を染める　fine 上質の、繊細な　leather 革　whatever ~がたとえ何であれ　product line 製品ライン　expert 熟練者、専門家　wrap ~の表面を装う　finish ~を仕上げる　provide ~ with … ~に…を提供する　highest-quality 最高品質の　tailored to ~ ~に合わせた　specifications 仕様　speedy 迅速な　worldwide 世界中の　guarantee ~を保証する　available 求めに応じられる　a variety of ~ さまざまな~　designer デザイナーによる　❷ automotive 自動車の　aviation 航空　seagoing 航海用の　dress shoes 礼装用の靴　footwear 履物　personal 個人用の　accessories （手袋などの）装身具

2 Eメール　tour 周遊する　seating 座席　❶ boat 船　texture 手触り　pleasing 魅力的な、満足な　thin 薄い　purpose 用途、目的　appropriate 適した　be concerned (that) ~ ~を心配している　easily 簡単に　tear 裂ける　worn out 擦り切れた　normal 通常の　❷ corporate 企業の　gala 祝賀会　naturally 当然ながら　comfortable 快適な　surface 表面　sturdy 丈夫な　durable 耐久性のある　withstand ~によく耐える、~に持ちこたえる　friction 摩擦　continual 継続的な　exposure さらされること　moisture 湿気　most importantly 最も重要であるが　stand up to ~ ~に耐久力がある　frequent 頻繁な　spill こぼれること　occur 起こる　beverage 飲み物　serve ~（飲食物など）を出す　issue 問題、問題点　in the past これまで、過去に　be certain to do 必ず~する　make the right choice 正しい選択をする　identify ~を見極める　material 素材　meet ~を満たす　❸ look forward to ~ ~を楽しみにして待つ　recommendation 提案、推薦

3 Eメール　❶ error 間違い　delicate 繊細な　❷ given ~ ~を考慮すると　usage 使い方、用法　be interested in ~ ~に興味がある　stain-resistant 汚れにくい、防汚加工された　treatment 処理　be subject to ~ ~にさらされる　repeated 繰り返された　add ~ to … ~を…に追加する　option オプション、選択肢　neutral color 中間色　originally 最初は　❸ be ready to do ~する準備ができている　place a full order 正式に注文する　client relations 顧客相談窓口

CD トラック・特典音声ファイル 一覧表

● CD1

Test	Track No.	Contents
サンプル問題	1	タイトル
	2	Listening Test Directions/ Part 1 Directions
	3	Q1
	4	Part 2 Directions
	5	Q2, Q3
	6	Part 3 Directions
	7	Q4-6
	8	Q7-9
	9	Part 4 Directions
	10	Q10-12
TEST 1	11	Test 1
	12	Listening Test Directions/ Part 1 Directions
	13	Q1
	14	Q2
	15	Q3
	16	Q4
	17	Q5
	18	Q6
	19	Part 2 Directions
	20	Q7
	21	Q8
	22	Q9
	23	Q10
	24	Q11
	25	Q12
	26	Q13
	27	Q14
	28	Q15
	29	Q16
	30	Q17
	31	Q18
	32	Q19
	33	Q20
	34	Q21
	35	Q22
	36	Q23
	37	Q24
	38	Q25
	39	Q26
	40	Q27
	41	Q28
	42	Q29
	43	Q30
	44	Q31
	45	Part 3 Directions

Test	Track No.	Contents
TEST 1	46	Part 3 Q32-34 会話
	47	Q32-34 問題
	48	Q35-37 会話
	49	Q35-37 問題
	50	Q38-40 会話
	51	Q38-40 問題
	52	Q41-43 会話
	53	Q41-43 問題
	54	Q44-46 会話
	55	Q44-46 問題
	56	Q47-49 会話
	57	Q47-49 問題
	58	Q50-52 会話
	59	Q50-52 問題
	60	Q53-55 会話
	61	Q53-55 問題
	62	Q56-58 会話
	63	Q56-58 問題
	64	Q59-61 会話
	65	Q59-61 問題
	66	Q62-64 会話
	67	Q62-64 問題
	68	Q65-67 会話
	69	Q65-67 問題
	70	Q68-70 会話
	71	Q68-70 問題
	72	Part 4 Directions
	73	Q71-73 トーク
	74	Q71-73 問題
	75	Q74-76 トーク
	76	Q74-76 問題
	77	Q77-79 トーク
	78	Q77-79 問題
	79	Q80-82 トーク
	80	Q80-82 問題
	81	Q83-85 トーク
	82	Q83-85 問題
	83	Q86-88 トーク
	84	Q86-88 問題
	85	Q89-91 トーク
	86	Q89-91 問題
	87	Q92-94 トーク
	88	Q92-94 問題
	89	Q95-97 トーク
	90	Q95-97 問題
	91	Q98-100 トーク
	92	Q98-100 問題

● CD2

Test	Track No.	Contents
TEST 2	1	Test 2
	2	Listening Test Directions/ Part 1 Directions
	3	Q1
	4	Q2
	5	Q3
	6	Q4
	7	Q5
	8	Q6
	9	Part 2 Directions
	10	Q7
	11	Q8
	12	Q9
	13	Q10
	14	Q11
	15	Q12
	16	Q13
	17	Q14
	18	Q15
	19	Q16
	20	Q17
	21	Q18
	22	Q19
	23	Q20
	24	Q21
	25	Q22
	26	Q23
	27	Q24
	28	Q25
	29	Q26
	30	Q27
	31	Q28
	32	Q29
	33	Q30
	34	Q31
	35	Part 3 Directions
	36	Q32-34 会話
	37	Q32-34 問題
	38	Q35-37 会話
	39	Q35-37 問題
	40	Q38-40 会話
	41	Q38-40 問題
	42	Q41-43 会話
	43	Q41-43 問題
	44	Q44-46 会話
	45	Q44-46 問題
	46	Q47-49 会話

次ページの「音声を使った学習例の紹介」を参考に、問題に解答した後の学習用教材としてもご活用ください。

音声ダウンロードの手順▶本誌 p.3　音声を使った学習例▶別冊 p.200

Test	Track No.	Contents
TEST 2	47	Part 3 Q47-49 問題
	48	Q50-52 会話
	49	Q50-52 問題
	50	Q53-55 会話
	51	Q53-55 問題
	52	Q56-58 会話
	53	Q56-58 問題
	54	Q59-61 会話
	55	Q59-61 問題
	56	Q62-64 会話
	57	Q62-64 問題
	58	Q65-67 会話
	59	Q65-67 問題
	60	Q68-70 会話
	61	Q68-70 問題
	62	Part 4 Directions
	63	Q71-73 トーク
	64	Q71-73 問題
	65	Q74-76 トーク
	66	Q74-76 問題
	67	Q77-79 トーク
	68	Q77-79 問題
	69	Q80-82 トーク
	70	Q80-82 問題
	71	Q83-85 トーク
	72	Q83-85 問題
	73	Q86-88 トーク
	74	Q86-88 問題
	75	Q89-91 トーク
	76	Q89-91 問題
	77	Q92-94 トーク
	78	Q92-94 問題
	79	Q95-97 トーク
	80	Q95-97 問題
	81	Q98-100 トーク
	82	Q98-100 問題

● 特典（ダウンロード）

Test	File No.	Contents
TEST 1	01	Part 5 Q101 問題
	02	Q102 問題
	03	Q103 問題
	04	Q104 問題
	05	Q105 問題
	06	Q106 問題
	07	Q107 問題
	08	Q108 問題

Test	File No.	Contents
TEST 1	09	Part 5 Q109 問題
	10	Q110 問題
	11	Q111 問題
	12	Q112 問題
	13	Q113 問題
	14	Q114 問題
	15	Q115 問題
	16	Q116 問題
	17	Q117 問題
	18	Q118 問題
	19	Q119 問題
	20	Q120 問題
	21	Q121 問題
	22	Q122 問題
	23	Q123 問題
	24	Q124 問題
	25	Q125 問題
	26	Q126 問題
	27	Q127 問題
	28	Q128 問題
	29	Q129 問題
	30	Q130 問題
	31	Part 6 Q131-134 問題
	32	Q135-138 問題
	33	Q139-142 問題
	34	Q143-146 問題
	35	Part 7 Q147-148 文書
	36	Q149-150 文書
	37	Q151-152 文書
	38	Q153-154 文書
	39	Q155-157 文書
	40	Q158-160 文書
	41	Q161-163 文書
	42	Q164-167 文書
	43	Q168-171 文書
	44	Q172-175 文書
	45-46	Q176-180 文書
	47-48	Q181-185 文書
	49-51	Q186-190 文書
	52-54	Q191-195 文書
	55-57	Q196-200 文書
TEST 2	58	Part 5 Q101 問題
	59	Q102 問題
	60	Q103 問題
	61	Q104 問題
	62	Q105 問題
	63	Q106 問題
	64	Q107 問題

Test	File No.	Contents
TEST 2	65	Part 5 Q108 問題
	66	Q109 問題
	67	Q110 問題
	68	Q111 問題
	69	Q112 問題
	70	Q113 問題
	71	Q114 問題
	72	Q115 問題
	73	Q116 問題
	74	Q117 問題
	75	Q118 問題
	76	Q119 問題
	77	Q120 問題
	78	Q121 問題
	79	Q122 問題
	80	Q123 問題
	81	Q124 問題
	82	Q125 問題
	83	Q126 問題
	84	Q127 問題
	85	Q128 問題
	86	Q129 問題
	87	Q130 問題
	88	Part 6 Q131-134 問題
	89	Q135-138 問題
	90	Q139-142 問題
	91	Q143-146 問題
	92	Part 7 Q147-148 文書
	93	Q149-150 文書
	94	Q151-152 文書
	95	Q153-154 文書
	96	Q155-157 文書
	97	Q158-160 文書
	98	Q161-163 文書
	99	Q164-167 文書
	100	Q168-171 文書
	101	Q172-175 文書
	102-103	Q176-180 文書
	104-105	Q181-185 文書
	106-108	Q186-190 文書
	109-111	Q191-195 文書
	112-114	Q196-200 文書

＊CDに収録の問題音声は全て、*TOEIC*®公式スピーカーによるものです。

＊特典音声は、CDとは別に収録したもので、標準的な北米発音を採用しています。

音声を使った学習例の紹介

『公式 *TOEIC*® Listening & Reading 問題集 7』は、付属 CD の音声の他、特典として TEST 1、2 のリーディングセクションの一部の音声を、スマートフォンや PC にダウンロードしてお聞きいただけます。以下に音声を使った公式問題集の学習法の一例をご紹介しますので、学習の参考になさってください。

準備するもの：別冊「解答・解説」（本書）、音声をダウンロードしたスマートフォンまたは PC

* Part 1 ～ 4 の音声は付属 CD でも聞くことができます。Part 5 ～ 7 の特典音声を含む全ての音声の利用は、abceed への会員登録（無料）とダウンロードが必要です。本誌 p. 3 の「音声ダウンロードの手順」に従ってサイトにアクセスし、『公式 *TOEIC*® Listening & Reading 問題集 7』をダウンロードしてください。リーディングの特典音声のスピードが速くて聞き取りが難しいと感じる方は、abceed のアプリなどのスピード調整機能を利用しましょう。初めのうちは 0.8 ～ 0.9 倍などで聞くことをお勧めします。

Part 1、2

1. 「解答・解説」で正解の英文の意味内容を正しく理解する。
2. 音声を聞き、発音やイントネーションを真似て音読する（リピーティング）。最初はスクリプトを見ながら行い、慣れてきたらスクリプトを見ずに行う。

> Part 1 では写真を見ながら正解の描写文だけを、Part 2 では質問と正解の応答を、音読してみましょう。自分が発話しているつもりで音読すると、表現が定着しやすくなります。

Part 3、4

1. 「解答・解説」でスクリプトの英文と訳を確認。知らない語の意味や英文の内容を把握する。
2. スクリプトを見ながら会話やトークを聞く。発話と同じスピードで英文を目で追い、即座に意味を理解できるようになるまで繰り返す。
3. スクリプトを見ずに会話やトークを聞く。聞き取りづらい箇所や意味が理解できない箇所をスクリプトで確認し、再び音声だけで理解できるか挑戦する。

> Part 3 ではスピーカー同士の関係や会話の目的、Part 4 では場面やトークの趣旨をまず把握し、徐々に理解できる範囲を増やしていくつもりで、細部の情報を聞き取るようにしましょう。

Part 5、6

1. 「解答・解説」で英文と訳を確認。知らない語の意味や英文の内容を把握する。
2. 本書の TEST 1、2 の該当ページ(p.42-48 と p.84-90)のコピーを取り、音声を聞いて空所の語や文を書き取る。知っている語彙や文法の知識も用いて空所を埋め、書き取ったものと実際の英文を比較する。最後に、もう一度音声を聞く。

> 聞き取れない箇所は、飛ばしたりカタカナで書いたりしても構いません。音声だけに頼らず、語彙力や文法の知識を用いて挑戦してみましょう。Part 5 は短い文なので、ディクテーションするのもよいでしょう。

Part 6、7

1. 「解答・解説」で英文と訳を確認。知らない語の意味や英文の内容を把握する。その際、読み方に迷った箇所に印を付けておく。
2. 音声を聞きながら英文を目で追い（初めはスピードを遅めにしても可）、英語の語順のまま理解できるようになることを目指す。分からなかった箇所は、適宜訳を確認する。
3. 1. で印を付けた、読み方に迷った箇所の言い方を確認する。
   例：数字や記号の言い方（日付、住所、飛行機の便名、価格、URL）など。

> 1 は構文や語彙の学習、2 は速読の学習です。2 では意味のまとまりを意識しながら英文を読み進めていくようにすると、取り組みやすいでしょう。3 は、実際の会話の際にも役立つので積極的に覚えるとよいでしょう。